Constitutional Dictatorship

TO

EDWARD S. CORWIN

AND

ROBERT E. CUSHMAN

In Alexander Hamilton's words
"The ablest adepts in political science"

Constitutional Dictatorship

Crisis Government
in the Modern Democracies

Clinton Rossiter

With a new introduction by
William J. Quirk

Transaction Publishers
New Brunswick (U.S.A.) and London (U.K.)

Library of Congress Catalog Number: 2002070330
ISBN: 0-7658-0975-3
Printed in the United States of America

Library of Congress Cataloging-in-Publication Data

Rossiter, Clinton Lawrence, 1917-1970.
    Constitutional dictatorship : crisis government in the modern democracies / Clinton Rossiter ; with a new introduction by William J. Quirk.
        p. cm.
    Originally published: Princeton, N.J. : Princeton University Press, 1948.
    Includes bibliographical references and index.
    ISBN 0-7658-0975-3 (pbk.: alk. paper)
        1. War and emergency powers. 2. Democracy. I. Title.

JF256 .R6 2002
321.8—dc21

2002070330

"Those republics which in time of danger cannot resort to a dictatorship will generally be ruined when grave occasions occur."

MACHIAVELLI

"The people's first intention is that the State shall not perish."

ROUSSEAU

CONTENTS

Introduction to the Transaction Edition

*The question you propose, whether circumstances do not sometimes occur,
which make it a duty in officers of high trust, to assume authorities beyond
the law, is easy of solution in principle, but sometimes embarrassing in
practice. A strict observance of the written laws is doubtless* one *of the high
duties of a good citizen, but it is not* the highest. *The laws of necessity, of
self-preservation, of saving our country when in danger, are of higher
obligation. To lose our country by a scrupulous adherence to written law,
would be to lose the law itself, with life, liberty, property and all those who
are enjoying them with us; thus absurdly sacrificing the end to the means.*
—Letter of Thomas Jefferson to John B. Colvin, Monticello,
September 20, 1810

How shall we be governed during the War on Terrorism? Definitely not as
we have in the past. Existing governing practices comprehensively failed to
protect the people and cannot be continued. Since we have been forced to face
the horrors of terror attacks on the United States we likewise need to consider
the sort of government such a war will force us to adopt. The "inescapable truth,"
Clinton Rossiter wrote in his classic study of modern democracies in crisis,
Constitutional Dictatorship, is that "No form of government can survive that
excludes dictatorship when the life of the nation is at stake." Saving the country,
as Jefferson wrote, is the highest obligation. Rossiter added the stunning thought
that dictatorships can be constitutional. Following the last forty years of judicial
superiority, his concept of a "constitutional dictatorship" is more shocking today
than when he wrote it.

Rossiter concluded, based on the most thoroughgoing study of the use of
emergency powers in modern democracies—Weimar Germany, France, England, and the United States—that the facts of history demonstrate that, from
time to time, constitutional dictatorship has served as an indispensable factor in
maintaining constitutional democracy. President Lincoln acted illegally when,
on April 27, 1861, reacting to Baltimore mobs interfering with troop trains
moving from Philadelphia to Washington, he authorized the Commanding General of the United States Army to suspend the writ of habeas corpus in Pennsyl-
vania, Delaware, Maryland, and the District of Columbia. When Chief Justice
Taney ruled in the circuit court case, *Ex parte Merryman*, 17 Fed. Cas. 146
(1861), that the president had no authority, Lincoln disregarded the decision. He
extended the suspension, in March 1863, to all other states. Civil liberty during
the Civil War was routinely restricted by arrest without warrant, detention without trial, and release without punishment. Lincoln, in effect, with popular sup-

port, suspended the Constitution, as did Woodrow Wilson in arming the merchantmen, and Franklin Roosevelt on the destroyer deal—and on a number of other occasions, including internment of 70,000 citizens of Japanese ancestry pursuant to Executive Order 9066, probably our greatest abuse of emergency power.

Francis Biddle, Roosevelt's attorney general, was asked later whether the Japanese internment decision was a difficult one for Roosevelt; he explained that he did not think "the Constitutional difficulty plagued him." Moreover, Biddle continued, the "Constitution has not greatly bothered any wartime President. That was a question of law which ultimately the Supreme Court must decide. And meanwhile—probably a long meanwhile—we must get on with the war."

Jefferson did not believe he had authority under the Constitution to buy the Louisiana Territory. He did it because it was essential for the country's future, and Napoleon's difficulties gave us an opportunity that might never be repeated. Elected officials, he wrote to Abigail Adams, must "risk themselves like faithful servants . . . and throw themselves on their country for doing for them unauthorized, what we know they would have done for themselves had they been in a situation to do it." The people, if they did not agree, could not give the Louisiana Territory back to Napoleon, but they could punish the president who bought it.

American law schools, however, teach today, as they have taught generations of lawyers, that the U.S. Constitution is never suspended; it is at all times in full force and effect. The law schools are correct that our Constitution—unlike the Weimar Constitution—makes no express provision for its suspension. Supreme Court doctrine, which is what the law schools teach, does not recognize any implied presidential power to suspend the Constitution: "The Constitution of the United States is a law for rulers and people, equally in war and in peace, and covers with the shield of its protection all classes of men, at all times, and under all circumstances." In short, "emergency does not increase constitutional power nor diminish constitutional restriction" (*Ex parte Milligan*).

The trouble with this view of course, is that it is inaccurate. Rossiter proves this over and over in his analysis of presidential action during the Civil War, World War I, the Depression, and World War II. The problem created by our law schools teaching Supreme Court rhetoric rather than historical truth is that the legal profession, critical in all aspects of the use of emergency power, is misinformed. They should all read Rossiter as soon as possible.

Rossiter's point is that although the normal rules do not apply there are other rules that do and that make the difference between a constitutional dictatorship and a dictatorship. Rossiter writes that every democracy, as a matter of survival, has a mechanism—either express or implied—to suspend the constitution when observing normal rules will endanger the continuation of the state. Is that our situation? Clearly, yes. The normal governmental practice of dealing with terrorism—since the downing of Pan Am 103—has been the criminal justice model. We have used police work, evidence, discovery and trials hoping to put terrorists in jail. The criminal law approach is counter-intuitive since police work is normally confined to a single jurisdiction which has agreed to a basic set of rules. Our government's new thought is that police work could be effective dealing with international terrorism because the emerging political world order had created an overall rule of law. Our government's law enforcement model, of course, was a mis-analysis. Its only virtue was that it was so ineffective that it did not arouse Arab emotions. A police force deters criminal behavior, apprehends and arrests perpetrators—it deals essentially with the consequences of criminal activity and will only incidentally prevent it; the military is designed to destroy forces and is morally permitted—unlike the police—to cause collateral damage. The military is used when the procedures appropriate to law enforcement are not realistic—when a state of war exists.

Rossiter wrote at the end of our last declared war, at a time when the country, of course, was fully committed. In the fifty-three years since, the country has engaged in at least a dozen foreign adventures, ranging from Korea and Vietnam to the Gulf War and Kosovo. But none were declared wars. The government did not believe the people were, or could be persuaded to be, fully committed. And if they were not fully committed to the war they were certainly not going to tolerate a suspension of normal constitutional rules. The country was fully committed to the Cold War, but the emergency powers needed for that war were largely non-intrusive. The ambiguity of congressional commitment is exemplified by the War Powers Act, pursuant to which Congress ceded its constitutional power of Declaration of War. The War on Terror, for the first time, finds the country as fully committed as it was during World War II.

Constitutional dictatorship, Rossiter explains, is based upon specific *principles*. He also explains the *dangers* inherent in the concept and its use (as in the *Weimar* Republic where a constitutional dictatorship degenerated into a dictatorship) and the *criteria* by which the concept's constitutionality can be tested. Rossiter outlines the *principles* of constitutional dictatorship as follows:

> *First, the complex system of government of the democratic, constitutional state is essentially designed to function under normal, peaceful conditions, and is often unequal to the exigencies of a great national crisis.*

> *Therefore, in time of crisis a democratic, constitutional government must be temporarily altered to whatever degree is necessary to overcome the peril and restore normal conditions. This alteration invariably involves government of a stronger character; that is, the government will have more power and the people fewer rights.*

xi

Finally, this strong government, which in some instances might become an outright dictatorship, can have no other purposes than the preservation of the independence of the state, the maintenance of the existing constitutional order, and the defense of the political and social liberties of the people.

The general principles and the particular institutions of constitutional dictatorship are, in Rossiter's phrase, "political and social dynamite."

The question "of first importance," of course, is to secure the democracy against the dangers inherent in the dynamite. The primary *danger* inherent in a constitutional dictatorship is that it will turn on the order it was established to defend. The crisis institutions of martial law, executive legislation, and the suspension of civil rights facilitate the overthrow of the constitution by revolutionary or reactionary interests.

The other major danger of the constitutional dictatorship is that the employment of special crisis institutions will work changes in the permanent structure of government and society: "No constitutional government ever passed through a period in which emergency powers were used without undergoing some degree of permanent alteration always in the direction of an aggrandizement of the power of the state." This risk is of particular significance in America's War on Terrorism since the crisis, we are told, will last indefinitely. It will not be ended, the Secretary of Defense tells us, by a signing on the deck of the *Missouri* in Tokyo Bay.

The emergency, in the case of the War on Terrorism, is open-ended. We are going on a permanent war footing. This makes it different from any of the emergencies analyzed by Rossiter, and which also makes more significant what Rossiter called the "final danger"—that the government by default, rather than design, may lose the *will* to resume its normal constitutional responsibilities, "that the people along with the rulers will fall into the habits of authoritarian government and fail to insist upon a reestablishment of democratic ways." After all, the goal is "not survival alone but survival as a free people." We do not mean to end up as a garrison state.

Rossiter proposed specific *criteria* to judge the worth and propriety of any resort to constitutional dictatorship. The eleven criteria are:

Initiation

1. *No general regime or particular institution of constituted dictatorship should be initiated unless it is necessary or even indispensable to the preservation of the state and its constitutional order. . . .*

xii

2. *The decision to institute a constitutional dictatorship should never be in the hands of the man or men who will constitute the dictator.*

3. *No government should initiate a constitutional dictatorship without making specific provision for its termination.*

Operation

4. *All uses of emergency powers and all readjustments in the organization of the government should be effected in pursuit of constitutional or legal requirements.*

5. *No dictatorial institution should be adopted, no right invaded, no regular procedure altered any more than is absolutely necessary for the conquest of the particular crisis. Certain it is that no normal institutions ought to be declared unsuited to crisis conditions unless the unsuitability be painfully evident.*

6. *The measures adopted in the prosecution of a constitutional dictatorship should never be permanent in character or effect. Emergency powers are strictly conditioned by their purpose, and this purpose is the restoration of normal conditions. The actions directed to this end should therefore be provisional.*

7. *The dictatorship should be carried on by persons representative of every part of the citizenry interested in the defense of the existing constitutional order. . . . Crisis government should be coalition government.*

Termination

8. *Ultimate responsibility should be maintained for every action taken under constitutional dictatorship.*

9.   *The decision to terminate a constitutional dictatorship, like the decision to institute one, should never be in the hands of the man or men who constitute the dictator.*

10.   *No constitutional dictatorship should extend beyond the termination of the crisis for which it was instituted.*

11.   *Finally, the termination of the crisis must be followed by as complete a return as possible to the political and governmental conditions existing prior to the initiation of the constitutional dictatorship.*

Rossiter's brilliant outline of the criteria provides a clear checklist for the people and Congress to judge the executive's actions. But the reader will note that much of his list rests on a premise missing today—the rapid return to normal government when the crisis is concluded. Most of Rossiter's criteria cannot be met if the emergency is open-ended. For example, "No government should initiate a constitutional dictatorship without making specific provisions for its termination" or "The measures adopted in the prosecution of Constitutional Dictatorship should never be permanent in character or effect." He explains that "emergency powers are strictly conditioned by their purpose which is the restoration of normal conditions." But we have been told at the beginning of this war that normal conditions are not going to be restored.

All previous emergencies have been for a well-defined purpose which could be accomplished fairly quickly. The people have been agreeable to a suspension of normal rules for a limited period. At the same time we can easily see that emergency powers are required—that there will be situations where searches and detention will be done without prior—or even subsequent—judicial authorization. There will be arrests without probable cause, searches without warrants, detentions without charges, and detentions without speedy trial. The executive will exercise those powers even if we choose not to recognize he is doing it.

Should America amend its Constitution to include some express provision for emergency powers? Article 48 of the Weimar Constitution provided:

If a state does not fulfill the duties incumbent upon it under the national Constitution or laws, the President of the Reich may compel it to do so with the aid of the armed forces.

If the public safety and order in the German Reich are seriously disturbed or endangered, the President of the Reich *may take the measures necessary* to the restoration of the public safety and order, and may, if necessary, intervene with the armed forces. To this end he may temporarily suspend, in whole or in part, the fundamental rights established in Articles 114 (inviolability of person), 115 (inviolability of domicile), 117 (secrecy of communication), 118 (freedom of opinion and expression thereof), 123 (freedom of assembly), 124 (freedom of association), and 153 (inviolability of property).

The President of the Reich must immediately inform the Reichstag of all measures taken in conformity with sections 1 or 2 of this Article. The measures are to be revoked upon the demand of the Reichstag. (emphasis added)

The critical language providing that the President "may take the measures necessary" is as broad as can be written. Would the German courts or legislature prevent the abuse of Article 48? The German courts—as Rossiter notes and readers will recall from the 1965 film, *Judgment at Nuremburg*—made only a small show of trying to restrain the use of Article 48. Indeed, it was even held that special courts could be established under Article 48. The special courts enforced the Nuremburg Race Laws of 1935. The legislature, which the Constitution set up as the primary guardian against the abuse of emergency powers, also failed. The Weimar Constitution's draftsmen's "fatal mistake" was to create the Reichstag as the oversight body, but then to give the president the power to dissolve the Reichstag. Of course, Weimar did not fail because of a drafting error. The Reichstag and German democracy failed. Chancellor Hitler, in 1933, issued his first decrees pursuant to Article 48. After that, he discarded the Weimar Constitution.

The Weimar model, of course, is not one we would want to follow, but some believe we would be better off if we openly recognized the benefits and problems of constitutional dictatorship. We could amend our Constitution to define the initiation, operation, and termination of emergency powers. We would be better off, the argument goes, if we dealt with the problem openly. Rossiter, on balance, disagrees for two main reasons: (1) the existence of such a provision would make the use of emergency powers more common—Weimar's Article 48 was invoked 250 times during its thirteen years of existence; and (2) the provision would likely be drafted too restrictively; it would probably limit the inherent or implied emergency power necessarily and properly used by Jefferson, Lincoln, Wilson, and Franklin Roosevelt.

The central and intriguing question is what would Rossiter suggest in our situation—a possibly permanent crisis—where a number of the Bill of Rights (Amendments 4, 5 and 6 come quickly to mind) assuredly will be disregarded. Probably the closest we can come to Rossiter's thinking is an article he wrote a few years after *Constitutional Dictatorship*, in which he applied his principles to what government would be like in the then dawning Atomic Age. He wrote that just as the defense of free speech is far more a question of public education than

XV

of laws, so the conditions of workable constitutional dictatorship "exist first of all in the minds and hearts of the American people and only secondarily in the constitution or any laws that we could ever work out." That is, "Political maturity, not paper, made this system work: political maturity, not paper, will save it from destruction." His thought is very close to Learned Hand's 1944 statement, "I often wonder whether we do not rest our hopes too much upon constitutions, upon laws, and upon courts. These are false hopes. Liberty lies in the hearts of men and women; when it dies there, no constitution, no law, no court can save it; no constitution, no law, no court can even do much to help it." In this nation, however, the lamp of liberty is hard to extinguish. As Rossiter remarked: "we are Americans, not Germans or Russians, and democracy is our most basic political and social tradition."

The president, of course, in a constitutional dictatorship, is the dictator and his actions are aimed at making it more effective. Rossiter suggests the *character* of the president, in a constitutional dictatorship, becomes more significant in both the quality of his judgment and his devotion to democracy. "The emergency powers are," as Rossiter said, "political and social dynamite." Congress is assigned the duty to assure that the dictator acts responsibly. The legislature's duty is to translate the Rossiter criteria into effective limits. Weimar failed because the Reichstag failed to perform its crucial function. Congress, in the current crisis setting, should be in continuous session. Ultimately, though, our system rests on the individual; it is the people's job to keep the Congress honest. The democracy can be preserved and, Rossiter writes: "If we will be resolute about this matter of constitutional dictatorship the future may be brighter than we have hitherto dared to think."

William J. Quirk
November 2001

Preface to the 1963 Edition

I send this book for the second time into the worlds of scholarly criticism and public debate with mixed feelings of gratitude and uneasiness. I am grateful because an author ought to be grateful for an unsolicited invitation to reprint a book that has been out of print for some years. I am uneasy because it must be reprinted in 1963 exactly as it was first printed in 1948.

Many things about this study of crisis government in the modern democracies—organization, style, terminology, definitions, distinctions, interpretations of fact, judgments of men and events, recommendations for action —plainly need to be rethought and reframed in the perspective of fifteen years. Yet even if I had the audacity (the audacity, that is to say, of the doctoral candidate of twenty-odd years ago) to write the new book that ought to be written on this subject, I would have to bow to the obdurate fact that my patience and energy are now completely mortgaged to other projects in other fields of political science. At the same time, the economic laws of paperback publishing forbid me to make even minor changes or to add even a few paragraphs. And so, having been persuaded by friends and colleagues that in this instance it is better to have an old book than no book at all, I hereby exhume *Constitutional Dictatorship* and bid its dry bones to live.

No one could be more aware than I of its limitations and faults. The most obvious of the former is that it makes too much of the law and too little of the sociology and psychology of crisis government; the most unsettling of the latter is the confusion I seem to have caused with my too ready assumption that "constitutional dictatorship" had been granted a secure place in the vocabulary of political science as the generic label for such government. That it has not been granted this place is a collective decision that I can protest but not alter. It is therefore likely that, if I had it to do all over again, I would replace the title of this book with the subtitle and restrict the application of "constitutional dictatorship" to those venerable but still lively institutions of martial rule, the state of siege and martial law.

When this book first appeared, it was subjected to a great deal of valid criticism by many scholars who had bothered to read it and to a small volley of abuse by a few polemicists who had not. I hope that all those who buy it in this Harbinger edition will do me the favor of reading it, and will read it as the work of a political scientist who is wholeheartedly committed to the principles, practices, and purposes of constitutional democracy. It is exactly because I cherish our Western style of democracy that I think we must be more knowledgeable and tough-minded about this recurring phenomenon of constitutional government called, for want of a milder and less controversial label, constitutional dictatorship.

This has never been an easy world for constitutional democracy, and it is plainly becoming less easy with each passing year. The future of such democracy—the only kind of democracy so far as we are concerned—may depend, therefore, to a large extent on the skill, courage, and devotion with which our future Lincolns and Churchills make use of autocratic powers and procedures in defense of our precious liberties.* Since I believe in the essential rightness of this harsh prediction even more profoundly today than I did fifteen years ago, I have permitted my feeling of gratitude to conquer (if not to obliterate) my feeling of uneasiness. If the republication of this book does nothing else, I hope that it will encourage others more competent than I in the skills of comparative government to carry on with the study of this fateful problem.

CLINTON ROSSITER

Ithaca, New York
July, 1962

---

*Those who are interested in the application of the lessons of this book to the horrid prospect of atomic war may wish to look at my "Constitutional Dictatorship in the Atomic Age," *Review of Politics,* XI (1949), 395, and "What of Congress in Atomic War?" *Western Political Quarterly,* III (1950), 602. These studies, too, need to be reworked and rewritten.

PREFACE

THIS is a book about dictatorship and democracy. Its treatment of these two patterns of government is not conventional. Instead of setting the one against the other, it proposes to demonstrate how the institutions and methods of dictatorship have been used by the free men of the modern democracies during periods of severe national emergency. It is written in frank recognition of a dangerous but inescapable truth: "No form of government can survive that excludes dictatorship when the life of the nation is at stake."

I can quote Lord Acton's dictum on the corrupting influence of power as approvingly as any man, and I am fully aware of the transient and long-range dangers to constitutional government inherent in this principle which I, following the lead of others, have chosen to call *constitutional dictatorship*. No person professing the democratic faith can take much delight in a study of constitutional dictatorship; the fact remains that it has been with us exactly as long as constitutional government, and has been used at all times, in all free countries, and by all free men.

My decision to devote this survey to four large modern democracies and no smaller ones was rather arbitrary. This I am frank to admit, and I wish that it could have been extended to the British Dominions, the Scandinavian monarchies, Holland, Belgium, Finland, and the rest. I can plead only the limiting factors of time and space. My original intention was to write about the United States, Great Britain, and France, the great and continuing western democracies. Along about the middle of my labors I decided that I could not possibly ignore or treat lightly the pitiful history of the German Republic of 1919-1933; first, because the Constitution of that unhappy democracy contained the most forthright provision for emergency dictatorship in modern constitutional history; secondly, because in the final reckoning this provision contributed heavily to the destruction of the Republic it was instituted to defend. The chapter on the Roman constitutional dictatorship may be ascribed to a classical education.

I have used the words *constitutional* and *democratic* almost synonymously in this book as adjectives descriptive of the form of government under which we live. This is wholly a matter of convenience, and I realize that there have been plenty of constitutional governments which were not at the same time democratic. This book deals with four governments which were both. Just for the record, I am one of the bitter-enders who believe that, even if a government can be constitutional without being democratic, it cannot be democratic without being constitutional.

The Machiavelli quoted opposite the title page is the republican-statesman who labored for years over *The Discourses*, not the Old Nick who dashed off *The Prince* in a vain attempt to wheedle a job out of Lorenzo de' Medici.

I would like to thank a number of "characters preeminent for ability and virtue" (another of Hamilton's phrases) for their criticism, help, and encouragement: Professor Mario Einaudi, Mr. John P. Roche, and Miss Ann Aikman of Cornell; Mr. Malcolm O. Young of Princeton; and Professor Frederick M. Watkins of McGill. My chief debts are acknowledged on the dedicatory page.

CLINTON L. ROSSITER

Ithaca, N.Y.
January, 1948

Constitutional Dictatorship

CHAPTER I

Constitutional Dictatorship

Is there in all republics this inherent and fatal weakness? Must a government of necessity be too *strong* for the liberties of its people, or too *weak* to maintain its own existence?" The man who posed that question was Abraham Lincoln. The date was July 4, 1861. The occasion was a message to Congress, a remarkably candid account of certain extraordinary measures which he had been forced to adopt during the first feverish weeks of the Civil War. If he had been living in 1942, he might have framed his question in more modern terms. He might have asked: "Can a democracy fight a successful total war and still be a democracy when the war is over?"

Mr. Lincoln never did get a direct answer to his question, nor did he really need one. He had already answered it himself with a series of unusual actions whereby he had personally initiated a military, administrative, and legislative program to suppress the rebellion of the southern states and preserve the American Union, and his answer was this: that in all republics there is *not* this inherent and fatal weakness, that a democratic, constitutional government beset by a severe national emergency can be strong enough to maintain its own existence without at the same time being so strong as to subvert the liberties of the people it has been instituted to defend.

In support of that answer this book proposes to examine the experiences with emergency government of four large modern democracies—the United States, Great Britain, France, and the German Republic of 1919-1933—and to see just what sort of unusual powers and procedures these constitutional states saw fit to employ in their various periods of national trial. The study will be partly historical; it will record the actions of some of democracy's great crisis governments and will present the personalities who sparked those governments and gave them leadership—Lloyd George, Clémenceau, Heinrich Brüning, Lincoln, Wilson, Franklin D. Roosevelt, and Winston Churchill. But it will be analytical too; it will examine these actions in terms of definite institutions and will demonstrate the recurring pattern which they have assumed in every democratic country. The modern version of Mr. Lincoln's question—"Can a democracy fight a successful total war and still be a democracy when the war is over?"—will be answered affirmatively by the incontestable facts of history.

3

Consider for a moment the government of the United States which piloted the American people through the crisis of the second World War. In the successful prosecution of a bitter struggle for survival the administration at Washington had continuous resort to actions that would have been looked upon as unconstitutional, undemocratic, and downright dictatorial in time of peace. Since it was a time of war these actions seemed altogether necessary and proper, and the American people generally gave them their support and applause. The ordinary citizen can list any number of unusual governmental procedures that were instituted in the four years of the war, procedures which only the paramount necessity of victory in an all-out war could have sanctioned: the Price Control Act, through which Congress handed over lawmaking power to the executive branch of the government; the history-making "destroyer deal," in which the President disregarded several statutes; the strict control of the American free economy by a host of temporary governmental agencies, most notably the WPB and the OPA; the direct invasion upon the freedom of the individual effected by rationing, the draft, and almost confiscatory taxes; military rule in Hawaii; the forcible removal of tens of thousands of American citizens from their homes on the Pacific Coast; the arbitrary suppression of the seditious words and periodicals of other American citizens; and the spectacular Army seizure of Montgomery Ward and Company. In these actions the government of the United States demonstrated conclusively that in the maintenance of its own existence it could possess and wield authoritarian power, and yet in the course of these same actions—whatever individual injustices and hardships may have been worked—the pattern of free government was left sufficiently unimpaired so that it functions today in full recognition of the political and social liberties of the American people, and in substantial accord with the peacetime principles of the constitutional scheme. We have fought a successful total war, and we are still a democracy.

What the ordinary citizen may not realize is that this more potent and less gentle government of his was pursuing in fact and theory a well-established principle of constitutional government, the principle of *constitutional dictatorship*. The word *dictatorship* should be no cause for alarm. The *dictator* in Mr. Webster's dictionary is primarily "one appointed to exercise, or one exercising, absolute authority in government, esp. in a republic." Indeed, the qualifying adjective *constitutional* is almost redundant, for the historical conception of dictatorship was that it could not be other than constitutional. The original dictatorship, that of the Roman Republic, involved the legal bestowal of autocratic power on a trusted man who was to govern the state in some grave emergency, restore normal times and government, and hand back this power to the regular authorities just as soon as its purposes had been fulfilled. The phrase *constitutional dictatorship*, hyperbole though it may be in many instances, will serve as the general descriptive term for the whole gamut of emergency powers and procedures in periodical use in all constitutional countries, not excluding the United States of America.

The principle of constitutional dictatorship finds its rationale in these three fundamental facts: first, *the complex system of government of the democratic, constitutional state is essentially designed to function under normal, peaceful conditions, and is often unequal to the exigencies of a great national crisis.* Civil liberties, free enterprise, constitutionalism, government by debate and compromise—these are strictly luxury products, and in but a fraction of the governments of man since the dawn of history has the pattern of government and society which the American people take for granted been able to thrive and prosper. "Democracy is a child of peace and cannot live apart from its mother," writes one noted publicist.[1] "War is a contradiction of all that democracy implies. War is not and cannot be democratic," adds a respected Justice of the Supreme Court.[2] Henry Sumner Maine's incisive reminder of the *fragility* of free government is perhaps more valid today than ever before. In the pages to follow it will be seen how frankly the responsible leaders of the modern democracies have admitted the inexpediency of normal constitutional government in periods of national emergency.

Therefore, *in time of crisis a democratic, constitutional government must be temporarily altered to whatever degree is necessary to overcome the peril and restore normal conditions.* This alteration invariably involves government of a stronger character; that is, *the government will have more power and the people fewer rights.* Considered in the light of the recent war, this is a rather astounding admission. At the very moment when the people of the United States were shouting about the differences between democracy and dictatorship, they were admitting in practice the necessity of conforming their own government more closely to the dictatorial pattern! The wartime inadequacies of their constitutional government were remedied in most instances by an un-

[1] William E. Rappard: *The Crisis of Democracy* (Chicago, 1938), p.265.
[2] Wiley Rutledge, in a foreword to "A Symposium on Constitutional Rights in Wartime," *Iowa Law Review*, XXIX (1944), p.379.

conscious but nonetheless real imitation of the autocratic methods of their enemies. The second World War was proof enough that crisis government means strong and arbitrary government, and that "in the eternal dispute between government and liberty, crisis means more government and less liberty."[3]

There are three types of crisis in the life of a democratic nation, three well-defined threats to its existence as both nation and democracy, which can justify a governmental resort to dictatorial institutions and powers. The first of these is *war*, particularly a war to repel invasion, when a state must convert its peacetime political and social order into a wartime fighting machine and overmatch the skill and efficiency of the enemy. The necessity of some degree of readjustment in the governmental structure and of contraction of the normal political and social liberties cannot be denied, particularly by a people faced with the grim horror of national enslavement.

The second crisis is *rebellion*, when the authority of a constitutional government is resisted openly by large numbers of its citizens who are engaged in violent insurrection against the enforcement of its laws or are bent on capturing it illegally or even destroying it altogether. The third crisis, one recognized particularly in modern times as sanctioning emergency action by constitutional governments, is *economic depression*. The economic troubles which plagued all the countries of the world in the early thirties invoked governmental methods of an unquestionably dictatorial character in many democracies. It was thereby acknowledged that an economic crisis could be as direct a threat to a nation's continued and constitutional existence as a war or a rebellion. And these are not the only crises which have justified extraordinary governmental action in nations like the United States. Fire, flood, drought, earthquake, riots, and great strikes have all been dealt with by unusual and often dictatorial methods. Wars are not won by debating societies, rebellions are not suppressed by judicial injunctions, the reemployment of twelve million jobless citizens will not be effected through a scrupulous regard for the tenets of free enterprise, and hardships caused by the eruptions of nature cannot be mitigated by letting nature take its course. The Civil War, the depression of 1933, and the recent global conflict were not and could not have been successfully resolved by governments similar to those of James Buchanan, William Howard Taft, or Calvin Coolidge.

[3] Cecil T. Carr: "Crisis Legislation in Great Britain," *Columbia Law Review*, XL (1940), p.1324.

Finally, *this strong government, which in some instances might become an outright dictatorship, can have no other purposes than the preservation of the independence of the state, the maintenance of the existing constitutional order, and the defense of the political and social liberties of the people.* It is important to recognize the true and limited ends of any practical application of the principle of constitutional dictatorship. Perhaps the matter may be most clearly stated in this way: the government of a free state is proceeding on its way and meeting the usual problems of peace and normal times within the limiting framework of its established constitutional order. The functions of government are parceled out among a number of mutually independent offices and institutions; the power to exercise those functions is circumscribed by well-established laws, customs, and constitutional prescriptions; and the people for whom this government was instituted are in possession of a lengthy catalogue of economic, political, and social rights which their leaders recognize as inherent and inalienable. A severe crisis arises—the country is invaded by a hostile power, or a dissident segment of the citizenry revolts, or the impact of a world-wide depression threatens to bring the nation's economy down in ruins. The government meets the crisis by assuming more powers and respecting fewer rights. The result is a regime which can act arbitrarily and even dictatorially in the swift adoption of measures designed to save the state and its people from the destructive effects of the particular crisis. And the narrow duty to be pursued by this strong government, this constitutional dictatorship? Simply this and nothing more: *to end the crisis and restore normal times.* The government assumes no power and abridges no right unless plainly indispensable to that end; it extends no further in time than the attainment of that end; and it makes no alteration in the political, social, and economic structure of the nation which cannot be eradicated with the restoration of normal times. In short, the aim of constitutional dictatorship is the complete restoration of the *status quo ante bellum.* That historical fact does not comport with philosophical theory, that there never has been a perfect constitutional dictatorship, is an assertion that can be made without fear of contradiction. But this is true of all institutions of government, and the principle of constitutional dictatorship remains eternally valid no matter how often and seriously it may have been violated in practice.

It is here that the need for the qualifying adjective becomes apparent. All the dictatorial actions in the recent war were carried on in the name of freedom. The absolutist pattern was followed and absolutist institu-

7

tions were employed for one great and sufficient reason: that constitutional democracy should not perish from the earth. The democracies fought fire with fire, destroyed autocracy with autocracy, crushed the dictators with dictatorship—all that they might live again under their complex institutions of freedom and constitutionalism. The wide gulf between constitutional and fascist dictatorship should need no demonstration. Like the Grand Canyon, it is there for anyone to see. It was and is a difference of kind as well as degree. However, there is one feature of constitutional dictatorship which sets it off most sharply from the Hitler variety: it is temporary and self-destructive. The only reason for its existence is a serious crisis; its purpose is to dispense with the crisis; when the crisis goes, it goes. The distinction between Lincoln and Stalin or Churchill and Hitler should be obvious.

It is important for the American citizen of 1948 to realize that his super-government of the past few years was nothing new or novel. Indeed, the leading characteristics of constitutional dictatorship are its antiquity and universality, for it is coeval and coextensive with constitutional government itself. The fact that the institutions of free government cannot operate normally in abnormal times has always been recognized. The striking power of autocracy has many times been used to preserve democracy, and more than one constitution has been suspended so that it might not be permanently destroyed. All constitutional countries have made use of constitutional dictatorship, none to any greater extent or with more significant results than the democracies of the twentieth century.

Constitutional dictatorship is a rag-bag phrase, and into it can be tossed all sorts of different institutions and procedures of emergency government. Just what these institutions and procedures are, what extent of governmental readjustment and invasion of civil liberty they involve, what type of crisis invokes their initiation, and how frequently they have been put to use will come to light in the chapters to follow. The present discussion is merely to introduce what lies ahead, and not until the final chapter will an attempt be made to give a precise definition to the major forms of constitutional dictatorship. Nevertheless, it would be of advantage at this early juncture to list the two or three outstanding institutions of constitutional dictatorship to be found in the history of all modern democracies and to add a few words of explanation to each.

In general, all institutions and techniques of constitutional dictatorship fall into one of two related, yet reasonably distinct categories: emergency action of an executive nature, and emergency action of a legislative nature. The crisis of rebellion is dealt with primarily in an executive fashion and calls for the institution of some form of military dictatorship. The crisis of economic depression is dealt with primarily through emergency laws (although these too have to be executed) and calls for lawmaking by the executive branch of the government. The crisis of war, at least total war, is dealt with in both ways. If a situation can be dealt with judicially, it is probably not a crisis.

The basic institution of constitutional dictatorship of an executive nature is *martial rule*; in one form or another it has existed in all constitutional countries. Martial rule is an emergency device designed for use in the crises of invasion or rebellion. It may be most precisely defined as an extension of military government to the civilian population, the substitution of the will of a military commander for the will of the people's elected government. In the event of an actual or imminent invasion by a hostile power, a constitutional government may declare martial rule in the menaced area. The result is the transfer of all effective powers of government from the civil authorities to the military, or often merely the assumption of such powers by the latter when the regular government has ceased to function. In the event of a rebellion its initiation amounts to a governmental declaration of war on those citizens in insurrection against the state. In either case it means military dictatorship—government by the army, courts-martial, suspension of civil liberties, and the whole range of dictatorial action of an executive nature. In the modern democracies the military exercises such dictatorship while remaining subordinate and responsible to the executive head of the civil government. Martial rule has a variety of forms and pseudonyms, the most important of which are *martial law*, as it is known in the common law countries of the British Empire and the United States, and *the state of siege*, as it is known in the civil law countries of continental Europe and Latin America. The state of siege and martial law are two edges to the same sword, and in action they can hardly be distinguished. The institution of martial rule is a recognition that there are times in the lives of all communities when crisis has so completely disrupted the normal workings of government that the military is the only power remaining that can restore public order and secure the execution of the laws.

The outstanding institution of constitutional dictatorship of a legislative nature is *the delegation of legislative power*. What this amounts

9

to is a voluntary transfer of lawmaking authority from the nation's representative assembly to the nation's executive, a frank recognition that in many kinds of crisis (particularly economic depressions) the legislature is unequal to the task of day-to-day, emergency lawmaking, and that it must therefore hand over its functions to someone better qualified to enact arbitrary crisis laws. On its face this would not seem to be a procedure of a particularly dictatorial character. When the age-old battles fought in all constitutional countries to thrust the executive out of the field of lawmaking are recalled to mind, however, it is obvious indeed that the transfer of legislative power from Parliament to Prime Minister or Congress to President is a highly unusual and even dictatorial method of government.

The delegation of power may be limited in time, made in and for a particular crisis, or it may be permanent, to be exercised by the executive in the event of some future crisis. Permanent delegations for emergency purposes have in modern times been cast in the form of statutes enacted by the national legislature. In some countries, however, the constitution itself has granted the executive branch of the government a provisional power of issuing emergency ordinances with the force of law. When the delegation of lawmaking power is a large scale proposition, that is, when the executive is empowered to make emergency laws for the solution of some or all of the nation's major problems, this device may be known as *the enabling act*.

Martial rule and executive lawmaking are both marked by a correlative technique or characteristic of constitutional dictatorship, *the governmental invasion of political or economic liberties*. The crisis expansion of power is generally matched by a crisis contraction of liberty. When a censorship of the press is instituted in time of war, when public meetings are absolutely forbidden in an area racked by rebellion, when a man's house can be legally searched without warrant, when a national legislature itself postpones the elections which it is supposed to face, or when a barkeeper is told in 1944 that he cannot sell a glass of whiskey for more than he charged in 1942—then political and economic rights of free men have been definitely abridged. That all these invasions of liberty and many more like them have been effected in periods of crisis by constitutional governments will shortly become apparent, and the ultimate reason in each case was apparently good and sufficient—the preservation of the state and the permanent freedom of its citizens.

There are many other devices and techniques of constitutional dictatorship: the cabinet dictatorship, the presidential dictatorship, the wartime expansion of administration, the peacetime emergency planning agency, the "war cabinet," the congressional investigating committee, the executive dominance of the legislative process—just to mention a few. Not all of them are necessarily dictatorial, but each can be regarded as an institution of constitutional dictatorship—a technique or device to which a constitutional government may resort in time of emergency. It is important to realize that they all overlap one another, and that there have been plenty of crisis governments, particularly those engaged in total war, which have made use of all of them at once. It is equally important to realize that they are legal and constitutional, that the people of the constitutional democracies have recognized openly that their leaders should have extraordinary power in extraordinary times.

It is perhaps unfortunate that the controversial *law of necessity* has to be mentioned at all. Actually this well-known doctrine is little better than a rationalization of extra-constitutional, illegal emergency action. The fact remains that there have been instances in the history of every free state when its rulers were forced by the intolerable exigencies of some grave national crisis to proceed to emergency actions for which there was no sanction in law, constitution, or custom, and which indeed were directly contrary to all three of these foundations of constitutional democracy. When Abraham Lincoln said: "Often a limb must be amputated to save a life, but a life is never wisely given to save a limb,"[4] he was grounding a number of unconstitutional and dictatorial actions on the law of necessity. The Constitution and certain statutes told him that he could not raise the limits of the army and navy, pay money to persons unauthorized by law to receive it, or contract a public debt for the United States—but Mr. Lincoln decided and candidly declared that the necessity for preserving the Union was sufficient cause for him to go ahead and do these things anyway.

"Every man thinks he has a right to live and every government thinks it has a right to live. Every man when driven to the wall by a murderous assailant will override all laws to protect himself, and this is called the great right of self-defense. So every government, when driven to the wall by a rebellion, will trample down a constitution before it will allow itself to be destroyed. This may not be constitutional law, but it is fact."[5]

[4] Lincoln to Hodges, J. G. Nicolay and John Hay: *Complete Works of Abraham Lincoln* (New York, 1905), II, p.508.
[5] S. G. Fisher: "The Suspension of Habeas Corpus during the War of the Rebellion," *Political Science Quarterly*, III (1888), p.485.

"The law is made for the state, not the state for the law. If the circumstances are such that a choice must be made between the two, it is the law which must be sacrificed to the state. *Salus populi suprema lex esto.*"[6]

This is the theory of *Not kennt kein Gebot,* necessity knows no law.[7] It isn't a very pleasant theory, because Hitler could shout "necessity!" as easily as Lincoln, but there is no denying the fact that responsible statesmen in every free country have broken the law in order to protect the nation in time of serious national emergency, and responsible statesmen will do it again. And the nation was always pretty solidly behind them. In Rousseau's words: "In such a case there is no doubt about the general will, and it is clear that the people's first intention is that the State shall not perish."[8]

There is one other feature of constitutional dictatorship that should be explained here, an obvious and even axiomatic feature, yet still deserving of passing mention. In the last resort, it is always the executive branch in the government which possesses and wields the extraordinary powers of self-preservation of any democratic, constitutional state. Whether the crisis demands the initiation of martial rule or an enabling act or a full-blown war regime, it will be to the executive branch that the extraordinary authority and responsibility for prosecuting the purposes of the constitutional dictatorship will be consigned. *Crisis government is primarily and often exclusively the business of presidents and prime ministers.* Where the forms of constitutional dictatorship have been worked out and given a legal or constitutional basis—as in the state of siege, the enabling act, or the statutes which give the President of the United States certain emergency powers—it is always the executive organ which is selected by the legislators to be the spearhead of crisis action. Where the forms have not been worked out, it is still the executive, this time selected by nature and expediency, which must shoulder the burden and deal with the emergency under the law of necessity.

[6] Joseph Barthélemy: *Problèmes de Politique et Finances de Guerre* (Alcan, 1915), p.121.

[7] The law of necessity was particularly dear to the German jurists of the pre-1914 era, and received its classic statement (complete, with authorities) in Josef Kohler's controversial *Not kennt kein Gebot* (Berlin, 1915), in which a famous legal authority set forth the philosophical justification of the German invasion of Belgium. The law of necessity found its practical application in the vindication of emergency executive lawmaking in the absence of the legislature. The best statement of this doctrine is, strangely enough, by the French writer L. Duguit: *Traité de Droit Constitutionnel* (2nd ed., Paris, 1921-1925), III, pp.700 ff. See also W. Jellinek: *Gesetz und Verordnung* (Vienna, 1887), pp.376 ff.; J. K. Bluntschli: *Allgemeines Staatsrecht* (Munich, 1857), II, p.109.

[8] *Social Contract,* IV, 6.

Locke could champion the supremacy of the legislature and bespeak the Whig fear of overweening executive power, but even he had to admit that it was the undefined power of this organ—the Crown's prerogative "to act according to discretion for the public good, without the prescription of the law and sometimes even against it"[9]—that was the ultimate repository of the nation's will and power to survive. It is never so apparent as in time of crisis that the executive is the aboriginal power of government.

The thesis and title of this book are both open to heavy and trenchant criticism. Dictatorship, even when softened by a popular adjective like constitutional, is a very nasty word. Webster's definition notwithstanding, dictatorship means exactly one thing to a world that has just rid itself of Hitler and Mussolini and still leaves a large variety of brown, red, and indifferent totalitarian regimes at large, and a lot of good people will resent its use in description of the valiant governments which brought them through the crisis and preserved their liberty. More than this, the line of argument in these first few pages may have exhibited a glib assumption that a constitutional democracy can use dictatorial powers and make abnormal readjustments in an emergency without making those powers and readjustments a permanent part of the constitutional scheme. If that be the impression, let it be corrected here and now. The general principle and the particular institutions of constitutional dictatorship are political and social dynamite. No democracy ever went through a period of thoroughgoing constitutional dictatorship without some permanent and often unfavorable alteration in its governmental scheme, and in more than one instance an institution of constitutional dictatorship has been turned against the order it was established to defend. Indeed, it is an inevitable and dangerous thing, and must be thoroughly understood and controlled by any free people who are compelled to resort to it in defense of their freedom. That is exactly what makes this problem so critical, for no free state has ever been without some method by which its leaders could take dictatorial action in its defense. If it lacked such method or the will of its leaders to use it, it did not survive its first real crisis. It is in this twentieth century and indeed in these very days that the age-old phenomenon of constitutional dictatorship has reached the peak of its significance. Men are just as willing today as they were in ancient Rome

[9] *Of Civil Government*, II, chap. 14, sec. 160.

13

to renounce their freedom for a little while in order to preserve it forever.[10]

[10] The literature on the problem of constitutional dictatorship is comparatively meager and inadequate. Special studies on the use of some particular form of emergency powers in some particular country are numerous enough, but comprehensive treatments of the problem in any one country or of some single device as it has been employed in several different countries are rare indeed. One excellent study of the comparative use of an instrument of crisis government is Herbert Tingsten: *Les Pleins Pouvoirs*, trans. from the Swedish (Paris, 1934), a survey of the enabling act in eight countries. The *Institut für ausländisches öffentliches Recht und Völkerrecht* in Berlin published a volume in 1928 entitled *Das Recht des Ausnahmezustandes im Auslande*, which presented a series of studies of emergency powers in six European countries.

A trail-blazing, if somewhat occasional work defining the distinction between constitutional and non-constitutional dictatorship was Carl Schmitt: *Die Diktatur* (1st ed., Munich, 1921). Schmitt, who was at the time advocating a broad interpretation of the emergency powers of the German President, separated all extraordinary public offices into two categories: the commissioned dictatorship (*kommissarische Diktatur*) and the sovereign dictatorship (*souveräne Diktatur*), but he lumped so many heterogeneous offices under the former category (the Roman dictator, Wallenstein, the "commissioners" of the Middle Ages, Lincoln) that he failed in the end to draw a sufficiently precise distinction between constitutional dictatorship and opportunistic Caesarism.

The best general discussion of the problem is presented by Frederick M. Watkins: "The Problem of Constitutional Dictatorship," in *Public Policy*, Friedrich and Mason, eds. (Cambridge, 1940), pp.324-379. See also the precise summaries written by Carl J. Friedrich: *Constitutional Government and Politics* (New York, 1937), chap. 13, and *Constitutional Government and Democracy* (Boston, 1941), chap. 13. See also Francisco Cambo: *Las Dictaduras* (3rd ed., Madrid, 1929); W. W. Willoughby and L. Rogers: *An Introduction to the Problem of Government* (New York, 1923), chap. 6; Théodore Reinach: *De L'Etat de Siège* (Paris, 1885); Heinrich Muth: *Das Ausnahmerecht* (Emsdetten, 1932).

That there have been and can be dictatorships other than the Nazi variety and that "dictatorship" is not always synonomous with "despotism" has been most recently and cogently asserted by Charles E. Merriam: *The New Democracy and the New Despotism* (New York, 1939), and by Robert M. MacIver: *Leviathan and the People* (Louisiana State University, 1939).

CHAPTER II

The Roman Dictatorship

THE assertion that constitutional dictatorship has always been an indispensable accessory to constitutional government finds convincing demonstration in the heroic history of republican Rome. The splendid political genius of the Roman people grasped and solved the difficult problem of emergency powers in a manner quite unparalleled in all history, indeed so uniquely and boldly that a study of modern crisis government could find no more propitious a starting point than a brief survey of the celebrated Roman dictatorship.

Whether a political institution of the ancient Romans can serve as a working model for the statesmen of modern times may well be doubted, so different are the social and economic conditions of this century from those of twenty-four centuries ago. And yet as a theoretical standard, as a sort of moral yardstick against which to measure modern institutions of constitutional dictatorship (particularly martial rule), the Roman dictatorship is invaluable. Nowhere in all history has the belief that a constitutional state can alter its pattern of government temporarily in order to preserve it permanently been more resolutely asserted and successfully proved than it was in the storied Republic of ancient Rome. Nowhere has constitutional dictatorship attained such a degree of institutional perfection and historical significance. For this reason the Roman dictatorship invokes the attention of all free men.

As a matter of fact, the history of almost all nations of antiquity presents instances of the concept and practice of constitutional dictatorship, although rarely was it raised to the level of a conventional institution. Aristotle tells in his *Politics* of an elective tyranny designed to restore law and order in a state which has been weakened by factional strife or the depredations of a neighboring power.[1] This was the institution of the *aesymnetes*, repeated occurrences of which are to be found in the history of many Greek cities. Only in republican Rome, however, was the constitutional dictatorship recognized as a regular instrument of government.

The dictatorship is a phenomenon which has intrigued almost all ordinary readers of history and almost no students of law and politics.[2]

---

[1] *Politics*, IV, 10.
[2] Conspicuous exceptions to this statement are those two great admirers of republican Rome, Machiavelli (*Discourses*, I, 34) and Rousseau (*Social Contract*, IV, 6), both of

15

If Macaulay's schoolboy knew "who imprisoned Montezuma and who strangled Atahualpa," he knew even better the noble legend of Cincinnatus, the aged Roman farmer who was called from the plow by his embattled countrymen and given despotic authority to repel the threat of alien tyranny; and who, after sixteen days of absolute power, in which the enemy had been routed in disgrace and the state had been saved, laid down the sword and again took up the plow. That the Roman dictatorship was never such a perfect ideal is a matter of history. This much, however, is certain: there did exist in ancient Rome a political phenomenon, the dictatorship, whereby in time of crisis an eminent citizen was called upon by the ordinary officials cf a constitutional republic, and was temporarily granted absolute power over its whole life, not to subvert but to defend the republic, its constitution, and its independence. Most significant of all, provision for this emergency institution was made in the fundamental laws of the state.

The Origins of the Dictatorship

THE historical origin of this office is shrouded in the mists of ancient history. Livy himself, although never one to resist the urge to state legend as fact when glorifying Rome's golden past, confessed his inability to ascertain exactly the genesis of the dictatorship—"nor can it be satisfactorily determined in what year the dictatorship was instituted. . . . nor who was the first dictator."[3] The majority of classical opinion assigns the honor of holding the first dictatorship to a certain T.

whom devoted many complimentary remarks to this institution. Algernon Sidney (*Discourses on Government*, II, 13) asserted: "I do therefore grant, that a power like to the dictatorian, limited in time, circumscribed by law, and kept perpetually under the supreme authority of the people, may, by virtuous and well disciplined nations, upon some occasions, be prudently granted to a virtuous man." Bodin (*Six Livres de la République*, III, 2) referred to the dictatorship as a "commissioned" office in contrast to an ordinary magistracy, and thereby set the stage for Carl Schmitt. Spinoza (*Tractatus Politicus*, x, 1) disapproved of the dictatorship as an instrument of government in an aristocratic republic, maintaining that even the briefest assumption by the republic of this monarchical form of authority was of more danger than value. In *Federalist*, no. 70, Hamilton pointed to the dictatorship as a unified and energetic executive that was indispensable to the cause of republicanism in Rome. Almost without exception the classicists have investigated the dictatorship "as a concern of antiquarianism, without attempting to fix its general significance as a concept of public law." Schmitt: *Die Diktatur*, I. In addition to the works cited in the various notes to this chapter, see Frank F. Abbott: *A History and Description of Roman Political Institutions* (Boston, 1907), chaps. 8 and 9; Pardon: *Die Römische Diktatur* (Berlin, 1885); Pauly-Wissowa: *Real-Encyclopädie der classischen Altertumswissenschaft* (Stuttgart, 1903), 9th half-vol., p.370; E. Servais: *La Dictature* (Paris, 1886); P. G. H. Willems: *Le Droit Public Romain*, 6th ed. (Louvain, 1884), pp.256 ff.

[3] Livy, II, 18.

Larcius Flaccus, who was named to the position sometime around 500 B.C. to conduct a crucial war against certain neighboring towns. Cicero writes that this took place "about ten years after the establishment of the first consuls."[4] It is of interest to note that there are two versions explaining the need of dictatorial leadership in this war—one asserting that the consuls had forfeited the confidence of the people through their sympathy for the exiled Tarquins, the other that the plebeians had chosen this crucial time to dramatize their grievances through the medium of a military strike. Whatever the reason, it is certain that it was not many years after the establishment of the Republic that the rulers of the new Rome were compelled by the stress of the times to go back to the recently discredited monarchical form of government as the only means of saving the state from extinction. The same men who had driven the kings out of Rome and had set up a constitutional government were now forced to admit in practice that this new government was inadequate to the task of its own preservation, and that only a temporary retreat to the kingly power could enable it to carry through to normal times. Once more a king, though by a different name and for a different purpose and for a much different length of time, was to rule in Rome.

The political origin of this office is another matter of dispute. Some authorities maintain that the dictatorship was an original part of the republican constitution instituted in 509 B.C., and thus stood ready for the use of T. Larcius Flaccus ten years later. Mommsen regarded the dictatorship as "an integral part of the republican constitution."[5] Others point out that it seems incredible that in the year in which the kings had been driven out such an office would be created by the Romans, and declare that the dictatorship was a later product, unprovided for in the original constitution and only instituted under the compulsion of events by a *lex de dictatore creando*.[6] All agree that the office was a relic of the monarchical system and was considerably influenced by analogous practices in other Italian towns.[7] There were such significant differences between the Roman dictatorship and the annual, collegial Latin dictators, however, that the Roman institution may be regarded as original with

[4] *De Re Publica*, II, 56.
[5] *Römisches Staatsrecht* (Leipzig, 1887), II, p.135. Otto Karlowa: *Römische Rechtsgeschichte* (Leipzig, 1885), I, p.211, agrees, and Arthur Rosenberg in his *Der Staat der alten Italiker* (Berlin, 1913), p.81, states: "Both offices, the Roman consulate and the Roman dictatorship, were created from a single political resolve."
[6] Livy, II, 18; Fritz Bandel: *Die Römischen Diktaturen* (Breslau, 1910), pp.5-6.
[7] See generally W. Soltau: *"Der Ursprung der Diktatur," Hermes, Zeitschrift für klassische Philologie*, XLIX, p.352.

that people, a product of their own history rather than an imitation of foreign practice.

The logical origin of the dictatorship is to be found in the peculiar political conditions prevalent in the early years of the Roman Republic. On the one hand, the Republic was continually beset by desperate wars without and bitter class struggles within; on the other, the Roman governmental scheme was unusually vulnerable to the impact of temporary emergencies. Rome was a constitutional state of an extreme type, a subtle fusion of aristocracy, direct democracy, and the representative system that found expression in an ever-increasing profusion of public officials and assemblies regulated by ideas of what was and what was not constitutional even more tenacious than those held twenty-four centuries later in England and the United States. At one and the same time there flourished three important assemblies, several smaller ones, and the famed Senate of Rome—a division of legislative authority quite without peer or precedent. It was for the institutionalization of executive authority, however, that the Romans reserved their most remarkable exercises of political inventiveness. Competence of an executive nature was parceled out amongst a myriad of officials, all of them severely and uniquely circumscribed in the performance of their duties. The unitary executive was completely alien to the normal scheme of government in Rome.

This unparalleled division of administrative authority did not arise at once in the republican structure and was not a reaction to executive power such as that manifested by the Americans of 1776. At the time of the institution of the dictatorship it was royal, not executive authority which was particularly feared. The revolution of 509 B.C. hardly deserved the name, for it was in reality nothing more than the substitution of two autocratic rulers for one. But it is true that the king, a single and powerful ruler, was expelled, and the consuls, a collegial and somewhat limited executive, were put in his place. Roman constitutional change was a slow process, and the real limitations on executive power, other than this original one of collegiality, were to come only with the passage of time. Indeed, the constitutional history of Rome had as one of its salient features the gradual weakening of executive power. The matrix of all power had been the king, who held in his hands those functions later to be performed by the Senate, the assemblies, and the whole hierarchy of administrative and judicial officials. From the king, and later from the consuls, powers were continually sapped by the repeated institution of new organs of government. The executive was further weakened by the gradual imposition of several important external checks.

In the great days of the Republic the executive authority was vested in two consuls, beside or beneath whom operated a number of other single or collegial magistracies. The consulate was an office coeval with the Republic, and was the legitimate heir of the authority and competence of the king. This competence, summed up in the mighty concept of *Imperium*, ran the gamut of the recognized types of political power—executive, judicial, legislative, administrative, military, and priestly. It may be conveniently tagged with the first of these labels, since the majority of the consul's duties were executive in nature.

Of importance to an understanding of the dictatorship is a clear picture of just how sharply the consuls, and indeed the entire catalogue of Roman magistracies, were limited in the exercise of their powers. The most significant limitation was the principle of collegiality, the distinctive mark of the Roman executive. Each consul was empowered with an absolute veto upon the acts of his colleague. The implications of this single fact leave no doubt of the logical origin of the dictatorship. Other shackles from which no consul or other executive official was ever free were the absolute veto of the tribunes on arbitrary magisterial actions (*intercessio*), the right of appeal from serious sentences to the centuriate assembly (*provocatio*), and the possibility of being held accountable to the people at the termination of his office. Another significant circumscription to the magisterial exercise of power was the dominant position of the Senate throughout most of the history of the Republic, a dominance that was finally to eventuate in senatorial absolutism. The "advice" of the Senate was rarely disregarded by any Roman official. Finally, the term of office of almost every magistracy was one year.

The Dictatorship

THE extreme and unparalleled vulnerability to crisis of this complex constitutional system had its natural counterpart in an instrument of emergency government equally extreme and unparalleled. To the obvious problem thus presented there could be only one solution for this city-state that meant to stay alive and republican in that turbulent world: an outright dictatorship, rigorously limited in time and purpose. Whenever the Republic should find itself immersed "in grievous wars or serious civil unrest,"[8] this complexity of power and functions was to

---

[8] Claudius: *Oratio Lugdunensis*, I, 28.

be united in one man. If collegiality was the distinctive mark of the consulate, unity was the distinctive mark of the dictatorship. To the Roman the one-man executive meant absolutism, and the substitution of two consuls for one king had been the most prominent advance in constitutional government in his nation's history. Yet, in a remarkable exhibition of political realism, he was willing to revert in dire necessity to the abandoned form, to use discarded absolutism to preserve present constitutionalism.

Whenever the Senate was convinced that the Republic was in grave danger and that the ordinary hierarchy of administrative officials was not competent to secure its safety, it could initiate a proposal that the consuls appoint a dictator. The consuls themselves could also propose that the dictatorship be employed, but the approval of the Senate remained necessary. The power of appointment resided constitutionally in the two consuls. They might act jointly, often in consultation with the praetor, or separately, in which case the consul who made the appointment was chosen by lot. In the selection of the dictator the consul followed peculiar religious rites to which he alone was competent. This prevented an unconstitutional appointment of a dictator, and bespoke the religious importance of this great bulwark of the state.

There was no check upon the consul in the discharge of this fateful duty. The otherwise omnipotent power of veto of his colleague or of the tribunes was not recognized. The various assemblies were without even advisory power in this matter. Constitutionally the Senate too was without power to disapprove his choice, although at the height of its authority in the old Republic this body not only passed on the advisability of instituting the dictatorship, but usually saw to it that its favorite was selected. Cicero regarded the nomination of the dictator as depending positively upon the Senate.[9] No dictator was ever named by another dictator. Not until the end of the history of the office was there any deviation from this method of instituting the dictatorship. After the shocking disaster at Lake Trasimenus in 217 B.C. the necessity of vigorous leadership was recognized by everyone in Rome. Almost spontaneously an assembly of citizens met under the leadership of a praetor and authorized the appointment of Q. Fabius Maximus as dictator.

The citizen selected as dictator had his *Imperium*, his sacred and absolute power, conferred upon him by a *lex curiata*, a matter of form only, but a constitutional procedure that gave the particular dictatorship

[9] *De Legibus*, III, 3, 9.

its stamp of legality. The whole process of instituting the dictatorship rarely consumed more than two or three days. The nomination to this exalted office was the highest honor which the Republic could confer. Therefore the man selected was invariably a well-known public figure, one who had prosecuted a successful career and was known for both his ability and his devotion to the Republic. In the early history of the office the non-consular dictators were as numerous as those of consular rank, but after 320 B.C. the dictators were invariably men who had held the consular office, a practice governed by what Mr. Dicey would have called a convention of the Roman constitution rather than by a specific law. A consul could not name himself, and only four or five times in the history of the dictatorship was a consul in office or a praetor chosen as dictator. This fact alone would serve to distinguish the Roman dictatorship from all modern constitutional counterparts, in that a new office was set up for the emergency and a private citizen was called upon to fill it.

The Purposes of the Dictatorship

THE *lex curiata* which gave legal sanction to the particular dictatorship defined the purpose of its institution. There were two varieties of constitutional dictatorship for time of crisis in Rome, the *dictatura rei gerundae causa* (literally, "the dictatorship for getting things done") and the *dictatura seditionis sedandae et rei gerundae causa* ("the dictatorship for suppressing civil insurrection"). Out of the total of about ninety dictatorships recorded in the three hundred year history of the office,[10] approximately fifty were *rei gerundae causa*. This was the appellation affixed to the true Roman dictator, the man called upon by the people to assume all powers and save the state from the threat of total defeat in war. The story of Cincinnatus, semi-legendary though it may be, is a perfect illustration of the use of the dictatorship in its purest form. The dictator *rei gerundae causa* was in the strict sense a military dictator, an all-powerful general of Rome's armies, but his *Imperium*, his authority and power, extended throughout the whole city and over the whole of Roman life. The line between things military and things civil was a tenuous one in ancient Rome.

The dictator *seditionis sedandae causa* was named at least four times. Internal strife between patrician and plebeian was his concern, and al-

[10] For complete (and in some particulars contradictory) lists of the dictatorships during these three centuries, see Bandel, *op. cit.*, who gives 88; Albert Dupond: *De dictatura et de magisterio equitum* (Paris, 1875), pp.45-48, who gives 86; and Felix Pichon: *De la Dictature* (Poitiers, 1888), pp.63-66, who gives a full 90.

though clear evidence on the matter is lacking, it seems certain that this variety of the dictatorship was a patrician weapon, the resort by the Senate to a device of crisis government ordinarily devoted to the maintenance of the whole state, but in this instance to the maintenance in power of the ruling class, threatened in its dominant position by the surge to equality of the plebeian multitude.[11] The hostility to the dictatorship of the people's party in Rome, the results of which will presently be noted, leaves little doubt of this fact. This by no means signifies that the dictatorship was the usual means by which the patricians sought to suppress the rise of the lower classes. This great struggle within the Roman state lasted for hundreds of years, and only four times was the dictatorship clearly resorted to as an oppressive weapon against the plebeians. And in several of these instances it was the state as much as the patrician class that was actually saved. The dictatorship could be used, however, as can all devices of constitutional emergency government, as an instrument of class warfare.

The dictatorship was also instituted for several other purposes. Not until 363 B.C. was there a dictator who was not either *rei gerundae causa* or *seditionis sedandae causa*, and it is obvious that it was for crisis purposes alone that the dictatorship was originally established. But in that year L. Manlius Imperiosus was appointed dictator *clavi figendi causa*, for the sole purpose of "driving in the nail," an ancient Roman religious rite designed to assuage the wrath of the gods, employed in this instance as the last resort in an effort to free the city from the ravages of a dire pestilence. The driving of the nail was a sacred ceremony to which an official of only the highest rank was competent, ordinarily the pontifex maximus. On this occasion a qualified person does not seem to have been available; therefore a dictator was chosen solely to perform this important ceremonial task. From this time on the dictatorship was employed with increasing frequency for purposes other than some grave national emergency. Thus this expedient was used some twenty times between 348 B.C. and 202 B.C. *comitiorum habendorum causa*, a dictator being appointed to conduct important elections in the absence or other incapacity of the ordinary magistrates. Other isolated objects for particular dictatorships were *feriarum latinarum constituendarum causa* ("for conducting religious festivals"), *ludorum celebran-*

---

[11] Montesquieu considered the dictatorship to be the means whereby the plebeians were intimidated rather than punished, and to him it was definitely a patrician device— *Esprit des Lois*, II, 3. See also Ludwig Lange: *Römische Althertümer* (Berlin, 1876-1879), I, pp.542 ff.; Dupond, *op. cit.*, p.3.

dorum causa ("for holding public games"), *quaestionum exercendarum causa* ("for special trials"), and *senatus legendi causa* ("for choosing the senate"). In each of these instances an unusual act of state to which no official was considered competent or for which the regular official was temporarily incapacitated demanded performance, and the dictatorship was chosen to fill the breach. Although the office was thereby weakened as an exemplary type of emergency government, its dignity and constitutional significance were not only attested but enhanced.

The Powers and Limitations of the Dictator

ONCE the Imperium had been conferred upon him, the dictator became as absolute a ruler as could well be imagined.[12] Freed from the many limitations put upon the ordinary magistrates, responsible to no one for his actions, possessed of all powers which might contribute to the successful pursuit of his assignment, the dictator was a constitutional magistrate unique in his capacity to move with dispatch and authority to all measures he might consider necessary to the preservation of the constitution which gave him authority and the Republic which gave him freedom. An examination of what few restrictions there were upon the dictator bears witness to the extreme liberty of action and breadth of competence which he enjoyed.

The one important formal limitation—and here is the characteristic most clearly distinguishing this dictatorship from all others that have ever existed—was the six-month term of office for which the dictator was chosen. This length of time is explained by the fact that the early Romans fought only in the summer. It was a restriction on the dictatorship that was never transgressed, by force or by law. Indeed, another convention of the Roman constitution bound the dictator to abdicate his office immediately his particular piece of business had been successfully terminated. Machiavelli wrote of the Romans he so greatly admired that "if any of them arrived at the dictatorship, their greatest glory consisted in promptly laying this dignity down again."[13] The tribunes could force him to resign if the emergency had clearly terminated. If he failed to do so he might, after having finally resigned, be prosecuted on a charge of having illegally prolonged his tenure of office. The L. Man-

[12] Albert Schwegler: *Römische Geschichte* (Tübingen, 1853-1858), II, p.120, describes the office as "a temporary reestablishment of the monarchy."
[13] *Discourses*, I, 30.

23

lius Imperiosus who was called up in 363 B.C. *clavi figendi causa* regarded his selection as due to military rather than religious reasons and assumed the role of a full-fledged dictator, but in the face of the unanimous opposition of the tribunes he was forced to resign from the office. There could be but one dictatorship in a single year, and no dictator could stay in office beyond the term of the magistrates who had named him. It is instructive to note the complete absence of any violation of these time limits. There could be no more convincing evidence of the constitutional character of the Roman dictatorship.

The dictator found a further restriction, of course, in the nature of the office he was called upon to fill. His sacred trust it was to maintain the constitutional order, and although to this end he was competent to resort to almost any measure, the Republic which he was chosen to defend could not be altered or subverted. There were three other restrictions upon the dictator, already limited in the time and scope of his office. First, he was entirely dependent upon the Senate in financial matters. Although he could not be held accountable for monies paid to him, the constitutional requirement that there be no withdrawal from the public treasury except by consent of the Senate was not relaxed. In the second place, the right of the people to decide on offensive wars was never conveyed to any dictator. Finally, the dictator as judge had no civil jurisdiction. In all other directions his competence was without restriction, and only the forbearance of his fellow citizens and the character of his trust acted as obstructions to the free play of his will. The sacred nature of the dictatorship demands particular attention, for in no other way can the fact be explained that never in the three hundred years of the office was this unshackled display of power used to subvert the constitutional order. No more ideal device for a monarchist or absolutist coup d'état was ever set up within the framework of a constitutional system, but it was never used except to preserve the existing order.

With the exception of these restrictions the dictator possessed full powers for the defense of the Republic. From the other restraints which sharply circumscribed the capacity of the consul or any other magistrate to act decisively in emergencies—the tribunician veto, the appeal from his sentences to the people, the responsibility after leaving office for his acts, and particularly the presence of a collegial official—the dictator was freed. The advisory control of the Senate was sharply decreased. The rights of the citizen underwent a sizable curtailment, as did the competence of the ordinary magistrates.

24

Whatever had to be done to repulse the enemy from the gates of Rome or abate the bitter strife of patrician and plebeian fell within the scope of his *Imperium*. As military commander his discretion was extreme. Without the order of the Senate no consul, by inflexible custom, could raise more than four legions. No such restriction hampered the dictator, who could call every man in Rome into the ranks. In his decisions as to strategy and the general conduct of campaigns he was not subject to the usual instructions of the Senate, and in the field he was generally relieved of the presence of the ubiquitous senatorial legates. Alone among all Roman generals it was the dictator who wielded an unshackled and independent military authority.

His command over the civil life of Rome was no less absolute. In addition to the general powers which attach everywhere to absolutism, the dictator had other and peculiarly Roman functions. He could convoke any of the assemblies and preside over them, and this power extended to the Senate. In the realm of judicial power his jurisdiction extended to all criminal cases affecting the safety of the state. To this end he possessed the power to execute summarily and without appeal, as well as to fix fines. His power of arrest overrode the intercession of the sacrosanct tribune. He could coin money, take the highest auspices, and freely dispose of booty and honors. According to Roman constitutional law the dictator could not legislate, that is, initiate and promulgate a *lex*; but he had the *ius edicendi*, and his decrees were, for the duration of his power, as good as laws and were published as such. *Quod dictatori placuit legis habet vigorem.*

Such were the powers and the freedom of the dictator *rei gerundae causa* or *seditionis sedandae causa*. The dictatorship was primarily a military office, instituted to save the state from the threat of foreign or rebellious arms, but the power of the dictator extended out from the army and its camp and embraced the entire state. The resort to the dictatorship converted the Roman Republic and its complex constitution into the simplest and most absolute of all governments—an armed camp governed by an independent and irresponsible general. This was martial law with a vengeance, the state of siege in its aboriginal form. The extreme position of the dictator may be illustrated by the fact that he was assigned twenty-four lictors, double the number granted to the consuls, and that this bodyguard, contrary to one of the strongest republican traditions, accompanied the dictator through the streets of Rome armed with their axes. The consuls could not appear before the dictator attended by their own lictors.

The dictator was constitutionally required to select a lieutenant, the so-called *magister equitum*, and in this choice he was uncontrolled. Nominally the *magister equitum* was in time of war the leader of the cavalry, while the dictator, originally known as *magister populi*, commanded the older and more important infantry. In practice, the *magister equitum* bore much the same relation to the dictator that Hess once did to Hitler in his capacity as *Stellvertreter des Führers*. He was a kind of "perfect substitute" for the dictator, and in the latter's absence could enjoy all his exceptional powers and freedom from restraint. If the dictator were in the field, the master of the horse could exercise his power at Rome. If the dictator were in the city, he could act for him as general of the forces in the field.

The Decline of the Dictatorship

IT IS obvious that this remarkable institution, despite the many successes it enjoyed as shield of the Republic, was from its inception the target of the popular party in Rome. Moreover, it was an object of some suspicion and fear to the senatorial aristocracy, which was forced to renounce much of its power whenever the dictatorship was instituted. It was the radical element in Rome, however, which distrusted this magistracy most deeply. Such a complete and unlimited concentration of power could hardly fail to be an object of fear, and the office could easily be used to quell an outbreak of the plebeians against the ruling class. Not content with seeing the first plebeian called up as dictator in 356 B.C., the radicals of ancient Rome were able by 300 B.C. to establish the right of appeal from the dictator's sentences, and near the close of the third century the power of the tribune to interpose his sacred veto was nailed into the laws.

Hedged in by these restraints, used more and more frequently for purposes other than the abatement of a severe crisis, initiated no longer after 217 B.C. by the Senate exclusively, the dictatorship had lost its pristine characteristics as an effective instrument of emergency government and therewith its reason for existence. The last constitutional dictator *rei gerundae causa* left office in 216 B.C., the last constitutional dictator of any sort in 202 B.C., and these dictators were in truth no dictators at all. Though the office was never abolished, it was never again employed. Sulla and Caesar each assumed the title of dictator, but except in name there was no similarity between their dictatorships and those under the old Republic. Both of these men were dictators in today's accepted sense of the word, with all powers and no restraints, and without any externally imposed limit on their term of office. After Caesar's death this dictatorship was abolished upon the motion of Antony,[14] and with the coming of empire the republican office fell into oblivion.

A number of other reasons suggest themselves to explain the decline of the Roman dictatorship. If this office had been rendered inadequate to the purposes for which it had been instituted some three centuries before, this meant nothing to the continued existence of the Roman state. Those purposes themselves, as well as the republican system, had also disappeared. The office had outlived its usefulness. The close of the great civil wars in 287 B.C. had been the last occasion for the dictatorship *seditionis sedandae causa*, and with the withdrawal of Hannibal to Africa in 203 B.C. the last threat of alien assault upon the gates of Rome or even against Italy had vanished. For the next four or five centuries Rome's wars were not to be even partially defensive in character. The crisis war was a thing of the past, and so too was the crisis governor and his sharply limited incumbency. The wars of a city on its way to world domination must be fought both summer and winter. The wars of aggression upon which Rome was now embarking had nothing to do with the maintenance of a republican constitution in a free state, the true purpose of the dictatorship.

More than this, the republican constitution was well in decline. The Senate had risen to a completely dominant if not absolute position, and from this time forward it was the maintenance of this dominance and not of a constitutional order that was to occasion extraordinary governmental action in Rome. It is a remarkable and instructive paradox that the Republic and the dictatorship reached the peak of their development side by side, and that the decline of the former was matched in time and degree by the decline of the latter. In the years following the close of the second Punic War there was no critical situation in Italy demanding exceptional measures. When the agitations of the noble Gracchi threw the city once again into turmoil, the Senate chose to resort to the consuls themselves as convenient repositories of its absolute power saying, "Let the consuls see to it that the state suffer no harm." It was by means of this simple delegation of emergency power to its magisterial servants, couched in the famed phrase *videant consules ne quid res publica detrimenti capiat*, that the Senate was to wage its bitter

---

[14] The dictatorship abolished by Antony was the Caesarian, not the constitutional dictatorship. See the note by F. Haverfield: "The Abolition of the Dictatorship," *Classical Review*, III (1889), p.77.

but futile struggle to maintain its ascendancy in the years between 130 B.C. and the rise of the empire. Constitutional government had passed into history; so too had the constitutional dictator. Emergency government of a legal nature had been replaced by emergency government in behalf of absolutism. Henceforth the government at Rome was to seek defense before the challenge of other groups and persons in quest of power through this delegation of senatorial omnipotence to magistrates better fitted to wield it in perilous situations. To Cicero as consul was directed this admonition in his suppression of the Catilinarian conspiracy, and weapon of absolutism as it may have been, it was to have its counterparts in many democracies of modern times.

Thus concludes this brief consideration of the most unique and successful constitutional emergency institution in all recorded history, most unique in that no other constitutional state ancient or modern so boldly asserted the periodic necessity of emergency government, and most successful in that it was the bulwark of the Republic through all the tumultuous centuries when the loss of any one of several wars could have led to the total obliteration of the Roman people, an event that might have altered radically the world's history. The lessons that Rome has taught the world have been many and significant, but none is of more present consequence than the pregnant truth imparted by the history of the famed dictatorship: that in a free state blessed by a high constitutional morality and led by men of good sense and good will, the forms of despotism can be successfully used in time of crisis to preserve and advance the cause of liberty.

"And truly, of all the institutions of Rome, this one deserves to be counted amongst those to which she was most indebted for her greatness and dominion."[15]

[15] Machiavelli: *Discourses*, I, 34.

Part One

CONSTITUTIONAL DICTATORSHIP IN THE GERMAN REPUBLIC

THE example of Rome, a republic which made specific provision in its constitution for the establishment of a dictatorship in time of national emergency, finds its most authentic modern parallel in the history of the ill-fated German Republic of 1919-1933. No constitutional democracy can compare with Weimar Germany in the varieties of its dictatorial experience—in its need for emergency government, in the frequency and consequence of its resorts to such government, or in the scope of constitutional provision therefor. This being Germany, theory kept pace with fact. The quantity of juristic discussion of the German constitutional dictatorship was prodigious. That the German Republic is dead and buried does not lessen, but rather enhances the importance of this study. There is much to be learned from its calamitous history, especially in the matter of constitutional emergency powers. A study of modern constitutional dictatorship could not possibly ignore the crisis history of the German Republic. This is particularly true because the techniques of constitutional dictatorship which had been designed and evolved for the defense of the Republic were in the end to play a considerable part in its destruction.

The most logical introduction to such a study is a glance at the "dictatorship article" of the Weimar Constitution itself, the famous Article 48.

If a state does not fulfill the duties incumbent upon it under the national Constitution or laws, the President of the Reich may compel it to do so with the aid of the armed forces.

If the public safety and order in the German Reich are seriously disturbed or endangered, the President of the Reich may take the measures necessary to the restoration of the public safety and order, and may if necessary intervene with the armed forces. To this end he may temporarily suspend in whole or in part the fundamental rights established in Articles 114 (inviolability of person), 115 (inviolability of domicile), 117 (secrecy of communication), 118 (freedom of opinion and expression thereof), 123 (freedom of assembly), 124 (freedom of association), and 153 (inviolability of property).

The President of the Reich must immediately inform the Reichstag of all measures taken in conformity with sections 1 or 2 of this Article. The measures are to be revoked upon the demand of the Reichstag.

In cases where delay would be dangerous, the state government may take for its territory temporary measures of the nature described in section 2. The measures are to be revoked upon the demand of the President of the Reich or the Reichstag.

A national law shall prescribe the details.

A few salient facts about Article 48 as an instrument of emergency government should be presented at this point. In the first place, despite recurrent proposals in the Reichstag as well as in academic and journalistic circles, the final sentence of this article was never acted upon, and throughout the history of the Republic Article 48 was the only written law on constitutional emergency powers. The definition of what could be regarded as "necessary measures" or a serious disturbance of "the public safety and order in the German Reich" was left to the President and his Cabinet. The absence of this supplementary law had no negative effect on Article 48 as a basis for emergency action; it was well understood that the government could act upon its authority alone.

Secondly, Article 48, because of its broad terms and the lack of a qualifying law, became the foundation for all sorts and degrees of constitutional dictatorship. In general, the types of crisis comprehended may be confined to two categories: the state of political disturbance (civil insurrection), for which Article 48 served as authority for measures reminiscent of the imperial or Prussian state of siege; and the state of economic disturbance (inflation, depression), for which it provided an emergency executive lawmaking power, a full-blown *Notverordnungsrecht*. Needless to say, Article 48 also stood ready for use in the event of a foreign war. Nowhere has the emergency power to overcome severe economic distress been more closely tied in with the power to abate the crises of war and rebellion. Article 48 was an inexhaustible reservoir of emergency power.

Thirdly, it is important to note that the ministerial countersignature of "all ordinances and orders" of the President of the Reich was established as a controlling principle of the German constitutional scheme by Article 50 of the Constitution. This served to make the use of Article 48 a group proposition and gave the Reichstag a further check upon it. It should be made clear, however, that the dictatorship was primarily a presidential prerogative. Without his consent the Cabinet had no power whatsoever to use Article 48; without the Cabinet's approval the President's prerogative was equally useless.

Finally, it is obvious that other articles of the Constitution conditioned the use of the dictatorship article—for example Article 54, which stated: "The Chancellor of the Reich and the Ministers require for the conduct of their offices the confidence of the Reichstag." It was a grant of extraordinary power to the executive branch of the government to be exercised within and in behalf of the constitutional scheme. The protection of the Republic was its sole purpose.

CHAPTER III

Article 48 in the Early History
of the Republic

THE life and death of the German Republic is in no small part a story of the use and abuse of Article 48 of the Weimar Constitution. In the thirteen-odd years of a constitutional Germany, recourse was had to this provision on more than 250 separate occasions,[1] and in the last of those years government in Germany functioned by virtue of the constitutional dictatorship alone. It is the purpose of the next two chapters to examine Article 48 as it was actually put to work in the German governmental framework. Its historical significance and its merits and demerits as a unique instrument of emergency government should in this way become apparent.

Article 48: Genesis and Background

ALTHOUGH the decision of the Weimar Assembly to introduce an emergency dictatorship into the new Constitution evoked considerable thought and discussion among the large proportion of scholarly delegates, Article 48 in its final form was more influenced by the circumstances of the year 1919 and by previous German experiences with emergency government than by any theoretical consideration of this problem. The question may well be asked: how was it that this democratic Assembly should have inserted in this democratic Constitution a governmental device copied from the "state of war" (*Kriegszustand*), one of the most autocratic institutions of the late and unlamented German Empire? The answer is plainly that Article 48 arose "out of the necessity of the time." As one of the sponsors of the dictatorship article stated before the constitutional committee:

"This power goes very far. But when we consider the events of these days, we shall find that this power is born out of the necessity of our time.

---

[1] A list of the 233 decrees issued on the basis of Article 48 up to September 1932 may be found in Lindsay Rogers *et al.*: "German Political Institutions—Article 48," *Pol. Sci. Q.*, XLVII (1932), p.576, pp.583-594. See also the three invaluable articles of Fritz Poetzsch-Heffter, each of them entitled *"Vom Staatsleben unter der Weimarer Verfassung,"* vols. XIII, pp.141-147, XVII, p.99, and XXI, pp.129-131 of the *Jahrbuch des öffentlichen Rechts*. Some of the decrees issued by the Hitler government on the basis of Article 48 are given in J. K. Pollock and H. J. Heneman: *The Hitler Decrees* (Ann Arbor, 1934).

It gives to the President a strong weapon which we cannot renounce under any circumstances. I welcome this strengthening of the presidential power most heartily."[2]

"The events of these days" to which he was referring are too well known to be repeated here. Virtual anarchy reigned in large portions of Germany, separatist movements and provincial rebellions threatened to dismember completely the bleeding corpse of the Reich, the spirit of the people lay broken beneath the vain sacrifices and hardships of the previous five years, extremists of right and left ran riot in their efforts to establish state and local governments of their own tastes, the allied blockade continued unabated, inflation had already begun its infinite skyward spiral, and unemployment was reaching threatening heights with the abandonment of war industries and the *Heimkehr* of the soldiers. Germany had indeed fallen upon evil times. It may well be doubted whether any republic was ever founded under more sinister and intractable conditions.[3]

It was under these conditions that the German National Assembly, chosen by the most democratic suffrage the world had ever known, met in Weimar on February 6, 1919.[4] One of the chief reasons for the selection of the town of Goethe and Schiller was the comparative quiet which it offered, in contrast to the turbulent extremities into which other and larger German cities had been plunged. Like the American fathers of 1787, the German fathers of 1919 did their work in peace, but it was the peace that exists in the middle of the maelstrom. The country was in an uproar, and it was thus inevitable that the problem of emergency powers should have received particular attention in the Assembly. The keynote of the debates was the hazardous state of the times, and therewith the necessity of government not only democratic, but strong. Not the least element of this democratic strength was to be a powerful executive. From the revolution of November 1918 until the establishment of the provisional constitution on February 11, 1919, Fritz Ebert and a small coterie of Social Democrats, attempting to fill the political vacuum left by the departure of the imperial government, had been forced in crisis situations to exercise dictatorial power without firm basis in the

[2] Dr. Ablass, quoted in C. J. Friedrich: "The Development of Executive Power in Germany," *American Political Science Review*, XXVII (1933), p.185, p.197.

[3] The most reliable accounts of the German revolution and the establishment of the Republic are Walter Jellinek: *"Revolution und Reichsverfassung," Jahrbuch des öff. Rechts*, IX (1921), pp.1-128, and R. H. Lutz: *The German Revolution* (Stanford, 1922).

[4] An excellent brief account of the Assembly's work is to be found in Fritz Stier-Somlo: *Die Verfassung des Deutschen Reichs vom 11. August 1919* (Bonn, 1920), esp. pp.19-74.

law. Now it became the purpose of the delegates at Weimar to provide a crisis dictatorship of a legal nature, and this was to be done in behalf of democracy and the Constitution. Despite the embittered opposition of the extreme left wing, a presidency was instituted which, although not the equal of the office of President of the United States, outstripped the French presidency in prestige and competence.[5] And to this chief executive, who was to govern in conjunction with a responsible cabinet, was given this unique grant of emergency powers.

The desire for a strong executive and the demand for adequate emergency powers were thus two answers to the same problem.[6] Article 48 became the particular concern of Professor Hugo Preuss, the "Father of the German Constitution." In the first draft of a constitution which he had been commissioned to lay before the Assembly, there appeared provisions similar to Article 48, and it was an easy task for Preuss and his followers to overcome the opposition expressed to the proposed emergency article. For the most part, discussion in the Assembly ignored the dangerous possibilities inherent in this clause and centered about the single feature of Reichstag control over presidential action. It was by a decisive majority that Article 48 was placed in the new German Constitution. The stress of the times had forced men to whom arbitrary government had been lifelong anathema, to put into their model charter a device of emergency government that was a relic of the past and a possible platform for despotism. It was their hope and somewhat over-confident expectation that only good democrats devoted to the cause of the Republic would ever be in a position to resort to this unusual fund of power. The pointed remarks of the leader of the Independent Socialists, Dr. Cohn, in which he lashed out at the complacency of the Assembly in assuming that a man true to the democratic cause and advised by a democratic cabinet would always occupy the presidential office, carried no weight. In 1932 his words were to stand as a remarkable and fatal prophecy, but in 1919 it was the belief of most of the delegates that the constitutional dictatorship was, in the words of Dr. Preuss, safely "built into the framework of the constitutional state."

Article 48 found its genesis in the events of 1919; it found its source in German history. The members of the Assembly were quick to make use of provisions that might be borrowed with profit from their old con-

[5] A concise summary of the office and powers of the President is found in F. M. Marx: *Government in the Third Reich* (New York, 1936), pp.53-61.

[6] A full consideration of the development of the presidency in the Weimar Assembly is given by Harlow J. Heneman: *The Growth of Executive Power in Germany* (Minneapolis, 1934), chap. 2.

stitutions. Once a decision had been reached to provide for a constitutional dictatorship, they resorted willingly to an examination of imperial forms as models for the proposed article. In the development of the Empire and its member *Länder* as constitutionally governed states, the use of emergency powers had been well established, and this example was not overlooked by the hard-pressed delegates at Weimar.

The chief emergency institution of imperial Germany had been the *Kriegszustand* or state of war, a standard form of constitutional dictatorship modeled directly on the French state of siege, although with certain alterations in keeping with the more autocratic character of the German Empire. A similar device was to be found in the various state constitutions, the *Belagerungszustand* or state of siege. Article 68 of the imperial Constitution was the basis for the state of war:

> The Kaiser can, if the public safety in the federal territory is threatened, declare the state of war in any part thereof. Until the enactment of an imperial statute regulating the conditions, the form of the proclamation and the effects of such a declaration, the provisions applying thereto shall be those of the Prussian statute of June 4, 1851.

No imperial statute was ever enacted, and this Prussian law of 1851 continued in force until the demise of the Empire.[7] It regulated carefully the form of the proclamation, the suspension of certain rights, and various other effects of the state of war. The proclamation of the state of war by the Kaiser resulted in the establishment of military courts for the trial of specified crimes, the suspension of numerous fundamental rights and most of the usual checks upon governmental action, and the transfer of executive powers from civil to military authorities. In the initiation of such measures the Kaiser was irresponsible, acting not as head of the state but as commander in chief of the armed forces. The stamp of the military was plainly affixed to the imperial *Kriegszustand*. In the state of war or siege pure and simple, the military always took control, but there was a lesser degree of the Prussian institution, the "minor" state of siege, in which such action was merely threatened, and all measures continued to be taken by the ordinary authorities.

In the forty years before 1914 there were but two occasions for the

---

[7] For the text of this law, see Wilhelm Haldy: *Der Belagerungszustand in Preussen* (Tübingen, 1906), p.74. Not all of its provisions were imported into imperial practice, for example Article 16 permitting an extraordinary regime without specific declaration, the so-called "minor state of siege," and Article 17 establishing the principle of executive responsibility to the chambers for declarations of the state of siege. See generally Karl Strupp: *Deutsches Kriegszustandsrecht* (Berlin, 1916); Hans Pürschel: *Belagerungszustand* (Berlin, 1916).

use of the state of war. However, in the four years of Germany's mighty war effort the state of war was resorted to with increasing frequency, particularly against left-wing elements obstructing this effort by word or deed. This brought the institution into disrepute with all liberal elements in the Reich. The leaders of the great Kiel mutiny of October 30, 1918 proposed as one of their most important reforms the abolition of the state of war or siege, but it was only the extreme left wing which clung to this view in the Weimar Assembly.

The results of this former experience convinced the delegates at Weimar that this sort of emergency institution could serve as the model for their dictatorship article, but with certain significant changes to comport with the transition from an imperial constitution to a democratic and republican one. These changes are obvious. For the irresponsible Kaiser was substituted the President and his responsible Cabinet, and indeed (by Article 48, section 3 and Article 54) the Reichstag. Moreover, in any action to be taken under Article 48, the military authorities were to be subordinate to the ordinary civil officials of the Reich government. These were the two liberalizing alterations of the old state of war.[8] On the other hand, by expressly reading the law of 1851 into its Article 68, the old Constitution had limited and qualified the use of the *Kriegszustand* more closely than did Article 48 the use of its broadly granted emergency powers.

In the Empire the use of emergency powers predicated the supremacy of the army over the civil authorities and was the prerogative of an irresponsible Kaiser. Under the Weimar Constitution the state of war had become a civil and republican institution.

Article 48: Its Use as a State of Siege in Early Insurrections

THE five years which followed the agonizing birth of the Weimar Republic brought the government and people no relief from the economic distress and unemployment, the violent attacks from right and left, the inclination to secession of many areas and elements in the Reich, or the occupation of German soil by the conquerors. It was just this sort

[8] See Johannes Heckel: *"Diktatur, Notverordnungsrecht, Verfassungsnotstand,"* *Archiv des öff. Rechts*, XXII (1932), p.257, p.263. The differences between the imperial and republican emergency institutions are summarized by Anschütz, *op. cit.*, p.277. See also Richard Grau: *"Die Diktaturgewalt des Reichspräsidenten,"* *Handbuch des deutschen Staatsrechts*, Anschütz and Thoma eds. (Tübingen, 1932), vol. II, p.275. The seven rights that could be suspended were copied directly from Article 5 of the Prussian law of 1851.

of nation-wide disorder and discord which the framers at Weimar had anticipated when they placed Article 48 in their democratic charter, and in these first troubled years it was used more than 130 times. Heroic and extraordinary (and occasionally ruthless) governmental action was necessary to the establishment and protection of the new Republic and to the security of its law-abiding citizens. Lacking the emergency competence provided in Article 48, the rulers of republican Germany could hardly have launched their infant democracy into the stormy seas of postwar Europe.

Armed with the one general and two specific grants of power, the first President of the Reich, Socialist Fritz Ebert, and his various Chancellors were able to proceed against civil discord with a variety of measures modeled directly on those adopted under the imperial state of war and similar to those which will be described at length in the chapters dealing with the French state of siege.[9]

In the suppression of a series of violent and widespread Communist outbreaks in 1920 the government made repeated use of Article 48. The suspension of the fundamental rights permitted the prohibition of public assemblies, the rigid censorship or abatement of newspapers and leaflets inciting rebellion, summary arrests and detentions, and other arbitrary police measures designed to aid in the forcible maintenance or restoration of public order. Special executive courts for the trial of certain crimes against the state were several times established.[10] The power of these courts-martial was broad and arbitrary, and when instituted for the trial of rebel violence they could punish with death. Other general measures adopted were the issuance of emergency decrees with the force of law, the temporary abeyance of the regular laws, and most important the use of troops in areas racked or threatened by insurrection. Pitched battles were fought at the barricades in the Ruhr area, and in every instance it was Article 48 which sanctioned the violent methods of the *Reichswehr* and police. In short, the government of the Reich made use of a constitutional power to wage war on its own rebellious citizens.

In some areas and cities a commissioner, to whom had been accorded all the freedom of the President in his choice and application of "neces-

[9] Poetzsch-Heffter, XIII, pp.2-28, presents a full technical account of the measures taken against Kapp, Hitler, the Communists, and other revolutionaries on the basis of Article 48. See also the excellent volume of Frederick M. Watkins: *The Failure of Constitutional Emergency Powers under the German Republic* (Cambridge, 1939), chaps. 2 and 3.

[10] For a concise account of these courts, see Watkins, *op. cit.*, pp.32 ff.

sary measures," was sent by the Reich government to restore public order. The commissioner might be either a military or a civil official, depending on the nature and gravity of the situation. If he were an army officer, his responsibility to the President went through the Reich Minister of Defense; if he were a civilian, it was the Minister of the Interior who controlled his actions in the name of the President. Often the two might work side by side, the military official having the final word in all important decisions.[11] The commissioners availed themselves of all the powers open to a dictator prosecuting a full state of siege or war. Any sort of action, no matter how severe and arbitrary, that has been recognized anywhere as a proper one under conditions of martial rule, could come within the competence of the authorities acting for the President.

A similar problem was presented when it was a state government itself that was in rebellion against the Republic. The usual procedure was the installation of a federal commissioner, who was to act in place of the state government until the crisis was past and a new administration was functioning in accordance with the principles of the Republic. In March of 1920 a precedent was set for the later conduct of such executions against recalcitrant state regimes by the appointment under section 2 of Article 48 (by all logic it should have been section 1[12]) of a *Reichskommissar* to supervise affairs normally under the control of the Thuringian cabinet. This commissioner was endowed by the national authorities with extensive military and administrative powers for the purpose of restoring public order.[13] It was his special task to bring the refractory government of Thuringia into accord "with the principles of the Constitution and the political life of the Reich."[14] In other words, he was commissioned to install a state government that conformed in organization and spirit to the important criteria of Weimar democracy, to

---

[11] On the use of commissioners in the execution of measures under Article 48, see Günter Meisner: *Der Kommissar* (Würzburg, 1933), p.31. Typical examples of the employment of the military commissioner may be found in *Reichsgesetzblatt* (1920), pp.41, 207, 1477; of the civil commissioner, *RGBl.* (1921), p.253.

[12] Section 1 of Article 48 was designed to deal with the peculiarly German problem of emergency government (inherited from the Empire) of "federal execution," and was derived directly from Article 19 of the imperial Constitution of 1871. It was a grant of extraordinary power to enable the central government to keep the states in line with the policies, laws, and Constitution of the Reich. The decision of the Weimar Assembly to provide for general emergency powers in the Constitution received considerable impetus from the recognition of the continuing need for this particular power of federal execution. In strict logic, it should have been left as a separate article, as had been originally planned. No action was ever taken by the Reich government on the basis of this section alone; all forcible attempts by state officials to resist its authority were met by measures based on section 2, or on sections 1 and 2 together.

[13] *RGBl.* (1920), p.343.   [14] Meisner, *op. cit.*, p.31.

guarantee to the people of Thuringia, whether they liked it or not, a republican form of government. A similar instance of Reich intervention was the case of Saxony-Gotha in April 1920.[15] The state government had attempted to set up a soviet, and it was the commissioner's special task to conduct new elections for the state assembly. Until the convocation of this assembly and the reconstruction of constitutional government he ruled the state with dictatorial powers, subject only to the advice of a specially chosen council. He was directly responsible to the Minister of the Interior. Having successfully presided over the birth of a young republic after the Weimar pattern, the commissioner was withdrawn and all his dictatorial measures were annulled.

It must be frankly and unhappily admitted that the suppression of revolutionary rightism was not blessed with equally favorable issue. The reason for this is obvious. In the prosecution of military measures under Article 48 the democratic Ebert regime had to rely upon an army whose sympathies were extremely reactionary and which itself dabbled in insurrection against the established authorities. The Kapp *Putsch* of March 1920, which sent the government packing from Berlin to Stuttgart, was rendered abortive by a general strike of the Social Democratic trade unions. President Ebert simply did not trust the *Reichswehr* sufficiently to call upon its direct assistance in the rout of Kapp and his followers, obviously because many of the followers were *Reichswehr* men themselves.

Hitler's Beer Hall fiasco of November 1923 was also thwarted by circumstances in which a resolute use of Article 48 played far too inconspicuous a part.[16] The national government went through all the motions of appointing a commissioner to deal with the uproar in Bavaria, but the commissioner himself was more interested in restoring the Bavarian monarchy than in vindicating the authority of the Reich in this most separatist of states. Not until the final march of the Nazi mob through the streets of Munich did the guns speak out with the authority of Article 48. At this same time, a leftist movement of a legal character in neighboring Saxony was being rather ruthlessly suppressed by the Reich officials.[17]

These few and typical instances should serve to give some idea of the powers and procedures of the Reich government in the use of Article 48 to quell insurrection. It is obvious indeed that certain of

[15] *RGBl.* (1920), p.477.
[16] Poetzsch-Heffter, XIII, pp.91-96. See also Karl Rothenbücher: *"Der Streit zwischen Bayern und dem Reich. . . ," Archiv des öff. Rechts*, VII (1924), p.71.
[17] Watkins, *op. cit.*, chap. 4; Poetzsch-Heffter, XIII, pp.96-99.

the instances were outright declarations of war against groups of German citizens who happened to be in violent disagreement with the authorities in Berlin. Article 48, mainly by reason of what it did not say, vouchsafed the government extraordinary power to suppress these uprisings, and although there were instances when this power was ladled out in doses far too strong for the correction of the particular social or political malady, it cannot be denied that had the young Republic lacked this constitutional provision for strong and even military action in times of acute crisis, it might not have survived those stormy years. Civil discord was conquered by a republican use of the imperial state of war.

Article 48: Its Use as an Enabling Act in Early Economic Crises

BY A decree of October 12, 1922 a new departure under Article 48 was effected. This presidential order set up regulations forbidding speculation in foreign currencies, surely one of the outstanding contributing factors to Germany's economic woes, and the dictatorship article was cited as the authority.[18] For the first time the President's emergency powers were employed not as the basis for stringent executive measures against civil insurrection, but for a decree dealing with an economic problem demanding a legislative rather than an executive solution. The entering wedge had been driven; the dual nature of the emergency grant in Article 48 was for the first time brought to light. President Ebert and Chancellor Joseph Wirth had determined that "the public safety and order" as understood in Article 48 could be "seriously disturbed and endangered" by economic as well as by political upheavals. Emergency economic decrees, decrees with the authority of law, were to be regarded as "necessary measures."

This new use of Article 48 was not so radical a step as might be imagined. To be sure, the Weimar framers had no conception of the dictatorship article as the basis for such a complete program of cabinet legislation as was eventually undertaken on the strength of this indefinite grant of emergency power, but there was no specific objection raised or prohibition leveled against the possibility of its being employed to such an end. The Weimar debates treat Article 48 as a political, not an economic cure-all, as a legal foundation for operations executive in character and modeled on the state of siege, and not for a general executive power of issuing emergency decrees.

[18] *RGBl.* (1922), pp.795, 847.

This problem of emergency decrees was discussed in another context and quite without reference to Article 48. It was proposed by some delegates that there be included in the Constitution a provision specifically authorizing the President to issue emergency ordinances with the force of law. Although there had been no such power granted to the Kaiser under the imperial Constitution, a majority of the pre-war state constitutions had authorized the executive to issue such decrees, even in derogation from existing law, whenever a serious emergency arose and the legislature was not in session. These grants of executive ordinance-making power had been abused by the state governments, and the framers at Weimar, led in this instance by Dr. Preuss, concluded that an enabling act proceeding from the Reichstag would be a more salutary method of providing for executive legislation in crises, and rejected all proposals for a specific power of crisis legislation to be lodged in the President. Article 48, Dr. Preuss intimated, stood ready to tide the government over in any really serious emergency. Its use as the foundation for a limited emergency decree power was thus not precluded. On the other hand, its use as the foundation for executive legislation on important subjects of Reichstag competence when that body was in session and able to act was certainly not foreseen. But once the entering wedge had been driven, and it had been acknowledged by the Reichstag itself that economic disturbances were of such a character as to come within the purview of Article 48's broad terms, what was to prevent an eventual resort to wholesale executive legislation? Such a possibility evidently never entered the minds of the delegates.

In all truth, there was no logical reason why, the Reichstag itself willing, this flexible grant of power bestowed in Article 48 should not have been adequate to provide legal authority for executive legislation in severe crises of any sort, political or economic.[19] Moreover, there was some precedent for this use of Article 48 to combat the country's economic troubles.

The old German state of war had nothing to do with economic distress. It was utilized not only primarily but exclusively to meet civil unrest. The procedures recognized under the state of war were administrative and not legislative in nature. In the years before 1914 Germany knew little of unemployment, inflation, and the other extremes of economic maladjustment which can imperil the order and even existence of a state as surely as can outright civil war.

[19] This broad view was sanctioned by several court decisions, *e.g. RGStr.*, vol. 56, pp.161 ff.

In the World War economic problems of a pressing nature came to the fore, and it was not long before the executive and military authorities were issuing emergency economic ordinances which, though nominally dealing with those economic problems directly concerned with the prosecution of the war, in fact encompassed a major part of German civil life, business, and industry, and thereby encroached upon the legislative reservation of the Bundesrat and Reichstag.[20] All of this legislative activity was based squarely upon the state of war or the state of siege, and constituted a radical departure from all previous practice and theory of these institutions. The German courts were in no position to obstruct this or any other effort to win the war, and they uniformly upheld a latitudinarian conception of the executive's power to issue such decrees. Any measure, although purely legislative in character, which contributed to the maintenance of public order and the success of the war effort was regarded by the courts as within the power of the authorities functioning under the state of war. The result was a plethora of decrees regulating the whole of the nation's economic life. The transitional government of President Ebert had continued this development and had issued decrees encroaching heavily upon all aspects of German life.

The decision of Ebert and Wirth to employ Article 48 to combat the evil practice of foreign speculation was thus not a revolutionary and unprecedented move, and it is remarkable how little objection was raised to this new interpretation of Article 48. Discussion was directed to the validity of particular measures, not to the general question whether the article could be expanded to permit such action. The theoretical case for this latitudinarian reading of the dictatorship article was good, the practical case was better. The problems of inflation were certainly as much a threat to the Reich as the insurrectionary activities of the extremist groups, and were often as impossible of legislative solution. The day-to-day vicissitudes of the German economy called for vigorous administrative lawmaking, and such action found a plausible basis in the generous terms of Article 48.[21] In the light of actual practice, the discussion was exclusively academic.

[20] See generally Ludwig Waldecker: "*Die Grundlagen des militärischen Verordnungsrechts in Zivilsachen während des Kriegszustandes,*" *Archiv des öff. Rechts,* XXXVI (O.S.), (1917), p.389.

[21] Ottmar Bühler: *Die Reichsverfassung vom 11. August 1919* (2nd ed., Leipzig, 1927), p.69.

A Digression on Enabling Acts

THIS use of the dictatorship article as a constitutional sanction for emergency decrees was actually rather hesitant. By no means was this broad reading of Article 48 completely accepted by the politicians and jurists of the time. In the severe crisis of 1930-1933 the Cabinet, as will be seen in the next chapter, enforced a strenuous economic dictatorship on the basis of Article 48, with the grudging approval of a hopelessly divided Reichstag. In the equally severe crisis of 1923-1924 the Cabinet had also regulated and rehabilitated the economic life of the Reich without the legislative interference of the Reichstag, but with this important difference in method: a large majority of the emergency decrees issued by the Cabinet in the earlier period found their legal basis in a series of enabling acts through which the Reichstag expressly authorized the executive to issue ordinances having the force of regular laws, while Article 48 was called into action only sporadically and interstitially.

In the chapters to follow it will become evident how important the delegation of lawmaking power has been for emergency governments in France, Great Britain, and the United States. Yet here in republican Germany, despite the blanket provision of Article 48, there was effected an instance of "delegated dictatorship" surpassing in scope and success any example these other countries could offer. It would therefore seem necessary and not too parenthetical to devote a few pages to these enabling acts of 1923-1924.[22]

The important legislative task of the Reichstag in the first years of its existence as a republican institution was that of shifting the Reich from a wartime to a peacetime economy. Already overburdened with political and social problems such as few legislatures, particularly infant legislatures, have ever been forced to face, and unable to enact statutes coping effectively with this particular problem, the Reichstag passed three important enabling acts in the first two years of the Republic, under which the Cabinet then issued a number of decrees directed to the specific purpose of reconversion.[23] Following a successful completion of this vital task, the practice was discontinued. During the next two years the Reichstag itself was able to meet all of Germany's problems through the ordinary procedures of legislation.

As time went on the German economic structure, burdened and com-

[22] See generally Watkins, *op. cit.*, chap. 5; Gustave Moulin: *"L'Expérience Allemande des Décrets-lois," Revue Politique et Parlementaire,* CXXX (1927), p.96; Poetzsch-Heffter, XIII, pp.206-216; Herbert Tingsten: *Les Pleins Pouvoirs,* pp.287-326.
[23] Poetzsch-Heffter, XIII, pp.207-212, lists these decrees.

44

plicated as it was with reparations, inflation, and unemployment, drew steadily nearer a state of collapse. Normal parliamentary methods were obviously unsuited to assault and dispel this danger. Article 48 was not yet regarded as the solution to all of the government's problems. The use of this grant in October 1922 was an isolated one, and this practice was not to be repeated for some time.

The precedent of the enabling act stood ready. Such an act was only possible with the assent of two-thirds of the membership of the Reichstag, for the delegation of legislative power was regarded among the jurists and politicians of republican Germany as something akin to an amendment to the Constitution. One of the methods of amendment provided in that document was that of a two-thirds vote of two-thirds the membership of the Reichstag. Until the invasion of the Ruhr too great a number of the deputies remained unwilling to surrender any sizable part of their legislative competence, and all efforts to secure the passage of an enabling act were doomed to failure. The march of French troops into Germany's great industrial center in January of 1923 caused a sudden change in this situation. The kind of force that a military command exerts cannot be answered by normal parliamentary methods. The problems that arose from the French occupation were plainly insoluble by the normal legislative procedures of the Reichstag. Article 48 could have provided the basis for the necessary Cabinet actions, but in the interests of a united nation the Cabinet chose to seek unimpeachable authority from the national legislature itself. The urgent request of the Reich government for a special grant of power was speedily honored by the requisite two-thirds majority of the Reichstag.

This enabling act of February 24, 1923,[24] empowering the Cabinet to proceed to all measures necessary to carry out Germany's campaign of resistance to the French invasion, was limited in time to June 1, but was later prolonged until October 31. The competence of the Cabinet was not a general one, but was confined to the problems arising from the occupation. All measures adopted were to be at once reported to the Reichstag, and were to be revoked in whole or in part upon demand. The use of this grant of power was not extensive, and the great campaign of passive resistance had more effect on the outcome of the struggle. A further precedent for this emergency device had nonetheless been established.

In the spring and summer of 1923 conditions in Germany grew steadily worse. The government blessed a policy of deliberate economic

[24] *RGBl.* (1923), p.147. Decrees listed in Poetzsch-Heffter, XIII, p.212.

breakdown in the Ruhr and thus committed itself to public support of thousands of employers and workers who would otherwise have been left to starve. The lavish expenditure thus involved spelled more inflation, and inflation spelled complete collapse of the Reich economy. Meanwhile the party-ridden Reichstag was showing itself to be not only technically but politically unable to provide any thorough solution to the nation's plight. The Reichstag lacked means and will alike to save the state from utter financial catastrophe. In point of fact, there was no common basis of action on which any legislative majority could hope to initiate a vigorous program of economic rehabilitation.

Gustav Stresemann, who had come into power as Chancellor on August 13, sought at first to meet this nasty situation by issuing economic decrees based on the President's authority under Article 48. There were five such occasions for the use of this article in the first two months of his incumbency, but these were faltering steps and hardly sufficient to the gravity of the conditions then prevalent in the Reich. Not yet had Article 48 come to be recognized by responsible opinion as the basis for a general power of emergency decree, and Stresemann was pursuing the ideas of the framers of the Constitution when he decided to attack this situation through executive legislation authorized by an enabling act of the Reichstag. In spite of embittered opposition from the extreme left, his request for such powers was answered with the passage of the enabling act of October 13, 1923.[25] The text of this highly important statute ran:

> The government of the Reich is authorized to adopt those measures which it considers to be absolutely necessary in the financial, economic, and social realms. Fundamental rights guaranteed in the Weimar Constitution may be disregarded in the process.
>
> This authorization does not extend to regulations affecting hours of labor, nor to the reduction of pensions, social insurance, or unemployment insurance.
>
> Decrees issued on this basis are to be reported at once to the Reichstag and to the Reichsrat. They are to be revoked at once upon the demand of the Reichstag.
>
> This law goes into effect on the day of promulgation. It shall cease to operate at the very latest on March 31, 1924, and shall lapse even before that time in case of any change in the party composition of the present government.

It was this final phrase "any change in the party composition of the present government" which explains the willingness of the Reichstag to

[25] *RGBl.* (1923), p.943. Decrees listed in Poetzsch-Heffter, XIII, pp.213-214.

grant the Cabinet this extraordinary power, for Stresemann's collection of ministers numbered members from every party true to the Republic, and the withdrawal of any one group would have automatically annulled the act. No more effective check on delegated legislative power could well be imagined.

From October 13 until November 2, when the Social Democrats abandoned the Stresemann government, thirty-six ordinances were issued covering the entire field of German economic life and laying the foundations for a comprehensive scheme of national financial rehabilitation. In the three short weeks of its competence the Cabinet was able to put a stop to "the debacle of the mark" by the creation of the *Rentenbank* and the *Rentenmark*, overhaul completely the finances of the Reich, organize the federal tax structure with more logic and precision, simplify the functioning of the Reich's social services, and provide for the betterment of the public health. The Stresemann Cabinet was not to fall for three more weeks, and in this time resort was had on eight occasions to the President's prerogative under Article 48 as a substitute for the defunct enabling act. The close affinity of the dictatorship article and the enabling act was thus clearly acknowledged.

The Cabinet of Centrist Wilhelm Marx, which included Stresemann and other members of his Cabinet, came to power November 30. While at first it continued the practice of using Article 48 as a stopgap authority for the decrees demanded by the exigencies of Germany's critical economic situation, it too preferred to act on the basis of Reichstag delegation; and the first piece of business presented to the assembly by the Chancellor was an outright demand for the passage of a new enabling act. The twin threat of dissolution and a concomitant resort to Article 48 was sufficient to secure the necessary two-thirds majority in the Reichstag. The text of this act,[26] promulgated on December 8, read in part:

> The government of the Reich is authorized to adopt those measures which it considers to be absolutely necessary in view of the distressing circumstances of the people and the Reich. Fundamental rights guaranteed in the Weimar Constitution may not be disregarded in the process. Before their issuance all ordinances are to be discussed in secret session with committees chosen by the Reichstag and Reichsrat, each to consist of 15 members.
>
> Decrees issued on this basis shall be reported without delay to the Reichstag and to the Reichsrat. They are to be revoked on demand of the Reichstag or of the Reichsrat. . . .
>
> This law shall cease to operate on February 15, 1924.

[26] *RGBl.* (1923), p.1179. Decrees listed in Poetzsch-Heffter, XIII, pp.214-216.

It is important to note the differences between this and the preceding enabling act. In one direction the capacity of the legislature to control the use of this grant of power was increased, by the provision of advisory Reichstag and Reichsrat committees. Moreover, the Cabinet was forbidden in the second act to invade civil liberties guaranteed in the Constitution. On the other hand, the term of the act's validity, although one of only two months, was not to be cut short by any change in the party lineup of the Cabinet. Most significant of all, the field of the Cabinet's legislative competence had been considerably enlarged by the removal of the restriction in the law of October 13 concerning hours of labor and other vital matters of social legislation. Only the abject fear of a Reichstag dissolution could have forced the Social Democrats to agree to the elimination of these prohibitions from the second act.

During the ten weeks which followed the promulgation of this law more than seventy legislative decrees were issued by the Cabinet. Not only were the chief problems of taxation, finance, and currency attacked, but also the revision of Germany's anachronistic judicial system, unemployment, and such matters as pensions and social insurance. One decree repealed the statute by which the Social Democrats had established the eight-hour day by law.[27] By the time the act expired the Marx regime could point with some pride to measures that had succeeded in stabilizing the currency of the Reich, organizing a workable budget, calling a halt to speculation, and reestablishing public confidence in the economic future of Germany. Through all this period the Reichstag was in recess, and while the deputies were home, Germany was being treated to one of the strongest doses of emergency legislation ever administered to any republic, whether by its executive or legislative organ.

Under the first enabling act the Cabinet exercised an economic dictatorship which the Reichstag itself never felt justified in equaling, nor in authorizing a second time. The Cabinet, whether it was initiating economic decrees under this act or under Article 48, was empowered to adopt legislative measures violating fundamental rights guaranteed by the Constitution, something that an ordinary law of the Reichstag could not do. In this respect the experience of Germany is unique, for the enabling acts utilized by the other modern democracies in their own periods of economic derangement never went so far as expressly to permit the executive to invade fundamental rights in the enactment of an emergency program of executive legislation. But then again, it was only in Germany that the practice of the enabling act was regarded as of such

[27] *RGBl.* (1923), p.1249.

fundamental importance as to require sanction by an extraordinary majority of the legislature. This question too is primarily of academic interest, for only in isolated instances did these executive decrees actually suspend any of the fundamental rights. An example was the so-called "seizing of securities" decree of September 7, 1923,[28] under which the President appointed a commissioner and authorized him to seize foreign securities and precious metals. The sanctity of domicile and secrecy of communications were expressly suspended by the decree.

The reconvening of the Reichstag on February 20 presented a potent threat to the Marx program, and it seemed for a few days that it was to be subjected to piecemeal criticism and amendment. On February 26 the Chancellor appeared before the Reichstag and declared flatly that his government insisted upon the whole collection of seventy decrees being either accepted or rejected as a unit. His plea went unheeded, and after several weeks in which the Reichstag continued to snipe away at the different ordinances, the President dissolved it and sent the deputies home. The elections of May 4 returned a legislature which refused to undo any part of the Marx program, and it is doubtful whether by this time it could have done so if it wished. The Stresemann-Marx government by emergency decree and the first effects of the Dawes plan had combined to set Germany well on the road to recovery.

Thus was concluded a remarkable experiment in emergency executive lawmaking, remarkable in its scope, remarkable in its degree of success. Out of the 150-odd legislative measures published between October 13, 1923 and February 15, 1924, about 110 were issued by the Cabinet by virtue of the two enabling acts and some 17 on the basis of Article 48. All but a few of this total of 17 were promulgated in the period between the demise of the Stresemann enabling act and the passage of the analogous Marx statute. The economic condition of Germany had been vastly improved; neither the responsibility of the Cabinet to the Reichstag nor the strength of parliamentary government had been seriously impaired; and with the close of this extraordinary era that had so imperatively demanded extraordinary governmental methods, the normal parliamentary system began to function once again. It would be difficult to find a more salutary instance of the use of this standard device of constitutional dictatorship. The cause of constitutional government might have come to an earlier death in Germany had not these bold and unparalleled steps been taken.

[28] *RGBl.* (1923), p.865.

CHAPTER IV

Article 48 in the Last Years
of the Republic

THE years 1925 to 1929 constituted the only period of political and economic well-being in the life of the German Republic. The young democracy was at last at peace with itself and with the world. The twin threats of inflation and civil insurrection had subsided, reparations payments had been put on a more stable basis by the Dawes commission, and foreign money was pouring into Germany. It was in this period that Paul von Hindenburg became the second President of the Reich.

From January 29, 1925 until July 16, 1930 Article 48 was employed only for the purpose of revoking decrees issued in the incumbency of President Ebert. Parliamentary government in Germany was functioning according to the plan of its originators, and normal governmental action was equal to the problems of the day. Some public men believed that the justification for Article 48 no longer existed, and that it should be stricken from the Constitution. No action was taken, however; the government was busy with other tasks, and Article 48 had served the Republic in danger too well to be thus lightly cast aside by the Republic in peace. Meanwhile the law anticipated by section 5 of the article failed to receive the attention which it surely deserved. If Germany's leaders had seen what lay ahead, they would have hastened to codify the use of Article 48 on the basis of the experience of the first five years. But what democracy at peace will prepare for war?

On March 27, 1930 Chancellor Herman Müller and the other Social Democrats in his coalition Cabinet resigned because of irreconcilable differences with his supporters in the German People's Party over the amount of money to be raised to meet the growing deficit in the Reich government's unemployment insurance fund. The following day Heinrich Brüning of the Center Party was asked to form a new Cabinet.

The constitutional government of the Republic was again in danger. The cruel storms of economic distress and social unrest were gathering to beat upon it from without; the foul acid of parliamentary decay had already begun to eat away its foundations from within. The years of peace and quiet were over, and Article 48 was again to assume an important role in the governance of Germany, indeed to become the whole basis of political authority in that country.[1]

Article 48 and the Economic Dictatorship

SOON after his entrance into power, Brüning was driven by declining receipts and mounting expenses to put forward proposals for a drastic increase in federal and local taxation. The Reichstag immediately showed its unwillingness to be responsible for such strong and unpopular measures by debating the issue for weeks and then entering into a legislative deadlock. On July 16, 1930 Brüning's budget was rejected by a vote of 256-193. Under German parliamentary procedure this did not necessitate a resignation of the Cabinet. The Brüning government, knowing no other Cabinet could be formed to put the necessary recovery measures through the Reichstag, decided on extraordinary action. On this very day two emergency decrees comprising the rejected Brüning tax and budget program were issued under Article 48. When the Reichstag, led by the Social Democrats, voted 236-221 to demand a revocation of these measures, he dissolved both the decrees and the Reichstag. The deputies having been sent home to stand for a new election, the decrees were reissued July 26 in substantially the same form, again by virtue of the President's competence under Article 48. The Chancellor had resorted to the extreme medicine of the Constitution in a resolute effort to save Germany from economic prostration and parliamentary irresponsibility. Unfortunately, he was staking out the lines for similar action in the future by men not devoted as passionately as himself to the cause of a republican Germany.

The Reichstag election of September 14 dealt a staggering blow to the democratic cause. The Nazis increased their seats in the Reichstag from 12 to 107, the Communists theirs from 54 to 77. The sworn enemies of the Republic had entered in force into the stronghold of German democracy.

Brüning was still able to remain in power, for at this point the Social Democrats, 143 in number, came to his support. Their fear of the extremist parties had overcome their dislike of the Centrists, and they had finally come to realize that only a united front of the Republic's friends could save Weimar democracy. On October 18 the Reichstag voted confidence in Brüning 318-236 and then adjourned. In the more

---

[1] The story of the last years of the Republic finds an extremely readable presentation in Frederick L. Schuman: *The Nazi Dictatorship* (2nd ed., New York, 1939), pp.142-201.

than twenty months of its existence (it was finally dissolved June 1, 1932) this Reichstag was to sit only six times, for a total of about twelve weeks. With one-third of its membership openly dedicated to the destruction of the parliamentary system, and with the largest single party (the Social Democrats) willing to support Brüning as Chancellor but not to cooperate with him in the legislative enactment of his drastic emergency program, the Reichstag was no longer a functioning mechanism in the constitutional scheme. Whether he liked it or not, Brüning had no choice but to assume the entire legislative function. Caught between the Scylla of parliamentary irresponsibility and the Charybdis of nation-wide depression, he fell back on Article 48 in a bold attempt to keep the Republic afloat.

From March 27, 1931 until May 8, 1932 the Reichstag was in session only twice, three days each time, merely for the sake of voting confidence in the Cabinet. A session from May 9 to May 30, 1932 produced two statutes by the regular procedure—two statutes in fourteen months, while the decrees under Article 48 in this period numbered about sixty, almost all of them measures of a legislative nature designed to meet the entire economic and social needs of the stricken Reich. Little by little, in a manner never anticipated by the Assembly of 1919, the decree power based on Article 48 encroached upon and finally encompassed the entire field of ordinary legislation: finances, taxes, customs, justice, governmental organization, and commerce. Brüning's Cabinet and the adaptable, ever-ready civil service governed Germany. The importance of the German bureaucracy, always entrusted with drafting a major part of the legislation introduced by the Cabinet into the Reichstag in the prosecution of government by Article 48, can hardly be over-estimated.[2]

On four separate occasions in the embattled months between December 1930 and December 1931, the Cabinet issued exhaustive decrees on the basis of Article 48 designed to prevent the collapse of public and private enterprise.[3] Wages and salaries of all governmental employees were progressively pared down to the subsistence level, new taxes and duties of all kinds were initiated while old levies were increased, war pensions and unemployment benefits were reduced, and drastic steps were taken to relieve the serious financial plight of the German municipalities. The famous "Fourth Ordinance," issued December 8, 1931, contained the "most radical measures ever promulgated

[2] Carl Schmitt: *Legalität und Legitimität* (Berlin, 1932), p.18.
[3] *RGBl.* (1930), p.517. *RGBl.* (1931), pp.279, 537, 779.

by a so-called capitalist government."[4] Wages, rents, interest rates, and commodity prices were all slashed in a valiant attempt to balance the budget. The rates of taxation were hoisted to the level of diminishing returns.

A quick glance at some of the other ordinances issued by the Brüning government should demonstrate conclusively that the democratic Chancellor and his democratic Cabinet, in default of any will on the part of a majority in the Reichstag to adopt the necessarily strong and inevitably unpopular measures to master this terrible crisis, were forced to employ Article 48 for the entire governance of the Reich. Provisions for the settlement by arbitration of industrial disputes; the absolute guarantee by the government of deposits in the great Darmstädter Bank which had closed its doors in July of 1931; the amendment of a regularly enacted Reich law governing bankruptcy proceedings of limited liability companies and cooperatives; the amendment of the notorious *Osthilfe* law of March 1931, whereby hundreds of millions of dollars were pumped into East Prussia to aid the agriculturists there in throwing off part of their huge burden of debt; the adaptation of property, inheritance, and land-purchase taxes to the fall in values in 1932—these are the sort of laws that proceeded not from the Reichstag, but from the German executive acting on the basis of Article 48.

National economy, social welfare, private business—all were sustained in these black days by this incredible program of executive law-making. Much of the New Deal legislation of 1933-1936 finds its counterpart in these measures. Americans who think their Congress was blacked out in the early days of the Roosevelt regime should throw a cursory glance at this German experience and see a real example of the term "executive legislation." The vacuum left by the abdication of Germany's irresponsible Reichstag was filled completely by Article 48.[5]

Article 48 and Civil Discord, 1929-1932

IN THE early years of the Republic the Nazis and Communists had learned the hard way that revolution in Germany was a practical impossibility as long as a democratic regime enjoying broad emergency

[4] Mildred Wertheimer: "The Financial Crisis in Germany," *Foreign Policy Reports*, VII (1932), p.468.

[5] For a concise discussion of the constitutionality of this program, see Karl Loewenstein: *"Zur Verfassungsmässigkeit der Notverordnungen vom Juli und August 1931,"* *Archiv des öff. Rechts*, XXI (1931), p.124.

powers flourished in Berlin. As a result the extremists adopted a "new technique of revolution."[6] Their failure to corrupt the loyalty of the armed forces and to seize authority over any sizable portion of the Reich by violent methods diverted their future activities into comparatively legal channels. A concerted effort was made to elect party members to official positions, and from these vantage-points the republican system was harassed with devastating effect. Most significant for Article 48, the revolutionary violence of the two extremist groups was now deflected from isolated assaults upon the government to unceasing assaults upon one another. The new technique brought to cities like Berlin a continuous crisis; this called for a continuous use of Article 48.

Revolutionary violence adopted a new form; so too did the use of Article 48 in suppressing such violence. The aim of the government was to maintain order by keeping the Nazis and Communists from each others' throats. To this end a number of severe decrees were issued under Article 48. The right of assembly was several times forbidden, semi-military bodies attached to political parties were ordered dissolved, and extremist publications were temporarily suppressed. One decree forbade the Nazi *Kleinbürger* to wear their brown shirts around the streets. The free exercise of individual rights was consistently interfered with by these decrees. The Nazi-Communist "battle for the streets" evoked stern measures of prevention and punishment from the regular authorities. As long as Brüning remained in power, justice was distributed to each of these warring extremes with a fairly even hand.

Government in republican Germany in these last years was authoritative and harsh, but the nature and intensity of the political (and economic) disturbances which threatened the peace and security of the Reich made such government inevitable. Few democratic governments have ever been faced with so virulent and insoluble a situation, for a good one-third of her citizenry was ardently committed to the destruction of the Republic, by violence if necessary. The indispensability of Article 48 in the government's attempts to combat this wholesale threat to German democracy should be obvious indeed.

The Final Abuse of Article 48

ON April 10, 1932 Paul von Hindenburg, supported by all defenders of Weimar democracy, was reelected President of the Reich over

[6] Watkins: *The Failure of Constitutional Emergency Powers under the German Republic*, chap. 5.

Hitler, the candidate of violent reaction, and Thälmann, the candidate of red revolution. It seemed possible that the Republic, with Article 48 as its chief bulwark, might yet weather the storm and return to the ways of true parliamentary government. At the Reichstag meeting of May 9 Chancellor Brüning retained a majority of 287-257, and thereby received renewed parliamentary support for his program of emergency legislation on the basis of Article 48.

The end came sooner than expected. Although the Brüning program of economic rehabilitation had frequently come into conflict with vested property rights, Hindenburg, whose consent to the use of Article 48 was constitutionally indispensable, had paid little heed to the cries of "bolshevism." In the days following his reelection, however, he was informed that his Chancellor was about to make use of Article 48 as authority for a decree dividing certain bankrupt eastern estates to aid the unemployed. The Junker President thereupon told the Chancellor that he refused to lend his name or prerogative to any program of "agrarian bolshevism," in spite of the fact that his chief support in the late election had been Brüning and his Centrists, the Social Democrats, and the trade unions. The Brüning Cabinet resigned May 30, although it still maintained its majority in the Reichstag. Without Hindenburg's consent the Chancellor could not use Article 48; without Article 48 he could not hope to govern. His resignation was therefore unavoidable. Franz von Papen was selected as the new Chancellor, and on June 4 the Reichstag was dissolved "since it . . . no longer conform(ed) to the political will of the German people."[7] The new Cabinet meanwhile governed by means of the dictatorship article.

From this day until the demise of democratic Germany the nation was ruled by a "presidential government." The Chancellor and his ministers were no longer a parliamentary, but a presidential Cabinet.[8] By virtue of the Reichstag's renunciation of its electoral and law-making functions, and by virtue of a latitudinarian and indeed revolutionary conception and exercise of his powers under the Constitution, President von Hindenburg became the absolute focus of government in Germany from the dismissal of Brüning to the advent of Hitler. The aged President (or rather the insidious clique that used him as a front) had finished with the parliamentary, party Cabinet. He now proposed to govern with one composed of a "non-party" Chancellor and non-party ministers. It was his hope that such a Cabinet would

[7] Poetzsch-Heffter, XXI, p.67, gives the text of this decree.
[8] See generally Horst von Hausen: *Das Präsidialkabinett* (Erlangen, 1933).

enjoy the confidence of the Reichstag. If a Chancellor of his choice were repulsed by that body, he intended to dissolve it repeatedly until one was returned that would grant the required confidence. The chief responsibility of the Cabinet was to him as President of the Reich, not to the Reichstag.

Brüning's repeated use of Article 48 as a remedy for the defects of German parliamentary government had thus resulted in the replacement of the parliamentary system by presidential government of the most extreme type. The technical means by which this constitutional revolution was effected, that is, the transfer of Cabinet responsibility from Reichstag to President, were: the President's right of dissolution under Article 25, by which he could send the Reichstag home for three months at a time; the presidential prerogative in the choice and dismissal of ministers under Article 53, in the exercise of which Ebert had shown considerable independence; the virtual abolition by the Reichstag of the necessity of a vote of confidence for the Cabinet to continue in power; the practice of non-convocation of the Reichstag; and finally, and most indispensable, Article 48, by which the President and his hand-picked Cabinet could govern the country without the presence of the legislature.

Hindenburg had adopted a conception of the presidency which had long been championed by certain German jurists, particularly Carl Schmitt. In the latter's noted and controversial book *Der Hüter der Verfassung*, published in 1931, there had been expressed this typically Germanic idea of the President as the pivot of the constitutional scheme, as a "neutral, mediating, regulating, and conserving" power set above all other branches to defend the Constitution and maintain the state.[9] The President alone was elected by the whole Reich; for this reason he had a peculiar claim to represent the people. He was to be above party and of no party, a neutral arbiter to regulate the play of the parliamentary system, and, in the event of its breakdown, to rule the country with Article 48 and a presidential Cabinet. Schmitt regarded Article 48 as the President's indispensable weapon in his capacity as guardian of the Constitution.[10] But as one observer has pointed out, Hindenburg was not the "Guardian" but the "Reformer" of the Constitution.[11] Whatever he was, he was the ruler of Germany in a way unforeseen by the Assembly of 1919—all by virtue of the dictatorship article and its ill-defined place in the constitutional scheme.

[9] Schmitt: *Der Hüter der Verfassung* (Tübingen, 1931), p.137.
[10] *Ibid.*, p.35.
[11] Heneman: *The Growth of Executive Power in Germany*, pp.242-243.

The two Cabinets that were to follow the departure of Brüning and precede the arrival of Hitler, the so-called "Junker Cabinets" of Papen (May 31, 1932-November 17, 1932) and Schleicher (December 2, 1932-January 28, 1933), were responsible to Hindenburg alone and governed the Reich by virtue of his power under Article 48. The Reichstag which had been elected July 31, 1932 sat only on August 30 and September 12. On this latter date it passed a vote of no confidence in Papen 513-32, but in the middle of the debate preceding this vote Papen seized the floor and made use of an undated order of dissolution which Hindenburg had previously given him. The Reichstag elected on November 6 sat December 6 to December 9 and cast no votes of any kind. Parliamentary government in Germany was dead. Through a revolutionary reading of his authority under the Constitution, Hindenburg, the man in whom the democrats had so fervently placed their trust, had precipitated a fatal transfer of power from those who sought to defend the Constitution to those who sought to destroy it. The dismal jeremiad of Dr. Cohn had come to pass. The enemies, not the friends of Weimar had claimed Article 48 for their own.

It was the devious Papen who perpetrated the most flagrant abuse of the President's emergency powers in the history of the Republic. This incident is known in German history as the "rape of Prussia."[12] On July 20, 1932 two decrees based on sections 1 and 2 of Article 48 were issued in the name of President von Hindenburg, one suspending all seven fundamental rights in Greater Berlin and the province of Brandenburg, and transferring the executive and police power in this area to the Reich Minister of Defense; the other appointing Chancellor von Papen himself as Reich Commissioner for Prussia, endowed with "all the powers of the Prussian government."[13] The official explanation for these extraordinary measures was the failure of the Prussian state authorities to suppress the bitter campaign of civil violence then at its height in the great industrial cities of that province. The real explanation was that Papen and his Cabinet, eager as they were for some sort of "modification" of the Constitution and the Republic, had come to regard the Social Democratic government of Prussia, headed by Otto Braun with Karl Severing as his Minister of the Interior, as a serious obstruction to their cause of reaction. The Braun government in Prussia and its potent police force had long been recognized as one of the three great

---

[12] See Schuman, *op. cit.*, pp.170 ff. for a keen account of this whole affair. Poetzsch-Heffter, XXI, pp.51-59, gives the important documents and letters connected with the incident.

[13] *RGBl.* (1932), p.337.

pillars of Weimar democracy. The other two were Hindenburg and the Brüning Cabinet, and they had already been pulled down by the reactionaries. Now this last one was doomed to destruction.

The fact is that disorders were prevalent throughout the Reich. The country was in the midst of an overheated Reichstag campaign which more resembled a civil war than it did an election. The Prussian government was doing no worse than any other state cabinet in the maintenance of order, and it could argue convincingly that the uproar in Prussia was largely due to the cancellation by the Papen government of the ban which Brüning had placed on the Nazi storm troops. (Papen was honoring a direct request of Hitler for this action.) It was a flagrant abuse of Article 48 by Papen to seek his selfish, reactionary ends. A few days after the deposition of the Prussian government Papen, in his capacity as Reich Commissioner for Prussia, proceeded to appoint a new state delegation to the Reichsrat. According to Article 63 of the Constitution, state representation in the Reichsrat was to consist of members of the state cabinets. The implications of the move were obvious: Papen intended to elevate this subordinate body to the position of power once occupied by the imperial Bundesrat, and control of the large Prussian delegation was the first and indispensable step.

Certain of the ousted Prussian ministers were not to be thus cast out without a show of opposition to this undisguised attempt to capture the last stronghold of democracy in Germany. The Prussian cabinet at once brought action in the *Staatsgerichtshof* against the government of the Reich for its intervention in Prussia. The decision of the court in this case is of some interest to American students. There was evidenced a clear-cut case of judicial review, even if couched in continental terms of formal competence, and even if the judges could have done a lot better had they been a little braver.[14]

The court refused to accede to the demands of the ousted Prussian cabinet and declare the whole decree of July 20 as beyond the competence of the President. It asserted that the conditions for federal intervention in Prussia actually existed, and that the Reich government was therefore within its powers in supplanting the Braun cabinet with a commissioner. The President's competence to initiate all measures necessary to restore order was vigorously reasserted. However, it was by this very criterion that the subsequent action of Papen in depriving the state

[14] The opinion is given in full in the *Frankfurter Zeitung*, October 26, 1932. For a thorough discussion of the decision, see J. Heckel: *"Das Urteil des Staatsgerichtshofs vom 25. Okt. 1932. . . ," Archiv des öff. Rechts*, XXIII (1933), p.183. Carl Schmitt was counsel for the Reich.

cabinet of its constitutional right to sit in the Reichsrat was judged by the court to be beyond the bounds of necessity in this case. As commissioner, Papen might temporarily wield all governmental power in Prussia, but this power did not extend to a permanent measure such as the alteration of its representation in an organ of the federal government.

The extremely controversial nature of this litigation had placed the *Staatsgerichtshof* in a most unwelcome position. Not possessed of the prestige of the American Supreme Court or its established power of judicial review, the highest German court could do little more than follow the facts advanced by the Reich government and thus validate the original decree of July 20. On the question of formal competence it could act and did, declaring that a Reich Commissioner exercising state authority in place of the normal government had no jurisdiction to oust permanently the regularly constituted ministry by substituting for it a new delegation in the Reichsrat.

Adolf Hitler's entrance into power January 30, 1933 brought the German Republic to its star-cross'd end. The Reichstag was again dissolved, and the new Chancellor issued the first group of his decrees on the basis of Article 48. An enabling act was passed by the new Reichstag March 24, 1933 giving Hitler full powers of executive decree, and the dictatorship article, having greatly simplified the initial labors of the Nazi revolutionists, was consigned to the scrap heap with the rest of the Weimar Constitution.

To summarize this confused story: Article 48 was used frequently and successfully between 1919 and 1924 to suppress insurrection aimed at the life of the new Republic. Toward the close of this period the interpretation of its phrases underwent an extensive expansion, and it became the authority for emergency decrees dealing with economic as well as political troubles. Between 1925 and 1930 Article 48 lay quiescent, and the German parliamentary system functioned according to plan. With the new upsurge of economic and political unrest and the rise of parties dedicated to the destruction of the parliamentary system, Article 48 came again into prominence. For several years it was the principal weapon of the men who were struggling to defend the Republic, and they resorted to it with increasing frequency to provide the Reich with some semblance of government. The downfall of the democrats was followed by the advent to power of Junker Cabinets responsible only to a senile President, and Article 48 became the possession of men who despised the whole idea of Weimar democracy. The Rock of the Republic was converted by Hindenburg and Papen into a bridge leading to despotism, and over this bridge marched Adolf Hitler to his evil power.[15]

[15] The Germans are not good Bourbons; they never learn, but they do forget. The postwar constitutions of three German states—Bavaria, Wurttemberg-Baden, and Hesse—have emergency provisions quite similar to Article 48. Legislative control has in each instance been strengthened. See J. K. Pollock *et al.*: *Change and Crisis in European Government* (New York, 1947), pp. 169-171.

CHAPTER V

Article 48 in Law and Theory

THE inordinate significance of Article 48 in the history of the German Republic must by now be apparent. But Article 48 is not primarily the province of the historian; the political scientist has an even more vital interest in this unique instrument of constitutional dictatorship. It is in recognition of the leading role played by the German jurists in the development and use of Article 48 that this chapter turns to an analytical rather than historical treatment of the German constitutional dictatorship.[1] Many aspects of this juristic discussion have already been considered in the previous two chapters and will therefore not be touched upon again.

The German Republic was unique among the four modern states examined in this book in that there was present in the Constitution itself specific provision for emergency powers in emergency situations. The dictatorship would surely have been an "alien element,"[2] an institution of government foreign to all accepted criteria of the constitutional state, had it not been "built into its framework." A weapon of reaction from Germany's imperial past had been republicanized and converted into a weapon of democracy. The power to dole out this extreme medicine resided in the hands of the regular civil organs of government, particularly the President of the Reich and the Cabinet, and their responsibility to Reichstag and people was in no wise circumscribed. Thus was the dictatorship made constitutional.

Article 48 in the Constitutional Scheme

FROM a strictly theoretical point of view the dictatorship had no place in the German pattern of government. German jurists agreed that Article 48 was not to be considered in relation to the normal structure of the separation of powers. The dictatorship was an all-inclusive fourth power to be held in abeyance as the peculiar expression of the

---

[1] Probably the best short theoretical discussion of Article 48 is Richard Grau's article in vol. II of the *Handbuch des deutschen Staatsrechts*, pp. 274-295, entitled "*Die Diktaturgewalt des Reichspräsidenten.*" A bibliography of the extensive literature evoked by Article 48 may be found in Karl Schultes: *Die Jurisprudenz zur Diktatur des Reichspräsidenten nach Artikel 48, Abschnitt II der Weimarer Verfassung* (Bonn, 1934), pp.ix-xviii. See also Gerhard Anschütz: *Die Verfassung des Deutschen Reichs* (14th ed., Berlin, 1933), pp.267-300.

[2] Grau, *loc. cit.*, p.274.

state's will to survive; when it was called into action, it combined all the other powers and something more. The dictatorship was a "fusion of the three categories of power, a union, a reestablishment of the original state of affairs that preceded the separation of powers."[3] Although no new powers attached to the dictator, the area of operation of his competence was broadened and deepened by the suspension of the seven fundamental rights. He was thus able to assert the total authority of the state in disregard of all the usual checks and balances and the guarantees of freedom set up to protect the German citizen from the arbitrary action of his government. It is important to recall again that, although by the "dictator" was specifically meant the President, all the other organs of the government were joined with him in the exercise of his prerogative. It was a magnificent assertion of the sovereignty of the German people, manifested in a forthright expression of the right of national self-preservation. "Dictatorship is rather government pure and simple—in the original, fundamental sense of the word—that is, *IMPERIUM*, or a disposition over the entire power of the state."[4] The possession and exercise of an authority analogous to the great Roman doctrine of *Imperium*—that was the unique characteristic of the constitutional dictator.

In its inception the use of Article 48 was not, as a reading of the article alone might infer, a purely presidential prerogative. The ministerial countersignature of all ordinances and orders of the President was established as an inviolable principle of the German governmental scheme. This joined the Chancellor and Cabinet with the President in any employment of Article 48. It has been seen that President von Hindenburg came to look upon Article 48 as his exclusive prerogative, a conception of his power which he was able to put into practice by reason of the presidential cabinet and the demoralized Reichstag. Throughout most of the years of the Republic, however, the dictatorship was definitely a group responsibility. Often the Cabinet took the initiative in the use of Article 48, sometimes the President did, but always the positive approval of both of these branches of the government was indispensable to such action.[5] And the positive disapproval of the Reichstag could prevent it.

[3] Schultes, *loc. cit.*, p.22.
[4] Heckel: *Archiv des öff. Rechts*, XXII, p.257, p.286.
[5] The accounts of many debates in the Reichstag demonstrate that this body considered the Cabinet rather than the President the actual bearer of responsibility for measures adopted under Article 48. See F. Blachly and M. Oatman: *The Government and Administration of Germany* (Baltimore, 1928), p.93.

Under certain conditions the dictatorial power could be exercised by the cabinet of a state within its own boundaries. This exercise, although provisional and immediately revocable by the President or the Reichstag, was an independent one; the state's power to act was derived directly from the Constitution.[6] The states were not agents of or subordinate to the President in their choice of measures under the dictatorship power. All the President could do was demand a revocation, or make the state decrees his own. He might prefer to issue an emergency ordinance dealing with the same situation. Under Article 13 of the Constitution (*Reichsrecht bricht Landesrecht*) this action would annul the state order. But until that moment the state would have been acting independently as possessor of some of the Reich's extraordinary power of survival.

The state cabinets were to exercise this power "solely and exclusively in place of the temporarily obstructed authority of the Reich, only on condition of such obstruction and only for the duration thereof."[7] The demand for revocation could not be disobeyed, but the state cabinet alone could revoke its own measures. Federal execution under section 1 of the dictatorship article was the corrective for a state's refusal to revoke. Such execution, though threatened,[8] was never consummated against any state for disobeying the President's demand for revocation. In the exercise of its competence under Article 48 the state could make use of the same powers and procedures as did the President of the Reich. It had no authority to command the services of the *Reichswehr*, but it could request them in case of inability to cope with a disturbance. The final decision on this point rested with the Reich Minister of Defense. On the whole, the employment of Article 48 by the state cabinets was sparing and successful.[9] In extreme conditions of disorder within a particular state the situation was usually regarded as a danger to the whole country, and intervention by the Reich government ensued directly.

[6] See generally R. Grau: *"Die Diktatur der Landesregierungen,"* Handbuch des deutschen Staatsrechts, II, pp.295-300; Karl Strupp: *"Das Ausnahmerecht der Länder nach Art. 48, IV der Reichsverfassung,"* Archiv des öff. Rechts, V (1923), p.187.

[7] Hugo Preuss: *"Reichsverfassungsmässige Diktatur,"* Zeitschrift für Politik, XIII (1924), p.110.

[8] For an example, see Johannes Mattern: *Bavaria and the Reich* (Baltimore, 1923).

[9] Lists of the decrees issued by the various state governments on the basis of Article 48, section 4, are to be found in Poetzsch-Heffter, XIII, p.155; XVII, p.99; XXI, p.139.

Limitations on the Use of Article 48

IF the study of constitutional law is essentially the study of constitutional limitations, then there could be no more effective means of determining the nature of Article 48 than to examine the restrictions, both practical and theoretical, placed upon its use. It was early established that the power of the President under Article 48 was sufficient to meet any type or degree of crisis. A decision of the *Reichsgericht* declared that the President under Article 48 could "unquestionably take any measure necessary to the restoration of the public safety and order. . . . Absolutely everything that the circumstances demand is to be allowed him in warding off the dangers that imperil the Reich."[10] The article was a bottomless well of dictatorial possibilities, and it has already been demonstrated how resourceful the two Presidents and their Chancellors were in their selection of "necessary measures," whether traditional or novel. One of the two great problems of constitutional government, that of power, had thus been solved. The problem of limitations remained.[11]

At this juncture it would seem advisable to repeat that the law foreseen and even demanded by section 5 was never passed. The enactment of such a statute regulating the scope and exercise of the powers granted by Article 48 might have averted many of the difficulties that arose from its application. Suffice it to say that, in default of such enactment, the only limitations upon the government in its use of this power remained those arising from the terms of the Constitution.[12] More than this, the definition of the important phrases of the article never achieved sufficient precision. The records of the republican Reichstag and the pages of Germany's law journals are studded with pleas for the passage of a qualifying statute, but action was never forthcoming. During the perilous first years of the Republic considerable reluctance was expressed toward laying any limitations upon the President in the use of this power. Preuss had voiced the opinion in the Weimar Assembly that this law could well be put off until a more peaceful time. With the return

[10] *RGStr.*, vol. 55, pp.115 ff.

[11] See generally Hans Kohne: *Umfang und Grenzen der diktatorischen Befugnisse des Reichspräsidenten* (Koslin, 1931).

[12] It was agreed among German jurists and was officially asserted by opinions of the Ministry of Justice that until the passage of this law the President should have "a completely free hand" in the use of Article 48. See W. Kronheimer: *"Der Streit um den Artikel 48 der Reichsverfassung," Archiv des öff. Rechts,* VII (1924), p.304, pp.306-307. All imperial and state laws regulating emergency situations were regarded as abrogated—Preuss, *loc. cit.,* p.108. See also R. Grau: *Die Diktatur des Reichspräsidenten und der Landesregierungen auf Grund des Artikels 48 der Reichsverfassung* (Berlin, 1922), p.31.

to more normal conditions, demands persisted for the passage of a statute defining the powers of the President, clarifying the relations of state and Reich in the use of Article 48, and guaranteeing more adequate legal remedies to the citizen whose person or property might have been unavoidably injured by measures taken during an emergency.[13] But still no action was taken. In the years of "Germany peaceful and republican" the whole question tended to drop out of sight. Liberty-loving people refuse to plan in time of peace the exact procedure by which their liberties are to be abridged in time of crisis—even when, as in this particular instance, it would entail a decrease, through definition, of the scope of emergency powers already provided. In the last years of the Republic, when this law was badly needed, its passage became a practical impossibility.

In the absence of this statute, what were the actual limits upon the competence of the government of the Reich in the use of Article 48?

Limits Found Expressly in the Constitution. A major portion of the debates concerning Article 48 in the convention at Weimar was devoted to the problem of checks upon the President in the utilization of his crisis powers. Preuss himself opposed demands for such restraints upon the President as countersignature by the whole Cabinet and the prior approval of the Reichstag. He expressed the opinion that these checks would vitiate the strength of Article 48, and that those provided in the article and the Constitution would suffice to restrict the authorities, in his mind all good democrats, to salutary and republican uses of Article 48, without at the same time depriving President and Cabinet of real striking power in emergency situations. The majority of delegates came to believe that there were sufficient checks thus provided. These were:

Countersignature: The requirement of ministerial countersignature meant that the President and his Cabinet would have to agree before any particular step could be taken. The Cabinet, responsible for its existence to the Reichstag, would refuse assent to any emergency action unacceptable to that body. The mere knowledge that the Reichstag would disapprove of a measure and evidence that disapproval through a vote of no-confidence was a healthy restraint upon careless or arbitrary use of Article 48.

Reichstag disapproval: A direct check upon the President and the

[13] The argument for the passage of such a law is best summed up in Hans Nawiasky: "*Das Durchführungsgesetz zum Artikel 48 der Reichsverfassung*," *Das Recht* (September 20, 1924), pp.455 ff. See also Richard Thoma: "*Die Regelung der Diktaturgewalt*," *Deutsche Juristen Zeitung*, no. 17-18 (1924), p.654. Carl Schmitt writes against this proposal in *Die Diktatur*, pp.254-257.

Cabinet was section 3 of the dictatorship article which required the executive to "immediately inform the Reichstag of all measures taken in conformity with . . . this article," and added that "the measures are to be revoked upon the demand of the Reichstag." An ordinance issued under Article 48 was not automatically suspended by such Reichstag action, but only by the President. Of course such a decree could be, and several times was, altered or annulled by a subsequent Reichstag statute. Although there were many motions introduced demanding a revocation of ordinance issued under Article 48, in thirteen years the Reichstag itself made but two formal requests. On December 16, 1921 a demand was made for the abrogation of a decree promulgated during the wave of terror which had reached its peak in September of that year. The revocation by the President followed on December 23.[14] The other demand for a revocation, that of July 18, 1930, and its results have already been discussed. The request was honored by Brüning, the Reichstag was dissolved, and the decrees were reissued a few days later. In 1932 Hindenburg, knowing that the Reichstag would make such a request, issued a decree of dissolution based on this very fact.[15]

Presidential responsibility: In his actions under the dictatorship article, as in his every action, the President of the Reich was liable to removal from office for abuse of power and trust. Under the terms of Article 43 of the Constitution he could be removed by popular vote on the proposal of two-thirds of the Reichstag. Under the terms of Article 59 he could be impeached before the *Staatsgerichsthof* by two-thirds of the Reichstag "for having culpably violated the Constitution or a law of the Reich." Finally, he could be prosecuted criminally with the consent of the Reichstag.

In summary, it is obvious that the vigilance of the Reichstag was the chief, if not the only barrier provided in the Constitution against the misuse of Article 48. Through the constitutional requirement of ministerial countersignature for presidential action and the principle of ministerial responsibility, as well as through the Reichstag's right to disapprove or amend any measure adopted by the President under Article 48, the representatives of the people constituted the foremost limitation on the employment of emergency powers in the Weimar Republic. The collapse of the Reichstag therefore meant the nullification of all effective checks upon the President and his Cabinet in their use of Article 48.

[14] For details of this incident, see Poetzsch-Heffter, XIII, pp.154 ff.
[15] September 12, 1932. See *RGBl.* (1932), p.441.

Limitations Arising From the Nature of the Constitution. There were other checks upon the executive in the use of Article 48 besides those specifically mentioned in the Constitution, checks which arose from the fact that the Republic existed under a written constitution, checks which, although without specific sanction, would have their ultimate warrant in the responsibility of the executive to Reichstag and people. In one sense these limitations existed only in theory. It was the presence of the Reichstag, not any vague prohibitions arising from the nature of the constitutional order, that conditioned and regulated the actual use of Article 48. And yet these "vague prohibitions" did offer an important restraint upon the actions of the President, sworn as he was to defend the Constitution. Moreover, they were the chief interest of the German publicists, engaged throughout all these years in a violent academic discussion of the dictatorship article. In no other country at any time has the problem of emergency government received the attention of so many eminent jurists, and it was the particular question of the inherent constitutional limitations upon the use of Article 48 which seems to have interested them most deeply. For this reason the question of the theoretical limits upon the use of the constitutional dictatorship cannot be overlooked.

In the first place, the nature of the dictatorship restricted the President to actions designed to restore normal conditions, so that the unaltered Constitution might again be set in effective operation. That is to say, the operation of the German dictatorship was, like its Roman forebear, conditioned by its purpose. That purpose was to reestablish public safety and order, and the executive was limited to measures directed to this end. He was not to employ this power to alter the form of the state or any of its functions or to create a new political situation, but was bound to restore the conditions existing prior to the outbreak of the disturbance.

A second inherent limitation on the use of these emergency powers was the unwritten but acknowledged principle that measures taken under Article 48 should be repealed as soon as possible, and should not extend beyond the restoration of public safety and order for which they had been adopted. Article 48 was always regarded as "limited in point of time by the achievement of the purpose of its institution."[16] The criminal division of the *Reichsgericht* had the following to say on this point:

[16] Poetzsch-Heffter, XXI, p.132.

"That the measures taken on the ground of Article 48 of the Reich Constitution are not finally valid for all time may be determined especially from the fact that they are only taken for the restoration of seriously disturbed or endangered public safety and order. But this in no wise prevents the President of the Reich from instituting such dictatorial measures for an unspecified period, if the public safety and order whose restoration he seeks would, in his opinion, if the measures were not continued, probably be increasingly disturbed or endangered for a long time."[17]

In other words, the President was bound to repeal all measures whose purposes had been fulfilled, but he could not be forced to do so against his positively asserted judgment. The measures adopted under Article 48 for the suppression of civil insurrection were as a rule repealed as soon as the danger to the state had been definitely allayed. Most of the emergency ordinances issued under the economic dictatorship were not limited in time. Measures as drastic as these, however, could hardly have been regarded by the government as permanent in nature.

Thirdly, the President was bound by solemn oath to observe and defend the provisions of the Constitution. Article 48 permitted him to abridge seven of the articles in that charter, but no others. It was the consensus of German juristic opinion that the use of the dictatorship article found an unconditional limitation in all the other provisions of the Constitution not singled out by section 2 as liable to suspension.[18] This inviolability of the Constitution arose from the so-called *argumentum e contrario* as well as from the constitutional character of the dictatorship. In both theory and practice, however, this point of view found considerable contradiction. Some jurists held that the President was not bound to leave untouched those constitutional guarantees subsidiary in nature to the seven fundamental rights which he was expressly empowered to suspend, for example, the guarantee of freedom of trade and industry under Article 151.[19] These jurists regarded all other provisions as untouchable. Others, notably Carl Schmitt and Erwin Jacobi, went further and asserted that a different approach must be made to this whole problem. The strictly legalistic interpretation of men like Preuss and Richard Grau they considered to be out of harmony with the facts, as well as with the nature of Article 48.

[17] *RGStr.*, vol. 59, p.30.
[18] Hans Nawiasky: *"Die Auslegung des Art. 48 der Reichsverfassung,"* *Archiv des öff. Rechts*, IX (1925), p.49; Strupp, *loc. cit.*, p.201; Preuss, *loc. cit.*, p.105; Grau: *Die Diktatur*, p.50. The jurisprudence of this "strict construction" school is summarized and criticized by Schultes, *op. cit.*, pp.23-47; the liberal interpretation of Carl Schmitt is summarized, pp.47-57.
[19] Fritz Muhr: *"Die wirtschaftliche Diktatur des Reichspräsidenten,"* *Zeitschrift für Politik*, XIII (1924), pp.483, 494-496, and 501.

Schmitt in particular expounded a latitudinarian conception of the President's dictatorial power, maintaining that the dictator might temporarily suspend almost all the articles of the Constitution, if necessary to save it, and not just the seven mentioned in Article 48 itself.[20] He could not permanently alter the Constitution, but he could temporarily prevent the operation of a large part of it. Schmitt advanced the idea that the operation of Article 48 itself provided for "an untouchable minimum of organization"—that is, there were several governmental organs (President, Cabinet, Reichstag) constitutionally joined together in the execution of those functions foreseen by Article 48; and these organs, their incumbents, and the constitutional conditions governing their activities (such as countersignature and responsibility) could not be altered by the President in his use of Article 48. Any temporary abridgment of other articles was not a serious and unconstitutional matter. Rather it was a necessary method of action permitted by Article 48, and was employed to save those articles for future operation.

In actual practice, even when German democracy was at its strongest, the Schmitt-Jacobi thesis was nearer the facts than was the strict and legalistic point of view. A number of provisions of the Constitution besides those specifically mentioned in Article 48 were clearly contravened by presidential decrees. Special courts were several times instituted, despite the explicit statement of Article 105 that exceptional courts were illegal and totally forbidden.[21] Moreover, there is ample evidence that the independence of the judges guaranteed by Article 102 was several times transgressed by persons executing the measures of the President under Article 48. Other articles that were violated with impunity were 129 (tenure of office and other rights of civil servants), 37 (freedom from restraint of Reichstag and Landtag deputies), and 45 (providing

[20] The Schmitt-Jacobi thesis finds its original and most cogent expression in the monographs presented by these two under the title "Die Diktatur des Reichspräsidenten," published in vol. I of Verhandlungen der Vereinigung der Deutschen Staatsrechtlehrer (Berlin, 1924). See also Schmitt: Die Diktatur, pp.242-254. The opposition to this thesis is best summarized and organized in Nawiasky, loc. cit., esp. pp.11-16. See also Heckel, loc. cit., pp.274-275. Kurt Häntzchel: "Die Verfassungsschranken der Diktaturgewalt des Artikels 48 der Reichsverfassung," Zeitschrift fur öff. Recht, v (1926), p.205, reviews this whole controversy.

[21] While the establishment of special courts under Article 48 was always bitterly attacked as unconstitutional by many authorities, the regular courts uniformly validated their institution as "special courts" (Sondergerichte), while the Constitution forbade "exceptional courts" (Ausnahmegerichte)! Exceptional courts were held to be those set up without any authorization, whereas Article 48 was regarded as sufficient authorization for special courts as "necessary measures" in the use of the article to suppress civil insurrection.

for the necessary consent of the Reichstag to treaties concerning subjects governed by national legislation).[22]

It seems strange now that so much juristic energy should have been expended on this question of how much of the Constitution could be disregarded by a President in the use of emergency powers, and so little in working out a law that would have settled many of the uncertainties and ambiguities surrounding Article 48. And yet this discussion merits at least passing mention, for it is the only occasion in juristic history when any country's first-rate political scientists turned in a body to an examination of some of the important and unsolved problems of constitutional dictatorship.

The Courts as Limitations on Article 48. A question that would readily suggest itself to the American reader is: what bounds, if any, did the courts of Germany set upon the use of Article 48? The answer: practically none. Although there was considerable discussion of this matter among the jurists of republican Germany,[23] nothing even closely approximating American judicial review was ever established. In the tradition of the civil law, the framers of the Weimar Constitution relied upon the legislature as the primary safeguard against the abuse of emergency powers, and judicial review was not seriously considered in this connection. Continental courts have always accepted as final the findings of the government on questions of fact, if supported by a bare minimum of evidence, and there was no deviation from this traditional rule during the history of the Republic. The courts held consistently that the existence of those conditions presupposed for the institution of any particular measure under Article 48 was a matter for the decision of the President of the Reich alone, or of the Reichstag, and thus foreclosed any judicial censorship upon the necessity of the various uses of this emergency power.[24] They also followed the lead of the government in refusing to limit the scope of the all-important phrase "necessary measures."[25]

This is not to say that the use of Article 48 was never challenged in

[22] See generally H. Schade: *"Ersatz der Zustimmung des Reichstags zu Staatsverträgen im Wege des Art. 48 der Reichsverfassung,"* Archiv des öff. Rechts, XXI (1932), p.364.
[23] R. Grau: *"Zum Gesetzentwurf über die Prüfung der Verfassungmässigkeit von Reichsgesetzen und Reichsverordnungen,"* Archiv des öff. Rechts, XI (1926), p.287; C. J. Friedrich: "The Issue of Judicial Review in Germany," *Pol. Sci. Q.,* XLIII (1928), p.188; Walter C. Simons: "Relation of the German Judiciary to the Executive and Legislative Branches," *American Bar Association Journal* (December, 1929).
[24] *RGStr.,* vol. 57, pp.384-385. *RGStr.,* vol. 58, pp.269, 271. Grau: *Handbuch,* II, p.294.
[25] *RGStr.,* vol. 59, pp.41 ff.

court. On the contrary, actions taken under the dictatorship article were repeatedly contested in the courts of the Reich, and these continental tribunals, quite capable of deciding questions of formal competence, had much to say on some of the controversial points which arose from the use of the article. Although they provided no substantial check upon this use, they certainly gave the jurists plenty to talk about, and incidentally put the stamp of judicial approval upon the latitudinarian conception of the scope of these emergency powers. Consider this passage from a decision of the *Reichsgericht*, asked to void an ordinance enacted under Article 48:

"He (the judge) must confine himself to the question whether the bearer of the dictatorial power of the decree under consideration has at least exhibited the purpose specified in Article 48 of the Reich Constitution. . . . Only so far as there can be established a manifest misconstruction of the legal requirements of procedure on the ground of Article 48 of the Reich Constitution, or a sheer willful misuse of authorization to the prosecution of a completely alien end, will the ordinance lack legal validity."[26]

In other words, the court would assume jurisdiction and examine the use of Article 48, but would not fail to uphold the government! These fine words may have salved the judges' continental consciences, but in fact provided no limit upon the decision to make use of Article 48, the measures taken under it, or their duration.

Such then were the actual and theoretical limitations which regulated the President's exercise of his dictatorial emergency powers. That these limitations did not prevent a use of Article 48 clearly deviating from the expectations of its framers, a use that was finally to become a shameful abuse, cannot be denied. But it would be unfair and unscientific to judge their intrinsic validity solely in the light of actual experience. In a country such as the United States where the electorate is vigilant, the legislature potent, and the Constitution a document of inordinate power and sanctity, these limitations would have sufficed to prevent any such abuse of constitutional emergency powers. In a country where two-thirds of the electorate were in a state of confusion and the other third committed to the violent destruction of the constitutional system, the legislature disorganized and impotent, and the Constitution a document without roots in the history or conscience of the people, these limitations could not prevent an abuse that was eventually to contribute materially to the overturn of the Republic.

[26] *RGStr.*, vol. 59, pp.185 ff.

It could well be questioned whether the balance adopted in Article 48 between the limitations on the dictator and his freedom of action was the proper one to guarantee a minimum of danger to the constitutional scheme and a maximum of striking power to the President and his Cabinet. An excellent case can certainly be made for the necessity of prior or subsequent positive approval by the Reichstag of all measures adopted under Article 48. Such a check might well have prevented the rise of the presidential Cabinet, and thereby strengthened the Republic. If the framers of the Constitution had realized that Article 48 would be used as the authority for presidential lawmaking, the positive approval of the Reichstag would doubtless have been provided. The burden of action lay far too heavily upon the members of the Reichstag. The registering of disapproval through a legislative demand for revocation was in its nature a difficult and inadequate procedure. With the Reichstag dissolved, the President had a completely free hand for several months. If positive approval had been required, the Reichstag would have had to remain in session as the prerequisite to any use of Article 48, and this would have provided a salutary check upon the President.

Certainly it was a fatal mistake, perhaps the cardinal defect of the Weimar Constitution, to give the President an almost unrestrained power of dissolution and then not provide for some method through which Reichstag oversight could be maintained in the interim between the dissolution of the old and the convocation of the new Reichstag. If the Reichstag was the chief means of control over the use of Article 48, this control should have been maintained at all times. When Brüning, to whom must unquestionably be assigned the blame for initiating this unholy alliance between the dictatorship and the power of dissolution, reissued the two economic decrees which the Reichstag had caused to be revoked and refused to listen to the complaints of the main interim committee of the dissolved Reichstag, he unwittingly dramatized the mortal defect of the dictatorship article, and Papen was not to disregard the implications of this drama. When the Reichstag reassembled several months later, it was in no position to revoke the Brüning decrees. The possibility that a newly elected Reichstag could demand and secure the revocation of decrees issued after the dissolution of the previous one was not a limitation but a rank delusion. The sterilization of the Reichstag by the physic of dissolution left the President and his Cabinet an undisguised dictatorship foreign to every principle of Weimar democracy. It was Article 48 which gave the reactionaries the lawful means to govern without the Reichstag.

Perhaps a case could be made for Article 48 as it stood, if only the Reichstag had been tenacious in the discharge of its duty. A good deal of the success which the users of this article enjoyed in the early years of the Republic might not have been achieved had the necessity of positive Reichstag approval been required by the Constitution. President Ebert and his Chancellors scored signal victories for the Republic with this power, and in large part this was due to the extreme freedom which they enjoyed in its use.

The framers of the Constitution were merely being optimistic in relying upon the normal responsibilities of the governmental order to prevent executive abuse of the dictatorship article. Ebert requited that optimism, Brüning betrayed it in spite of his good intentions, and both Papen and Hitler made excellent use of it to destroy the Weimar system. That German constitutional morality and parliamentary democracy were to deteriorate so completely as to permit this shamefully unconstitutional abuse of the dictatorship could hardly have been foreseen by Dr. Preuss and his co-workers.

Never has the chief danger to constitutionalism from its instruments of emergency government—that such instruments may be turned *against* the constitutional order—been so graphically illustrated. Never has the simple fact that power is one thing in the possession of good men and another in the grasp of evil men been brought home so forcefully to the democratic understanding. In 1922 Article 48 was a blessing, in 1932 it was a curse. The only moral can be: never let an enemy of democracy get his hands on a weapon of democracy. And a corollary: don't overwork your weapons.

Yet it would be a fatal error to ascribe the demolition of the German Republic to this single defective institution of emergency government. What Montesquieu said of a lost battle and Holmes of the passage of a law—that if either of these "has ruined a State, there was a general cause at work that made the State ready to perish by a single battle or law"—can be said of republican Germany's Article 48. If constitutional dictatorship helped destroy it, still there was a far deeper cause at work to make republican Germany ripe for destruction.

Perhaps the men of Germany could not have worked *any* constitution, while the "men of Massachusetts" could have made a ringing success of the Weimar Constitution and its Article 48.

Part Two

CRISIS GOVERNMENT IN THE
FRENCH REPUBLIC

A FREE PEOPLE with a history full of wars and revolutions are bound to be well acquainted with the uses, dangers, and problems of constitutional dictatorship. In the 160 turbulent years since the first attempt to establish a workable popular government in France, the people of that unlucky country have known many wars and revolutions, many constitutions, many periods of emergency dictatorship. Some of these dictatorships were legal and constitutional, instituted by governments of a constitutional France to preserve the state from the perils of some grave national emergency, and in many instances they were marked by eminent success. To an examination of the adventures in constitutional dictatorship of the third of France's Republics, the next four chapters are directed.

The history of France is peculiarly deserving of such examination. French institutions of law and government have always served as models for nations throughout the world, and this is as true of France's devices of constitutional dictatorship as it is of its Code Napoleon. In the first place, the foremost emergency institution of modern times, the state of siege, finds its birthplace in France. The state of siege was the model for similar instruments of constitutional dictatorship in the German Empire and its member states, in almost all other civil law countries, and even in Anthony Hope's mythical Ruritania. It is a particularly important institution of government in the Latin-American nations. Secondly, the pattern of the French government of the first World War can serve as an admirable model for all democracies engaged in a large-scale war of defense. Finally, the postwar experience of France with the emergency institution of the enabling act has had few equals in scope and consequence. The preeminence of France in the general field of law and politics is clearly carried over into the particular problem of constitutional dictatorship.

77

CHAPTER VI

The State of Siege in History, Law, and Theory

THE fundamental crisis institution of the French Republic is the famed *état de siège*, the state of siege. It is in this typically French solution to the ancient problem of constitutional dictatorship that modern emergency government reaches its peak of institutional and legal perfection. To the civil law tradition of France the idea of a legally anticipated device to place the nation in a state of emergency is altogether logical and unavoidable. The French have always acknowledged without hesitation the ineluctable necessity of emergency government and have chosen to provide for it in their constitutions and laws; they have been through too many wars and rebellions to think they could get along without some clear provision for a constitutional dictatorship. The state of siege is eminently a product of history and eminently an institution in law.

It is this extreme legality which most clearly distinguishes the state of siege from its counterparts in the constitutional systems of England, the United States, and even Germany. The French jurists have never tired of emphasizing that theirs is a legal institution,[1] established in law and finding inviolable limitations in the nature and structure of the French constitutional scheme. In contradistinction to the "unprecedented looseness" of Article 48 of the Weimar Constitution or to the regimes of martial law unregulated by statute in England and the United States, the French state of siege has always been foreseen and methodized in detail by laws of Parliament.

The State of Siege in History

For all its regulation by law, the state of siege is more a product of history than of legislative activity. Its nature and place in the French pattern of law and government cannot be understood without some

---

[1] For example, Joseph Barthélemy: "*Le Droit Public en Temps de Guerre*," part I, *Revue du Droit Public*, XXXII (1915), p.137: "The extraordinary regime in periods of trouble is still a legal regime." Esmein-Nézard: *Eléments de Droit Constitutionnel* (8th ed., Paris, 1928), vol. I, p.30, n. 84: "But today the rule of law is not even suspended by the state of siege." For the best definition of the French concept of *légalité*, see L. Duguit: *Traité de Droit Constitutionnel* (2nd ed., Paris, 1921-1925), III, p.681.

reference to French history.[2] As all traditional and executive forms of constitutional dictatorship the state of siege has a military origin—in this instance, as its name indicates, in the ancient practice of conferring full powers of government upon the general in command of a besieged fortress.[3] The development of the state of siege in history involved the gradual conversion of this purely military institution to one that was political in character, one in which the state of siege became *fictif*, a term to indicate that an open, civil area menaced by invasion or rebellion was to be regarded in law as "besieged," and that the government should have powers in that area analogous to those of a general in command of a beleaguered fortress.

The history of the state of siege begins with the French Revolution. No civil institution of crisis government existed under the *ancien régime*. It is unnecessary to suspend rights that do not exist or augment powers that are already absolute. Since the days of the Revolution, however, France has been ruled the major part of the time by a government constitutionally restricted in its competence, and the state of siege in some form has always been available for use in periods of national emergency. The starting point for the conversion of the strictly military and occasional state of siege into a civil and political institution was the law of July 10, 1791, "concerning the conservation and classification of military areas."[4] This statute established the conditions and forms of action of a state of siege in regard to fortresses and military posts. It was provided that in the event of an attack by enemy troops "all the authority with which the civil officers are clothed by the constitution for the maintenance of order . . . will pass to the military commanders." In this military state of siege, applicable only to fortified places, was the seed of the modern state of siege.[5]

The development from military to political, from *réel* to *fictif*, was given impetus by a law of the tenth Fructidor of the year 5 (August 27, 1797).[6] This law assimilated all *communes de l'intérieur*, that is to say

---

[2] See generally Fernand Velut: *Le Régime de l'Etat de Siège avant la Loi du 9 Août 1849* (Paris, 1910) ; Théodore Reinach: *De l'Etat de Siège* (Paris, 1885), pp.89-124; Paul Romain: *L'Etat de Siège Politique* (Albi, 1918), pp.31-161.

[3] Fritz Mandry: *Das Ausnahmerecht in Frankreich* (Berlin, 1928), p.9; Maurice Hauriou: *Principes de Droit Public* (Paris, 1916), p. 457, n. 2.

[4] Carette: *Lois Annotées*, 1st series (1789-1830), p.121.

[5] The *état de siège proprement dit*, the state of siege which places the absolute command of a defended town besieged by the enemy in the hands of the commanding military officer, still exists in French law. The two states of siege are to be clearly distinguished. See the speech of M. Bardoux, proposer of the law of 1878, *Journal Officiel*, April 3, 1878.

[6] *Bulletin des Lois*, An. v, bull. no. 139, p.14.

open cities, to the *places de guerre* of the law of 1791, and provided that rebellion as well as foreign invasion could justify the establishment of the state of siege. The *effectif* character of this new state of siege was maintained by the prerequisite of actual invasion or rebellion for its initiation. Nevertheless, the dichotomy of the two states of siege had been established. The early years of the political state of siege were marred by repeated abuse, for the Directory and thereafter the First Consul found ample occasion to use this law in the pursuance of their schemes for absolute power.

The history of the modern state of siege begins with the collapse of the July monarchy and the accompanying demise of the *Charte* of 1814 as France's fundamental law. In the turmoil which accompanied the birth of the Second Republic a decree of the Constituent Assembly issued on June 24, 1848 placed the city of Paris in a state of siege, and conferred a "commissioned dictatorship" upon General Cavaignac to maintain public order in the area. This state of siege was not lifted until October 12. The commendable performance of the general and the remembrance of perils past had much to do with the insertion of this article in the new Constitution of November 4, 1848:

> 106. A law will fix the occasions in which the state of siege can be declared, and will regulate the forms and effects of this measure.

The result of this provision constitutionalizing the state of siege was the law of August 9, 1849,[7] still in force as the fundamental law of constitutional dictatorship in France. The political state of siege was thereby clearly distinguished from the military, which continued to be governed by laws coming down from Revolution and Empire, and was regulated minutely as to declaration, effects, and suspension of civil rights. Napoleon III made considerable use of the law of 1849 both as President and Emperor, particularly in the former capacity, and indeed turned it against those who had fathered the idea in the Constituent Assembly. Article 12 of his Constitution of January 1852 had the effect of transferring the right of declaring the state of siege from the legislature to the head of the state alone, with the Senate in the role of advisor. During the Franco-Prussian War and the ensuing internal agitation the institution was employed on a scale hitherto unknown. More than forty Departments were placed under the state of siege for several years, and in four large Departments this emergency govern-

[7] *Bull. des Lois* (1849), sec. 2, p.146.

ment was not brought to an end until April 4, 1876. Needless to say, this indiscriminate use of the state of siege aroused a good deal of responsible opposition.

The French constitutional laws of 1875 reorganized fundamentally the structure of the French government. Concerning the state of siege, and many another important matter, this peculiar Constitution had nothing to say. As a result the law of 1849 no longer conformed in its organizational aspects to the government of France. A new law on the state of siege was therefore proposed and debated, and went into effect April 4, 1878. The law of 1849 was not superseded. Rather it was brought up to date and into conformity with the new structure of the French government. With the passage of this law of 1878 the historical development of the state of siege as a political and republican institution had come full circle.

The State of Siege in Law

THE texts of these two vital statutes run as follows:

The law of 1878:

1. The state of siege can only be declared in the event of imminent danger resulting from a foreign war or an armed insurrection.

Only a law can declare the state of siege.

This law will designate the communes, arrondissements, and departments to which it is to apply. It will fix the period of its duration.

At the expiration of this period, the state of siege ceases automatically, unless a new law shall prolong its effects.

2. In the event the Chambers are adjourned, the President of the Republic can declare the state of siege, on the advice of the Council of ministers; but then the Chambers meet automatically two days later.

3. In the event the Chamber of Deputies is dissolved, and until elections shall have been entirely completed, the state of siege cannot, even provisionally, be declared by the President of the Republic.

Nevertheless, in the event of a foreign war, the President, on the advice of the Council of ministers, can declare the state of siege in the territories menaced by the enemy, on the condition that he convoke the electoral colleges and reassemble the Chambers in the shortest possible delay.

4. In the event that communications with Algeria are interrupted, the governor can declare all or part of Algeria in a state of siege, under the conditions of this law.

5. In the occasions foreseen by articles 2 and 3, the Chambers, as soon as they shall have reassembled, shall maintain or lift the state of siege. In the event of a disagreement between them, the state of siege is lifted automatically.

82

6. Articles 4 and 5 of the law of August 9, 1849 are hereby maintained, as well as the provisions of its other articles not contrary to the present law.

The pertinent provisions of the law of 1849:

7. As soon as the state of siege has been declared, the powers of police and those others with which the civil authority has been clothed for the maintenance of order pass in their entirety to the military authority.

The civil authority continues nevertheless to exercise those of its powers of which it has not been dispossessed by the military authority.

8. The military courts may take jurisdiction over crimes and offenses against the safety of the Republic, against the Constitution, against public peace and order, whatever be the status of the principal perpetrators and their accomplices.

9. The military authority has the power, (1) to conduct searches by day or night in the homes of citizens; (2) to deport liberated convicts and persons who do not have residence in the areas placed in the state of siege; (3) to direct the surrender of arms and munitions, and to proceed to search for and remove them; (4) to forbid publications and meetings which it judges to be of a nature to incite or sustain disorder.

11. Despite the state of siege, citizens continue to exercise the rights guaranteed by the Constitution whose enjoyment is not suspended by the preceding articles.

13. Following the lifting of the state of siege, the military courts continue to recognize crimes and offenses over which they have already assumed jurisdiction.

The general provisions of these two laws remain today the legal foundation for the state of siege—the law of 1878 regulating its organization, the law of 1849 its effects. It should be added that the French military authorities are governed by exhaustive codes of their own production in the prosecution of their duties under this institution. It is important to note that these two laws are not constitutional provisions, but ordinary statutes proceeding in the ordinary manner from the legislative authority. As such they have never bound the French Parliament in any formal way, and are completely alterable at the latter's discretion. However, they do constitute a definite moral sanction on the legislature, being organic laws of long standing and fundamental importance.

The State of Siege in Theory

THE nature of the state of siege is manifest in the terms of these two laws. Two of its main characteristics have already been noted, the stamp of legality and its thorough regulation by statute. A third characteristic is that of parliamentary supremacy. By law and custom the legislature

83

of the Third Republic was almost always in decisive, positive control of the state of siege, a far different situation from that which existed in regard to Article 48 of the Weimar Constitution. Dufaure, Minister of the Interior in 1849, even characterized the state of siege as a "parliamentary dictatorship." As the report of the parliamentary commission on the law of 1878 made clear, the power to suspend the laws should always be lodged in the hands of those to whom the people have entrusted their making.[8] "The right to suspend the rule of the laws can belong to no one but the power which makes them."[9] The execution of the state of siege is the responsibility of the Cabinet and the army, but by the grace of Parliament alone do they function. This legislative ascendancy in the use of the state of siege is likely to be even more pronounced in the Fourth Republic than it was in the Third.

The reasons for this vital fact of parliament supremacy (which finds expression in the necessity of positive legislative declaration of the state of siege) are plain enough. The law of 1878 has been characterized as "a law based on a reaction to the abuses of the state of siege."[10] In particular it was a reaction against an executive abuse of this device. The continuous use of the state of siege in the Franco-Prussian War and its ensuing commotions had not been forgotten in 1878. More than this, the pretensions to power of Marshal MacMahon were still a burning issue of the day, and it is no wonder that the control of the state of siege should have been so firmly placed in the keeping of the legislature. MacMahon's dissolution of the Chamber of Deputies in an attempt to have a representation of monarchical character returned had an even more important effect on the state of siege and indeed on the whole history of the Third Republic. From that day forward the President's power to dissolve Parliament was a dead letter, and no Cabinet ever felt competent to ask for a dissolution. This definitely insured parliamentary supremacy over the use of the state of siege. How different the sad story of Article 48 might have been if the dissolution of the Reichstag had also been a practical impossibility!

Circumstances invoking the state of siege. The state of siege is an emergency institution reserved for crises of only the most severe nature. Article 1 of the law of 1878 makes this certain by forbidding its declaration except in the actual presence of foreign invasion or armed

---

[8] This interesting report by M. Franck-Chaveau is in *Revue Générale d'Administration*, 1 (1878), pp.603 ff.

[9] Franck-Chaveau in the Chamber of Deputies February 6, 1878—*Journal Officiel*, February 7, 1878.

[10] Barthélemy, *loc. cit.*, p.147.

insurrection. The disparity between this provision and section 2 of Article 48 may be more one of degree than of kind, but there is no doubt that the formula for the establishment of the state of siege is a far more restricting one than the broad terms of Article 48. Moreover, it must be remembered that the French state of siege embraces only half the province of the German dictatorship article, for it most certainly does not impart any sort of an emergency ordinance power to the Cabinet or army. The state of siege, like martial law and the old German state of war, is a purely executive form of constitutional dictatorship.

Article 1 of the law of 1849 had authorized a declaration of the state of siege in the event of an "imminent danger to internal or external security." The lawmakers of 1878, having had their fill of the state of siege under both the little Napoleon and the provisional governments of 1871-1875, proceeded to narrow the conditions for its declaration, in order to prevent any further promiscuity in its use. The more general terms of the 1849 statute, easily adaptable to include strikes and minor riots, were championed in the Senate, where the emphasis was on a state of siege more preventive than repressive in character, but to no avail.

Declaration. MacMahon's abortive coup d'état of May 16, 1877 left its mark upon more than one provision of the law of 1878. Article 1 placed the authority for declaring the state of siege squarely in the hands of the Chambers. The right of the head of the state to do this, long an executive prerogative in France and in the other countries that have borrowed this institution from her, was reduced to a merely provisional power. Article 3 was also a direct reaction to MacMahon's escapade. He had been advised by many of his extremist supporters to dissolve the Chambers a second time and, in the hope of obtaining a monarchist Parliament, to hold the new elections under a state of siege. Although this extraordinary action was never realized, the deputies of 1878 were quick to take preventive measures against any such abuse of the state of siege in the future. They had no desire for a *dictatura comitiorum habendorum causa*! With the Chamber of Deputies (now the National Assembly) dissolved, the President, in conjunction with the Cabinet, can declare the state of siege; but only in the event of a foreign war, which undoubtedly signifies the actual invasion of French soil, and only in territories directly threatened by the enemy. He is immediately to convoke the electoral colleges and thereafter the Chambers. Even this provision for presidential declaration in case of war was adopted with a great deal of hesitation and opposition. More concerned

85

with executive pretensions to power than with the logic of the matter, the lawmakers of 1878 made no provision for a state of siege in case of armed rebellion if at the same time the Chambers were dissolved.

Effects of the state of siege. The state of siege has a number of definite and predictable effects upon the government and life of the country. The first of these (by article 7) is the devolution upon the army of the powers of police ordinarily exercised by the civil authorities, "the characteristic feature of the French state of siege."[11] This means that the enforcement of local justice and the maintenance of local order pass from the hands of prefects, sub-prefects, mayors, and other civil officials to the military commanders stationed in the area or sent in for this specific purpose. This grant of police power to the military is permissive, and it has always been expected that the civil authorities will continue to exercise part of their normal competence to keep the peace, particularly those duties of a preventive nature. This is provided for specifically in the same article 7. Of course, the mayors, prefects, and other officials continue to pursue their other tasks of local government. The military authorities have no power to meddle with local business of a strictly civil character. They cannot raise a tax-rate or appoint a dog-catcher or approve a municipal loan. The two powers are to work side by side in a spirit of cooperation to keep local government functioning as efficiently as possible in troubled conditions and to exert every effort to restore those conditions to normal.

Secondly, the military arm is granted four additional and extraordinary powers, permitting the infringement of several important rights of French citizens. These provisions are to be strictly construed and are not regarded as giving the military a power over civilians comparable to that exercised over its own soldiers. It is in the abridgment of his fundamental rights that the citizen has brought home to him the dictatorial impact of the state of siege. It is of interest to compare these provisions with the analogous suspensory clauses of Article 48.

A third effect of the state of siege is established by article 8, which authorizes the military courts to assume jurisdiction over all crimes and other offenses against the security of the Republic, the Constitution, and the public safety and order—whatever the status of the perpetrators and their accomplices. Thus an ordinary citizen who commits a crime of a public nature in an area under the state of siege is liable to trial and punishment by a court-martial. Here again the article is permissive in character, and if the military authorities agree, the ordinary courts

---

[11] Reinach, *op. cit.*, p.156.

can hear litigations not connected with the maintenance of public safety and order.

Finally, it is implicit in the nature of the state of siege that the Cabinet, as agent of the legislature and advisor to the President, shall be entrusted with a competence of supervision and decree that would seem abnormal in ordinary times. This by no means signifies that this organ is granted extraordinary powers of legislative decree. Rather it indicates that the pertinent ministers—the Premier, and the Ministers of War, Interior, and Justice—benefit by an enlargement of their regular power of issuing administrative ordinances.

Otherwise, the structure and functions of government and the lives of the people of France are left unaffected by the state of siege. The citizen who minds his own business may hardly know that it has been declared, contrary to the experience of the ordinary German who learned all about Article 48 from his tax bill. As for the government, the two main relationships, that between Parliament and Cabinet and that between the civil authority (at the national level) and the military, remain unaltered. Parliament continues to function as the legislative and controlling authority of the French constitutional scheme, the source of all laws, and the guardian of the Republic against any abuse of executive or military competence. The responsibility of the French Army to the Ministry of War and thence to the representatives of the people remains unimpaired.

Limitations on the state of siege. The checks placed upon the initiation and administration of the state of siege are several and important. Even a cursory review of them should substantiate the claims of the French jurists for the unique *légalité* of their great crisis institution, and should demonstrate that the knotty question of limitations has been far more successfully answered than it was in the case of Article 48. Most of these checks are to be found in the laws of 1849 and 1878. Further restraints are implied in the constitutional scheme of the French Republic.

The chief limitation upon the declaration of the state of siege is Parliament itself. Whether the original declaration is made by the Chambers or is first, in the event of their being out of session, to be initiated by the President and Cabinet, in either instance it is a law, a positive expression of the will of the people's chosen representatives, which alone can make the state of siege effective and lasting. Whereas the framers of Germany's Article 48 made the important limitation of parliamentary control a negative one, the French lawmakers of 1878 made the decision to establish a state of siege depend upon the positive initiative or positive approval of both houses of the national legislature.

Two formal limitations upon the declaration of the state of siege are to be noted in the law of 1878. It is specifically declared that the law (or decree) establishing the state of siege shall fix the limits of its duration. The law of 1849 contained no such provision, but the legislators of 1878 remembered that parts of France had recently been more than five years in a state of siege, a good part of that time to no obvious purpose. It has always been the consensus of French juristic opinion that this duration is to be expressed in terms of weeks or months, not in a general phrase such as "for the duration of the present emergency." In addition to this restriction of time there is a restriction of space. The declaratory law is to designate the specific areas to which the state of siege is to apply. This provision was designed to prevent further careless extension of the state of siege to areas not actually in a state of emergency.

The authority to control the employment of these emergency powers is no less firmly lodged in the hands of the French legislature. The execution by Cabinet and army of their duties under the state of siege is sharply restricted by the fact that at any time whatsoever another simple law of Parliament can bring their powers to an abrupt termination. Moreover, the responsibility of the Cabinet to Parliament continues, and acts as a strong deterrent upon arbitrary executive action. In this way the general manner in which the state of siege is conducted must conform to the wishes of the Chambers. Although there has never been a statute governing the matter, it has been generally understood that the Chambers are to remain in session for the duration of the state of siege.[12]

The individual acts of the authorities are, to be sure, only indirectly restrained by parliamentary surveillance, and this would seem to conform to the theory of the state of siege in particular and emergency government in general. The act of 1849 advances a number of extraordinary powers to the authorities, allows them to encroach upon certain rights of citizens, and forbids by letter and spirit the further extension of those powers or the suspension of other than the designated rights. Within the sphere of action thus delineated, these authorities are able to act speedily and often arbitrarily in defense of the Republic.

The Courts. The civil law courts of France provide absolutely no check upon the declaration of the state of siege, neither at the time of

---

[12] See a discussion of this point in Joseph Carret: *L'Organization de l'Etat de Siège Politique* (Paris, 1916), pp.46-54; Mandry, *op. cit.*, pp.23-24.

the proclamation nor after the disturbed conditions have been allayed. The declaration is clearly an *acte de gouvernement* or *acte politique* and in no way subject to judicial review.[13] Even if the executive declares the state of siege without any possible reason, it is not up to the courts but to the legislature to protect its prerogative in this respect.[14] This is one of the chief distinctions between the continental state of siege and its common law counterpart of martial law.

Nor do the regular courts offer a sure refuge to the citizen mistreated by the arbitrary procedures of government which the state of siege sets in motion. It is generally agreed that the courts, especially the two highest French tribunals, can test the competence of the authorities to proceed to any particular act in the same way that executive acts are tested in normal times, which still isn't saying very much. It is in the *Cour de Cassation* or the *Conseil d'Etat* that the injured citizen has his one real chance of judicial retribution. In the light of the important political character of the state of siege, even these high and independent courts are not much of a sanctuary. The *recours pour excès de pouvoir* is the normal way to proceed against a flagrant abuse of power, and the *Conseil d'Etat* might annul a measure beyond the competence of the official and also indemnify the injured citizen.

Finally, it need hardly be emphasized that the fundamental purpose of France's chief emergency institution provides significant material limitations upon the extent and manner of its utilization. The constitutional scheme and the Republic are to be maintained, not impaired by the state of siege. The political responsibility of President and Parliament to the French people provides the ultimate restriction upon the use of the state of siege, and maintains its character as a republican and legal device of constitutional dictatorship.

The end of the state of siege. Only one method is foreseen by the law of 1878 for the raising of the state of siege which has been declared by law. At the expiration of the period fixed by the declarative law the state of siege comes to an automatic end, unless an entirely new law shall prolong its life. If a special act of the legislature to terminate the life of any particular state of siege is not necessary, nevertheless it is not forbidden. The legislature can pass a law raising the state of siege at any time before it has run its full course. It is certain that the President cannot lift the state of siege by decree once it has been declared

---

[13] Carret, *op. cit.*, pp.95-105 ; Duguit, *op. cit.*, II, pp.259-260.
[14] Edouard Laferrière: *Traité de la Jurisdiction Administrative* (2nd ed., Paris, 1896), II, p.36. Henry Berthélemy: *Traité Elémentaire de Droit Administratif* (9th ed., Paris, 1920), p.443, disagrees.

by law, even in the case of Parliament's prorogation or dissolution. As a matter of fact, the prorogation or dissolution of the legislature is not regarded as constitutional when the state of siege is in effect in any part of the nation. Finally, the Chambers can prescribe by a simple law other ways of ending this emergency regime, for example, by delegating such power to the discretion of the President.

The end of the state of siege brings a virtually complete return to normal government and civil life. The regular authorities are immediately invested with their former competence, the suspended rights are restored to their pristine status, the ordinary courts replace the military tribunals. One exception is to be found in the law of 1849, article 13, which provides that the permanent military courts shall continue in the adjudication of cases already commenced. Only a statute of Parliament can alter this continued jurisdiction.

In conclusion, it is important to recognize that the French state of siege is not characterized by an expansion of power so much as it is by a transfer thereof. This instrument of constitutional dictatorship is based upon the idea that the ordinary powers of government are sufficient to meet even the most dire threats to the security of the Republic, if only these powers are used in a more unified and decisive manner and by a more powerful and less political authority. To be sure, the military in prosecuting its tasks under the state of siege is given specific competence to invade certain fundamental rights of the French people, this constituting a definite expansion of power; but the bulk of authority of both military police and courts results from the transfer of the usual powers of the civil administration. In the suppression of open rebellion, of course, the state of siege, like Article 48, can authorize what amounts to an open declaration of war on the rebellious citizenry.

If the state of siege does not quite match Article 48 as an emergency device for situations of violence, still it is for a democratic, constitutional state a remarkably adequate instrument of self-preservation. It gives to those organs best fitted to exercise it a sizable competence of administrative action, which if necessary can be exercised in disregard of the fundamental rights of the French citizen. As such its powers as a republican device of crisis government are indeed sufficient to its purpose. If the authorities cannot save the Republic by acting on the basis of the state of siege, then they cannot save it at all.

CHAPTER VII

The State of Siege in Fact: The First World War

THE organization of these chapters on French emergency government was not designed to create an impression that the state of siege in fact and the state of siege in theory are two different things. On the contrary, throughout the history of the nation the state of siege in practice has conformed rather closely to the general pattern which has just been outlined. There have been deviations and abuses, particularly in the difficult times which followed the Franco-Prussian War, but no more than in any institution of government, which is always one thing in the minds of its framers and another in the hands of its users.

It is now proposed to examine the foremost role of the state of siege, as the backbone of France's civil government in the Great War of 1914-1918. France made use of other emergency devices in these years of sustained crisis, but the state of siege was, as it was intended to be, the basic authority for the maintenance of public order in the Republic's darkest hours of trial. It was the state of siege which determined the wartime relations of state and citizen and placed the Republic in the condition of watchful emergency which enabled it to stand up to the exorbitant demands and bitter hardships of the first of the total wars.

On August 2, 1914 President Poincaré of the French Republic issued a decree placing the entire country in a state of siege.[1] The explanation of this wholesale resort to the state of siege, the first in the history of the Third Republic and the most complete in the history of France, was the necessity of maintaining public order while general mobilization was in progress. Incidentally, the fact that this declaration was the first in almost forty years illustrates perfectly the economy of utilization which was one of its chief characteristics. Only minor disturbances had occurred in France since the events of the 1870's, and to minor disturbances the state of siege, in contradistinction to the flexible Article 48, was not directed. Although unnecessary in view of article 2 of the law of 1878, a summons went out to the recessed Chambers to assemble August 4. At the opening of this session the Cabinet proposed a law

[1] *Journal Off.*, August 3, 1914.

declaring the state of siege, and on the following day this law was promulgated :[2]

> The state of siege which was declared by the decree of August 2, 1914 in the 86 French departments, the territory of Belfort, and the three departments of Algeria is hereby maintained for the duration of the war.
>
> A decree of the President of the Republic, issued on the advice of the Council of Ministers, can lift the state of siege and, after it has been lifted, reestablish it in part or all of this area.
>
> The present law, deliberated upon and adopted by the Senate and the Chamber of Deputies, is to be executed as a law of the State.

It is obvious that in the very declaration of the state of siege there were several features contrary to all prevailing opinion concerning the law of 1878. In the first place, the inclusion of the entire country in the purview of both the President's decree and the subsequent law was a violation of the "imminent danger" formula of article 1. Secondly, the term established, "for the duration of the war," did not conform with any previous conception of the time limit stipulated in this same article 1. The provision for presidential suspension and reestablishment of the state of siege was no less a departure from the regulations of the law of 1878. French jurisprudence had a field day discussing the legality of these provisions and their nonconformity with the law of 1878. Such discussion, in the light of Parliament's power to deviate at will from both laws on the state of siege, was purely academic. France faced a crisis of the first magnitude, and the French legislature did not stickle to resort on a wholesale scale to the nation's chief weapon of constitutional dictatorship.

The state of siege thus instituted throughout France was not lifted until October 12, 1919. For more than five years the citizens of France were governed largely by virtue of this emergency institution. During the first bitter months of the war this regime was one of far greater severity than the prewar legislation had contemplated. This severity had its natural reaction in vociferous demands for the repeal of the law of August 5, 1914, crystallized in a proposal to that effect introduced in the Chamber of Deputies by Paul Meunier on March 4, 1915. Although no legislative action ensued, instructions were issued in September 1915 from the Ministries of Interior and War restoring the normal powers of police to the prefects and mayors in the interior areas. Nevertheless, the military retained its extraordinary competence unimpaired and as its exclusive prerogative. Many areas in France returned to almost

[2] *Journal Off.*, August 6, 1914.

normal conditions of government. To the end of the war (and a full year after) the effects of the state of siege were felt throughout France in varying degrees of intensity. It must be constantly remembered that the declaration of the state of siege placed certain powers in the hands of the executive and military organs of government, enabling them to oppose any sort of civil crisis with resolution and force. It was not intended that powers should be arbitrarily employed or rights summarily suspended unless there was ample cause. The capacity for sudden and effective action always belonged to these officials, but after the first year of the war the actual application of this power fell short of what was possible or of what might have been endured by the people.

By the terms of article 7 of the law of 1849 the proclamation of this state of siege automatically substituted the local military authorities for the civil officials in all matters of police. The maintenance of law and order throughout France was placed squarely in the hands of the French Army. In point of fact, the state of siege in the World War resulted less in a substitution of the military for the civil authority than in a collaboration of these two in the prosecution of the problems of local administration. This collaboration, in which the civil authorities might do most of the actual work of law enforcement but with the military retaining final control, was logical and in accord with previous practice and theory of the state of siege. The army officials had been given instructions to cooperate as far as feasible with the civil authorities. This passage from the military code on the state of siege illustrates the character of French local and regional administration during the World War.[3]

In the exercise of its powers, the military authority will attempt to alter as little as possible the normal functioning of the civil services, in order to avoid on the one hand the inconvenience which would result for itself in taking these over, and on the other hand the derangements which these alterations would occasion. Therefore, dispossession (of the civil authorities) will be the exception.

In areas directly menaced or actually invaded, the army would take over the entire governance of civil life and run things according to army conceptions of authority and liberty. In September of 1914 Paris was handed over completely to the military dictatorship of General Gallieni. With the retreat of the Germans and the return of the national government from Bordeaux, a good share of the municipal authority

[3] *Ministère de la Guerre, Instruction Réglant l'Exercice des Pouvoirs de Police de l'Autorité Militaire sur le Territoire National en État de Siège,* October 1913.

reverted to the prefectoral government. In areas far from the front the army, busy with other and more important matters, would leave the problems of government to the regular authorities, although always retaining and occasionally exercising its extraordinary competence under the law of 1849. Local decrees of a police nature were often issued bearing the joint signatures of the pertinent representatives of the civil and military powers, for example, the prefect and the commandant-general of a particular region. The prefects and mayors continued in the exercise of their other duties and were only deprived of their powers of keeping the peace. In their own tasks they were often aided by the army; in the latter's tasks they would in turn lend considerable assistance. The result was a joint administration of a large part of local and departmental France.[4] The powers under the state of siege were great, but like all great powers they were often of most value when held in reserve.

The Military Courts

THE outbreak of the war was accompanied by an immediate application of article 8 of the law of 1849.[5] The government was counting on the energy of the army to secure public order, and it was a logical step to institute military courts to provide the aid for military authority that civil courts would in normal times accord to the civil authority. The military courts offered several advantages to a regime more concerned with the maintenance of internal peace than with the scrupulous protection of individual rights: an equitable but summary procedure, a personnel intimately concerned with the successful prosecution of the war, and a scale of penalties in harmony with the exigencies of the times. The nearer to the front, the more summary the trial and the more rigorous the penalty. Penalties for violating police ordinances had been established in the penal code, and neither the military authorities nor the courts had any power to fix their own penalties.

There were permanent army courts in each military district, as well as ample provision in law for the institution of special courts. *Conseils de révision*, on which professional jurists were not represented, sat as

[4] This was not the case in the Franco-Prussian War, there being in that period a definite and often hostile cleavage between civil and military authorities. On the subject of local government in the World War see the series of four articles by Louis Rolland: *"L'Administration Locale en Temps de Guerre," Rev. Dr. Pub.*, XXXII (1915), and XXXIII (1916); see also his chapter of the same title in *Problèmes de Politique et Finances de Guerre* (Alcan, 1915), pp.167 ff.

[5] See generally J. Barthélemy: *"Le Droit Public en Temps de Guerre," Rev. Dr. Pub.*, XXXIII (1916), pp.95-108.

courts of appeal from the sentences of these tribunals. The whole system was one of extreme severity, unparalleled in the experience of any of the countries discussed in this book. It is true that the competence of these tribunals was permissive, and that the ordinary courts could continue to sit in judgment on crimes over which the military courts did not express a desire to assume jurisdiction. As a rule the military and civil courts worked together, in pursuance of an understanding by which the former heard all important cases. At Paris, in the Palace of Justice, there was a *bureau anonyme*, composed of both civil and military members, which had the final decision on the distribution of important cases. The decisive authority at the local or regional level remained the military. No civil court had a right to a case which the local military courts had expressed a desire to adjudicate.

In actual practice the military tribunals did not hesitate to deal with civilians accused of crimes of any sort that might be considered as falling within the loose terms of article 8, even though these terms had been qualified in subsequent ordinances of the Ministries of Justice and War, as well as in various sections of other legal codes. The interpretation of this article was extremely broad. Assaults upon or resistance to citizens charged with some public duty, frauds in connection with the quality of provisions furnished the armed forces or in their sale, attempted robbery in a railroad station, insults to public officials engaged in their duties, the misdemeanor of *vagabondage*, the embezzlement of letters by a post-office agent—these were but a few of the crimes and offenses of civilians regularly tried and punished by the military courts. In assuming this power these courts were following the commands of their superiors in Paris. For instance, it was a circular of the Ministry of War of October 29, 1914 which ordered all military courts to take jurisdiction over robberies committed in railroad stations.

The severity of this situation kept pace with the increasing severity of the times. By decrees of August 10 and September 8, 1914 the government applied to the whole country the rules of procedure established for courts-martial at the front. Although the summary procedure thus instituted was not always utilized by courts in the interior, nevertheless it was ready for their use in the more flagrant cases, the sort which in normal times usually receive the fairest and most thorough sort of trial.

The end of the great German threat of 1914 brought a stiff reaction to the country-wide regime of military courts. The grievances against the harshness and broad jurisdiction of these courts were given a thorough airing in the two houses of the French legislature.[6] It was generally agreed by both Parliament and Cabinet that the competence of the military courts ought to be restricted, and that of the civil courts expanded to encompass many of the offenses having no direct relation to the prosecution of the war or the maintenance of public order. The first results of this sentiment were two long overdue circulars, one dated December 17, 1915, the other April 18, 1916, issued by the Ministry of War and directing commanding officers to restrict the military tribunals to crimes clearly within their jurisdiction. Then on April 27, 1916 a significant statute was enacted by the Chambers defining minutely the cases in which a civilian was amenable to the jurisdiction of the military courts.[7] In addition to a number of important crimes listed in the penal code, the military jurisdiction over civilians was to include cases of espionage, treason, communicating or trading with the enemy, incitement to insurrection, and finally of any crime or offense "interfering with national defense." The courts were empowered to find extenuating circumstances and grant reprieves, the rights of the defense were established in law, and further provision was made for appeals. This exceptional regime was to cease *de plein droit* at the signature of the peace.

Thus in law and practice was the rule of the *conseils de guerre* considerably mitigated, although hardly emasculated. The important fact is that in the middle of the war the legislature had seen fit to put some bounds to the competence of the extraordinary courts under the state of siege. The moral effect of this action transcended its legal consequences. As the war progressed other innovations concerning procedure, appeal, and pardon were instituted to relax further this harsh regime. It came to an end with a decree of December 24, 1918. The contrast of the military courts of 1914 and those of 1917-1918 provides an instructive lesson in constitutional dictatorship. The former were overburdened with the consideration of petty offenses, unnecessarily severe in their dealings with civilians, and generally inefficient in the performance of their duties; the latter were restricted to the more important offenses against the state, far more equitable in their treatment of civilians, subject to higher revision of their decisions, and operating efficiently in aid of the war effort. This French experience furnishes an excellent pattern for any future use of special courts during an extended period

[6] See generally Paul Meunier: *Les Conseils de Guerre* (Paris, 1919).
[7] See Romain: *L'Etat de Siège Politique*, pp.434 ff., for a thorough account of the proposal, debate, and passage of this law. See also Barthélemy: *Rev. Dr. Pub.*, XXXIII, pp.295 ff.

of emergency. Moreover, no more salutary example of parliamentary control of the state of siege could be advanced. From the people's representatives proceeded the initiative and the laws that tempered the severe rule of the military courts.

Civil Liberties under the State of Siege

THE control of civil liberty under the permissive terms of the state of siege constituted an efficient aid to the French government in the prosecution of the war.[8] That there were abuses of power by the army officials cannot be gainsaid, but on the whole the regime of the military was surprisingly liberal. The military competence under article 9 of the law of 1849 was held in close check by the higher authorities, and there was no general or arbitrary use of these powers that did not have superior sanction. Whenever interference with various freedoms did take place, it was generally necessitated by the exigencies of the situation.

The courts provided little check upon the military and civil authorities entrusted with duties under the state of siege. Measures adopted by the military under article 9 of the law of 1849 were rarely attacked judicially. There were a few instances where injured citizens were able to win retribution by an appeal to the *Conseil d'Etat* on a plea of *excès de pouvoir* or to the *Cour de Cassation* on the assertion of criminal action by the authorities, but generally the broad interpretation of their extraordinary powers by the officials was upheld in both of France's high courts.[9] In this respect there was a marked deviation from previous theory. It was the intention of the framers of the law of 1849 that it should be interpreted restrictively, but in practice the decisions of the courts were based upon the principle that the specific competence of the military arm under article 9 of that law was not to be construed so as to impair its operation in support of the state of siege.[10] In actual fact this meant that just about anything the authorities chose to do on a local or regional level was upheld by the courts as within their powers under the state of siege.

Inviolability of domicile. The law of 1849 had authorized military invasion of the sanctity of the French home. Even the most squeamish

[8] See generally Henri Plait: *L'Etat de Siège et la Restriction des Libertés Individuelles pendant la Guerre 1914-1919* (Auxerre, 1920).

[9] See Barthélemy: *Rev. Dr. Pub.*, XXXII, pp.547-553, for a concise account of the almost universal acquiescence of the French courts in the actions of the authorities under the state of siege.

[10] Gaston Jèze: "*Interprétation de la Loi du 9 Août 1849 sur l'Etat de Siège*," *Rev. Dr. Pub.*, XXXII (1915), p.700; *Rev. Dr. Pub.*, XXXIII (1916), p. 407.

could hardly deny the necessity of summary search and seizure in respect to all dwellings in an area threatened by war or insurrection. There was no logical reason why spies and enemy sympathizers should be permitted to hide behind the right of inviolable domicile and force the authorities to get out a warrant every time they wanted to search a suspicious dwelling. The use of this dictatorial power by the police was extremely effective in the capture of spies and saboteurs.

Freedom of assembly. Throughout the war, gatherings of citizens to discuss controversial subjects were generally prohibited. The ordinary Frenchman might curse the police for denying him his right to run around the streets or for sending him home if he insisted on running around anyway, but the assistance of this arbitrary power in the maintenance of public order was indispensable. In this way the authorities were able to move summarily against professional agitators whose only hope of success depended upon their ability to gather a crowd. The chief opposition to this police power of prohibiting assemblies of a nature to disturb public order came from those citizens of the Republic who insisted on fighting the war and running the government from the safety of the bistros. A number of barroom brawls in different parts of France resulted in the complete or partial prohibition by many of the local authorities of the dispensing of liquor in public places. Gatherings of citizens in bistros were broken up and forbidden by the police on the theory that these were meetings within the meaning of the law of 1849. A decision of the *Conseil d'Etat* upheld the general power of the military to take this dictatorial action.

Freedom of the press.[11] The question of censorship was of vital importance to the French war effort. Gallic curiosity and Gallic indiscretion in the effort to satisfy that curiosity have always made the press an unpredictable feature of French public life, and thus well deserving of a bridle in time of crisis. In the War of 1870 the Germans had derived much valuable military and diplomatic information from the French newspapers, and the regime of 1914 was fully decided to prevent the recurrence of any such costly folly. The liberty of the press was not to obstruct the effort of the Republic to stay alive.

Article 9 of the law of 1849 had authorized the military arm to forbid all publications of a nature to excite disorder. This provision was regarded as not sufficient to the task in hand, and in the famous session of

[11] See generally Barthélemy: *Rev. Dr. Pub.*, XXXII, pp.310-359; A. Capus: *"La Presse pendant la Guerre,"* *Revue Hebdomadaire* (March 13, 1915) ; Plait, *op. cit.*, pp.50-74.

August 4, 1914 the government secured the passage of a law suppressing "indiscretions of the press in time of war."[12] This statute forbade the publication of information regarding military operations not communicated by the pertinent authorities, as well as any evaluation of military or diplomatic events that might assist the enemy or influence unfavorably the morale of army or nation. The military courts were to punish infractions, and severe penalties were provided.

Grounded in these two laws of 1849 and 1914, an effective repressive and preventive censorship was instituted and maintained for the duration of the war—by various "understandings" between the government and the press, by the institution of a central press bureau whose "advice" the newspapers constantly sought (and disregarded at their peril), and by the extension of this sort of practice throughout the local military regions of France. This does not mean that the French press was forced into unanimous support of the government. On the contrary, a full discussion of vital problems was carried on throughout the war. It does mean that all articles of a disloyal or particularly abusive and violent character and all articles that might give information to the enemy were strictly forbidden. It was the license, not the liberty, of the press that was curtailed under the compulsion of war and the state of siege. The Paris newspapers and important periodicals were censored by the central bureau under the law of 1914; the local journals were controlled by the local military authorities under the state of siege. Censorship committees, to which the prefect was allowed to name a civilian member, were the chief instruments of censorship throughout the country. In less imperiled areas a prefectoral committee might take over this task.

As the war progressed the cooperation foreseen by the law of 1914 became rather one-sided, and obligatory censorship became the rule, especially in Paris. The result was a healthy airing of complaints on the floor of the Chambers which served as a warning to the censors to take more care in their operations. To the end of the war the censorship was maintained, often bungling and abusive, but generally salutary and indispensable. Before Clémenceau came to power in November of 1917 he had been the most feared opponent of the press bureau and its censorship; after he had come to power he left it in full operation. The wartime control of the press came to an end October 12, 1919, when both the state of siege and the press law of August, 1914 were abolished.

Freedom of person and trade. The years of war witnessed severe administrative and military restrictions upon the freedom of the citizen

[12] *Journal Off.*, August 5, 1914.

to travel about and pursue the normal pleasures of civilian life. These were generally based on the belief that the competence of the military authorities to keep the peace extended to the adoption of all measures convenient to that end, even though the enjoyment of rights other than those mentioned in article 9 of the law of 1849 might thereby be impaired. Although this was a clear departure from the law and theory of the state of siege, it was with the acquiescence of the French people, who realized the necessity of such measures. That these restrictive procedures, to which by law the military authorities were alone competent, were on occasion exercised by civil officials caused even less of a stir. Other measures were justified quite without reference to the state of siege, on an enlargement of military power occasioned by the simple fact of war—a claim which the courts were generally disposed to favor.[13] It was not always possible to determine the legal foundation for some arbitrary governmental action.

Among the restraints upon civil life adopted by the police authorities were curfew hours, the prohibition of the sale of absinthe, the rationing of food and other necessities, and the establishment of business hours. These measures were all upheld in various decisions of the *Cour de Cassation*. Among the restrictions expressly voided by this court were the unlimited prohibition of trade in alcohol and the closing without just cause of a bistro.[14] Regional and national decrees were issued providing for strict regulation of all travel. For example, it was forbidden anyone to leave Paris by train for a trip of over 150 kilometers except by special permission of the police.

It was agreed that these measures could find no basis in article 9 of the law of 1849, and they were regarded as being adopted "by virtue of the unwritten rule of law which charges the government with securing public order and the defense of the nation."[15] In effect there was inserted into article 9 a fifth clause permitting the authorities to infringe upon other and subsidiary rights whose unrestrained enjoyment would contribute to public disorder. Absinthe can drive a man crazy; crazy men are a nuisance in times when public order must be maintained; therefore the freedom of Frenchmen to indulge in absinthe was suspended for

[13] On the theory of *pouvoirs de guerre* see Gaston Jèze: *"Théorie des Pouvoirs de Guerre et Théorie des Actes de Gouvernement,"* Rev. Dr. Pub., XLI (1924), p.572, esp. pp.594-599; A. Bosc: *"Les Actes de Gouvernement et la Théorie des Pouvoirs de Guerre,"* Rev. Dr. Pub., XLIII (1926), p.186, esp. pp.233-257.

[14] *Cour de Cass.*, July 15, 1916; Dalloz (1916), I, p.23; *Cour de Cass.*, June 2, 1916; Dalloz (1916), I, p.129.

[15] Barthélemy: *Rev. Dr. Pub.*, XXXII, p.157. The noted jurist regarded this as evidence of the futility of prior regulation of the police power in times of emergency.

the duration of the war. It was on the basis of the theory of *pouvoirs de guerre* that the courts upheld the authorities and denied retribution to citizens suffering an impairment of rights other than those expressly singled out by the law of 1849. These measures, the courts held, were necessitated by the general interest of the Republic at war. That this practice constituted an element foreign to the whole idea of the French state of siege is obvious, but this supplementation of article 9 and derogation from article 11 of the law of 1849 disturbed juristic far more than it did public opinion.

The rights of labor. In France as in the other democracies it was recognized by government and people alike that the rights of labor, particularly the right to strike, would suffer considerable abridgment under the compulsion of war.[16] Although the state of siege did not impinge directly upon the right to strike, except when this right was exercised in connection with a condition of armed rebellion, it would nevertheless seem logical at this point to consider those reductions in normal freedom that French labor did suffer during the war. On the whole, the rights of the working man suffered no serious impairment. At no time was an anti-strike or general compulsory arbitration law passed, and the reduction of the number of strikes in the war period was largely the result of a voluntary renunciation of this right and of the informal efforts of various of the ministries to effect a conciliation of those industrial disputes which threatened to erupt into a strike. Sanctions for these efforts were found in the authority of the government to send deferred workers to the front and to take over the operation of factories. The number of strikes in 1914 and 1915 was far below the prewar level, but in the later years of the war there was a steady increase under the compulsion of rising costs and stable wages, never serious enough to necessitate drastic governmental action. Although certain provisions of the labor laws were roughly treated in the effort to get French industry into high gear, no such device as a general conscription of labor was ever employed. "Civil mobilization" was often talked of, but action of this sort was not forthcoming. It was free labor that waged the war behind the front.

In these many ways did the citizen undergo a contraction of his peacetime liberty in France's years of sustained crisis. A large majority of the measures adopted to this end were based upon the existence of the state of siege. It can hardly be doubted that this contraction was essen-

[16] On French labor in the war, see generally W. Oualid and C. Picquenard: *Salaires et Tarifs, Conventions Collectives et Grèves* (Paris, 1928).

tial to the maintenance of a home front prepared to give the fullest moral and material support to the forces in the field. Whether it was the prohibition of the sale of absinthe or the legislative postponement of elections (all parliamentary and almost all municipal elections were suspended during the war), the departures from the normal pattern of French civil and political liberty were valuable adjuncts to the successful prosecution of the war. The ample but not undue provisions for the suspension of these liberties attest the foresight of France's lawmakers; the strong and efficient yet comparatively restrained use of these provisions attests the usually calm efficacy of her World War army; the general acquiescence in the necessity of these measures attests the peculiar sense of reality of the French people and their continental respect for military authority; the success of this program and the speedy return to the full enjoyment of civil rights at the close of the war should bear witness that the emergency suspension of the liberties of a free people can be an effective technique of constitutional dictatorship.

Thus the state of siege in fact. That in many particulars it did not comport with pre-1914 juristic and official ideas is obvious. The fact is that the France of 1878 and the France of 1914-1918 were two different propositions. To expect a law drawn up in peacetime and based on a reaction to executive authority to answer fully the needs of a country suddenly become the battlefield of one of history's decisive conflicts would be asking too much of the foresight and ingenuity of mortal man. The lesson for the student of politics is that the workings of crisis government cannot be completely foreseen. Whether the logical conclusion is, as many have maintained, that they ought not be foreseen at all is another question for another time.

The deviations of the state of siege of the World War period from the practice, theory, and law of the past may be summed up in the assertion that it was converted under the pressure of events from a *repressive* into a *preventive* institution of emergency government. Originally the state of siege was to be called into action only when the perils of invasion or rebellion had assumed a serious magnitude, and only in areas directly threatened. The extraordinary competence of the military police and courts was to be exercised with dispatch and vigor in an area where violence was a present reality, as an adjunct to outright martial rule, a major state of siege. In the World War, however, the French Parliament, as was its undoubted right, chose to use this institution over an extended area and for an extended period of time, in order to maintain order on the home front and strip all enemies of the Republic and other obstructionists behind the lines of the usual guarantees of law and civil justice. In this transition from a major to a minor state of siege the character of the institution was thus partially altered, and so too were some of the procedures adopted under it. The state of siege was still available as a repressive instrument of emergency government and took on this character in areas near the front.

The history and the lawmakers of France had combined to fashion a potent weapon of constitutional dictatorship, the state of siege. In the hours of France's great trial this weapon was wielded by the government in a manner conforming remarkably closely, in the light of the crisis, to the letter and spirit of the laws.

CHAPTER VIII

The Government of France in the First World War

CONSTITUTIONAL dictatorship comes into its own in a war of defense. Let a country be invaded by an enemy aggressor, and even the anarchists rally 'round the flag and call for a sweeping increase of governmental power. World War France is a striking example of this assertion. Driven to the wall by one of the most violent aggressions in all history, the French people, democratic and individualistic as they were, acquiesced in a government that was always strong and sometimes dictatorial, a government which prosecuted a victorious war and then effected a virtually complete return to normal conditions. This French government can thus be regarded as an excellent example of the constitutional dictatorship which guides a free people through the perils of a sustained national emergency.

The most notable feature of this government was the relative scarcity and unimportance of the emergency alterations in the peacetime constitutional scheme. In the first bitter months of the German onslaught parliamentary government in France was almost completely eclipsed, but with the successful defense of Paris and the deceleration of the war of movement the government returned to more normal conditions. For the remainder of the war the various organs of the French constitutional scheme did their usual jobs in pretty much the usual way. It has been truly written: "Among the great belligerent states it was France which passed through the crisis while remaining most faithful to its traditions and its constitutional principles."[1]

The concern of this chapter is an examination of those changes which took place at the national level. The state of siege will receive only passing mention. This does not signify that this institution lacked importance in these national changes and in the successful conduct of the war by the government in Paris. Indeed, the prominence of the role played by the state of siege in this government can hardly be overestimated. It was the means whereby local government was adapted to the many problems of the crisis, and it formed the basis for the marked contraction of French civil liberty. More than this, it was the state of siege which

[1] Pierre Renouvin: *Les Formes du Gouvernement de Guerre* (Paris, 1925), p.147.

placed the people in a psychological condition of readiness to meet the demands of the emergency measures invoked by the national government. The last chapter should have demonstrated the incalculable importance of the state of siege for the success of France's war government.

In direct contrast to the legal provisions for the state of siege, scarcely one piece of important legislation preparing the government for war was on the statute books.[2] There was statutory anticipation for the nationalization of the railroads, for the allocation of military command, and for the military power of requisition. A number of bills covering such matters as mobilization of the armed forces were filed in various offices of the Ministry awaiting immediate introduction into Parliament and equally immediate enactment in case of war, but there were no measures in legal form dealing with the organization of the government or with the administration and its powers. Whether the parliamentary system would function as usual, whether the executive would have any power of legislative decree, whether the Cabinet would undergo structural changes—none of these major problems had been foreseen by statute, and most of them advisedly not. It was believed that this parliamentary system could adapt itself in due course to the exigencies of almost any crisis. Thus it was only in time and through experience that Cabinet, Parliament, and military command assumed their proper roles for the struggle. A few more detailed laws might have helped this orientation, but it cannot be said that the lack of statutory preparedness was detrimental to the war effort.

Parliament and the War

SUCCESSFUL modern war and parliamentary democracy are not mutually exclusive social phenomena. This is the lesson of World War France, a country where, in the midst of a great struggle for national survival, the legislature was neither effaced from the governmental scene nor even forced into a position of secondary importance, as had been expected by the majority of the prewar publicists. On the contrary, the French Parliament played an important role in the war effort and played it to

[2] *Ibid.*, pp.11-18. Renouvin goes on to discuss a number of interesting prewar proposals for war government in France, none of which admitted "that French institutions were easily adaptable to a state of crisis," and some of which suggested the outright effacement of parliamentary government. See for example the two books of Eugene Pierre: *L'Organisation Intérieure du Pays en Cas de Guerre* (Paris, 1890) and *Du Pouvoir Législatif en Cas de Guerre* (Paris, 1890); see also Marcel Sembat: *Faites un Roi, sinon Faites la Paix* (Paris, 1913).

the hilt. It was a role characterized by several marked innovations in keeping with the nature of the times : permanence of sessions, acceleration of the legislative process, the development of new controls and the modification of old ones, the express or tacit transfer to the Cabinet of certain powers of legislation, the abandonment of *la lutte des partis,* and the assumption of a general tone of sincerity and dignity that it was never again to enjoy.

In the first six months of the war France was without a legislature. On August 4 the Chambers met in the white heat of the *Union Sacrée,* declared the state of siege, approved the request of Viviani's government for decree powers enabling the Cabinet to govern the country alone for an extended period, and then adjourned in an expression of supreme confidence in the government's ability to prosecute this "war of but a few weeks." Many members went on active military duty. Parliament was prorogued on September 7 by the President, and there were few protests, although this was a violation of the best conceptions of the state of siege. In the ensuing months, the most perilous in France's history, the country was ruled by a cabinet and military dictatorship. The war was to be of short duration. Action and not debate, emergency ordinances and not permanent laws were the measures to overcome this perilous but transient crisis. The sudden violence of the war had created a situation in which public opinion and effective government could both do without a legislature for the time being. Not until December 22 were the Chambers reconvened, and then only to sanction measures already taken and to vote provisional credits for the coming year.

This voluntary abdication by the Chambers of their powers and position in the French constitutional structure came to an end on the second Tuesday of January 1915, when they assembled *de plein droit* according to their constitutional rights. From this day until almost a year after the cessation of hostilities the French Parliament was in permanent session, and the President's power of prorogation remained in abeyance. The prospect of an extended war had effected a reversion to more normal methods of government. Legislation of a permanent nature was needed, and the traditions of democratic France demanded that the legislature should perform its regular functions, even in time of crisis. Throughout the ensuing years of the war this legislation was forthcoming. Although the executive enjoyed some of Parliament's powers of legislation, the major part of the load remained upon the shoulders of the Chambers. Nor did they fail in this responsibility, but in accordance with the exigencies of the times enacted some of the most vital statutes in the history of the Republic.

In the passage of these laws the regular procedure was followed, although speeded up considerably. The luxury of aimless debate and the more picayune proceedings of France's powerful legislative committees were both foregone. Standing orders of the Chambers were modified in harmony with this spirit of "action rather than debate." For example, in January 1917 the Chamber of Deputies instituted *une procédure spéciale d'urgence* whereby the committee hearings and debates on a particularly vital government bill might be cut to the least possible time and still comply with the accepted methods of parliamentary government. In a case of absolute necessity the Cabinet had the right to demand a vote on a bill within twenty-four hours. The ordinary procedure on voting the budget was altered to grant the Cabinet added leeway in the allocation of funds. In these various ways did the French Parliament accelerate its legislative activities without surrendering its ascendancy in this field or its right to debate thoroughly any vital subject.[3]

Even in time of peace the power of Parliament to control and direct the activities of the Ministry has always been as important as its power to legislate. Through interpellations, questions, committee hearings in both Chambers, and repeated and often irresponsible unseating of Cabinets, the French legislature has always imposed a check upon the functions of the Cabinet quite as significant for French democracy as the statutes it has enacted. What was true in peace was true in war. The importance of Parliament in the war government lay more in its well-played role as defender of democracy than in its legislative activities.[4] The Cabinet and the army were charged with the active conduct of the war; as such they leaned strongly to arbitrary measures. The Parliament, backed by public opinion, provided a check on those leanings. The resulting balance between power and limitations, between dictatorship and democracy, between the demands of war and the demands of the democratic tradition was precisely what was needed for the prosecution of a victorious constitutional dictatorship.

The Parliament did not hesitate to maintain a check upon the Cabinets whose creation it had ordained. The four years of the war saw seven

---

[3] Ernst von Hippel: "*Die Entwicklung des öffentichen Rechts in Frankreich seit 1914*," *Jahrbuch des öff. Rechts*, xv (1927) p.149, pp.159-160.

[4] Duguit: *Manuel de Droit Constitutionnel* (3rd ed., Paris, 1918), pp.201-208, 452-454; Barthélemy: *Problèmes de Politique et Finances de Guerre*, pp.131 ff.

Cabinets and five Premiers,[5] which is just about par for the French course. Only one Cabinet, that of Painlevé, was actually turned out by express vote of Parliament (November 14, 1917), but the others retired because they sensed a definite weakening of the confidence of the Chambers. Parliament was as anxious as the executive to get on with the war, and once the right Cabinet was found, it followed its lead to the end. The Ministry of Clémenceau lasted from November 16, 1917 to January 20, 1920. Parliament had not abandoned its electoral competence, but had found in the Tiger what England had found in Lloyd George, someone who could be a dictator in conformity with the desires of the legislators and of the people of France. The changes of Ministry, resulting from the pressure of public opinion on Parliament and Parliament on Cabinet, in the end contributed to rather than detracted from the efficiency of this crisis government.

The other methods of parliamentary surveillance underwent a change to comport with the necessities of the times. The right of interpellation, the stumbling block of many French Cabinets, could not be exercised in a normal manner, since the government was unable to reply in public session to many of the members' questions, nor was it in accord with the exigencies of wartime government that the Cabinet should be continually harassed by open questioning in Parliament. In this as in other matters the Chambers themselves renounced their usual prerogative. For about a year and a half in 1916-1917 secret sessions were held for the purpose of permitting interpellation, but with the advent of Clémenceau this innovation was discarded. The practice of written questions suffered no diminution, but rather developed considerably in the course of the war. In the single year 1915 almost 7000 questions were addressed to the Ministry or its pertinent departments, many of them at the instigation of the public.

It was the great committees, particularly those on the budget, navy, army, and foreign affairs, which exercised the most effective control by Parliament of the Ministry. In normal times the members of the Ministry defend government bills before the committees of both Chambers; parliamentary control of administrative activities is thereby considerably strengthened. In war this became almost the sole means of day-to-day check, and these groups, acting in place of the two Chambers, were not remiss in exercising a thorough surveillance of the pertinent ministers. The Army Committee of the Chamber of Deputies maintained a particularly vigilant control over the Minister of War and thus

[5] There is a complete list of these in Renouvin, *op. cit.*, Appendix II.

over the French Army itself. Whether this control worked for the best efficiency of Ministry and army is debatable, but it was an interesting and effective species of democratic restraint upon executive activity. In the last two years of the war several of the committees of Parliament undertook an appreciable amount of investigation and supervision at the front itself, a practice generally harmless to the war effort and reassuring to the people.

The record of the French Parliament in the first World War provides conclusive proof that the type of constitutional dictatorship which extends over a period of years does not exclude a maintenance of the parliamentary system. The legislature must realize the necessity of vigorous executive action, must modify its own procedures in keeping with the nature of the crisis, and must abstain from irresponsible nagging and upsetting of the cabinets to which it delegates large amounts of its lawmaking competence. It was not the role of the French Parliament to conduct the war, but its continual presence never failed to bring home to the army and the administration the sobering truth that it was a war of freedom in which the Republic was engaged. The law of April 27, 1916 which put a bridle on the military courts, the instructions of September 1915 which restored powers of police to the civil authorities in the interior, the maintenance of civil control of military plans and activities—these were but a few of the healthy results of Parliament's energy. The spirit and the institutions of parliamentary democracy were kept strong without detriment to the success of the war effort.

The Cabinet and the War

To the Council of Ministers, acting as agent of Parliament and in the name of the President, fell the chief responsibility for getting on with the business of war. This was not the result of a legislative decision but of the indisputable truth that war is something to be dealt with primarily in an executive way. The army did the fighting and Parliament legislated and maintained its controls, but it was the Cabinet which repeatedly took the initiative in the important measures that won the war, whether administrative, legislative, or strategic.

The record of World War relations between Cabinet and Parliament falls into three distinct periods. In the first six months of the struggle there was no Parliament; the Cabinet found its only responsibility in the political conscience of its members. After January 1915, the legislature grew stronger in its relations with the Cabinet, and the latter was gradually reduced to its prewar status as agent of Parliament, although the Chambers did not indulge in the usual practice of unseating Ministries for political and personal reasons. The high point of this development came with the banishment of Painlevé's government. In the middle of France's most bitter war Parliament had dramatically reasserted its supremacy over the Cabinet. With the advent of Clémenceau and his program of vigorous, final action—*"Je fais la guerre"*—the Cabinet was once again in the ascendant, and the Chambers were now ready to acquiesce in his dictatorship, having confidence that this was the man to finish the war. Had they lacked that confidence, he could have been turned out like Painlevé. The independence of Clémenceau was maintained until after the peace conference at Versailles, and no Premier ever enjoyed a stronger moral and electoral parliamentary position.

The Cabinet itself instituted remarkably few innovations in its own structure to meet the exigencies of wartime activity, and most of these were abandoned after a short trial. For instance, Viviani, who was Premier at the beginning of the war, became the first President of the Council in the history of the Third Republic who was not also the head of a specific ministerial department—a sensible break with peacetime practice but one not repeated by any of his successors. A number of plans to erect a policy determining inner cabinet were initiated and then discarded before a final one was adopted as satisfactory. Briand first established five "Ministers of State," who joined the Cabinet without portfolio to provide ministerial solicitude for those over-all problems of the war which the overworked heads of departments had no opportunity to contemplate. This action turned the meetings of the Cabinet into a sort of miniature parliament. Next Briand, under the influence of British practice, attempted to establish a war cabinet. Here again the objections were many and the successes few. The French *Comité de Guerre* did not enjoy the responsible and authoritative status of its English model, and after the departure of Briand it was abandoned.

In point of fact, the Council of Ministers was expanding rather than contracting in numbers as new undersecretaryships were set up in answer to the novel problems arising from the war effort. Revived by Painlevé in September of 1917, the *Comité de Guerre* was finally given real authority and responsibility under Clémenceau. To the end of the war he made his more consequential decisions in company with four or five of the important ministers, a rump cabinet which supplanted the larger Council in the political direction of the war. It comprised the Ministers of War (Clémenceau himself), Marine, Foreign Affairs,

Blockade, Armament, and sometimes Finance. The Chief of Staff could attend but not vote. Clémenceau also instituted a secretariat for the Premier, to relieve himself of certain less vital duties and to harmonize the diffused activities of the Council. Both the war cabinet and the secretariat were abandoned with the return of peace.

The increase in powers which the Cabinet enjoyed arose from three main sources.[6] In the first place, it has already been seen that the state of siege put the country, especially government at the local level, in a position receptive to the strong measures which the government was forced to adopt. Although the state of siege itself did not grant the Cabinet any extraordinary power of decree, nevertheless "instructions" issuing from the particular ministries supervising the execution of this emergency institution had the practical effect of law, especially when dealing with the special competence which the military enjoyed under article 9 of the law of 1849. Many questionable decrees of the Cabinet were regularized by general reference to the state of siege.

Secondly, the Cabinet was accorded wide powers of emergency legislation by express grant of Parliament. At no time during the war was there any complete enabling act authorizing the Cabinet to become the chief source of law in France, and but one outright attempt was made to secure the passage of such a statute. On December 14, 1916 the Briand government introduced a bill into the Chamber of Deputies which would have permitted the Cabinet to decree "all measures . . . required by national defense." In the face of open hostility it never had a chance of passage. It was referred to a special committee and was killed by a vote of 23-2. Such a wholesale delegation of legislative competence was too odious to the republican tradition to be thus effected, even in time of war. The deputies gagged hardest on provisions in this bill authorizing the Ministry itself to fix the penalties for nonobservance of its decrees.

Delegation for specific purposes was a common occurrence throughout the war. In the historic session of August 4, 1914 the Cabinet was empowered to decree measures necessary to "facilitate the performance or suspend the effect of commercial or civil obligations," in other words to institute a moratorium "in the general interest," as well as to open provisional credits "necessary to the needs of national defense" by

[6] See generally Barthélemy: *Rev. Dr. Pub.*, XXXII, pp.135-155; see also the same author's article *"Du Renforcement du Pouvoir Exécutif en Temps de Guerre"* in *Problèmes de Politique et Finances de Guerre*, esp. pp.105-108.

decrees validated by the *Conseil d'Etat*.[7] Parliamentary ratification was required if these measures were to continue indefinitely with the character of regular law. Even after the reestablishment of Parliament in the constitutional scheme in early 1915 this practice of specific delegation prevailed, particularly in regard to subjects concerning which Parliament was incapable of enacting detailed statutes. The Cabinet also made use of certain powers of decree under laws enacted before the outbreak of war. For example, a law of March 27, 1910 gave it power to adopt measures of a legislative character against a country which had discriminated against French commerce, while a law of September 17, 1814 still in force permitted it to suspend or reestablish the export of French products in certain exigencies. The immediate approval of Parliament was necessary. Price-fixing of certain important commodities was another significant form of delegated legislative activity.

The Clémenceau Cabinet received a grant of power in fact almost as sweeping as that denied Briand, but made more palatable by the exclusion of any ministerial power to fix penalties for the violation of its decrees. The Cabinet was empowered by a statute of February 10, 1918 to regulate by decree "during the war and the six months following the cessation of hostilities" the production, transport, and sale of produce serving as food for men and animals.[8] This enabling grant was broadly construed to authorize government action not only in questions of food supply, but also in any transport or other labor crisis bearing on them. All decrees were to be ratified by Parliament within one month, but a refusal to ratify was not to annul the effects of ordinances adopted in the interval.

Finally, the Cabinet found a source of increased competence in what Barthélemy has labeled the *"initiative envahissante de l'exécutif."* A number of times during the war, particularly during the nonparliamentary period of 1914, the Cabinet issued decrees having the force of regular law or suspending the effects of parliamentary statutes—all without any apparent sanction in the laws or Constitution of France. The state of siege had no effect upon the power of the Cabinet to enact emergency legislation, nor in many instances could the specific delegations by the Parliament to the Cabinet be relied upon as authority for these decrees, not even by the most latitudinarian construction of such

[7] For a criticism of this statute and the broad approval placed upon its use by the *Conseil d'Etat*, see Gaston Jèze: *"Le Pouvoir Exécutif en Temps de Guerre," Rev. Dr. Pub.*, XXXVII (1920), p.243.

[8] See Louis Rolland: *"Le Pouvoir Réglementaire du Président de la République en Temps de Guerre et la Loi du 10 Février 1918," Rev. Dr. Pub.*, XXXV (1918), pp.542-580.

delegations. The plain fact remains that the Cabinet invaded the field of Parliament's competence and enacted legislation pure and simple. There was some precedent for emergency executive legislation of this kind,[9] and the Cabinet did not hesitate in unavoidable circumstances to resort to this dictatorial practice.[10] The power of executive ordinance-making is traditionally a much broader one in France than in the United States or England. As a result this practice was not as radical a step as it would have been in these other democratic nations at war, and in the few instances where the French courts were called upon to determine the validity of such decrees they were able to retreat with relative ease to the theory of *pouvoirs de guerre* or even to the old doctrine of necessity.[11]

Instances of this sort of decree, all of them in direct derogation from existing law, were: that of September 9, 1914 providing that men exempted from military service were subject to a new medical examination; that of September 6, 1914 setting up special and summary *cours martiales* at the front; that of September 27, 1914 forbidding trade with the enemy; and that of September 9, 1914 permitting the government to dispense with the services of generals without regard for the guarantees secured them by law. These measures, if indispensable, were definitely contrary to law. At other times the government issued decrees of this character to initiate unpopular measures which the more politically minded Chambers might hesitate to pass. On January 7, 1915 a decree was issued prohibiting the sale of absinthe and the opening of any new saloons, this despite the imminent reassembly of Parliament. It would appear that the government doubted the enthusiasm of the Chambers in this controversial matter and decided to present them with a *fait accompli*.[12]

Most of these decrees were subsequently ratified by Parliament on the

[9] At the time of the great railroad strike of 1910 Premier Briand had gone so far as to state: "If, in the face of an eventuality which would have put the country in danger, the government had not found in the law the means to defend the existence of the nation by safeguarding its frontiers, if it had not been able to assure itself of the disposition of its railroads, that is to say instruments essential to the defense of the nation— in short, had it been necessary to resort to illegal means, it would have resorted to them; its duty would have been to resort to them." Quoted in Mandry: *Das Ausnahmerecht in Frankreich*, p.26, n. 39.

[10] On this World War practice, see Barthélemy: *Rev. Dr. Pub.*, XXXII, pp.557 ff.

[11] For example, the case of Verrier, *Conseil d'Etat*, August 30, 1915, which is discussed at length in a note by Jèze in *Rev. Dr. Pub.*, XXXII, p.479. For a rejection of this doctrine of necessity, see the judgment of the *Cour de Cass.*, November 3, 1917; Sirey (1917), I, p.145.

[12] Barthélemy: *Rev. Dr. Pub.*, XXXII, p.564. He describes this illegal regime as *"de la dictature très bonne, excellent, admirable, nationale, patriotique, démocratique . . . mais c'est de la dictature."*

theory that, had it been in session, it would have enacted them itself. Some were replaced by more detailed statutes and some were merely tolerated. A few were declared illegal by the courts as beyond the competence of the Cabinet. None of them had any effect as permanent legislation. This sort of action faced the enmity of both courts and Parliament, especially after the bitter days of 1914, and the demand for enabling acts was the natural result. The grant of decree power to Clémenceau in 1918 was in particular the result of parliamentary and judicial protests against unauthorized Cabinet legislation.

It is not the province of this discussion to review the literature which this practice evoked nor to ventilate the general conceptions of the *Not kennt kein Gebot* theory of executive legislation.[13] It must suffice to relate the fact that the French executive, in the absence of Parliament and in the most perilous hours of France's national existence, issued important decrees that were in direct violation of all existing law. Unquestionably the government should have demanded a far more sweeping grant of authority, on August 4, 1914. Lacking this grant of power, it had no choice but to act illegally and seek subsequent parliamentary approval.[14]

Of the three great democracies at war there was danger only in France that the army might get out of hand and dominate the civil government, contrary to the most essential dictates of constitutional democracy. It can be happily asserted, however, that the military, although its importance in the French government was many times magnified, remained throughout the war in its proper place in the constitutional framework. By this test France further demonstrated its adherence to the democratic tradition. At no time did the French Army exercise any such authority over civilian affairs as the military was increasingly doing in Germany. On the contrary, except for the agonizing month of September 1914, when the government had fled to Bordeaux and Paris was seriously menaced, the army command was clearly under the control of the national government.[15] The vicissitudes of the high command,

[13] The consensus of French opinion on the doctrine of necessity as a plea for executive decrees in derogation from existing law is well expressed in Duguit, *op. cit.*, III, pp.696 ff.

[14] As a matter of fact, it was the government of Belgium which made the broadest use of this practice during the World War, due to the impossibility of ordinary parliamentary activity. The courts of that democratic and constitutional state upheld the government on the basis of this very theory of necessity. See generally Ernst Schmitz: *Der Ausnahmezustand in Belgien* (Berlin, 1928).

[15] See generally J. Barthélemy: *Les Pouvoirs Public et le Commandement Militaire* (Paris, 1917); Renouvin, *op. cit.*, pp.76-85.

which assumed several forms in the course of the war, indicate the continuous and decisive interest of the civil government in the most vital army affairs. Freedom of action and decision the military enjoyed, especially Joffre and Foch, but the ultimate predominance of the civil authority was always maintained. As Parliament checked the Cabinet so the Cabinet checked the army. Clémenceau and Foch had pretty much their own way, but only because their political superiors, supported by the people, were willing.

Finally, it seems hardly necessary to remark that the socialistic nature of modern war was clearly illustrated in the experience of France in the first World War. Without precision of plan or purpose, but also without interruption, the control of the state was increasingly extended until the nation's entire economy was subject to the dictates of the national government. Freedom of production, commerce, and consumption were almost obliterated by the legislative and administrative activities of the state. Drastic laws were enacted placing the control or management or operation of all vital industry in the hands of the various ministries, and the administrative structure underwent a tremendous expansion in its effort to cope with the problems arising from such widespread governmental intervention. It was in this respect that the government actually sustained its most radical changes in the course of the war. This is not the place to describe the particulars of French control of industry during the World War.[16] It must be enough to state as a general proposition that democratic France, in order to win this long war, was forced to erect state controls over the French economy to a degree that would have been unthinkable in 1913. A noted observer could write: "France has had the feeling that it has been governed, strongly governed,"[17] yet this vigorous rule proceeded from the regular organs and through the regular channels.

The government of World War France faced and subdued a crisis of sinister magnitude. In so doing it maintained surprisingly unaltered the institutions and procedures of parliamentary democracy. Deviations and adaptations there were, but so far as was reasonably possible this parliamentary system, bolstered for the crisis by a sizable expansion of legislative competence and the establishment of the state of siege, did its work in a fairly normal way and did it very well. Although the liberties

[16] This problem is exhaustively treated in Arthur Fontaine: *French Industry during the War* (New Haven, 1926).

[17] Barthélemy: *Problèmes de Politique et Finances de Guerre*, p.110.

of the people were put at the disposal of the government by the state of siege, they were not limited beyond the evident necessities of the struggle. World War France gave the lie direct to those critics of parliamentary democracy who denied that an effective fighting machine could be constructed within its framework, to men like Marcel Sembat who had written: "I do not think that we could ever extract from the Republic those qualities demanded by the politics of war." For all its faults and falterings, this was true and successful constitutional dictatorship.

CHAPTER IX

Crisis Government in Postwar France

THE happy conclusion of the first World War was followed closely by a complete reestablishment of the normal procedures of parliamentary democracy. An exacting and almost fatal crisis had been met and conquered through a sizable readjustment in French politics and government, and the return of peace found neither the framework nor the processes of this system damaged or permanently altered. Constitutional dictatorship had recorded a signal victory.

But the years of war had wrought lamentable changes in the nation's economic and social fabric, changes that were not undone or corrected but rather were intensified by the return to peacetime ways. Where one great crisis had been put down, a score of lesser ills arose to plague the land and force the government to seek the salvation of the Republic through the use of emergency procedures that were a retreat towards absolutism. In postwar France, as in almost every other nation in the world, the crisis was basically economic, although it had serious social and political repercussions.[1] And in France, as in most other nations, the instrument of constitutional dictatorship called upon to save the country's economy from collapse was a wholesale resort to executive lawmaking, based on acts of delegation by the legislature itself. It was the crisis of a disrupted financial structure which first turned the government away from the tried mechanisms of parliamentary procedure to the dangerous device of the enabling act. When a more ominous threat to the existence of the Republic arose in the last years before the second war, the enabling act continued to be utilized, in this instance to meet the crisis of abject unpreparedness before the horrible menace of totalitarian aggression.

The state of siege was not declared at any time between 1919 and the outbreak of the second World War. It must again be asserted that this instrument carried with it no power of executive decree, and that it was reserved by law and custom for emergencies of a violent nature. It certainly was not adapted to use in economic crises as was Weimar Germany's flexible Article 48. The strikes and riots which followed hard upon the economic disturbances of the 1930's were never of a proportion

---

[1] The events of these years find reliable treatment in two books by Alexander Werth: *France in Ferment* (New York, 1935) and *Which Way France?* (London, 1937).

to be dealt with under the state of siege, and it may well be doubted whether the French people would have countenanced the employment of this emergency instrument. The leftist parties demanded a declaration of the state of siege in the February 1934 riots of their extremist enemies on the right, and in the days immediately preceding the general strike of November 30, 1938 the government let it be known that it was contemplating such a declaration. In neither instance did the Cabinet feel secure enough to ask for a declaration by Parliament or the President.

The Enabling Act in Postwar France

THE story of crisis government in the France of 1919-1939 is almost exclusively one of the emergency delegation of lawmaking power by Parliament to the Cabinet. Exactly how far this recourse to a most dangerous instrument of emergency government was necessitated by an inherent parliamentary incapacity to attack the problems of fast changing economic disturbances with vigorous and timely legislation is difficult to say. The smoothest functioning and hardest working legislatures must go through periods when even their best efforts are inadequate to meet the vicissitudes of a serious crisis, whereas legislation by fiat of a small group of men may master the intricate problems thus presented with relative ease. But it is certain that there was in France (as in Germany) another sort of peril which contributed heavily to this wholesale employment of the practice of executive lawmaking—that of par...amentary irresponsibility.

Often, particularly in the last years of the Republic, the members of Parliament were simply unwilling to accept the political responsibility, unpopularity, and hard work that a program of emergency legislation would have entailed. It is doubtful whether any thoroughgoing enabling act would have been absolutely necessary at any time during these troubled years if an able and courageous French Parliament had existed. Its function of legislation, however, it could not or would not discharge. As in the case of Germany, the legislature was able to shirk its duty only because a satisfactory substitute was available. In Germany it was Article 48; in France it was the enabling act. The men who formed the Cabinets during these troubled years had no choice but to demand and receive legislative competence. The result was the substitution of the Cabinet for Parliament as the legislative branch of the French government. Contrary to German practice and theory, the French government did not regard this radical step as something akin to a constitutional amendment, and all of the many delegations of legislative authority were effected by the passage of a simple statute.

The enabling act in postwar France had most of the usual features of this standard crisis weapon. Only a regularly enacted statute of both Chambers could devolve this power of executive lawmaking. The grant was qualified and confined to a specific purpose, and a time limit was always inserted in the act. Its terms generally required that each decree be placed before Parliament within a given period. This did not mean that they had to be confirmed to have lasting effect. Parliament could ratify a decree by formal act, this action giving it the form and validity of a regular law as of that moment. Usually it took no action at all. This tacit and negative approval left the decree with all the force but none of the formal character of law. To the good people of France it was all the same.

In actual practice the requirement that decrees be submitted to Parliament had little significance. Often it was a practical impossibility to repeal or amend an ordinance that had already taken effect and possibly even run its course before the Chambers ever got around to looking it over. Moreover, the decrees were usually submitted in groups, a practice that made it quite unlikely that any particular decree would be singled out and examined with any hope of repeal or amendment. Positive refusal to ratify voided the decree from the time of rejection, but all acts taken under it remained valid. In short, these decrees could for all purposes be regarded as laws pure and simple. They could alter existing law and could not themselves be modified or repealed except by express vote of Parliament. To be sure, the issuance of such ordinances remained, by reason of their source, acts of an administrative character and thus reviewable by the *Conseil d'Etat* for *excès de pouvoir*. In actual fact, however, the courts were extremely reluctant to invalidate decree-laws which had passed the bounds laid down in the terms of the enabling act. They seemed to regard this question as a political one, for the decision of the legislature alone.

It was almost a constitutional necessity that only Cabinets of an obvious coalition character be accorded the power to legislate by decree,[2] and most of the Cabinets thus empowered were conspicuous in their maintenance of the composition and title of "governments of national union." Finally, the legislature's temporary surrender of its power to make laws was not accompanied, as had been the situation in Germany,

[2] Gustave Moulin: "*L'Expérience Allemande des Décrets-Lois*," *Revue Pol. et Parl.*, CXXX (1927), p.99.

119

by a simultaneous abdication of its powers of control or of its insistence upon the inexorable necessity of ministerial responsibility. The Cabinet made laws, but only because the Chambers were willing. Since the latter always retained the right, they could at any time have reassumed the legislative function. Moreover, they could and did unseat Cabinets that had been accorded this extraordinary competence. In the matter of control at least, this practice remained faithful to the tenets of parliamentary government. Parliament had empowered an agent to act temporarily in its place; it could cut off that agent at a moment's notice.

The history of enabling acts in the Third Republic begins with the World War.[3] Prior to 1914 there had been scattered instances of delegation to the government of an emergency power of decree for specific purposes, and in the war period itself there were many such laws of Parliament authorizing the war government to issue decrees with the force of law. A complete renunciation by the Chambers of their legislative capacity was never effected. A general enabling act was refused Briand in 1916, and the only instance of broad delegation during the war was the law of February 10, 1918 giving Clémenceau's regime an ordinance power in the matter of food supply. With the close of the war this statute was repealed, and it was agreed among French publicists and politicians that it had been a temporary aberration in a state of utmost necessity that was not to be repeated.

The beginning of the new year 1924 found France in a condition of severe economic distress. The immediate cause of concern was the imminent collapse of the franc, and the Poincaré Ministry demanded prompt and emp. ꞏꞏic legislative action to keep the state on a solvent basis. Parliament, far too concerned with *"ses passions politiques et ses préoccupations électorales,"*[4] was unable to act with speed and unwilling to act with severity. As a result, the embattled Poincaré introduced a law into the Chamber of Deputies on January 17 which would have given the Cabinet the power to issue decrees with the force of law, cutting governmental expenses by at least a billion francs (through administrative reorganization) and increasing taxes by twenty per cent.[5] All decrees which operated to alter or suspend regular laws were to be submitted for parliamentary approval within six months. The proposal met vigorous resistance from those opposed to the Poincaré regime under any circumstances, and also from moderates like Paul-Boncour and

[3] See generally Herbert Tingsten: *Les Pleins Pouvoirs*, chap. I.
[4] Esmein-Nézard: *Eléments de Droit Constitutionnel*, II, p.112.
[5] See generally Louis Rolland: *"Le Projet du 17 Janvier et la Question des Décrets-Lois,"* Rev. Dr. Pub., XLI (1924), p.42; Tingsten, *op. cit.*, pp.22 ff.

Herriot,[6] who emphasized the incompatibility of enabling acts and true parliamentary government and in the encounter beat a labored retreat to the crumbling fortress of *potestas delegata non potest delegari*.[7] The bill was finally passed on March 22 with a time limit of four months. Before Poincaré could make use of it elections had intervened, and a new Cabinet headed by Herriot refused to inherit this Poincaré legacy. It was repealed still unused on June 11, but a precedent had been set.

The failure of parliamentary or executive action resulted in a continued drop of the franc. By 1926 it was realized that, if the debacle of the German mark were not to be repeated in France, drastic action would have to be taken. In July of that year the Briand-Caillaux Ministry made a flat request for emergency decree powers, but the former was no more fortunate in receiving such a grant than he had been ten years before, and his Cabinet was forced to resign. Poincaré returned to office and finally succeeded in receiving parliamentary authorization for his Cabinet of "National Union" to issue decrees in an attempt to alleviate the economic crisis. The enabling act of August 3, 1926 empowered his government to initiate sweeping administrative reforms in the interest of national economy and to adjust customs duties to the new value of the franc. The authorization was to terminate by December 31, 1926, and all decrees dealing with administrative reforms necessitating "changes in organization, formalities, or procedures fixed by law, or the annulment of appropriations" were to be submitted for parliamentary ratification within three months. Under the terms of the act more than one hundred decrees were issued abolishing and consolidating local governmental agencies and decentralizing local administration. None was ever ratified by Parliament, and almost all were repealed by statutes forced upon the not unwilling Chambers by local vested interests.[8]

From these rude beginnings the enabling act developed into the chief

---

[6] Herriot, quoted in Tingsten, *op. cit.*, p.29: *"Ce n'est plus la république; c'est l'empire."*

[7] The whole question of the delegation of legislative power has been quite thoroughly thrashed out in French jurisprudence. An excellent summary of the various theories held on this matter is to be found in Tingsten, *op. cit.*, p.36 ff. The classic statement of the French version of the "strict construction" school is an article by Esmein: *"De la Délégation du Pouvoir Législatif,"* Rev. Pol. et Parl., 1 (1894), p.200. See also Esmein-Nézard, *op. cit.*, II, pp.82, and 113 ff., and the article by Duguit: *"Des Réglements faits en vertu d'une Compétence donnée au Gouvernement par le Législateur,"* Rev. Dr. Pub., p.313.

[8] See generally Roger Bonnard: *"Les Décrets-Lois du Ministère Poincaré,"* Rev. Dr. Pub., XLIV (1927), p.248. He lists and analyzes the more important of the decrees. See also Jean Devaux: *Le Régime des Décrets* (Paris, 1927).

emergency institution of postwar France. Whether the legislation which France so sorely needed was the kind that the slow mills of regular parliamentary procedure are not geared to grind out, or whether, as seems nearer the truth, the French Parliament just did not have the courage or unity to make the difficult attempt, the fact remains that the men who formed the Ministries and offered to take authority and responsibility—men like Doumergue, Tardieu, Daladier, and Blum—were forced to demand dangerous powers of executive lawmaking to provide France with government. As in Germany, so in France this procedure was as noxious as it was helpful, probably more so. The ever-ready Article 48 permitted the German legislators to evade their duties with relative impunity. The enabling act did the same for the French deputies. The result was to destroy the efficacy of the regular processes of legislation for even the most unimportant sort of laws. And where Germany had a Papen, France had a Laval! A brief review of the important enabling acts from 1934 onward should suffice to illustrate the scope of this emergency government.[9]

The law of February 28, 1934.[10] Under the terms of this statute the Doumergue-Tardieu government of "national unity" was empowered to take "all measures necessary to balance the budget," this grant of power to terminate on June 30. This particular government had decided to attack the problems of the prevalent depression through a program of deflation. Rather than be forced to endure a bitter fight on the floor of Parliament, it chose to legislate itself and then seek approval. The decrees issued under the government's policy of retrenchment were bitterly opposed by labor and the bureaucracy, and the two succeeding Cabinets of Flandin and Bouisson were refused their demands for similar acts.

The law of June 8, 1935. The victory of the forces in Parliament backed by the Bank of France resulted in an enabling act intended "to avoid monetary devaluation" and authorizing the new Laval Ministry "to issue decrees having the force of law designed to prevent speculation and to defend the franc." All measures adopted were to be submitted for parliamentary sanction before January 1, 1936. Under the terms of this grant the Laval government turned out more than five hundred decree-laws while Parliament was adjourned for the summer. The re-

[9] This problem is treated at some length in Otto Kirchheimer: "Decree Powers and Constitutional Law in France under the Third Republic," *Am. Pol. Sci. Rev.*, xxxiv (1940), p.1104.
[10] The text of this law, and those of the other enabling acts, may be found in the *Journal Officiel* for the day following its passage and promulgation.

sult of this executive lawmaking was a complete deflationary program which played havoc with private obligations and often went far beyond the limits of economic policy stated in the act. Public salaries and pensions were reduced, interest on government securities was lowered, rents and utility rates were fixed—there was even one decree regulating the possession of carrier pigeons by alien residents.[11] By the time the Chambers had reconvened most of these decrees were already in effect and were allowed to run their course without subjection to any serious consideration.

The Laval program aroused bitter reaction, and the *Front Populaire* campaign of 1936 leveled some of its most powerful guns at this "fascistic" practice. One of the first acts of the Blum regime was to demand and receive the repeal by the new Parliament of the bulk of the Laval measures, including those specifically ratified by the previous session. The Blum program of social reform was enacted by normal parliamentary procedure. In June of 1937, however, new financial difficulties forced the Popular Front to ask in its turn for a grant of *pleins pouvoirs* to devalue the franc, raise taxes, and establish exchange control. The Chamber voted to meet the Blum request, but the more conservative Senate balked at such a sweeping donation of lawmaking power to the archenemy and his Popular Front. As a result the Blum Ministry resigned.[12] This demand, even though refused, was of considerable significance, for it symbolized the final acceptance of the enabling act as an emergency institution by all divisions of French politics. Every major party had at one time or another consented to the use of this crisis device; as a result it had become a recognized fixture of French constitutional practice. No longer was there debate in the Chambers over the nature of the enabling act and its compatibility with parliamentary democracy. The question now was not whether decree powers ought to be bestowed at all, but rather whether they should be bestowed upon a particular government. The debates from this time forward were over political and not constitutional principles.

The law of June 30, 1937. The grant of power to the hybrid Chautemps Cabinet which succeeded the departed Blum government ran:

The government is authorized until August 31, 1937, to take by decree adopted in the Council of Ministers all measures to assure the suppression of attempts to weaken public credit, to fight against speculation, to advance

---

[11] The *Journal Officiel* for October 31, 1935 lists more than three hundred of these decrees.

[12] See Lindsay Rogers: "M. Blum and the French Senate," *Pol. Sci. Q.*, LII (1937), p.321.

economic recovery, price control, budget balancing, and without control of exchange to guard the gold holdings of the Bank of France.

These decree-laws were to be laid before the Chambers within three months, or at the latest before the first extraordinary session of 1937. The words "without control of exchange" constituted the first specific prohibition in a French enabling act and indicate the compromise character of the delegation. Under these powers the second Popular Front government, with non-Socialists occupying the key positions of Premier and Minister of Finance, released a new covey of decrees detaching the franc from its gold parity and increasing taxes. Elevated to the premiership in March of 1938, M. Blum again found the Senate a stumbling block in his demands for decree power and again he preferred to resign.

The Four Daladier Enabling Acts

EDOUARD DALADIER assumed the presidency of the Council of Ministers on April 10, 1938. From this day until almost the end of the Third Republic he governed France, and during this time the normal procedures of parliamentary democracy were in a state of suspension. It mattered little whether Parliament was in or out of session—as a legislative organ its days were over. Coerced against his better judgment by the bankruptcy of parliamentary responsibility and the stark necessities of the time, Daladier went to Parliament on four separate occasions and received decree power enabling the Cabinet to supplant the legislature almost completely as the lawgiver of France. Europe was "on the eve," and in the hours before the night it was this instrument of crisis government with which France chose to gird herself for combat with the total states. France was ruled as completely by the decree system as Germany had been in 1931 and 1932.

The law of April 12, 1938 was limited to the end of the regular session or to July 31, and authorized the Daladier "Cabinet of National Defense" to adopt all measures necessary to both national defense and economic recovery. While Parliament's legislative productivity in this period fell to the zero mark, the Daladier Cabinet was enacting a set of decree-laws dealing with the entire problem of French defense and economy.[13] The mention of a few of the matters dealt with—public utility regulations, reorganization of the French Red Cross, reform of local finances, coordination of transportation, customs duties, reorganization of the military hierarchy, housing, agriculture, the entire defense

[13] *Journal Officiel*, June 26 and 29, 1938.

effort, and even the reestablishment of the Blum-abolished practice of exile of criminals to Guiana—should demonstrate that the legislature of France was no longer Parliament but the Council of Ministers.

The law of October 1, 1938 followed directly upon the dramatic return of Daladier from Munich and empowered the government to issue decrees "in order to effect an immediate recovery in the financial and economic situation of the country." The decrees which flowed from this grant constituted an almost complete annihilation of the Blum social reforms, and this wholesale resort to government by decree had severe political repercussions. The Daladier government issued a decree which extended the hard won forty hour week to fifty or more hours in industries vital to national defense. As a result, and in protest against the whole regime of decree-laws, the C. G. T. issued a call for a one-day general strike of all French labor for November 30, 1938. The Daladier government moved decisively against this threat, and once again the decree-law was chosen as the primary emergency weapon. The state of siege was threatened but not declared. Under the law of July 11, 1938 on the organization of the nation in time of war, the government issued a decree mobilizing all laborers of a public character and requisitioning the railroads. The army was alerted to proceed against any manifestations of violence, and the jurisdiction of the military courts was broadened to include public crimes of any of the mobilized workers. The strong show of authority and the decisive measures thus adopted caused a complete collapse of the strike and a complete victory for the Daladier government. It was doubtful authority that Daladier had used, but there was no one who was able to question it effectively.

The law of March 19, 1939 was in every respect an emergency piece of legislation. In the debate preceding its enactment Daladier pointed to the parlous state of affairs in France and to the menace of Nazi Germany, and stressed heavily all the advantages enjoyed by the totalitarian states in the feverish efforts to prepare for the war to come—particularly the ability of their executives to act in a legislative manner independently, secretly, and rapidly. The idea he was trying to put across was obvious, and the terms of the resultant act eliminated parliamentary lawmaking from the French political scheme as a procedure of government compatible with crisis conditions. The Daladier government was empowered to decree "all measures necessary for the defense of the country." The decree-laws issued under this grant of power dealt comprehensively with preparations for war and in so doing effaced the last remnants of the Blum social program.

The fourth and final enabling act was passed after the outbreak of war, December 8, 1939, and was still in force at the death of the Third Republic. It was inserted into article 36 of the law of July 11, 1938 concerning the "General Organization of the Nation in Time of War." As amended this article ran:

During the duration of hostilities the Chambers exercise their powers in legislative and budgetary matters as in time of peace.

However, in case of immediate necessity, the Government is authorized to take, by decrees considered and approved in the Council of Ministers, measures enjoined by the exigencies of national defense.

These decrees are to be submitted to ratification within one month or, in case of absence of the Chambers, at their first meeting.

Under the terms of this statute the procedure of legislation by executive decree was introduced into French law as a permanent emergency institution for time of war. There was no time limit set except "the duration of hostilities," nor was the grant reserved to any specific Cabinet. From this time forward the entrance of France into war was automatically to empower the French Ministry to legislate by decree on any urgent matter "enjoined by the exigencies of national defense." In the months that followed, the Cabinets of both Daladier and Reynaud employed this permissive competence to the full.

The last years of the Third Republic witnessed the complete substitution of Cabinet for Parliament as the legislative organ of the French government. Whether this employment of the enabling act was absolutely necessary to meet the earlier threat of economic collapse or the late threat of German assault may well be doubted. The plain fact remains that Cabinets of every political texture felt impelled to make use of executive legislation as the only means of governing the country in troubled times. At the end of this period the practice had been so completely accepted as an instrument of emergency government that it was converted by statute into a permanent wartime device.

In France as in Germany the enabling act was invoked by those willing to accept hard work and responsibility as the only alternative to anarchy. It remains an indispensable weapon in the arsenal of constitutional dictatorship, but it should be reserved for crises that exist *outside* the government itself. When the enabling act is used too often and too carelessly, it intensifies rather than cures the fevers and ills of the parliamentary system. The French Constitution of 1946 acknowledges this truth in its Article 13: "The National Assembly alone may vote the laws. It may not delegate this right." It remains to be seen whether this will be anything more than a pious hope.

The War of 1939-1940

THE significance of the short war which ended in the unhappy oblitera-tion of the Third Republic lies in the government's deviations from the practices of the first World War. On the whole, the pattern of 1914-1918 was followed rather closely by this new war regime.[14] There were two vital and interesting differences that ought to be noted. In the first place, the wholesale propagation of decree-laws by the Cabinet was a pronounced departure from the system of the first World War. In the last months of their existence as a free people the French were gov-erned completely by executive decrees. In direct contrast to the experi-ence of the first war, the Cabinet had become the one real source of law in France. Even the important step of postponing elections was adopted in the form of a decree.

Secondly, France was governmentally prepared for this war by the thoroughgoing law of July 11, 1938, which regulated minutely the changes in government and administration to be effected in case of war. No such statute had been ready for use in 1914, and experience alone dictated the many alterations now foreseen in this comprehensive law. This time France was ready, if only on paper. In the civil law tradition of the state of siege the French lawmakers had told the people in peace-time what changes were to take place in war. Other laws and decrees were enacted or prepared for enactment to supplement this statute and put even more of the informal and extra-legal or even illegal procedures of the last war into statutory form. An example of this was the replace-ment of the extra-legal system of World War censorship by a decree of August 27, 1939 establishing a legal, preventive control of the press.

Except for these two significant changes the government of France in 1939 was a conscious imitation of that of 1914-1919. The state of siege was invoked throughout the nation; the rights of the people singled out by the law of 1849 were once again at the mercy of the au-thorities and in fact were much more tactlessly and unnecessarily vio-lated; the relations between the government and the high command were the same; a war cabinet was eventually instituted; industry and labor were controlled closely but not dragooned; and most important of all,

---

[14] See generally Roger Bonnard: *"Le Droit Public et La Guerre," Rev. Dr. Pub.,* LVI (1939), p.549, and *Rev. Dr. Pub.,* LVII (1940), p.90.

Parliament, although it had renounced all pretensions to the status of a lawgiving body, retained and exercised its powers of control. It was in session throughout most of this period and was clotured only once, October 5 to November 30, to enable the government to take harsh action against the Communist deputies thus deprived of their parliamentary immunity from arrest. During this hiatus the demands for convocation, particularly from the left wing, were many and vociferous, and when Parliament finally reassembled it stayed in session until April 26, 1940. It adjourned itself until May 16, but when that date arrived Paris was under military command, and for obvious reasons the session did not last very long.

The interpellation in secret session, the only means by which the Cabinet could be forced to give an account of its work, was repeatedly demanded of Daladier and finally voted against his will. Committees continued to exercise control, and Cabinet responsibility in the strict sense was shown still to exist when on March 19 the Daladier government, voted the "confidence" of Parliament 239-1 with almost three hundred abstentions, resigned from office. This peculiar vote was regarded by most people as a parliamentary demand for a substantial reshuffling of the Daladier Cabinet, but he himself chose to consider it as a summons to resign. The Reynaud government, given a vote of confidence on March 23 by a tally of 268-156 with 111 abstentions, got off to a shaky start, but grew stronger as the weeks progressed, and on April 20 received a 515-0 vote of support with but 16 abstentions. The least that can be said of the unhappy French legislature is that it still retained ultimate control over the actions of its agents in the Ministry. Otherwise the Cabinet had been given the competence to fight the war as executive and legislature together.

The sole interest of this chapter in the Pétain government which ruled France during the years of the Nazi occupation is the so-called "Constitutional Act No. 2," promulgated by the Marshal July 11, 1940. Article 1, section 8 of this authoritarian decree gave him, as head of the French State, an uncontrolled power to declare the state of siege in all or part of France. No more conclusive evidence of the wide gulf between the Third Republic and the Pétain regime could possibly be adduced. In the Fourth Republic the power to declare the state of siege is back with the legislature where it belongs. As to the Fourth Republic generally, it is still far too early to record or evaluate its experiences with the institutions of constitutional dictatorship. Indeed, since a relatively stable constitutional order is a general prerequisite of true constitutional dictatorship, it would seem more accurate to describe the first troubled years of the Fourth Republic as a period of constitutional infancy, not constitutional dictatorship. Suffice it to say that the moderates, who fortunately have been able to stay in power despite de Gaulle on the right and Thorez on the left, have made repeated use of the emergency administrative decree to protect the interests of the Republic from a variety of economic and political threats. The Communist-led strikes and riots of late 1947 might well have evoked a declaration of the state of siege; instead the Schuman government asked and received stringent (though temporary) anti-sabotage powers from the French legislature. Parliament's show of determination, partial mobilization, and stern though judicious use of troops and police all contributed to a successful weathering of this most recent storm.

The Third Republic owed a sizable debt to its institutions of constitutional dictatorship, a natural debt for any democracy that would seek to remain a democracy and live on the continent of Europe. As a parliamentary democracy the Third Republic has been held up to students of political science as everything that a parliamentary democracy should not be. But as a government which scored conspicuous victories in its use of constitutional emergency powers, France can serve as a model to be thoughtfully studied by all free men. No instrument of crisis government conforms so closely to the theory of constitutional dictatorship as the famed and widely-imitated state of siege. Few governments at war have achieved so successfully as did World War I France the delicate balance between democracy and dictatorship which makes effective use of the latter to preserve the former. Nor even in the repeated use of enabling acts to meet the perils of depression and unpreparedness was the French experience a complete failure. With the collapse of the Republic this instrument of emergency government unquestionably had something to do, but the collapse would have come anyway.

No crisis institution, no matter how skillfully employed, could have made the Third Republic ready for total war or saved it from the impact of the German war machine. There are obvious limits to the services which constitutional dictatorship can render constitutional democracy.

Part Three

CRISIS GOVERNMENT IN GREAT BRITAIN

No one can say that twentieth century Great Britain hasn't had its fair share of experience with constitutional dictatorship. The first World War and the economic crisis of 1931-1932 were both occasions for the democratic use of autocratic powers, and in the second war with Germany the island itself was for years in a virtual state of siege. The siege has been raised, the wartime dictatorship has come to an end, and the government, despite its energetic programs of national austerity and man-power control, functions today in conformance with the essential dictates of parliamentary democracy. But the difficult years of 1939-1945 are not forgotten. Never in their history were the British people forced to renounce so many of the liberties and luxuries of a democratic, constitutional society. Never was their political system geared so completely to the mandates of efficiency and high resolve. Yet never were they so acutely conscious of the strength of their liberty and their free government. The organization and the laws of the British government of 1939-1945 spoke of dictatorship, but the men who made those laws, as well as the men who obeyed them, spoke only of democracy. This was constitutional dictatorship in fact as it ordinarily exists only in theory.

For the readjustments in their government and lives worked by this bold adventure in constitutional dictatorship the English people were ready and willing, and they went down into the arena fully aware of the changes that would be forced upon them by the exorbitant demands of total war. Constitutional dictatorship had become institutionalized and anticipated in Great Britain in much the same way that it had always been in France. This fact constitutes a pronounced break with the history of British law and government. The institutionalization of emergency powers is out of harmony with the traditions of English politics and with the common law. The textbooks have always treated Britain as the country with the system of government most unfriendly to legally provided emergency powers of the French or German variety. The new editions are being revised, however, for crisis government of the nature of the state of siege is now an accepted element of the British Constitution. England is still a long way from an Article 48, but constitutional dictatorship is today an increasingly more significant reality of British law and politics, as a glance at any newspaper will serve to demonstrate.

CHAPTER X

Crisis Government in Great Britain Before 1914; Martial Law

THE history of crisis government in Great Britain divides into two distinct periods: the centuries before 1914 when there was little need and therefore little provision for instruments of constitutional dictatorship, and the years since 1914 in which both need and provision have outstripped the experience of almost all other democracies. Probably the most striking feature of this history is the cleavage between the traditional and modern patterns of crisis government in England. Rarely does British government indulge in revolutions of this sort. The explanation is not far to seek, but proceeds from the facts of history. Of all the great nations of Europe in 1914, England was the least acquainted with aggressions and rebellions, depressions and periods of anarchy, "alarums and excursions." While France and Italy, Germany and Spain could look back on histories replete with revolutions, abrupt and illegal changes of government, and invasions by hostile armies, the development of England had been a comparatively peaceful evolution to parliamentary democracy in which an executive-fearing Parliament had generally held the whip hand, and in which those emergencies which did arise had been met forcefully but without the necessity of a sizable departure from the normal functioning of a uniquely competent governmental system.

It was just these facts of relative peace and quiet within the realm, freedom from fear and actuality of invasion, distrust of overweening executive power, and a parliamentary system capable of handling any situation that came along which gave English emergency government its classic stamp of non-institutionalization and set it off so sharply from the continental and civil law type of constitutional dictatorship exemplified by the French state of siege. The rise of the British Cabinet to a dominant position around the turn of the present century strengthened the inherent capacity of this parliamentary government to meet every crisis as it arose. Ramsay Muir could dramatize and excoriate England's "cabinet dictatorship,"[1] but in so doing he was simply point-

[1] *How Britain is Governed* (3rd ed., Boston, 1935).

135

ing out the unexampled crisis flexibility of this greatest of cabinet governments.

The cleavage between the realities of emergency government in England and France had its counterpart in a cleavage in theory, resulting in a rather absurd clash between some of the more chauvinistic publicists of these two nations. French jurists have always regarded statutory provision for emergency powers as indispensable to *légalité*, their criterion of the constitutional state. English jurists, on the other hand, looked upon the French state of siege as contrary to "the rule of law," their own criterion of free government.[2] Each school was proud of its own system, contemptuous of the other's. Today these writers could no longer indulge in this holier-than-thou criticism of the other's plan (or lack of plan) for emergency dictatorship. Indeed the victory, whatever it may be worth, belongs to the French. Under the impact of modern war and economic depression England has been forced to abandon traditional ways and has begun to adopt the continental pattern of crisis government. The first World War caused more development in this respect than did all the previous centuries of English history. The years which followed the war were to witness the passage and use of a statute which ranks with the most important and controversial instruments of constitutional dictatorship,[3] and the events of the 1930's and 1940's have carried this constitutional revolution even further along the road to the continental principles of emergency powers.

The theory and practice of emergency government throughout most of English history were: a minimum of statutory provision for situations of national danger; action by Parliament itself (led by the Cabinet) to meet any serious crisis that had arisen; and, where Parliament was unable to function, independent executive action based on the royal prerogative or the common law. Such executive action usually took the form of martial law, the basic English institution of constitutional dictatorship.

Although no laws existed comparable to the French statutes of 1849 and 1878 instituting and regulating the state of siege, Parliament had enacted several statutes which were ready for the government's use in the event of an emergency incapable of solution by legislative action.

[2] For the classic example of English contempt for the state of siege, see A. V. Dicey: *Law of the Constitution* (8th ed., London, 1915), pp. 283-284, 288-289. See also Frederic Harrison: *National and Social Problems* (New York, 1908), chap. 10. The case for the *dictature prévue* is strongly advanced by all French authorities on the state of siege, for example, Romain: *L'Etat de Siège Politique, concl.*

[3] The Emergency Powers Act of 1920. See below, p.172.

Archetype of these laws was the celebrated Riot Act,[4] passed in 1714 to enable the government to cope with the disorders generated by the supporters of the Stuarts, at that moment quite busy expressing violent opposition to the newly-imported Hanoverians. This statute provides that wherever twelve or more persons are riotously assembled, a magistrate shall make a proclamation in the name of the King commanding them to disperse—a ceremony incorrectly but popularly known as "reading the Riot Act." It is a felony for the rioters to continue together for more than one hour after the issuance of this proclamation, and if they refuse to disperse they may be seized and incarcerated. The army and any other subjects may be called upon to assist in the dispersal, and if in so doing any citizen or public servant should injure or kill a rioter, he is to be indemnified both criminally and civilly. It was this sort of isolated and rather antiquated statute by which Parliament made provision for the maintenance of public order in England.

The statutes preparing the nation for war and depression were equally few and uncomprehensive. In the latter part of the nineteenth century Parliament began to make additional statutory provision for emergencies, but here too the efforts were scattered and unconnected. Examples of statutes authorizing executive action in emergencies were the Telegraph Act of 1863 and the Wireless Telegraphy Act of 1904 empowering the government to take over the nation's means of communications, the Regulation of the Forces Act of 1871 permitting the government to nationalize the railroads, the Bank Holidays Act of 1871 authorizing the closing of the banks, the Customs Laws Consolidation Act of 1876 sanctioning the prohibition by proclamation or Order-in-Council of the importation of any goods, the Customs and Inland Revenue Act of 1879 and the Exportation of Arms Act of 1900 conferring a similar power to forbid exports, and the Mines Regulation Act of 1908 providing that the Crown might suspend the operation of this law "in the event of war or imminent national danger or great emergency or in the event of any grave economic disturbance."[5]

In the absence of any comprehensive provision for governmental action in sudden crisis, it was left to Parliament to act through the processes of normal legislation, or to the Cabinet or other executive officials to act under the royal prerogative or the common law. Most of the crises

[4] 1 Geo. 1, Stat. 2, ch. 5. A number of American states have statutes modeled on this act.

[5] These statutes are respectively: 26 & 27 Vict., ch. 112, sec. 52; 4 Edw. VII, ch. 24; 34 & 35 Vict., ch. 86, sec. 16; 34 & 35 Vict., ch. 17; 39 & 40 Vict., ch. 36, sec. 43; 63 & 64 Vict., ch. 24; and 8 Edw. VII, ch. 57.

of English history were of a nature to be met by determined parliamentary action. The more of a reality Cabinet leadership became, the easier it was for this government to proceed to any arbitrary action made unavoidable by the sudden precipitation of a national emergency. The increasingly intimate conjunction between the legislative and executive branches of the British government, with the latter just as increasingly in the ascendant, created a system uniquely prepared to take prompt and drastic steps in time of crisis. The last of England's great wars with France, continuing over a period of some twenty years, was almost wholly conducted through acts of Parliament. Two of the more noted examples of parliamentary exertion in the face of emergencies, neither of which has been employed within the boundaries of England for generations, were the so-called Suspension of Habeas Corpus Act, by virtue of which the government might defer until less troubled times the trial of persons apprehended for rebellion or other treason against the kingdom,[6] and the Coercion Act, a sort of legislative declaration of martial law placing the government of a disturbed area in the hands of the executive and military authorities.[7] The Coercion Act was unknown in constitutional England, but was used occasionally in Ireland.

The ultimate weapon of emergency government in Great Britain—and it is still in the arsenal today—was that of executive action taken on the responsibility of the actor, and based upon the royal prerogative or upon principles of the common law which he could plead in the regular courts of England.[8] Such actions were always undertaken with the hope and expectation of a parliamentary indemnity act, and this procedure by which an omnipotent legislature registered *ex post facto* approval of some unusual executive act could extend to any sort of action, whether it had a legal basis or not. A leading example of illegal executive initiative made legal by subsequent parliamentary approval occurred in 1766. In the presence of a serious food shortage and in the absence of Parliament, the King, on the advice of Pitt and his ministers, permitted the promulgation of a royal proclamation laying an embargo on all ships laden with wheat and flour, in direct derogation from existing law. The responsible ministers were eventually indemnified by Parliament, but not without some difficulty. This famous "forty days tyranny" was frankly defended by its principals on the basis of the law

---

[6] For an example, see 34 Geo. III, ch. 54. [7] Dicey, *op. cit.*, p.227.

[8] The classic statement of the ultimate significance of the executive prerogative—"this power to act according to discretion for the public good, without the prescription of the law and sometimes even against it"—is given by John Locke: *Of Civil Government*, II, chap. 14.

of paramount necessity.[9] This action was unique in modern English constitutional history, and can hardly be said to have set a precedent. It does illustrate clearly the unbounded possibilities of emergency competence then and now open to any English Cabinet enjoying an undoubted majority in and control over its Parliament. The British Cabinet has long been capable of any crisis action which Parliament would subsequently indemnify, no matter how dictatorial or illegal or unconstitutional it might be. That this has not happened since 1766 is evidence of the comparatively smooth tenor of English history as well as of the constitutional maturity of the English people.

Martial Law in England

THE institution known as martial law is the classic and characteristic device of constitutional dictatorship within the realm of England, the British and common law counterpart of the French and civil law state of siege. The same circumstances give rise to both martial law and the state of siege: an invasion or insurrection. The same procedures are followed: suspension of civil rights, institution of military courts for civilian crimes, substitution of the military arm for the regular police. The same purpose dictates the efforts of the British and French authorities: to restore public order and normal government. But there the similarity ceases, for martial law and the state of siege arise from different theories of the nature of constitutional emergency powers, from different legal systems, and from different political and military histories.

Although it has been practically superseded, or at least relegated to a secondary status by the statutory developments of the past twenty-five years, and although it has not been instituted in England itself for over 150 years,[10] nevertheless martial law deserves thorough consideration as a much copied, much debated, and still possible instrument of constitutional dictatorship. There has been an immense amount of literature written on the subject of martial law, the chief result of which has been a good deal of unnecessary confusion on the subject. Indeed, the most remarkable thing about martial law is "the haze of uncertainty

[9] *Parl. Hist.*, XIII, pp.250-313. There were several less obvious examples of this sort of emergency action in the long war with France.

[10] The last instances of martial law in England, none of them particularly serious, were in 1715, 1740, and 1780. See generally C. M. Clode: *The Military Forces of the Crown* (London, 1869), II, pp.163 ff.

which envelops it."[11] The bewildering confusion which surrounds the cardinal instrument of emergency government of both England and the United States arises chiefly from the traditional failure of jurists, historians, politicians, and generals[12] to distinguish the various forms of government and law to which the general label martial law has been affixed. This phrase was originally applied to that law administered in early times by the Court of the Constable and the Marshal, in Coke's words "the fountain of marshal law."[13] Since then it has been used with equal facility to indicate the military law governing soldiers in the service of the Crown,[14] the military government of conquered areas, the efforts of the Stuart Kings to extend the peacetime jurisdiction of their "military commissions" to civil crimes,[15] any sort of arbitrary government in which military power plays the dominant role, and finally that emergency rule "which obtains in a domestic community when the military authority carries on the government, or at least some of its functions."[16]

It is this last type of martial law, *the extension of military government to domestic areas and civil persons in case of invasion or rebellion,* that is to be considered here. It can and must be clearly differentiated from military law and military government, although all of these, like the several states of siege, have common historical and logical roots.[17] This type of martial law is in every sense of the word an instrument of constitutional dictatorship, for it is a suspension of normal civil government in order to restore it, and has civilians for its subjects and civil areas for its loci of operation. Once this particular type of martial law is isolated and examined, much of the doubt and confusion disappears, and it can be understood how unnecessary most of its polemic history has been.

[11] Charles Fairman: *The Law of Martial Rule* (2nd ed., Chicago, 1943), p.19. This work is the best brief legal treatment of martial law in England and the United States and does much to clear up this confusion.

[12] The Duke of Wellington described both military government and martial law as "nothing more nor less than the will of the general."

[13] *4th Inst.,* 123.

[14] This is the martial law of Coke and Blackstone (*Commentaries,* Cooley's 2nd ed., I, p.412).

[15] See Sir James F. Stephen: *A History of the Criminal Law of England* (London, 1883), I, pp.208-210. The Petition of Right of 1628 excluded in undoubted terms the legality of this practice in time of peace, but left room for debate whether it outlawed such martial law in time of war.

[16] Fairman, *op. cit.,* p.30; Stephen, *op. cit.,* I, pp.207-208.

[17] On the history and development of martial law in England, see W. S. Holdsworth: "Martial Law Historically Considered," *L.Q.R.,* XVIII (1902), p.117; Fairman, *op. cit.,* chap. 1; Stephen, *op. cit.,* I, pp.201 ff.; James M. Lowry: *Martial Law Within the Realm of England* (London, 1914).

It was this confounding of martial rule with military law, military government, and even military dictatorship which put the term martial law under a cloud throughout most of English history and helped to give emergency government in England prior to 1914 its peculiar feature, its almost complete lack of institutional status. It is in this respect that martial law differs most sharply from the state of siege—the absence of statutory foresight for its initiation and use. Whereas the French law-givers reacted to executive abuse of the state of siege by making it a legal institution and placing it in the keeping of the legislature, the English, indulged in their distaste for emergency government by the elementary facts of their history, refused to provide at all in their statutes for full-fledged crisis powers of the executive variety. The executive institution of an "English state of siege" has occasionally been found necessary, however, and rather than leave a possible instrument of government outside their imposing legal structure, the English courts and jurists have brought martial law within the bounds of the common law and the rule of law.

A few of the English jurists, however, have wandered even further from the idea of legally anticipated emergency government and have denied absolutely the possibility of martial law in England as a legal institution, except by express declaration of Parliament. Professor Corwin writes: "It was a Whig dogma following the Glorious Revolution that the English Constitution did not know martial law, except as it was authorized from year to year by parliament for the government of the army."[18] This dogma, a direct result of the hatred for the insolence of executive authority entertained by the men who framed the Petition of Right, was enshrined in glib maxims such as "the common law knows nothing of martial law," "it is the most unconstitutional procedure conceivable," and "it is totally inaccurate to state martial law as having any place whatever within the realm."[19] The Parliament of 1628 thought it was outlawing completely the application of military law to civil persons, and such worthies as Hale, Blackstone, Lord Loughborough, and Lord Chief Justice Cockburn subscribed wholeheartedly to this doctrine. In the nineteenth century martial law as a legal concept or a practical institution can hardly be said to have existed in England itself. It is true, however, that it was still an actuality and something of a burning issue for the colonies and Ireland, and in this way martial law

[18] "Martial Law, Yesterday and Today," *Pol. Sci. Q.*, XLVII (1932), p.103.
[19] Fairman, *op. cit.*, pp.20-21.

141

was kept alive as a product and a part, although an extraordinary part, of English law.[20]

The honors for the salvaging of martial law from the scrapheap of oblivion, confusion, colonial and Irish exile, and downright negation must be divided between Professor A. V. Dicey and Sir James Stephen. Thanks to them and to the discussions which their writings evoked, the institution of martial law has been revived and made ready for further use in England—if the necessity should ever arise. It is agreed today that there is an institution of constitutional dictatorship known as martial law, and that it may be initiated legally to provide for the dictatorial governance of British civilians under conditions of serious public disorder.

What is Martial Law?

PROFESSOR DICEY defines martial law as "the power of the government or of loyal citizens to maintain public order, at whatever cost of blood or property may be necessary."[21] Sir Frederick Pollock adds that martial law is "an unlucky name for the justification by the common law of acts done by necessity for the defence of the Commonwealth when there is war within the realm."[22] Given a condition of emergency in England that would call for a declaration of the state of siege in France, the government (or a local magistrate or military commander)[23] has the power to do just about the same things that French officials can do under the state of siege. The authority to adopt whatever arbitrary measures are necessary to restore public order proceeds directly from the common law right and duty of the Crown and its subjects to "repel force by force in the case of invasion or insurrection, and to act against rebels as it might against invaders."[24] Correlative common law rights are those of the citizen to abate a nuisance, to defend himself against illegal assault, and to arrest any person whom he knows to have committed a felony or whom he sees committing a breach of the peace. In short, there is a common law justification of whatever summary meas-

[20] For instances, see Fairman, *op. cit.*, chaps. 4 and 7. Internal disturbances in England in the late eighteenth and early nineteenth centuries were dealt with through repressive acts of Parliament. See H. M. Bowman: "Martial Law in England," *Michigan Law Review*, xv (1916), pp.119-123.

[21] *Op. cit.*, p.286; in complete accord is Stephen, *op. cit.*, I, p.214.

[22] "What is Martial Law?", *L.Q.R.*, xviii (1902), p.156.

[23] And in theory at least any private citizen has this power, although in fact the competence of the individual is a thing of the past—Karl Heck: *Der Ausnahmezustand in England* (Berlin, 1928), p.198.

[24] Stephen, *op. cit.*, I, p.208.

142

ures the authorities may be compelled by the force of events to adopt in time of war or rebellion. The very conditions where there is no law or peace make normally illegal measures legal. What would be a felony in time of peace becomes a public duty in time of war.

Whether this power to act under martial law is, as maintained here, an example of the common law right to employ force to repel force, or is rather a prerogative of the Crown remains an unsettled question. The former view is that of Dicey, Holdsworth, and Pollock; the latter finds its broadest expression in the writings of H. W. Finlason.[25] Although the common law theory is favored by most jurists, actually it makes little difference, as long as the existence of the institution is acknowledged.[26] There is another theory which holds that all actions under martial law must be regarded as illegal in the first instance, and that the authorities must proceed to these admittedly unlawful acts in the hope of an act of indemnity. The truth, however, seems to rest with this statement of Pollock's:

"But this, it is submitted, imputes gratuitous folly to the Common Law, which cannot be so perverse as to require a man in an office of trust to choose between breaking the law and being an incompetent officer and a bad citizen. In the absence of positive authority we are entitled, and indeed bound, to suppose the law to be reasonable."[27]

The legal nature of martial law finds expression in proceedings before the regular courts of England. Those who wield this extraordinary authority must stand ready to prove to the courts, when normal government has returned, that general conditions were likewise extraordinary and thus justified martial rule. They must further be prepared to prove that the particular measures adopted were warranted by the exigencies of the situation, for these measures may be proceeded against both civilly and criminally.[28] This fact sets martial law off sharply from the state of siege. Under the latter the legislature is the sole limit upon arbitrary use of the extraordinary competence of the officials, and the regular courts offer scant refuge to the individual injured during the condition of emergency. Under martial law the courts are the chief obstruction to wanton acts of an official nature. While the legislature maintains a continual check under the state of siege, the courts act only at the con-

[25] *A Treatise on Martial Law* (London, 1866); *Commentaries upon Martial Law* (London, 1867); *A Review of the Authorities as to Repression of Riot and Rebellion* (London, 1868).

[26] Lord Halsbury: *The Laws of England* (London, 1907-1917), VI, p.402.

[27] Pollock, *loc. cit.*, p.156.

[28] See the old case of *Wright v. Fitzgerald* (1799), 27 St. Tr. 659.

clusion of martial law. In neither instance are the limitations as effective in practice as they are in theory.

It is true that Parliament would be just as interested in a declaration of martial law as the French legislature is in the establishment of the state of siege. In the first place, Parliament itself can declare martial law, although ordinarily this remains an executive act. More than this, the hope of an indemnity act conditions the exertions of the officials acting under martial law as much as the expectancy of standing trial for misuse of power. Through this device Parliament may and almost always will give statutory sanction to the measures adopted by the authorities and the sentences imposed by the courts-martial which they have seen fit to ordain. This precludes judicial examination of these measures and sentences, and demonstrates that the English legislature too has the last word in the use of the country's chief institution of emergency government.

The nature of the indemnity act has been disputed by some of the leading authorities, but it seems sufficient to characterize it as a law passed "to obviate any question as to the legality of the measures . . . taken" under martial law.[29] Whether Parliament takes this step "from necessity or out of abundant caution," that is, whether the acts thus sanctioned were clearly illegal and would have been declared so by any regular court, or were doubtless legal and demanded by the necessities of the situation and were thus made doubly good, makes little difference.[30] The act of indemnity is thus the usual postlude to a regime of martial law; its significance rests in that it maintains parliamentary, popular control over the executive in the exercise of his emergency authority. The government must always act with an eye on Parliament as well as on the courts. Incidentally, lest the act of indemnity be converted into a general sanction for everything done under a regime of martial law

[29] S. C. Pratt: *Military Law* (19th ed., London, 1915), p.267. Cockburn's charge to the grand jury in *Queen v. Nelson and Brand, Annual Register* (N.S.) (1867), p.230, cited the practice of the indemnity act as evidence of the illegality of martial law. In the case of *Philips v. Eyre* (4 Q.B. 242-243) he stated that every act of indemnity involves "a manifest violation of justice."

[30] Pollock, *loc. cit.*, p.157: "An act of indemnity is a measure of prudence or grace." Dicey regards the act as the legalizing of an illegality and as having no effect on any action already legal, *op. cit.*, pp.547-549. Harold Laski believes that all acts of indemnity should require at least a two-thirds vote of the legislative assembly for passage, this guaranteeing a more scrupulous and intelligent exertion of executive crisis authority— *A Grammar of Politics* (London, 1925), pp.558-559. In July 1944 Home Secretary Herbert Morrison announced to the House of Commons that he had failed through a grave oversight to lay a series of National Fire Service Regulations before Parliament, as had been required by their authorizing statute. The result was an outright Act of Indemnity (7 & 8 Geo. vi, ch. 35).

144

and thus debar judicial scrutiny and retribution in the case of clearly wanton exertions of authority, such an act is generally framed to protect only those actions undertaken in "good faith," an elastic standard if ever there was one.

The Measures Taken Under Martial Law

THE particular measures which may be lawfully employed under martial law are determined by the stringency of the disturbed conditions which force its initiation. Invasion and insurrection, both of them conditions of violence, are the factual prerequisites of martial law, and as they vary in intensity, so will vary the severity of the measures adopted. The rights of person and property present no obstruction to the authorities acting under such a regime, if the acts which encroach upon them are necessary to the preservation or restoration of public order and safety.[31] *Princeps et res publica ex justa causa possunt rem meam auferre.* All the procedures which are recognized adjuncts of executive crisis government, more specifically all those actions which are so carefully described in the French law of 1849 on the state of siege, and other measures too, are open to the persons who bear official authority under martial law. The government may wield arbitrary powers of police to allay disorder,[32] arrest and detain without trial all citizens taking part in this disorder and even punish them (in other words, suspend the writ of habeas corpus),[33] institute searches and seizures without warrant, forbid public assemblies, set curfew hours, suppress all freedom of expression, institute courts-martial for the summary trial of crimes perpetrated in the course of this regime and calculated to defeat its purposes, and generally govern the particular area as a general governs a besieged fortress—in brief, do absolutely anything that the exigencies of the moment demand and that the courts and Parliament will recognize as having been necessary. For the duration of a regime of martial law

[31] See H. E. Richards: "Martial Law," *L.Q.R.*, XVIII (1902), pp.133, 135 ff., for a lengthy discussion of the manner in which martial law may invade personal and property rights.

[32] The limits and character of military aid to the civil authorities are defined in the report of the special commission on the Featherstone Riots—*Parl. Papers*, 7324. As British subjects the military authorities may if necessary act independently of the civil government but they too must meet the subsequent tests of courts and Parliament and pay the penalties for illegal action.

[33] The legalists still insist that the executive cannot suspend the right of habeas corpus; the conditions of disorder make the issuance of the writ impossible, they maintain, and the executive merely recognizes this fact.

the ordinary citizen can consider himself practically a member of the armed forces.

The certainty of subsequent judicial or legislative scrutiny must not discourage the authorities from proceeding to the actions demanded by the circumstances, for these actions are a duty as well as a right. The officer acting under martial law would be liable for criminal prosecution for negligence if he failed to do "all that could be reasonably expected from a man of ordinary prudence, firmness, and activity, under the circumstances in which he was placed." In short, in the prosecution of measures found necessary under martial law, the middle line between the too weak and the too strong must be discovered and followed. As the court stated in the celebrated case of *King v. Pinney*, the official is "bound to hit the precise line of his duty."[34]

Martial law and the acts taken under it do not normally depend upon the proclamation that accompanies the initiation of this emergency institution.[35] The proclamation is a declaration of an existent fact and a warning by the authorities that they have been forced against their will to have recourse to strong means to suppress disorder and restore peace. It has, as Thurman Arnold has written, merely "emotional effect" and cannot itself make up for the absence of the conditions necessary for the initiation of martial law.[36]

Martial law is thus nothing more than a state of fact based upon a condition of necessity. In the words of Sir James Mackintosh:

"The only principle on which the law of England tolerates what is called Martial Law is necessity; its continuance requires precisely the same justification of necessity; and if it survives the necessity on which it alone rests for a single minute, it becomes instantly a mere exercise of lawless violence."[37]

"Necessity" is the plea of the government to the courts (or to Parliament) for the justification of all actions adopted under a regime of martial law. There is a healthy difference of opinion concerning what this criterion permits, both in the inauguration and continued maintenance of martial law. Pollock believes that the courts should sanction all acts which may have been fairly regarded as necessary during the emer-

---

[34] (1832), 3 B. & Ad. 947.

[35] *King (Ronayne and Mulcahy) v. Strickland* (1921), 2 Irish Rep. 333.

[36] See his article "Martial Law" in *The Encyclopedia of the Social Sciences.* "Whether a state of war exists within British territory is always a matter for judicial determination, and a mere proclamation to that effect has no authority."—Thomas Baty and H. J. Morgan: *War: Its Conduct and Legal Results* (London, 1915), p.6.

[37] Quoted in Clode, *op. cit.,* ii, p.161.

gency.[38] Dicey, who labels Sir Frederick's assertion the doctrine of "political expedience," would extend judicial sanction only to those actions justifiable on the grounds of "immediate necessity,"[39] while Richards considers the plea of good faith as sufficient to cover any acts undertaken by those charged with the execution of martial law.[40] The doctrine of immediate necessity is supported by the bulk of English jurisprudence,[41] but Pollock's view that martial law may extend to areas merely threatened by rebellion and invasion, and thus may permit measures of a preventive nature, is more in conformity with the realities of the situation. A German invasion concentrated around the Dover area would unquestionably have warranted a Cabinet declaration of martial law from Land's End to John O'Groat's, and it is certain that, even if Parliament had given the courts a chance to hear litigations involving the legality of official measures adopted under this state of martial law, the declaration itself could not possibly have been questioned, and all acts taken in good faith would have been regarded as "necessary."

The Courts-Martial

MOST people identify martial law with a regime of courts-martial which supplant and act for the regular courts. This idea is not quite true. While in France the declaration of the state of siege automatically substitutes military tribunals for the civil courts, under martial law the latter are not superseded by the proclamation, but by the fact that conditions are so disturbed that they cannot sit. Martial law "only exists by reason of those tribunals having been practically superseded."[42] It is true that under certain conditions of martial law the ordinary courts may be open for business, but in this case they exist only at the sufferance of the military authorities. Indeed, the status of the ordinary courts is one of the chief tests of the necessity of martial law. "The fact that the courts are open and undisturbed will in all cases furnish a powerful presumption that there is no necessity for a resort to martial law, but it should not furnish an irrebuttable presumption."[43]

[38] Pollock, *loc. cit.*, pp.155 ff.   [39] Dicey, *op. cit.*, pp.545 ff.
[40] *Loc. cit.*, pp.133 ff.
[41] Bowman, *loc. cit.*, pp.111-112, cites the authorities.
[42] Joint Opinion of Sir John Campbell and Sir S. M. Rolfe on the power of the Governor of Canada to proclaim martial law, January 16, 1838—Forsyth: *Cases and Opinions on Constitutional Law* (London, 1869), p.199.
[43] W. W. Willoughby: *The Constitutional Law of the United States* (New York, 1910), II, p.1251. *Ex parte Marais* (1902), A.C. 109, established the doctrine that martial law may exist while the courts are still open. See Cyril Dodd: "The Case of Marais," *L.Q.R.*, XVIII (1902), p.143.

It is in the discretion of the official or general executing martial law whether the void generally left by the enforced abdication of the regular courts is to be filled by courts-martial. Nine times out of ten it is so filled, but it need not be if the authorities refuse to regard it as a necessary step. The cleavage between English and French practice receives a further confirmation. Under both martial law and the state of siege special courts will ordinarily be instituted, but only the latter makes this certain by fixing it in law. The authorities in England may detain prisoners without any sort of trial whatsoever, or they may institute a full-fledged military trial for crimes against the state. In any case, the proceedings of these courts "derive their sole authority from the existence of actual rebellion, and the duty of doing whatever may be necessary to quell it, and to restore peace and order."[44]

Thus dependent upon the whim of the executive the courts-martial of English (or American) martial law are no courts at all, but administrative organs charged with aiding in the restoration of public order. They are little more than proof of good faith on the part of the authorities prosecuting the state of martial law. These authorities might choose to punish and execute without trial, but instead initiate special courts to give punishment or execution some sort of institutional form. Lord Halsbury went so far as to declare that to regard these courts as courts of justice is "quite illusory."[45] To be sure, in more extended periods of martial rule courts-martial must perforce be established to handle those civil and criminal cases whose solution is necessary to a successful regime of martial law, and which in their nature demand some sort of immediate trial. A system of tribunals, with the possibility of appeal to a higher judge-advocate, might be regarded as "necessary." Even then it would be a matter of executive discretion whether or not they were to be instituted. So too is the procedure of these courts discretionary, although it is almost mandatory that they should follow recognized forms of military-judicial procedure and "act in accordance with the principles of justice, honor, humanity, and the laws and usages of war."[46] The good faith of the commander and the English concept of fair play are the indispensable criteria for the initiation and actions of these courts.

The courts-martial come to an abrupt end with the restoration of order. Their existence in time of peace to punish suppressed rebellion

---

[44] *King v. Allen* (1921), 2 Irish Rep. 241.
[45] *Tilonko v. Attorney General* (1907), A.C., 95.
[46] Quoted in Fairman, *op. cit.*, p.264.

is forbidden by the Petition of Right, and with the reestablishment of normal conditions they must hand over their prisoners to the civil powers.[47] It is uncertain in English law whether the sentences of the courts-martial lapse with the termination of martial law. In this regard, as in many others, the practice of the indemnity act has precluded a judicial determination of the question. These sentences would seem to be for the regular courts to approve or repeal, in the absence of parliamentary action.

What then is the meaning of martial law in England today? Does it have any significance at all as an institution of emergency government? The answer would seem to be in the affirmative. The statutory developments of the last twenty-five years have pushed martial law well into the background, and quite possibly it may never again be used within the realm of England. Thurman Arnold would relegate martial law to the status of a "handy dialectic tool," in which case it would still have significance as the symbol of the British government's absolute competence to take any arbitrary action that the necessities of any particular crisis—e.g. an atomic attack—might demand.

But what if the great crisis had come, and Parliament had found it impossible to convene and make a statutory declaration of martial law? Then, in the hour when Hitler's hordes invaded England, the Cabinet or some ranking and responsible official or general in a local area— Mr. Churchill, the Lord Mayor of Bristol, Sir Auckland Geddes, K.C.B. (as Regional Commissioner for Sussex), or perhaps even Mr. George Bernard Shaw (as Mr. George Bernard Shaw)—could have proceeded with autocratic authority to any action necessary to secure or restore order in a threatened or invaded area: imprisoned suspected citizens without warrant, deployed the Home Guard or the police, evacuated the civil population, suspended all rights including the privilege of habeas corpus, and instituted summary courts for the trial and even execution of British citizens. And when peace had been restored, he could have walked into any court of the land, asserted the necessity of the actions assailed, and justified these measures as legal and indeed a public duty arising from the common law itself. And it is certain that, before any of these gentlemen ever got near a court room, Parliament would have passed an act of indemnity allaying all doubts concerning his actions and thanking him for having proceeded in this manner which, though extraordinary, was foreseen by the law of England.

[47] *Wolfe Tone's Case* (1798), 27 St. Tr. 613.

"I conceive that it is the better opinion that the law of England, born and nurtured in times when war within the realm was very possible, is not without resources in the face of rebels and public enemies; that a right arising from and commensurate with the necessity is a part, though an extraordinary part, of the Common Law."[48]

[48] Sir Frederick Pollock: *The Expansion of the Common Law* (London, 1904), p.105.

CHAPTER XI

The Government of Great Britain in the First World War

O F all the nations that went to war in 1914, Great Britain was the least prepared to undergo the protracted and grievous rigors of the first of the total wars. In England the ideals and actualities of free government for free men flourished most tenaciously. In England could be found the model of all parliamentary systems, evolved through generations of peace within the realm and geared to a continuation of peace. A potent army, legislation to put the nation on a wartime footing, time-tested devices of emergency government, provisions for the control of popular liberties—all these England lacked. A stout navy, stout leaders, and stout hearts she could summon up to meet the crisis, but beyond this the British were ill-prepared to carry off the colossal task of defeating an autocratic war power. Since 1904 a "Committee of Imperial Defence," composed of leading members of the Cabinet and representatives of the armed forces, had been evolving plans for war.[1] Their proposals were to prove of inestimable value in effecting the conversion to wartime methods of government, but in early August of 1914 they were still nothing but proposals.

Of all the nations, then, Great Britain was forced to experience the most radical alterations in governmental organization and, comparatively speaking, the most sweeping invasions of civil and economic liberties. The transition from Germany at peace to Germany at war worked little transformation in the powers and organization of the government or in the relations of citizen to state. The transition from Britain at peace to Britain at war was almost a revolution. More than this, it was an eloquent testimonial to the political aptitude of the British people and to the infinite elasticity of their cabinet government. A good deal of this departure from the ways of the past was destined to be only temporary. Some changes, however, were to become permanent, and not the least significant of these was an entirely new constitutional theory of emergency government. The important readjustments in the framework of English government undergone in the first World War were: a sizable increase in the power and prestige of the Cabinet, a con-

---

[1] W. Ivor Jennings: *Cabinet Government* (Cambridge, 1936), pp.228 ff.

comitant reduction in the power and prestige of Parliament, a fundamental alteration in the structure of the Cabinet and of the cabinet system, a radical governmental intrusion into the hallowed field of English liberties, and an expansion of governmental activity to control the entire economic life of the British people.

The declaration of war found the British government already making use of every statutory emergency power within its grasp as well as the long-dormant royal prerogative. The latter was disinterred to authorize the initiation of a one month moratorium on the payment of bills of exchange and to forbid trading with the enemy.[2] The government showed its doubts concerning its power to do this by immediately securing legislation on these same two subjects—the Postponement of Payments Act and the Trading with the Enemy Act.[3] The prerogative was used without subsequent parliamentary sanction to authorize the Admiralty to requisition English ships and to brand as treason the giving of financial assistance to the enemy.[4] On August 4 a royal proclamation was made to the people of England in which "all our loyal subjects" were called upon for obedience, aid, and fidelity.[5] Just what the government had in mind in the issuance of this proclamation, without the formal approval of the Privy Council or Parliament and merely as an act of kingly prerogative, is not entirely clear. Some writers seem to think that the "prerogative of the Crown in connection with the public safety and the defence of the realm" was thereby to be revived and employed.[6] Others believe that it was simply a reminder to the citizens of their common law duty to support the Crown in danger and to obey all lawful acts and orders of the government.[7] Nothing was ever done on its authority—Parliament was in session and ready to act. Britain fell back upon the ancient method of facing moments of national peril: action by Parliament itself.

The product of Parliament's first few days as a wartime legislature may have been conventional in form, but not in content or method of

[2] Alexander Pulling, ed.: *Manual of Emergency Legislation* (September, 1914), pp.238, 375.
[3] 4 & 5 Geo. v, ch. 11, p.87.   [4] *Manual* (1914), pp.386, 177.
[5] *Ibid.*, p.145.
[6] Heck: *Der Ausnahmezustand in England*, pp.203-214; Tingsten: *Les Pleins Pouvoirs*, pp.179-180. This view was subscribed to in *Grieve v. Edinburgh and District Water Trustees* (1918), S.C. 700.
[7] S. W. Clarke: "The Rule of DORA," *Journal of Comp. Legis. and Int. Law*, 1 (3rd ser.), (1919), pt. 1, p.37; Gaston Jèze: *L'Exécutif en Temps de Guerre* (Paris, 1917), p.17. The prerogative of the Crown to legislate has long since been restricted to isolated subjects such as the prescription of prize regulations.

enactment. The Cabinet went into Commons and demanded the immediate passage of a remarkable aggregation of emergency laws, and these laws, prepared in advance by the pertinent ministries or by the Committee of Imperial Defence, were suddenly spewed forth without debate, without alteration, and without protest. The laws thus enacted dealt with everything from the problem of enemy aliens to the expansion of the army, and in most instances presented broad discretionary powers to the Cabinet. One of these statutes stands out from the rest as perhaps the most radical parliamentary enactment in the history of England, indeed in all the history of constitutional government. This was the renowned Defence of the Realm Act of August 8, 1914,[8] a statute which not only came close to being a legislative declaration of martial law throughout England, but also delegated the government out-and-out legislative power. It was indeed "a marked departure from Anglo-Saxon legal traditions."[9] Two weeks later the Act was strengthened to conform even more completely to the pattern of the state of siege, and on November 27 it was further broadened and given final form.[10] The pertinent parts of the Defence of the Realm Consolidation Act of 1914 read:

I. (1) His Majesty in Council has power during the continuance of the present war to issue regulations for securing the public safety and the defence of the realm . . . ; and may by such regulations authorize the trial by courts-martial, or in the case of minor offences by courts of summary jurisdiction, and punishment of persons committing offences against the regulations. . . .

(3) It shall be lawful for the Admiralty, Army Council, Air Council, or the Minister of Munitions—[11]

(a) to require that there shall be placed at their disposal the whole or any part of the output of any factory . . .

(b) to take possession of and use for the purpose of His Majesty's naval or military or air-force service any factory . . .

(d) to regulate or restrict the carrying on of any work in any factory, . . . or to regulate and control the supply of metals and materials that may be required for any articles for use in war; . . .

and regulations under this Act may be made accordingly.

(4) For the purpose of the trial of a person for an offence under the regulations by court-martial and the punishment thereof, the person

[8] 4 & 5 Geo. v, ch. 29.
[9] Lindsay Rogers: "The War and the English Constitution," *The Forum* (July, 1915), pp.27-28.
[10] 4 & 5 Geo. v, ch. 63; 5 Geo. v, ch. 8.
[11] The reading of section 3 as here given is its apparent final form after several amendments, particularly by the terms of the Defence of the Realm (Amendment) No. 2, Act of March 16, 1915—5 Geo. v, ch. 37.

153

may be proceeded against and dealt with as if he were a person subject to military law . . .

    Provided that where it is proved that the offence is committed with the intention of assisting the enemy a person convicted of such an offence by a court-martial shall be liable to suffer death.

    (5) For the purpose of the trial of a person for an offence under the regulations by a court of summary jurisdiction . . . the maximum penalty which may be inflicted shall be imprisonment . . . for a term of six months or a fine of one hundred pounds, or both . . . , but any aggrieved by a conviction of a court of summary jurisdiction may appeal in England to a court of quarter sessions. . . .

The Defence of the Realm Act—known to the British people of the last war as DORA—established a virtual state of siege, brought the entire scope of English life and liberty under the control of the government, exalted the Cabinet, and deflated Parliament. It was the foundation for all government in Britain in the first World War.

The Cabinet and the War

It was in the Cabinet, the executive organ of the British government, that the direction of the war effort was naturally centered. World War England affords a striking example of the assertion that "crisis government is primarily and often exclusively the business of the executive branch," for it presented to the world the extraordinary spectacle of the greatest and oldest of parliamentary governments resolving itself into a thoroughgoing cabinet dictatorship. The most remarkable feature of this dictatorship was the ease and spontaneity with which it came to be instituted.

    It should be obvious that of the two chief forms of modern constitutional government, the cabinet and the presidential systems, the former is better suited to the exigencies of crisis rule. If successful constitutional dictatorship involves either a union of the ordinarily separated powers or a simple disregard of that hoary principle of constitutionalism, then it would seem axiomatic that the less rigidly a government conforms to the theory of the separation of powers, the more easily it can adapt itself to the rigors of any particular crisis. The cabinet system possesses a distinct advantage over the presidential variety in its ability to forge the close union of executive and legislative powers so often indispensable in an extended period of national emergency. The former guarantees the existence of a working harmony between the executive and the legislature, the latter does not. Moreover, as Walter Bagehot pointed out,[12] a cabinet government is designed to change its leaders suddenly and without too much fuss, and choose the man and men best qualified to lead the people in time of crisis. In a presidential government such as the United States there is no telling what sort of President might be in office in a period of national emergency, and there is no convenient method of replacing an incompetent man with a strong one (or even a dangerous man with a good one). The British do not have to wait until the next election to find themselves an able man to lead them through an emergency. Finally, a legislature will be more easily persuaded to delegate legislative power to a cabinet which it can unseat at any moment than to a president over whom its control is tenuous or nonexistent. Whatever their relative merits in time of peace and prosperity,[13] there can be no gainsaying the superiority of cabinet over presidential government in time of national emergency. Presidential governments can overcome the crisis disadvantages of the separation of powers principle and function admirably in desperate situations, but crisis government is likely to be more successful in a country under the cabinet system.

The crisis advantages of the cabinet system are more evident in the experience of World War England than in that of World War France. So too are its dangers and disadvantages. Far more completely than in France was the Cabinet freed from legislative control and granted lawmaking capacity. Far more decisively did it dominate the workings of the legislative process and see to it that its bills were put through speedily and in unaltered form. Cabinet dictatorship was a reality in England to a degree that it never was in France. The chief danger of the cabinet, parliamentary system—that the cabinet will attain such ascendancy that it can cast itself loose from the legislature and leave the latter a recording machine capable only of registering automatic approval to executive decrees—was graphically illustrated in the experience of World War Britain.

The reason for this contrast is not far to seek. In Great Britain the rise of the Cabinet to a dominant position was a political fact long before the outbreak of the war.[14] This development was quite in contrast to France where the Parliament, composed of a number of strong and

[12] *The English Constitution* (New York, 1920), pp.99-100.
[13] The literature on this subject is too plentiful to note here. A concise review of the best discussions of the relative merits of the two systems is in Henry Hazlitt: *A New Constitution Now* (New York, 1942), chap. 2.
[14] See Sidney Low: *The Governance of England* (London, 1904), pp.80-81.

ordinarily irreconcilable party groupings and protected from dissolution by constitutional custom, dominated the Council of Ministers. The latter was always a minority or coalition combination and never enjoyed the unique blessing of support in Parliament by a disciplined one-party majority. It is not to be supposed that Parliament was completely erased from the governmental scene in World War England or that the Cabinet effected some revolutionary means for doing away with its responsibility to that organ. It is nevertheless true that, to a much greater degree than in contemporary France, the British Parliament sustained a significant reduction in its legislative and electoral functions. The reverse of this picture means that the Cabinet assumed unusual powers of legislation, was virtually freed from the necessity of a parliamentary vote of confidence (and of the fear that such a vote would not be forthcoming), and enjoyed an almost complete immunity from the legislative oversight ordinarily exercised through the debates and committees of the House of Commons.

The Delegated Dictatorship

THE exclusive responsibility for legislation in the World War rested with the Cabinet. Whether it was the overstuffed and ineffective Cabinet of Mr. Asquith or, after December 10, 1916, the brilliant combination piloted by Lloyd George and his revolutionary War Cabinet, it was upon the shoulders of the Ministry (and the Civil Service) that the legislative burden was squarely placed. Whereas actually as well as nominally the chief producer of important laws in France remained the Chambers themselves, and the government's demand for a large-scale delegation was repulsed with vigor, in England the emergency instrument of the enabling act was resorted to at the outset of the war. Therewith the focus of lawmaking authority in Britain shifted from Parliament to the Cabinet.[15] The Defence of the Realm Act granted the government a sweeping legislative competence, even if the measures thereby authorized were disguised under the label of "regulations." It was always understood that any fundamental measure, particularly one abrogating or amending existing law, would be adopted in the form of a regular statute. Nevertheless, the Defence of the Realm Act constituted the foundation for a major part of the government's legislative activity in this war, and the regulations issued

[15] See Tingsten, *op. cit.*, pp.181 ff., for a discussion of DORA in the light of the enabling acts of other countries.

thereunder were able to derogate from existing law with relative impunity. Moreover, additional authority of this character was presented to the government as the war progressed. The statutes authorizing the creation of the new Ministries of Food, Munitions, Labour, Shipping, National Service, Reconstruction, Pensions, and Air all carried with them broad donations of legislative competence. It must be emphasized that this executive lawmaking was based almost entirely on these delegations, and not on any revival of the long-dead royal prerogative of legislation.[16]

This grant of competence—"His Majesty in Council has power during the continuance of the present war to issue regulations for securing the public safety and the defence of the realm"—gave the Crown "the power to do almost anything for the prosecution of war except spend and tax."[17] An executive that can neither spend nor tax without parliamentary approval cannot be said to have been delegated *pleins pouvoirs* in the strict sense, but a subservient Parliament stood ready to comply with every demand of the government concerning financial matters. As a result, the fiat of the Cabinet was the law of England. Except for budget and tax acts and statutes of the importance of the Military Service Act of 1916, the laws which governed Great Britain in this war came straight from one of the offices in the Ministry and usually cited DORA for their authority. The practice of delegating legislative capacity to departments and boards had long been employed in Britain,[18] but never before on such a scale. The regulations filled volumes and comprised the entire governance of the war effort from the acquisition of huge factories and the strict control of the pressing problems of food supply on down to the regulation of dog shows and the supply of cocaine to actresses.[19] DORA was no trivial delegatory statute employed in isolated instances to aid in the execution of other parliamentary enactments, but a broadly permissive law which provided the legal foundation for a thoroughgoing government by administrative decree. That the grant was originally effected by a Parliament which held a limited conception of its terms is certain. No one had a clear idea how much legis-

---

[16] The leading case confirming the principle that DORA "does not purport to embody in the form of an enactment the Crown's existing prerogative" was *Attorney General v. De Keyser's Hotel* (1920), A.C. 508.

[17] W. Ivor Jennings: *Parliament* (Cambridge, 1940), p.455.

[18] *Ibid.*, pp.451-491; Sir William R. Anson: *The Law and Custom of the Constitution* (4th ed. by A. B. Keith, Oxford, 1935), II (pt. 1), chap. 4; Courtenay Ilbert: *Legislative Methods and Forms* (London, 1901).

[19] The important regulations issued in the course of the war may be found in the *Defence of the Realm Manual* (7th ed., London, 1919), edited by Sir Charles Cook.

lative power was being thus transferred to the Crown-in-Council. The result, if not the original grant of authority, was a delegated dictatorship. "From this grain of mustard seed sprang a goodly forest of regulations."[20]

Neither the Act, Parliament, nor the courts placed any serious limitations upon the Cabinet in the exercise of this competence to enact regulations as far-reaching as regular laws. Only two broad conditions were imposed by the statute itself: the Orders-in-Council were to be made during the war, and for the purpose of securing the public safety and the defense of the realm. The first regulation issued under DORA stated:

> The ordinary avocations of life and the enjoyment of property will be interfered with as little as may be permitted by the exigencies of the measures required to be taken for securing the public safety and the defence of the Realm. . . .[21]

All persons carrying out these regulations were admonished to observe this general principle, and it was for Parliament to see to it that the regulations and the actions taken under them were necessary and proper. Actually, Parliament was almost valueless as an instrument of control over this government by administrative decree. Parliamentary approval of the regulations was not provided in the statute, the members apparently clinging to the mistaken belief that it was not legislative power which they had delegated but simply the authority to issue supplementary rules and orders. Although some decrees were attacked in Parliament, none was ever withdrawn as a direct result, nor was there ever in all the years of the war a general debate on the Defence of the Realm Act.

Being in form nothing more than administrative rules, these regulations, unlike acts of the sovereign Parliament, could be challenged in the courts as *ultra vires*. In practice, however, the courts were no more effective than Parliament in restraining the Cabinet's use of this sweeping grant of power. There were isolated instances of a regulation being voided by a court as beyond the competence of some particular minister,[22] but every one of these came after the conclusion of the war.

[20] Cecil T. Carr: *Delegated Legislation* (Cambridge, 1921), p.18.
[21] *Defence of the Realm Manual* (1919), p.41.
[22] *Chester v. Bateson* (1920), 1 K.B. 829; *Newcastle Breweries v. King* (1920), 1 K.B. 854. The leading decision upholding the broad scope of the regulations issued under DORA is "Zadig's Case," *King v. Halliday* (1917), A.C. 260. The dissent of Lord Shaw of Dumferline is an eloquent plea for circumspection in the use of DORA and in behalf of the Rule of Law. Sir Frederick Pollock in writing to Justice Holmes

The Orders-in-Council issued under DORA were as little subject to judicial review as ordinary laws of Parliament, and thus for all purposes were of statutory character.

The War Cabinet

LONG before 1914 it had become apparent that the peacetime Cabinet was not at all suited to vigorous action, particularly action of an emergency character. It was expected by most observers that the advent of war would force a substantial readjustment in the British executive branch, especially a reduction in size. The "inner cabinet" had always been a problem and occasionally an actuality of British politics.[23] Now in the World War it was to come into its own as the driving force of Britain's constitutional dictatorship.[24]

The outbreak of war found a Liberal Cabinet in office, headed by Henry Asquith and composed of some twenty chiefs of the important ministerial departments. The parliamentary support of this Cabinet was the Liberal Party, which itself failed to constitute a majority in Commons, and the Irish Nationalist and Labour Parties. Contrary to contemporary events in France, there was no spontaneous urge to an *union sacrée*. The Asquith Cabinet, having effected a political truce with the Unionist (conservative) opposition, and having managed to push through its program of emergency legislation, did not alter its Liberal composition except to admit Lord Kitchener as Secretary of State for War. This appointment was itself a two-fold deviation from established practice, for a non-party man was admitted to the Cabinet and a military officer was placed at the head of the War Office. For ten months it was this large, one-party group which was entrusted with the revolutionary powers found necessary for the prosecution of the war. As time went on it began to be more and more seriously questioned in and out of Parliament whether the political composition and size of

(May 14, 1917) expressed surprising impatience with Shaw's opinion and stated: "It is my private opinion that in time of war there is no such thing as the liberty of the subject."

[23] The problem of the inner cabinet is discussed by A. Lawrence Lowell: *The Government of England* (new ed., New York, 1914), I, p.59; Sidney Low: *The Governance of England*, pp.162 ff.

[24] See generally Robert L. Schuyler: "The British War Cabinet," *Pol. Sci. Q.*, XXXIII (1918), p.378; "The British Cabinet, 1916-1919," *Pol. Sci. Q.*, XXXV (1920) p.77; Sidney Low: "The Cabinet Revolution," *Fortnightly Review* (February, 1917); John A. Fairlie: "British War Cabinets," *Mich. L.R.*, XVI (1918), p.471; Jennings: *Cabinet Government*, pp.232 ff.

England's executive organ were in conformity with the exigencies of the times.

The initial result was the establishment on June 3, 1915 of a coalition Cabinet, a radical departure from one of the strongest traditions of parliamentary government in England only made constitutional by "a clear and urgent case of national necessity."[25] In ceding to the threats of the Unionist leaders that either the political texture of the Cabinet be altered or they could no longer maintain their self-imposed restraint of criticism in Parliament, and in forming a Cabinet whose twenty-two members included the chief men in all three of the major parties, Asquith acquiesced to a virtual revolution in the British parliamentary system. There had been coalition Cabinets in England before, but they had been only partially of this character; none had gone to this extent of including the leaders of all the responsible parties in the House of Commons. (The Irish Nationalists were offered representation but declined to serve until Irish Home Rule should be effected.) Eighty-eight per cent of the membership of the lower chamber was now represented in the Cabinet. The English and their Prime Minister had come to realize what seems to be one of the essential prerequisites of constitutional dictatorship in general and of a dictatorial cabinet in particular, that it should be representative of every part of the community interested in the conquest of the crisis and in the maintenance of the constitutional order.

The problem of size remained for solution, and it was soon advocated with vigor in press and Parliament that a smaller body be created within the framework of the Ministry, to be composed of the key men of the British war effort and to be solely responsible for its prosecution. Why give a Cabinet absolute power, it was asked, if it cannot by reason of its size and composition make adequate and vigorous use of it? The consequence of this agitation was the establishment in November 1915 (after several false starts) of a smaller directing body within the confines of the regular Cabinet—the so-called "War Committee," consisting of the Prime Minister, the Secretaries of State for War and for Colonies, the First Lord of the Admiralty, the Minister of Munitions, and the Chancellor of the Exchequer. Founded on the prewar Committee of Imperial Defence, this group was granted the assistance of a military, naval, and diplomatic staff, and was entrusted with the over-all direction of the war effort. The Cabinet at large was to be kept informed of its decisions and was to be consulted before any vital steps were

[25] Asquith, quoted in *The Times History and Encyclopedia of the War*, v, chap. 90, p.316.

taken. Unfortunately this War Committee began shortly to take in the heads of other important departments and eventually became as large as the regular Cabinet itself.

The coalition Cabinet of Mr. Asquith with its steadily distending inner circle was to last another year and finally fall before the trenchant criticism of the press, in which was reflected the evident desire of the people for a more strenuous prosecution of the war.[26] The dénouement came in December 1916 when David Lloyd George, Secretary of State for War, made a proposal that a council of war be constituted from which the Prime Minister was to be excluded, and was rebuffed in this demand. His resignation was followed shortly by that of Asquith and the whole Cabinet. The King turned first to Bonar Law as leader of the Unionist Party, but the latter was unable to form a satisfactory Ministry. Thereupon Lloyd George was called to power. Britain's cabinet system had taken a long time about it, but at last had produced and had established in authority a true crisis executive.

From this time until the termination of the emergency Lloyd George conducted a vigorous cabinet dictatorship, operating through a constitutional innovation even more revolutionary than the coalition composition of the Ministry—the renowned "War Cabinet." The Ministry, swollen under the pressure of war to almost ninety members,[27] was left intact, and the department heads continued their usual tasks. But the system of a Cabinet of twenty-odd "tired men," containing within itself a smaller War Committee composed of several of these same tired men, was now abandoned. In its stead was created one Cabinet of five men which assumed the whole responsibility for the direction of the war effort, and these men were to devote all their time to that end. This revolutionary nucleus was the only Cabinet in the government. All other heads of departments were shunted into the mammoth and formless Ministry. The War Cabinet was composed of Lloyd George (Liberal) as Prime Minister, Lord Curzon (Unionist) as President of the Council, Bonar Law (Unionist) as Chancellor of the Exchequer and leader of the House of Commons, and Lord Milner (Unionist) and Arthur Henderson (Labour) as Ministers without portfolio. Only Bonar Law held an important administrative post. The men who were

[26] The attack in the press was led by Northcliffe's *Daily Mail.* Its most vigorous editorial against the Asquith government and its "twenty-three men who can never make up their minds" is given in E. M. Sait and D. P. Barrows: *British Politics in Transition* (Yonkers, 1925), pp.36-39.

[27] A complete list of the ministers of the World War period may be found in John A. Fairlie: *British War Administration* (New York, 1919), pp.53-58.

to formulate and execute the war policy that was to bring victory to Britain had cut themselves loose from active direction of administration and henceforth wielded only a casual control over the ever-multiplying myriad of administrative departments. This radical departure from the ancient prescriptions of the British Constitution was not the result of a parliamentary vote or a decision taken in the Crown's Council, but of a simple agreement between the leaders of the various parties dictated by the indispensable Lloyd George.[28] Such are the ways of the greatest of parliamentary governments.

The members of the War Cabinet not only abandoned all duties of an exclusively administrative nature; they also withdrew themselves from participation in the proceedings of Parliament and became an executive quite apart from the legislature, a radical departure from the tenets of parliamentary government and a near approach to the separation of executive and legislative branches exemplified in the American presidential system. Lloyd George gave up his position as leader of the House of Commons and attended its sessions only on special occasions. The constant stream of ministers, generals, diplomats, dominion representatives, and other experts who attended the sessions of the omnipotent five were occasionally given explanations of some of his important policies, but the nation's representatives in Parliament were virtually ignored. After a few months Bonar Law retired from the War Cabinet; there remained no member of this body whose regular attendance in Commons was to be expected. Only a sufficient amount of contact was maintained with the emasculated Parliament to allay distrust and to keep it from acting up. The people and Parliament acquiesced in this constitutional revolution because it seemed the necessary step to take.

Among the minor innovations instituted in the course of the war were: the abandonment of the collective responsibility of the Ministry, although the War Cabinet itself remained collectively responsible; the renunciation of the ancient custom of Cabinet secrecy with the initiation of minutes; the establishment of a permanent secretariat; the inclusion of General Smuts as an active member of this inner circle in 1917; and the exclusion from a policy-determining Cabinet of the Secretaries for War and Foreign Affairs as well as the First Lord of the Admiralty.[29]

The crisis potential of the cabinet system of government has never

---

[28] Lloyd George's defense of this plan is printed in Sait and Barrows, *op. cit.*, pp.39-41. See also his *War Memoirs* (Boston, 1933-1936), III, pp.1063-1064.

[29] These innovations are outlined and the procedure adopted by the Cabinet summarized in *The War Cabinet: Report for the Year 1917* (London, 1918), pp.1-3.

been more dramatically illustrated than in this British experience of the first World War. The manner in which the world's leading parliamentary government was gradually converted into an unvarnished cabinet dictatorship is a fascinating and instructive chapter in the history of British government and politics.

Parliament and the War

THE rise of the Cabinet was matched step for step by the decline of Parliament, and the role of the British legislature in World War I was much less effective than that played by its French counterpart. The legislative function was given away by Parliament with the passage of the Defence of the Realm Acts, and although all the more important laws enacted in the course of the war were in the constitutional form of regular statutes, the members and committees of Parliament had precious little to do with their evolution and passage. The vital statutes which regulated the British war effort were worked out in detail in the ministries and railroaded through Parliament without amendment or protest. The normal processes of Parliament were abbreviated or abandoned. Debate was cut short and measures of the highest importance became law with bewildering speed. Whenever the downtrodden back-benchers raised serious objections to a particular bill or clause, it was dropped to reappear a few days later in the form of a DORA regulation. Particularly in financial matters was the status of Parliament that of "a machine for registering magisterial edicts."[30] The practice of parliamentary initiative was abandoned in early 1915, "the first occasion in the history of any Parliament in which it (had) been formally surrendered for an indefinite period."[31] Never once in all the course of the war did Parliament show that it retained any of its ancient independence and initiative in legislative matters. Its only value was to give a democratic form to the dictatorial edicts of an autocratic Cabinet.

In the last resort, it was the emasculation of Parliament's usual powers of election and control that permitted this cabinet dictatorship to rule England's destiny through all these years.[32] In the consequential alteration of the Asquith Cabinet in June 1915 the Parliament played practically no part, following meekly the leadership of the party chiefs in

[30] F. A. Ogg: *English Government and Politics* (New York, 1929), p.129.
[31] "The United Kingdom: Parliament" in *Political Quarterly* (May, 1915), p.163.
[32] Indeed, it can hardly be said that Parliament exercised any of Bagehot's five functions—the electoral, expressive, teaching, informing, or legislative—to any extent in the course of the war. See Bagehot, *op. cit.*, chap. 5.

their revolutionary decision to form the first outright coalition Cabinet in the history of England. In the elevation of Lloyd George to power it played even less of a part. The chiefs of the different parties, all of them members of the Cabinet itself, made the decisions concerning the composition and character of this group to be charged with the execution of the war, and the back-benchers voted approval without protest or hesitation. The Northcliffe press wielded more influence in this incident than Parliament itself. The separation of the executive and legislative branches which became a reality in the last part of the war was personified in Lloyd George, who in actual fact drew his strength from outside Parliament and owed his unquestioned independence and ascendancy "to a kind of informal and irregular, but unmistakably emphatic plebiscite. The House of Commons did not make him premier; it is doubtful whether it could unmake him."[33] Had Parliament not wanted Lloyd George, it could have unseated him; but the impeachment of a President of the United States would hardly have caused more difficulty and excitement.

The day-to-day powers of parliamentary control also fell into disuse, and few efforts were made to resuscitate or revamp them as was successfully done in France. The initiative in the suspension of the usual practices of parliamentary criticism and questioning was taken by the opposition party itself in August 1914. The forbearance of the Unionists lasted until June 1915, when the possibility of a sudden outburst of criticism in Commons was forestalled by the formation of Asquith's all-party Cabinet. From this time until the end of the war organized opposition was nonexistent, the burden of parliamentary criticism falling upon a small group of independent radicals and Socialists who sniped away with no evident success at Lloyd George's "committee of public safety." Indeed, the House of Lords had a much better record than Commons in the liberalism and effectiveness of its debates. Most of the ministers, most conspicuously the members of the War Cabinet, practically ceased attendance at the sessions of Parliament, overburdened as they were with their manifold duties and realizing that it was unnecessary to go down to a House of Commons which had no power to turn them out. Discussions of war policy went on in Commons throughout the war, but many times there was not one responsible minister on hand to defend the government against the inquiries of the handful of members of Parliament who had not entered the Ministry or the armed

[33] Low: "The Cabinet Revolution," *Fortnightly Review* (February, 1917), p.212.

forces. Many of the Ministry had no seat in Parliament at all, another departure from normal constitutional practice.

The status which the British Parliament occupied in the first World War has been described by one political writer as "humiliating,"[34] a judgment as true as it is harsh. Hear too the testimony of an eminent Englishman who was on the spot to witness the dismal decline of the Mother of Parliaments: "At the present time the idea of parliamentary government in this country is nothing more than a farce."[35] Like the Senate of Rome, the sovereign legislature of Great Britain withdrew from the field of battle, saying: *"Videant consules ne quid res publica detrimenti capiat."*

The War and British Liberty

THIS substantial alteration in the structure and operation of the British government had its counterpart in a substantial alteration in the relations between the government and its subjects, manifesting itself in a significant invasion of the peacetime freedom of the ordinary citizen. For the duration of the war the ancient British liberties—consecrated in such documents as Magna Charta, the Petition of Right, and the Bill of Rights—were at the mercy of the government. It was the Defence of the Realm Act which initiated this change in the British political pattern, a change which may be regarded as nothing more or less than a preventive state of siege, as "martial law and something more."[36] The Act itself and the regulations issued under it "struck down with a single blow the personal liberties and rights of property which had been held as the most sacred tradition of the British Constitution."[37] The ordinary citizen who minded his own business suffered little hardship and may scarcely have realized that his liberties were actually mere playthings of the government, but in case of necessity the authorities were prepared to and did invade such rights as those of personal freedom, property, public assembly, speech and press, inviolability of domicile, and jury trial.

Personal freedom was severely limited by such regulations as No. 55 empowering "any person authorized for the purpose by the competent

[34] Charles G. Fenwick: *Political Systems in Transition* (New York, 1920), p.86.
[35] Lord Parmoor in the House of Lords: *Parl. Deb.* (1917), Lords, XXIV, p.418. In this powerful speech he contrasted vividly the respective roles played by the French and English Parliaments in the war.
[36] Baty and Morgan: *War: Its Conduct and Legal Results*, p.111.
[37] Fenwick, *op. cit.*, p.90. "The English Defence of the Realm Regulations . . . struck a rather vicious blow at the Rule of Law, but the time was abnormal."—Willoughby and Rogers: *An Introduction to the Problem of Government*, p.96.

naval or military authority" to "arrest without warrant any person whose behavior is of such a nature as to give reasonable grounds for suspecting that he is acting or has acted or is about to act in a manner prejudicial to the public safety or the defence of the Realm," or 14B permitting the government a somewhat circumscribed power of detention of persons of "hostile origin or associations." By virtue of other such regulations the right to move about or reside as one pleased was sharply abridged and subjected to governmental requirements. Public assemblies were controlled more strongly than usual by the police, although they were not forbidden outright. The inviolability of domicile could not be allowed to obstruct searches and seizures undertaken to detect and foil enemy espionage activity. Regulations under DORA empowered the competent military or police authorities to institute searches and seizures without warrant by day or night on the sole ground that there was "reason to suspect" the premises were being used for purposes prejudicial to the public safety or defense of the realm.[38]

The freedoms of speech and press were both subjected to the control of the government by the provision in the Defence of the Realm Act authorizing the issuance of regulations designed "to prevent the spread of false reports or reports likely to cause disaffection to His Majesty or to interfere with the success of His Majesty's forces by land or sea or to prejudice His Majesty's relations with foreign powers." Under this provision a number of regulations were published providing severe punishment for any spoken or printed word that might be regarded as obstructing the prosecution of the war.[39] Supplementing the regular laws of libel, sedition, and treason—the "Law of the Press"—these regulations produced what amounted to a voluntary self-censorship of English journalism. A press bureau was set up in the Home Office, and doubtful articles were submitted to its scrutiny.[40] Under the guidance of this bureau and the various departmental offices a preventive censorship of war and diplomatic news and all cabled material was maintained. The consequence was the usual desultory but reasonably effective democratic wartime control of the press—part outright censorship, part cooperation, part threat, and once in a while punishment by suppression, fine, or even imprisonment. There was the usual grumbling, some of it warranted, and there were mistakes; but on the whole the control of the press in wartime England answered the requirements of emergency gov-

[38] Regs. no. 51, etc.
[39] Regs. no. 27, 27A, 27B, 27C.
[40] Sir Edward Troup: *The Home Office* (London, 1925), pp.244-245.

ernment and democracy alike.[41] Essential information was kept from the enemy, irresponsible criticism and demoralizing slander were almost nonexistent, and yet the press remained free and powerful enough to play a vital part in such an important governmental change as the overturn of the Asquith government and the induction into power of Lloyd George.

Unquestionably the most dictatorial abridgment of English liberty was effected by the provisions of the Defence of the Realm Act authorizing the trial and punishment by courts-martial, or in minor offenses by courts of summary jurisdiction, of persons violating the regulations issued under the Act. This amounted to an outright deprivation of the ancient right of trial by jury, for in the proceedings before the court-martial the person apprehended was to be "dealt with as if he were a person subject to military law and had in active service committed an offence under section five of the Army Act." According to this section the maximum punishment is imprisonment for life, but the Defence of the Realm Act of November 27, 1914 provided the death penalty for offenses committed by persons "with the intention of assisting the enemy." The practical results were the suspension of the writ of habeas corpus and the extension of military law to the entire population. For the first time in generations an Englishman could go to a legal execution without benefit of trial by jury. The remarkable thing is how little comment this evoked in English public life. The compliant House of Commons passed this drastic amendment to the original Defence of the Realm Act without a word of dissent; vigorous but fruitless opposition was registered in Lords by Halsbury, Loreburn, and Bryce.[42]

To be sure, the possible far outstripped the actual. It is not to be understood that a complete regime of military courts was instituted throughout Britain for the duration of the war. On the contrary, the government never made use of the possibilities authorized in the Defence of the Realm Act on a scale likely to arouse public suspicion and protest. Regulation No. 1 under DORA had provided that "ordinary civil offences will be dealt with by the civil tribunals in the ordinary course of law," and throughout the war the regular courts adjudicated all but the most flagrant offenses against the state. The Ministry used

[41] See generally Gaston Jèze: *"Le Régime Juridique de la Presse en Angleterre pendant la Guerre,"* a series of five articles, *Rev. Dr. Pub.*, XXXII and XXXIII (1915-1916).

[42] The case against the courts-martial is summarized in Baty and Morgan, *op. cit.*, chap. 3. They regard the death penalty by court-martial as "a blot on the Statute-book," and DORA in general "as the kind of legislation hitherto exclusively reserved for uncivilized protectorates."

its extensive competence with evident restraint and circumspection. Nevertheless, popular pressure and the determined exertions of several eminent members of the House of Lords finally resulted in an amendment to the Defence of the Realm Act on March 16, 1915,[43] giving an accused Briton the right to jury trial for offenses previously liable to trial before a court-martial. The trial of aliens by the civil courts was left to the option of the government. Even as to British subjects, the right thus established, or rather reestablished, could be suspended by the Crown in case of invasion or other emergency, and the trial by court-martial be reinstituted.

The World War experiences of France and England in this matter of military trials of civil offenses were remarkably similar. In each instance provision was made for a complete regime of military courts, and in each instance popular opinion and governmental self-restraint brought a significant diminution of the power of the special courts. Trials were held as much as possible according to normal methods, although the extreme military procedure was always retained for instantaneous use in case of emergency.

There were other rights whose unrestricted enjoyment in time of peace contributed to the maintenance of England as a democratic and constitutional state, but whose unrestricted enjoyment in time of war might have constituted a fatal obstruction to victory. One of the great rights, or more correctly luxuries, of English citizenship was a unique freedom from compulsory military service. It took the government a long time to proceed to the radical, if admittedly provisional step of conscription (the Military Service Act was finally promulgated January 27, 1916), but the step was one which had to be taken. Thereby a democratic duty replaced an accidental privilege. Another significant abrogation of a normal democratic right was effected through a series of statutes postponing general and by-elections to the House of Commons for the duration of the war, as well as local elections. The statutory limit for the duration of Commons fixed in the Parliament Act of 1911 was about to expire in 1915 when a bill was enacted extending the life of the House for several months.[44] Subsequent statutes prolonged this until December 1918. A general election, it was agreed by all, was impractical and dangerous *durante bello*.

The right to strike, although never suppressed in wartime Britain by any comprehensive statute or governmental action, was seriously cur-

---

[43] 5 Geo. v, ch. 28.   [44] 5 & 6 Geo. v, ch. 76.

tailed by various laws and administrative measures.[45] There were plenty
of strikes throughout the war,[46] none of which was of serious proportions or a rebellious character. Several might well have been disastrous,
but trouble was forestalled by strenuous governmental action based on
the Defence of the Realm Acts or other statutes. For example, continued strikes in the coal mines forced the government to take over the
entire industry. Most strikes were one or two day affairs, designed to
dramatize the usual grievances of rising prices and employer profiteer-
ing. Voluntary renunciation of the right to strike by the trade unions
was an important means of cutting down the number of industrial disputes. In 1915 the unions made an open promise to the government to
surrender their acknowledged freedom to strike. Especially in those industries which eventually came under direct governmental control or
operation—the railroads, munitions factories, shipyards, and mines—
was the peacetime conflict between employer and employee suppressed in
keeping with the exigencies of the war. An example is the munitions industry, where the practice of compulsory arbitration before the Board of
Trade was introduced by the Munitions of War Act of 1915.[47] The emergency and provisional character of this procedure was frankly admitted
in the Ministry of Munitions Act.[48] In other industries boards were set
up to arbitrate or conciliate the reciprocal grievances of labor and capital.
By legislation, regulations, pleas for moderation, formal and informal
cooperation, and in a few instances outright coercion and the imprisonment of union leaders under DORA, the government brought the freedom of labor into conformity with the demands of the crisis. Although
repeatedly advocated, no conscription of labor was ever introduced; all
efforts in this respect were of a noncoercive character.

Finally, the experience of World War England, like that of World
War France, offers conclusive proof of the universality of some degree
of "state socialism" as an accessory to emergency government in periods
of extended crisis. To investigate the ramifications of this economic aspect of war government in Britain would be to digress too far from the
limited scope of this book. It must be sufficient to state the facts in brief:
that England, the country of Adam Smith and the Manchester Liberals
(but also of Robert Owen and the Fabians), was driven by the necessi-

[45] The entire problem of labor and the war is exhaustively treated by M. B. Hammond: *British Labor Conditions and Legislation During the War* (New York, 1919).
See chap. 10 in each of the War Cabinet *Reports*.
[46] See the table in Hammond, *op. cit*, p.235.
[47] 5 & 6 Geo. v, ch. 54. See also 5 & 6 Geo. v, ch. 99; 7 & 8 Geo. v, ch. 45.
[48] 5 & 6 Geo. v, ch. 51.

ties of a long war to an increasingly vigorous control and management of privately owned and operated institutions of production and supply.[49] In characteristic democratic fashion this control was established only gradually by piecemeal legislation and regulations. The outbreak of war was followed by state intervention in the railroad industry, the tenets of free enterprise being satisfied by compensation to the owners, but otherwise the Asquith Ministry resorted to only "tentative action" and relied on voluntary methods for the necessary readjustments of British business and industry to the abnormalities of war. The second Asquith government proceeded to "determined regulation," and DORA was used more and more frequently to provide strict control of the important industries. The socialization of the munitions industry was based upon the Munitions of War Act of 1915. Finally, the advent of Lloyd George ushered in a policy of "stringent regulation," and throughout the remainder of the war British economic life was severely controlled or directly managed by the many departments of the Ministry. Food, textiles, shipping, mines, munitions, transport—all were governmentally regulated or operated. By March of 1917 every coal mine in Britain was being managed directly by the government. By 1918 the country was well on the road to socialism.

[49] See generally H. L. Gray: *Wartime Control of Industry; The Experience of England* (New York, 1918) ; C. W. Baker: *Governmental Control and Operation of Industry in Great Britain and the United States During the World War* (New York, 1921) ; War Cabinet *Reports*: (1917), chap. 13; (1918), chap. 12.

CHAPTER XII

Crisis Government in Great Britain, 1919-1939

THE return of peace was followed shortly by the reestablishment of the normal pattern of British government. Although the impact of this supreme war effort had wrought permanent changes in the whole fabric of English economy and society, the political life and institutions of the nation were comparatively unaffected and were not long in reverting to prewar ways. Parliament began to rise from the Slough of Despond immediately after the elections of December 1918, and although it has never regained its nineteenth century status of independence, prestige, and factual superiority, it must be remembered that the ascendancy of the Cabinet was a political fact even before the war. The experience of 1914-1919 only served to strengthen that dominant position. The War Cabinet, as well as most of its accompanying innovations, was abandoned by Lloyd George in the face of growing criticism in October 1919. The hopes of the reformers that a radical reconstruction of the Cabinet would be instituted for peacetime purposes were shattered by a complete restoration of the old twenty-man executive.[1] The separation of policy-determination and administration was not regarded as salutary in England at peace, however successful this innovation had been in England at war. The only lasting change was the establishment of the Cabinet secretariat on a permanent basis.

The several liberties and privileges of the people which had undergone a sizable restriction in the years of the war were restored to their full stature. Much of the control of industry was relaxed (unquestionably a bit too hastily), but much was retained. (This is one crisis alteration that is very difficult to erase completely upon the return of normal conditions.) Finally, the regulations enacted under the Defence of the Realm Acts were either established by statute on a permanent basis, repealed expressly by other regulations or orders, or allowed to die a natural death. An Act of Indemnity was passed in 1920 staying all legal proceedings "in respect of any act, matter or thing done . . . during the war . . . if done in good faith, and done or purported to be done . . . for the de-

---

[1] The indispensability of the small Cabinet in war and its unsuitability in peace is well stated by Harold Laski: *Parliamentary Government in England* (New York, 1938), pp.205-207.

fence of the realm or the public safety."[2] The competence of the government under DORA came to an official end August 31, 1921, the date declared by the Crown-in-Council (empowered by the Termination of War Act of 1918)[3] as the legal termination of the war. England was back to normal. The crisis had been mastered, and the Constitution again held sway throughout the land. But in the darkness of war a new and revolutionary idea had crept into English constitutional law and was now allowed to remain: the continental theory and practice of emergency powers.

The Emergency Powers Act of 1920

THE clean break with the tradition of the common law and martial law, indeed with the whole of British constitutional development, was effected in the Emergency Powers Act of 1920.[4] The most important provisions of this significant statute run:

An Act to make exceptional provision for the Protection of the community in cases of Emergency.

I. (1) If at any time it appears to His Majesty that any action has been taken or is immediately threatened by any persons or body of persons of such a nature and on so extensive a scale as to be calculated, by interfering with the supply and distribution of food, water, fuel, or light, or with the means of locomotion, to deprive the community, or any substantial portion of the community, of the essentials of life, His Majesty may, by proclamation . . . declare that a state of emergency exists.

No such proclamation shall be in force for more than one month. . . .

(2) Where a proclamation of emergency has been made, the occasion thereof shall forthwith be communicated to Parliament, and, if Parliament is then separated by such adjournment or prorogation as will not expire within five days, a proclamation shall be issued for the meeting of Parliament within five days, and Parliament shall accordingly meet and sit . . . and continue to sit. . . .

II. (1) . . . it shall be lawful for His Majesty in Council, by Order, to make regulations for securing the essentials of life to the community, and those regulations may confer or impose on a Secretary of State or other Government department, or any other persons in His Majesty's service or acting on His Majesty's behalf, such powers and duties as His Majesty may deem necessary for the preservation of the peace, for securing and regulating the supply and distribution of food, water, fuel, light, and other neces-

---

[2] 10 & 11 Geo. v, ch. 48.
[3] 8 & 9 Geo. v, ch. 59. But the Act itself did not leave the statute book until 1927.
[4] 10 & 11 Geo. v, ch. 55.

sities, for maintaining the means of transit or locomotion, and for any other purposes essential to the public safety and the life of the community. . . .

Provided that nothing in this Act shall be construed to authorize the making of any regulations imposing any form of compulsory military service or industrial conscription.

Provided also that no such regulation shall make it an offence for any person or persons to take part in a strike, or peacefully to persuade any other person or persons to take part in a strike.

(2) Any regulations so made shall be laid before Parliament as soon as may be after they are made, and shall not continue in force after the expiration of seven days from the time when they are so laid unless a resolution is passed by both Houses providing for the continuance thereof.

(3) The regulations may provide for the trial, by courts of summary jurisdiction, of persons guilty of offences against the regulations; . . . the maximum penalty . . . shall be imprisonment with or without hard labor for a term of three months, or a fine of one hundred pounds, or both. . . .

(4) The regulations so made shall have effect as if enacted in this Act. . . .

III. (2) This Act shall not apply to Ireland.

It is obvious that the Emergency Powers Act, directed as it is toward one part of the community and one narrow type of emergency, sets up an extremely controversial instrument of constitutional dictatorship. Wisely or unwisely, the Parliament of England found it necessary to make provision for an emergency device based on the continental pattern—to guarantee that the people would be fed and warmed whenever widespread strikes should threaten to disrupt the normal production and distribution of necessities. As such, this statute is clearly a constitutional instrument of crisis government. That it is uniquely available as an instrument of reaction cannot be denied, but the truth of the matter is that every device of constitutional dictatorship is in its nature ideally suited to be employed as a weapon of reaction and class struggle. Article 48 could first maintain and then destroy democracy in Germany; the Emergency Powers Act could also be used to further or obstruct the progress of a constitutional England. Everything depends upon the men who wield emergency authority. That a Labour government stood ready to use this controversial crisis power will shortly be noted.

The Emergency Powers Act was passed October 29, 1920 upon the urgent request of Lloyd George's government, at that very moment bogged down in a swamp of political confusion in its attempt to solve a bitter strike in the coal mines as well as to forestall the possibility of a general strike. The government felt keenly the need for extraordinary authority to proceed to the drastic measures necessary to protect the

173

community at large from the sudden halt in the production of an indispensable commodity. With the remembrance of DORA and the power it had brought them still fresh in their minds, the members of the Cabinet decided to ask Parliament for a direct grant of emergency competence, couched in terms of a permanent statute. In the heated debates in Commons the Prime Minister insisted strongly on the continuity of this statute with the Defence of the Realm Act,[5] regarding the new proposal as a peacetime substitution for the latter and an invaluable adjunct to the maintenance of order in the social and economic community. Bonar Law, in introducing this bill, had also linked it with DORA and had pointed to similar provisions in the laws of other countries.[6] The government itself was forced to admit the extreme inopportunity of the moment to demand the passage of such a statute, and yet it was put through over the bitter protests of the Labour members of Commons by a vote of 238-58 after but one week in parliamentary transit. It is interesting to note the lack of speculation in the debates concerning the constitutional and comparative nature of this law, most of the argument centering upon the burning question whether or not it was an outright attempt to coerce the miners. Although the opponents of the measure did not fail to appeal to the Constitution and the "ancient liberties" as forbidding such a law,[7] the revolutionary nature of this grant of extraordinary power was at no time clearly expressed. The speeches of the opposition were aimed at the government rather than at the bill, and cries of "dictatorship," "coercion," and "reaction" filled the air. Although the opposition could not block the passage of the Act, it did manage to mitigate several of its more severe provisions by sensible amendments. Thus was nailed into the laws of England "the first Coercion Bill since the days of Castlereagh."[8]

Ever since 1920 then, the British government has been armed with emergency powers foreseen and foreordained in the approved continental manner. The Emergency Powers Act is a much less dictatorial weapon than was DORA, for a number of powerful limitations are placed upon its arbitrary or excessive use. When compared with Article 48 of the Weimar Constitution, its potency and flexibility as a weapon of emergency rule appear to be almost unreliable. The time limit of one month

[5] *Parl. Deb.* (1920), Commons, CXXXIII: p.1451.
[6] *Parl. Deb.* (1920), Commons, CXXXIII: p.1399.
[7] See Chih-Mai Chen: *Parliamentary Opinion of Delegated Legislation* (New York, 1933), p.121, n. 27.
[8] Willoughby and Rogers: *An Introduction to the Problem of Government*, p.97. They attest the revolutionary character of this Act by calmly informing Professor Dicey that he "will have to rewrite *The Law of the Constitution*," p.100.

on the extent of any one proclamation, the obvious restriction of its application to strikes of only the most serious nature and the most pressing inconvenience to the national community, the immediate convocation and continued sitting of Parliament for the duration of the emergency, the necessity for positive parliamentary approval within seven days for the continued validity of all regulations issued by Order-in-Council, the fixing of a maximum penalty in the Act itself for the punishment of violations of regulations issued under it—all these are limitations completely and unfortunately absent from the loose terms of Article 48. All of them are limitations which go a long way toward guaranteeing a circumspect employment of the extraordinary freedom of action which the Emergency Powers Act affords.

It is important to note two other restraining provisions in the Act, provisions particularly designed to vitiate its potentialites as a strike-breaking instrument in disguise: the specific prohibition against military and industrial conscription—a provision precluding any such solution to a general strike as was effected by the French Cabinet in the fall of 1938 when it mobilized all workers of a public character—and that against the issuance of any regulation making it an "offence for any person or persons to take part in a strike, or peacefully to persuade any other person or persons to take part in a strike." Finally, the Emergency Powers Act, in authorizing the issuance of regulations having "effect as if enacted in this Act," takes on the character of a permanent if limited enabling statute. Thus was established in English law a permanent instrument of constitutional dictatorship, an innovation whose revolutionary character has been recognized by most British jurists.[9] Its purpose was not so much to provide a mechanism designed to deal with violent rebellions, although it might conceivably be employed to such an end, but rather to bestow an extraordinary if well-guarded competence upon the executive branch of the government to act swiftly and drastically in the event of calamitous strikes in industries vital to the security and welfare of the realm, that is, to prevent any serious interference with the freedom of transport or with the production, supply, and distribution of a commodity essential to the health and well-being of the nation.

The Emergency Powers Act of 1920 has been used on three separate occasions to enable the government to maintain public safety and welfare before the distressing effects of widespread industrial unrest. The

[9] See for example A. B. Keith: *Constitutional Law: Being the Seventh Edition of Ridge's Constitutional Law of England* (London, 1939), p.216.

great coal strike of 1921 was the signal for a royal proclamation of emergency based on the "immediate threat of cessation of work in the coal mines."[10] An Order-in-Council, prepared by the Home Office after consultation with the various departments, was immediately promulgated, conferring all powers necessary to guarantee the continued flow of this fuel so vital to the British nation.[11] New proclamations under which the Cabinet was able to ration the available stock of coal were issued April 30, May 27, and June 27. The emergency ceased with the termination of the strike on July 4. The country had been able to proceed in a reasonably normal manner despite the three months' stoppage of coal production. Again in 1924 serious strikes in major industries threatened, although Britain's first Labour government had just taken office. Under the compulsion of a London transport strike a proclamation of emergency was announced March 28,[12] but was immediately revoked when the government managed to settle the issue before a full strike was called. The significant feature of this abortive crisis was the apparent willingness of Labour in power and responsibility to make use of this Act which it had opposed so bitterly, and was to oppose even more bitterly again.

Finally, the great General Strike of 1926 evoked a series of emergency proclamations, the first on April 30,[13] the last on November 20. A succession of drastic regulations was issued as Orders-in-Council and was approved by the government's secure parliamentary majority.[14] The protests of the Labour members that the Act was tyrannous and unconstitutional were met by Conservative debaters who pointed to the willingness of the MacDonald Cabinet to make use of this power in 1924. A complete code of regulations was promulgated by the government, greatly facilitating the maintenance of a sufficient supply of public essentials without inciting any serious clashes between police and strikers. These ordinances were chiefly directed to the production and distribution of fuel and food. Ministers were given power to requisition necessities and property of a public character, as well as to fix prices, and individual liberties suffered sizable abridgment. The regulations authorized summary police action against attempts to incite disaffection. The government pursued a policy of employing regular courts and judicial procedures for the trial of all offenses against the regulations or breaches of the peace, even the serious crime of train-wrecking. The end of the strike was followed by a cancellation of these emergency powers and

[10] *London Gazette*, May 1, 1921.
[12] *London Gazette*, April 1, 1924.
[14] *S.R.O.* (1926), pp.485 ff.
[11] *S.R.O.* (1921), pp.1612-1617.
[13] *London Gazette*, May 1, 1926.

the remission of almost all sentences for crimes committed in the furtherance of the strike itself.

Since 1926 there has been no resort to the Emergency Powers Act. It remains available for the use of the government in the event of a recurrence of the industrial strife of the 1920's. The sincere and successful use of crisis authority in any country and under any circumstances calls for statesmanship of the highest caliber, in no instance more so than in the case of the Emergency Powers Act, this English "minor state of siege." It can be used as an instrument of oppression and reaction; it can be used as an invaluable means of providing the people with the necessities of life in the event of a serious strike in a manner unprejudicial to the interests of either of the factions locked in the struggle. It is for other methods of government to discover where the right in the matter resides and to effect a settlement. It is for the authorities under the Emergency Powers Act to see to it that the nation is kept at peace and in health, without reference to the merits of the dispute. Whether it is to be judiciously and democratically employed is for English statesmanship to decide, not the terms of the statute itself. Whatever else it is, it is a revolution in English politics and government.

The Crisis of 1931-1932

POSTWAR Great Britain, a country where politics remained a means rather than an end and where constitutional democracy showed itself to be rooted in the lives and consciences of the people as it never was in Weimar Germany, was happily spared the ravages of the political and social decay which was eating the heart out of half the democracies of Europe. The malignant cancer of political extremism and the dry rot of parliamentary irresponsibility could never find a sufficiently vulnerable spot in the English body politic. With the exception of the General Strike of 1926, the British government was not once called upon to meet a serious national crisis engendered by social or political maladjustment. In regard to the economic maladies of this era, however, the experience of England was no different from that of the other nations of the world. Although the total collapse of the mark and the near collapse of the franc were not paralleled by the postwar career of the pound sterling, the several world-wide depressions of the 1920's and 1930's had the same general impact on Britain as they did on the less stable countries of Europe—unbalanced budget, severe unemployment, calamitous depreciation of security values, industrial stagnation, and a dangerous weakening of the entire financial structure. To meet the recurrent economic crises of these years the government was generally able to work through Parliament itself, and drastic emergency laws were enacted in the normal manner. Throughout the large part of the postwar period the modern British parliamentary system—a dominant Cabinet and a well-disciplined majority in the House of Commons—was flourishing at its strongest, and the ordinary procedures of legislation were able to produce whatever solutions were thought necessary for the nation's urgent economic problems.

One of these economic upheavals, however, was of such magnitude as to appear to the government to defy suppression by ordinary parliamentary methods. This was the severe economic depression of 1931-1932, when England like the rest of the world was beset by all the symptoms which portend a serious collapse of the national economy. To face this ominous situation the Cabinet decided to have recourse to the standard crisis device of the enabling act. Parliament was asked to empower the government to adopt measures, in the guise of Orders-in-Council or departmental regulations, which would ordinarily require statutory enactment. The trend toward the practice of delegated legislation had been pronounced since the war, but this was the first instance since the Emergency Powers Act of 1920 of a large-scale delegation of lawmaking power for emergency purposes. In the debates on the statutes which gave the Cabinet this power, their emergency character was emphasized by repeated reference to DORA and the Emergency Powers Act. Prime Minister MacDonald remarked that emergency legislation had "characterized the whole history of Parliamentary government in this country. First one emergency and then another has had to be dealt with, not by maintaining the normal procedure of the House of Commons, for the simple reason that the House of Commons, in the circumstances, could not maintain its normal procedure."[15]

The "National Government" of Ramsay MacDonald was granted temporary powers of executive lawmaking by five separate statutes. The Gold Standard (Amendment) Act of September 21, 1931,[16] besides effecting an abandonment of the gold standard and indemnifying the Bank of England for acting in the previous three days (at the request of the Cabinet) as if that standard had already been abandoned, empowered the Treasury to adopt all measures necessary "to meet difficulties arising in connection with the suspension of the gold standard."

[15] *Parl. Deb.* (1931), Commons, CCLVI: p.419.
[16] 21 & 22 Geo. v, ch. 46.

This grant was limited to six months' duration, but was extended to March 20, 1933 by a statute of March 17, 1932.[17]

The National Economy Act of September 30, 1931 authorized the issuance of Orders-in-Council effecting drastic economies in the fields of education, health, unemployment insurance, police, and public works, and in respect to "remuneration . . . of persons in His Majesty's Service."[18] Parliament gave the Cabinet exactly one month to slash the salaries of all servants of the King as well as expenditures in the public services specifically mentioned. Furthermore, the Cabinet could proceed to "the modification or termination of statutory or contractual rights, obligations and restrictions subsisting at the date when the provisions of the Order take effect." Although existing law and contracts could be suspended or abrogated by a simple decree, there was no provision for direct parliamentary oversight of these regulations. This was indeed a radical grant of delegated power for emergency purposes.

In connection with the three other emergency acts delegating legislative competence, the express approval of Parliament was required. The Foodstuffs (Prevention of Exploitation) Act of October 7, 1931 empowered the Board of Trade to issue statutory orders "for preventing or remedying shortages in, or unreasonable increases in the price of . . . any article of food or drink of general consumption."[19] The power to prescribe trial by courts of summary jurisdiction for offenses against such regulations was granted, the statute itself fixing penalties and forbidding the alteration of existing procedure in criminal cases or punishment without trial. All orders were to be laid before each House "as soon as may be after they are made," and either House could void such order within twenty days through an address to the Crown. The Act was limited to six months' duration, but was also extended to March 20, 1933. The Abnormal Importations (Customs Duties) Act of November 20, 1931 authorized the Board of Trade, with the concurrence of the Treasury, to levy or raise customs duties up to 100 per cent *ad valorem* on certain manufactured articles "being imported into the United Kingdom in abnormal quantities."[20] It was provided that each order under this grant of power should be laid before the House of Commons at once and should cease to have effect in twenty-eight parliamentary days unless the House should approve it by resolution. The

---

[17] 22 Geo. v, ch. 13.   [18] 21 & 22 Geo. v, ch. 48.   [19] 21 & 22 Geo. v, ch. 51.
[20] 22 Geo. v, ch. 1. The Import Duties Act of February 29, 1932, the statutory impulse to the abandonment of free trade, also delegated a good deal of legislative power to the government, but it was the establishment of a new and permanent policy, and although undoubtedly hastened by the crisis, the delegation was a matter of convenience.

Act was limited to six months and expired without further extension. Finally, the Horticultural Products (Emergency Customs Duties) Act of December 11, 1931 granted an identical power for one year to the Minister of Agriculture and Fisheries in regard to certain food products.[21]

These five statutes, together with other important legislation enacted by normal parliamentary methods, were the basis of the MacDonald government's reasonably successful exertions to prevent any further weakening or a collapse of the national economy. Extensive and drastic use was made of this program, and Britain was subjected to a protracted period of government by administrative decree. It was generally agreed that this experiment in economic crisis government achieved results which the slower processes of Parliament might not have realized. The enabling act was not employed again until the outbreak of World War II. The sad experience of the Third Republic was not repeated in England, where Parliament was something less than intransigent and the Conservative "cabinet dictatorship" could secure parliamentary acceptance of all its reasonable desires, emergency or otherwise.

This brief account of the emergency delegation of lawmaking power does not present the entire picture of the changes worked in the English political system under the stress of these troubled times. The MacDonald "National Government," to which this unusual power was granted, was marked by several constitutional innovations, most of them explained by its apologists as indispensable to the mastery of the economic crisis. The detached observer finds it difficult to regard several of these innovations as resulting from a conscious determination to adopt unusual procedures to rout the perils of the depression. The actions of the Prime Minister in the crisis, characterized as everything from "the most courageous and sincerely patriotic political deed of our day" to "the rankest apostasy to the cause of labour and democracy alike," defy satisfactory explanation in the simple terms of the financial difficulties of 1931. At least it can be asserted that there was a clear-cut crisis, and that in the course of the government's exertions to alleviate it certain pronounced departures from normal constitutional practice were initiated.[22]

[21] 22 Geo. v, ch. 3.
[22] The most incisive critical analysis of this whole affair is that of Harold Laski: *The Crisis and the Constitution: 1931 and After* (London, 1932). The parts played by the Prime Minister and the King are branded a "palace revolution." See also his *Parliamentary Government in England*, pp.339 ff. For the criticism of a leading Liberal,

The facts are these: August of 1931 found Ramsay MacDonald and a Labour Cabinet in power, supported in Commons by the Labour Party (288 members) and the Liberals (59), and opposed generally by the Conservative Party (260). Parliament had adjourned in July, and in the ensuing weeks the nation's financial troubles grew steadily more parlous. For some months the idea of inter-party cooperation in the face of this growing crisis had been germinating in the minds of the leaders of all three parties in Commons—the Prime Minister, Stanley Baldwin, and Sir Herbert Samuel. MacDonald knew full well that he could count on no specific aid from the other parties for a program of drastic emergency legislation unless they were presented with seats in the government. He knew fully as well that his own party and the trade unions were bitterly opposed to any retrenchment by way of a cut in unemployment benefits,[23] but that this step was an indispensable prelude to the securing of a foreign loan to bolster the failing resources of the Bank of England. Finding his hands thus tied, but unwilling to renounce the power which he knew to be his, Mr. MacDon .ld—after a significant consultation with the King and an even more significant *lack* of consultation with his Cabinet, the House of Commons, or the Labour Party —resigned as Prime Minister of a Labour government August 24 and immediately became the head of a "National Government," supported in this unprecedented move by his former opponents in the Conservative Party and bitterly opposed by his own comrades in the Labour Party.

A ten-man Cabinet was formed consisting of four members of the Labour government, four Conservatives (including Chamberlain, Hoare, and Baldwin), and two Liberals. All other ministerial offices, filled mostly by Conservatives and Liberals, were left outside the Cabinet. It was publicly announced that the National Government was an emergency innovation, and that its "national" and emergency character would not be maintained once the crisis had been safely passed. "There is no question of any permanent coalition," said Stanley Baldwin, and the Prime

---

see Ramsay Muir: *The Record of the National Government* (London, 1936). The best account of one who participated is that of Snowden in *An Autobiography* (London, 1934), II, pp.947-954. See also Sidney Webb: "What Happened in 1931: A Record," *Political Quarterly*, III (1932), p.1.

[23] The real or apparent instability of British finance in this crisis was in large part due to the policy, initiated by Baldwin and carried on by the Labour government, of uncontrolled borrowing to deal with unemployment. *The Report of the Committee on National Expenditure*, the so-called May Committee (Cmd. 3921, 1931), had advocated a reduction in unemployment benefits. The gloomy picture painted in this report and *The Report of the Committee on Finance and Industry*, the MacMillan Committee (Cmd. 3897, 1931), had done much to weaken faith in the British economy.

181

Minister expressed confidence that the normal positions of the political parties would be resumed within a few weeks. Parliament convened September 8 and voted confidence in the new government by a majority of sixty, with 242 of the 256 Labour members in stunned and bitter opposition. A constitutional revolution had been consummated. Whether he had seen no other way to pull Britain through, or whether he had abandoned the fervently held socialist creed of his early years and had become a Conservative in everything but name, MacDonald, by resigning as Prime Minister of a one-party government and becoming Prime Minister of a government composed of his former enemies and the floating center, had effected the "greatest Constitutional experiment since party government was introduced some two hundred years ago."[24] Apostle Paul or Judas Iscariot, his was a crisis government.

The new government jammed through the first three delegating statutes and the emergency budget bill over the obdurate opposition of the Labour Party, which had read MacDonald and his chief henchmen right out of its ranks. The Prime Minister then dissolved Parliament to go to the people for approval of what had already been done and to ask further for the famed "Doctor's mandate," a blank check to do whatever he might find necessary in the future to remedy the nation's economic woes. The National Government had decided that its objective was not yet fulfilled, and that its life was not to be, after all, a matter of a few weeks. The results of a campaign of unparalleled bitterness, in which the Conservatives, Liberals, and MacDonald's renegade Labourites fought pretty much as a unit, were in keeping with the incredible tenor of the times. 554 government supporters were returned as against but 52 members of the Labour Party and nine assorted independents and Lloyd George Liberals, a parliamentary representation actually quite out of line with the division of the popular vote. The Prime Minister referred to the outcome as "embarrassing."

The new Cabinet, still headed by MacDonald and now of normal size, put through the remainder of its emergency program, including the last two delegating statutes, with consummate ease. MacDonald continued as Prime Minister until his retirement in 1935, but after this election the National Government was nothing more than a Conservative government with a conservative Prime Minister, supported by one of the most considerable majorities in the history of the British Parliament. All claims to the status of anything but an old-line party government

[24] *Law Journal,* August 29, 1931.

were lost when the Liberals and Snowden resigned from the government over the issue of protection in October 1932, and a few months later "crossed the floor" and went into open opposition. MacDonald was the political prisoner, and a willing one, of the Conservative Party. From this date until the outbreak of the second World War Britain's difficulties were met by ordinary legislation prepared by the government and railroaded through a well-disciplined Parliament.

This hasty sketch gives little idea of the complex circumstances surrounding the "National Government" of 1931-1932. It should have sufficed to indicate the constitutional innovations instituted in the crisis, whether for emergency reasons or not. The first MacDonald coalition and the independent actions of the Prime Minister in the formation of the Cabinet; the still mysterious role played by the King, which passed well beyond the established boundaries of consultation, encouragement, and warning (for the royal exhortation and blessing played an indispensable role in the MacDonald apostasy and the assurance of the support of Baldwin and Samuel); the ten-man Cabinet; the cavalier disregard of the party system; the "Doctor's mandate" campaign; and the five enabling acts—all were significant departures from the accepted ways of English government and politics. A further innovation was the decision of the Cabinet at its meeting of January 22, 1932 (when it decided to abandon free trade) to allow the Liberal members to oppose this policy publicly. Cabinet solidarity was thus abolished for a period of about six months.[25] Coalition government and the enabling act were more firmly established as instruments of crisis government in England; the revival of the King as a political factor in any national emergency and the idea of a Prime Minister as someone above party and able to flit from one group to another for support most certainly were not.

[25] Laski: *The Crisis and the Constitution*, pp.59-64. See also Lindsay Rogers: *Crisis Government* (New York, 1934), pp.76-85, for an interesting discussion of the constitutional and political issues involved in the crisis of 1931.

CHAPTER XIII

The Government of Great Britain in the Second World War

I F ever in history a British government had clear title to the powers and instruments of constitutional dictatorship, it was the resolute group of men who led the nation through the second World War. The protracted hardships of the Battle of Britain, accompanied as it was by the baleful threat of Nazi invasion, was the most formidable crisis in modern English history. It is not too much to say that in the hands of the Churchill government was reposed not only the final destiny of the English people, but for several years at least a major responsibility for the future of democracy itself.

It is therefore not surprising that the trusted leader and his colleagues were granted dictatorial powers, or that the government sustained radical alterations in the course of this bitter trial—in organization, in methods of operation, in relations between citizen and state and, not least important, in spirit and resolve. And yet it remains a debatable question which feature of this most recent British adventure in constitutional dictatorship was the more remarkable—the scope of the autocratic power handed the Churchill government or the democratic and restrained manner in which that power was employed. Another leading characteristic of this government was its similarity to that of the first World War. The lessons of 1914-1919 were not forgotten, and the pattern of those victorious days was in most respects faithfully retraced. The important deviations from World War I experience arose from a conscious desire to avoid repetition of the real or alleged mistakes of that era or were forced upon the government by the more "total" nature of this second global conflict.[1]

It was Hitler's invasion of the remnant of Czechoslovakia in March 1939 which finally convinced even the most shortsighted members of the British government that a general European war was imminent. As

---

[1] "The war was planned, by the Chamberlain government, in almost conscious imitation of the war of 1914"—E. P. Chase: "The Government of England in Wartime" in *Government in Wartime Europe and Japan*, Zink and Cole, eds. (New York, 1942), p.1. See also Professor Chase's article "The War and the English Constitution," *Am. Pol. Sci. Rev.*, XXXVI (1942), p.86, for an excellent brief appraisal of the impact of war on both the practical and philosophical aspects of the British Constitution.

summer of that fateful year drew on, the Chamberlain Cabinet, supported in Commons by a large and docile majority, exerted its limited energies in preparation for war. If the output of this effort in terms of plans drawn up by the Committee of Imperial Defence and the various ministries far exceeded the output in terms of planes and tanks, nevertheless the almost fatal deficiency of the latter should not obscure the significance of the paper preparations.[2] Institutionally Britain was better prepared for this war than for the previous one, although not nearly so thoroughly as she ought to and might have been. It is an historical commonplace that the Chamberlain government was not spiritually forearmed for the great trials to come, and this fact was reflected in a persistent refusal to proceed to any radical reorganization of the defense system until even the most obvious changes were forced upon it by the naked reality of war.

The activities of the government at the outbreak of war paralleled closely those of 1914. The Crown called upon the people for obedience and sacrifice, the Cabinet made use of the various emergency powers granted to it by previous laws,[3] Parliament's first few sessions of the war were spent in registering automatic and vigorous approval of more than forty war statutes prepared under the supervision of the Cabinet and the Committee of Imperial Defence,[4] and a comprehensive enabling act for the defense of the Realm, a rejuvenated and expanded DORA, was speedily enacted. The Emergency Powers (Defence) Act,[5] passed with only six dissenting votes in a special session of Parliament on August 24, just one week before the German attack on Poland, was the 1939 counterpart of the Defence of the Realm Acts of 1914, and it was equally as important for the war governments of Chamberlain and Winston Churchill as the Acts of 1914 were for the war governments of Asquith and Lloyd George.

[2] See Lord Hankey: *Government Control in War* (Cambridge, 1945), chap. 4, for an outline of the organizations contributing to war-planning "between the wars."

[3] Among the new emergency statutes passed since the last war were the Air-Raid Precautions Act of 1937 (1 & 2 Geo. vi, ch. 6), the Civil Defence Act of July 1939 (2 & 3 Geo. vi, ch. 38), the Incitement to Disaffection Act of 1934 (24 & 25 Geo. v, ch. 56), the Public Order Act of 1936 (1 Edw. viii & 1 Geo. vi, ch. 6), and a whole crop of Army, Navy and Air Force Acts.

[4] These laws are in 2 & 3 Geo. vi, chs. 63-103. On but one bill, that imposing general conscription, was there a dissenting vote. For a survey of this legislation, see Ivor Jennings: "Emergency Legislation" in the *Annual Survey of English Law: 1939,* published by the London School of Economics (London, 1940).

[5] 2 & 3 Geo. vi, ch. 62. By all odds the best technical treatment of the Act and its Defence Regulations is C. K. Allen: *Law and Orders* (London, 1945), pp.206 ff. This book is a valuable survey of the general problem of delegated legislation.

I. (1) Subject to the provisions of this section, His Majesty may by Order in Council make such Regulations . . . as appear to him to be necessary or expedient for securing the public safety, the defence of the realm, the maintenance of public order and the efficient prosecution of any war in which His Majesty may be engaged, and for maintaining supplies and services essential to the life of the community.

(2) Without prejudice to the generality of the powers conferred by the preceding subsection, Defence Regulations may. . .

(a) make provision for the apprehension, trial and punishment of persons offending against the Regulations, and for the detention of persons whose detention appears to the Secretary of State to be expedient in the interests of the public safety or the defence of the realm;

(b) authorise—

(i) the taking of possession or control, on behalf of His Majesty, of any property or undertaking;

(ii) the acquisition, on behalf of His Majesty, of any property other than land;

(c) authorise the entering and searching of any premises; and

(d) provide for amending any enactment, and suspending the operation of any enactment, and for applying any enactment with or without modification.

The new DORA went on to make specific provision for the sub-delegation of ordinance power to the authorities carrying out the regulations issued under the Act, the validity of all regulations despite their derogation from existing law, and the immediate submission of all Orders-in-Council containing "Defence Regulations" to Parliament, which might—through the resolution of either House adopted within twenty-eight days—annul any regulation. Furthermore, the Treasury was empowered to impose and recover charges "in connection with any scheme of control contained in or authorised by Defence Regulations," with the positive approval of Commons within twenty-eight days required for the continuance of any specific scheme. This was a conscious attempt to vest the government with a power which the Law Lords had regarded as a violation of the Bill of Rights in litigation following the first war.[6] Expressly forbidden was the use of the Act for military or industrial conscription or for the trial of civilians by court-martial. The duration of the Act was limited to one year, although an Order-in-Council, pursuant to an address of both Houses, could extend this period for another year.[7] The Crown was further empowered

---

[6] *A.G. v. Wilts United Dairies* (1922), 38 T.L.R. 781.

[7] Amended to read "two years" by the Emergency Powers (Defence) Act of 1940, s. 1 (3).

to declare the termination of the emergency "that was the occasion of the passage of this Act" and therewith the termination of the Act itself. The 1939 Act contained (contrary to DORA) a "saving clause" in regard to the royal prerogative. The internment and control of enemy aliens proceeded largely on the authority of the prerogative.

The general similarity of the Emergency Powers (Defence) Act to the Defence of the Realm Acts of 1914 is more significant than the particulars in which it differs from or goes beyond the 1914 laws. These differences and additions are apparent in a reading of the two principal Acts. Most significant are the provisions in the 1939 Act for parliamentary disapproval of defense regulations, the prohibition against courts-martial for civilians, the time limit (included at the request of the opposition), and the power of the Treasury to initiate a tax in connection with the regulations. Some clauses in the 1939 Act put into statutory form practices which were recognized as valid but never made strictly legal in the first war, for example the provision for the validity of a regulation even though inconsistent with existing statutes. In the course of the war there were more than 250 amendments or suspensions of English statutes effected by defense regulations, ranging from the Act of Settlement on down. The major regulations issued under the Emergency Powers (Defence) Act far outstripped in volume and consequence those promulgated under DORA in the last war. The Cabinet of Winston Churchill governed England by administrative decree as surely as did the Cabinet of Lloyd George.[8]

This statute was twice amended to increase the government's authority. The Emergency Powers (Defence) Act of May 22, 1940, passed at the moment when the German assault in the west was at its highest pitch, put into the hands of the government an almost "complete control over persons and property."[9] The government was authorized to issue regulations

making provisions for requiring persons to place themselves, their services, and their property at the disposal of His Majesty, as appears to him to be necessary or expedient for securing the public safety, the defence of the

---

[8] See the excellent discussion of the implications of this Act and the regulations under it for the "Rule of Law" in Ivor Jennings: "The Rule of Law in Total War," *Yale Law Journal*, L (1941), p.365, esp. p.380. His conclusion is that the Rule of Law, in the Diceyan sense, has long since disappeared in England, but that parliamentary control of arbitrary power (which the classic theory almost ignores) is still effective. "The law rules because Parliament rules."

[9] 3 & 4 Geo. VI, ch. 20. These are the words of Clement Attlee in introducing this drastic bill into the House of Commons—*Parl. Deb.* (1940), Commons, CCCLXI: p.152.

realm, the maintenance of public order and the efficient prosecution of any war in which His Majesty may be engaged and for maintaining supplies and services essential to the life of the community.

This Act permitted industrial conscription, as well as military conscription of conscientious objectors and other groups omitted in the National Service Act. The Emergency Powers (Defence) (No. 2) Act of August 1, 1940,[10] put through Commons only after a keen debate in which amendments were forced upon the government, permitted the establishment of special courts (not courts-martial) for the trial without jury of civilians in areas to be designated as war zones "by reason of recent or immediately apprehended enemy action." A third statute supplementing the Act of 1939 was the Treachery Act of May 23, 1940,[11] hurried through Parliament when the importance of the fifth column to German victories was for the first time being clearly realized and an invasion of England was regarded as imminent. Treachery (punishable by death) was defined in the light of the modern standards of the fifth column, and trial by court-martial of enemy aliens accused of acts of sabotage and espionage was provided. This Act, taken with the ensuing Act of August 1, 1940, again meant that an Englishman could go to his death by execution without benefit of trial by jury.

The high point of dictatorial power was reached in the National Service (No. 2) Act of December 1941,[12] which stated:

It is hereby declared that all persons of either sex for the time being in Great Britain are liable to national service, whether under the Crown or not, and whether in the armed forces of the Crown, in civil defence, in industry or otherwise.

This is the *levée en masse* of democracy in total war. It is apparent that the Churchill government possessed an autocratic power to meet any crisis of any intensity, whether of invasion, disaffection, or starvation. The Crown-in-Council could do anything but borrow money, levy taxes, and acquire land. Needless to say, the dictatorial potentialities of these Acts were never realized. Although the liberties of the people might have been completely suppressed, labor conscripted, property ruthlessly appropriated,[13] and industry socialized—these steps were never taken.

[10] 3 & 4 Geo. VI, ch. 45.   [11] 3 & 4 Geo. VI, ch. 21.   [12] 5 & 6 Geo. VI, ch. 4.
[13] In case of necessity, the common law provides ample authority for governmental appropriation of private property in return for just compensation. Was Coke thinking of 1940 when he wrote: "But when enemies come against the realm to the sea-coast it is lawful to come upon my land adjoining to the same coast, to make trenches or bulwarks for the defence of the realm, for every subject hath benefit by it."? (Coke: XII *Rep.* 12; *The Case of Saltpetre.*)

The cardinal fact is that they could have been, and it was the British Parliament which had almost unanimously authorized this dictatorial competence.

The War Cabinet

THE most fundamental readjustment of the British government to the exigencies of the second World War was the reestablishment of the "cabinet dictatorship" of 1916-1919. For Lloyd George and his War Cabinet and his mammoth Ministry there were now Winston Churchill and his War Cabinet and his mammoth Ministry. The executive duties of the Cabinet were swollen tremendously under the bruising impact of war, not the least of that body's tasks being the daily oversight and direction of a military, naval, and logistical strategy which embraced the five continents and the seven seas. The legislative burden fell completely upon the Cabinet and Ministry, by virtue of the delegation and sub-delegation authorized in the Emergency Powers (Defence) Act. More than this, the executive and legislative ascendancy of the Prime Minister and his Cabinet were set in bold relief by the concomitant reduction, even if largely potential, of the political and economic freedom of the British people. That the Cabinet was a dictatorship can hardly be denied, but it remained an eminently constitutional one. The people were behind it almost to a man, and its use of its autocratic powers was restrained and circumspect. Historians must go back to the younger Pitt to discover a Prime Minister and Cabinet with the electoral and moral preeminence of the government of 1940-1945.[14]

The War Cabinet of Churchill was not the War Cabinet of Lloyd George. Although he discoursed repeatedly on the inestimable value of colleagues not burdened with departmental duties, Churchill never did manage to separate the twin functions of policy-making and administration, and his final War Cabinet was constituted almost entirely of men with heavy ministerial responsibilities. The Prime Minister himself clung tenaciously to the post of Minister of Defence. The Churchill War Cabinet was an "above-the-line" group carved out with the knife of expediency from the Ministry itself, and in many respects this idea of a War Cabinet had little more than emotional value. Moreover, it was somewhat larger than its predecessor of 1916-1919. Although its devia-

[14] That the classical theory of the Prime Minister as *primus inter pares* did not hold in this crisis (and in fact is probably done away with permanently) is made clear by Harold Laski: "Some Reflections on Government in Wartime," *Political Quarterly*, XIII (1942), p.57.

tions from that model met with some criticism, the best opinion would seem to be that of Professor Finer: "The system of Lloyd George may have suited Lloyd George, but Mr. Churchill is entitled to the organization which suits him."[15]

The declaration of war was accompanied by a basic reorganization of the Cabinet and Ministry. Some ministers experienced a sizable increase in power; others—Home Secretary, Food, Economic Warfare, Shipping, Information—were set up for the first time. More than twenty new ministries were established in the course of the struggle. The Committee of Imperial Defence was dissolved and absorbed into the War Cabinet itself. Although many observers had predicted a war executive on the pattern of Lloyd George's unorthodox five, Chamberlain preferred a Cabinet of nine men within the framework of the Ministry: himself as Prime Minister, Sir John Simon as Chancellor of the Exchequer, Churchill as First Lord of the Admiralty, Hore-Belisha as War Secretary, Kingsley Wood for Air, Lord Halifax for Foreign Affairs, Lord Hankey without portfolio, Hoare as Lord Privy Seal, and Lord Chatfield as Defence Coordination Minister. This government was almost exclusively a Conservative affair, for the Liberal and Labour parties refused to take part, awaiting the advent to power of a leader in whom they could really put their trust.

The leisure of the "phony war" enabled the opposition in Parliament and press to campaign for the formation of a smaller War Cabinet, stocked with more imaginative and vigorous members. The continued refusal of the Labour members to serve under Mr. Chamberlain finally bore fruit in the aftermath of the Norwegian debacle and the assault on the Low Countries. On May 10 Winston Churchill formed his first government. He had decided on a War Cabinet of five men: himself as Prime Minister and Minister of Defence; Chamberlain, still the leader of the Conservative party, as Lord President of the Council; Halifax as Foreign Minister; and two leaders of the Labour party, Clement Attlee as Lord Privy Seal and Arthur Greenwood without portfolio. Here was a War Cabinet worthy of the name. Composed of five men, two of whom were chiefs of the former opposition and three of whom were relieved of ministerial duties, this group seemed to be an ideal compromise between Lloyd George's idea of a purely policy-making Cabinet and Chamberlain's belief that the administration of both de-

[1] "The British Cabinet, the House of Commons, and the War," *Pol. Sci. Q.*, LVI (1941), p.348.

fense and foreign affairs should be a direct concern of the men at the top.

Almost from the date of its establishment this War Cabinet began to grow in numbers. Mr. Churchill was forced to yield to other realities and to accept into the inner circle the heads of several of the more important ministries. By early February 1942 the Cabinet numbered ten members, including Lord Halifax as Ambassador to the United States. The shocking blows of that month aroused in press and Parliament a demand for readjustments impressive enough to compel the Prime Minister to do some house-cleaning. The result was the reduction of the War Cabinet to seven men, and it was this organization—with a few minor changes in offices and personnel—which carried on to the end of the German war. The Cabinet at the peak of its efficiency and ascendancy was thus constituted: Churchill as Prime Minister and Minister of Defence; Attlee as Deputy Prime Minister and Lord President of the Council; Oliver Lyttleton as Minister of Production; Anthony Eden as Foreign Secretary and Leader of the House of Commons; Ernest Bevin as Minister of Labour and National Service; Herbert Morrison as Home Secretary; and Sir John Anderson as Chancellor of the Exchequer. Lord Woolton became an eighth member in November 1943 as head of the newly created Ministry of Reconstruction.

The War Cabinet did its work through a system of committees directly responsible to it, some headed by members of the Cabinet itself, others headed and staffed by ministers or officials not in the Cabinet at all. Examples of this interesting departure were the Defence Committee, the Chiefs of Staff Committee, and the Lord President's Committee (for the coordination and determination of the nation's economic policy). These committees were in effect junior war cabinets, and generally made important decisions for which the War Cabinet itself was responsible. The sessions of Lloyd George's all-powerful quintet (which Lord Curzon once likened to an Indian durbar) were paralleled in this second war, and numerous ministers, officials, generals, and dominion and allied representatives (such as Ambassador Winant and Harry Hopkins) participated in its deliberations. A remarkable innovation in English practice was effected in the 1942 shakeup of the Cabinet and Ministry. The elevation of Sir James Grigg from the post of Permanent Undersecretary for War to the Secretaryship itself was the first instance in modern times of the appointment of a civil servant to head his department. Shortly after the same shakeup Churchill took a leaf from Lloyd

191

George's book and named Richard G. Casey, Australian envoy in Washington, to the War Cabinet as Minister of State to deal with Middle Eastern affairs.

Mr. Churchill's organization was the target for a lot of well-deserved criticism throughout the war, but it did the job in a satisfactory manner. The energetic Prime Minister fashioned a medium through which he believed his own and his colleagues' talents might operate most effectively in the successful prosecution of the war, and that this medium was different from that of Lloyd George should occasion no great surprise. It is to the credit of the English system that, in its unparalleled flexibility, it could mould itself to the personalities and preconceptions of each of these great wartime leaders.

The War Parliament

THE status of Parliament in the war government of 1939-1945 was in many, but not all ways similar to that which it had held in the first war. As a legislative and electoral body the House of Commons lost most of its peacetime significance. As in 1914-1919 it met, except on special occasions, as a rump parliament, so many of its members were engaged in ministerial work or were in the armed forces. Its membership was "frozen" for the duration. The general elections scheduled for November 1940 were postponed repeatedly. The Beaverbrook press campaigned vigorously for a general election *durante bello*, but the House was conforming to the general will of the British people in prolonging its own life by statute until the crisis was past. An inter-party truce was established early in the war, and by-elections went uncontested except by various types of independent candidates. Twelve of these gentlemen were elected over the candidate backed by the full force of the three major parties.

The legislative function was renounced in exactly the same manner as in the first World War. By virtue of a sweeping grant of legislative competence to the executive—and this time there was no sham, for the Emergency Powers (Defence) Act specifically provided that the defense regulations would have validity despite derogation from the terms of existing statutes—Parliament again expressed its inability to legislate in answer to the changing demands of a protracted crisis. All matters fundamental to the English Constitution and the democratic tradition were enacted in the form of regular statutes. Hampden may sleep; the Crown still cannot tax by Order-in-Council. The House of Commons was given the opportunity to debate and vote upon such vital subjects as conscription, taxation, appropriations, and normal social legislation, but the result was never in doubt. Nine times out of ten a bill prepared in one of the ministries went through all the parliamentary stages with haste and without amendment. Only over extremely controversial bills such as the Emergency Powers (Defence) (No. 2) Act of 1940 was there a prolonged debate, a concession by the government, and a show of opposition on the vote.

As the electoral college of the British system the work of Commons was done in May 1940, except as it was occasionally able to convince the Prime Minister of the necessity for a new face in one of the departments. Winston Churchill could no more have been turned out by Parliament in the late war than President Roosevelt could have been by Congress. Churchill demanded a vote of confidence January 29, 1942 and, despite a long series of successive calamities (*Barham, Prince of Wales, Repulse*, the production muddle, Hong Kong, the Rommel offensive, and the imminent loss of Singapore) he was upheld 464-1. In fairness to Parliament it must be recognized that Churchill was overwhelmingly the choice of the British people. It is instructive to note, however, that Neville Chamberlain, unfitted for wartime leadership as he always appeared, was never voted out of office at all. On May 8, 1940 he received from his dependent, and therefore dependable Conservative majority a vote of confidence of 281-200. The two hundred who had turned from toleration to active opposition were too much to stomach, however, for they numbered the entire Liberal and Labour Parties and forty-three Conservatives, numbering many Privy Councillors out of office and nearly all the Conservatives in uniform. In other words, an irreducible majority of Commons was willing to let this failure continue the war, and he only resigned in the face of the reiterated refusal of the opposition parties to join in any government of which he was to be the leader. The House of Commons had upset a government by minority action, something that could hardly happen except in an epic crisis where the unanimous support of all those loyal to the Crown-at-War was more necessary than the maintenance in power of any one man.

The fact is that the House of Commons, despite great difficulties, not the least of which was the destruction of its place of business, played a starring role in this drama. The descent to the "humiliating status" of 1914-1918 was not repeated. Although severe restrictions were placed upon its normal operation by the exigencies of war, and although in the making of laws and leaders it lost most of its significance, nevertheless the House of Commons established itself firmly in the war government by reverting consciously to its Bagehotian functions of teaching and informing, and of expressing the will of the people as manifested in public opinion. It might be said that Commons also assumed the King's functions—"the right to be consulted, the right to encourage, the right to warn." The main task of Parliament in the war was "sensing, focusing, intensifying, and concentrating upon the Ministers the mood and feeling of the time."[16] As the Prime Minister stated in a debate on January 22, 1941:

> "I think I have said before that to try to carry on a war, a tremendous war, without the aid and guidance of the House of Commons would be a superhuman task. I have never taken the view that the Debates and criticisms of this House are a drag and a burden. Far from it. I may not agree at all with the criticism—I may be stunned by it, and I may resent it; I may even retort—but at any rate Debates on these large issues are of the very greatest value to the life-thrust of the nation, and they are of the very greatest assistance to His Majesty's Government."

And Churchill was true to his word. Although Parliament had been expected to pass into virtual oblivion with the absorption of the opposition into a "truly national" government, the reverse was true. While Commons displayed far more confidence in its leaders than ever before, it nevertheless intensified its role as critic and became an extremely healthy factor in the war effort. The government was forced to come down to Parliament and answer the questions, limited though they often were by fear of giving valuable information to the enemy.[17] The debates in the House of Commons came to be one of the most salutary and reassuring features of Britain's war government. Every burning question was thoroughly thrashed out on the floor of the House. Tobruk, Greece, Crete, blockade, air-raid shelters, propaganda, production (undoubtedly the most important subject debated), civil liberties, war aims, Russia, unpopular ministers, Singapore, the release of Oswald Mosley, reconstruction, the Home Secretary's power of detention—all these controversial issues were debated in full by a Parliament that refused to abdicate its last and noblest duty, that of expressing the will and whim of the people of England. The main issue of confidence may no longer

---

[16] Finer, *loc. cit.*, p.324.
[17] On the relations of Cabinet and Parliament, see Harold Laski: "The War Cabinet and Parliament," *The New Statesman and Nation*, December 14, 1940.

have been a matter for discussion, but Commons showed no signs of ridding itself of "its associated function of vigilant supervision and the voicing of popular feeling."[18]

These debates were participated in by responsible members of the Cabinet and Ministry, often Mr. Churchill himself, a situation far different from the Lloyd George dictatorship of the first war. The tonic of the vigorous three-day debate which followed Churchill's return from America in January 1942 had a wondrous effect on the government and people, and it left many Americans speculating how beneficial it might be if their system required the executive to go down to the floor of Congress and face the questions and criticisms of the legislators, and then come back up again with some invaluable advice, with the air cleared of nasty rumors and innuendoes by the candor of the debates, and with a heartening vote of confidence.

It was in one sense unfortunate that the expression of the popular feeling of the moment could not always have been reciprocated, and that some of the most vital debates could not have been as much a cause of public opinion as a result. Although most of the important questions were aired in an open House, with the nation being treated to the stimulus of a full-fledged parliamentary debate, there were several important secret sessions about which the Germans learned little and the public less. It was generally agreed that this practice was sometimes necessary, in order to keep valuable secrets out of the enemy's hands, but it was and remains a departure from normal to be resisted as much as possible.[19]

There could be no more convincing proof of the inherent vitality of England's democratic institutions than this readjustment of the oldest of Parliaments to the crisis of 1939-1945, this spectacle of a House of Commons deprived willy-nilly of its legislative and electoral significance converting itself into a high council of state, a critical and heeded adviser to a government and leader in whom its ultimate confidence was unbounded. The debates and questions in Commons promoted war efficiency and protected democracy, and for those two accomplishments the people of Britain can be truly thankful. This performance was all the more amazing when it is recalled that this particular House had been

---

[18] H. R. G. Greaves: "Parliament in Wartime," *Pol. Q.*, XII (1941), p.202. This article continued a series in *Pol. Q.*, XI and XII, by Ivor Jennings. See also Albert Viton: "The British Parliament in Total War," *Virginia Q. R.* (Winter, 1945), p.19.

[19] See particularly the well-aimed blast of Ivor Jennings in his *Parliament Must Be Reformed* (London, 1941), pp.9 ff.

elected in 1935 on issues having nothing to do with the crisis, and was actually quite unrepresentative of the spirit and politics of the British people at war. The British Parliament of 1942 and 1943 was a far cry from that of 1916, or even 1938, where a well-disciplined majority obeyed the requests of an ineffective cabinet dictatorship, while government supporters who criticized the government were accused of "fouling our own nests." It is to the added credit of Winston Churchill, nettled though he sometimes was by searching criticism of some of his associates in power and some of his policies, that he remained, as he himself phrased it, a "good House of Commons man" and recognized the right of Parliament to speak to him with the voice of the people "with its persistent, tenacious, constructive questioning."[20]

"The House of Commons is really a symbol of what we are fighting for; it is part of our war and peace aims, and I hope we will not take any steps which will prevent its shining during the war as brightly as it has done all down the centuries."[21]

British Liberty in the Second World War

ONE of the most impressive features of the British government of the recent war was the scrupulous and consistent regard for the civil liberties of the people maintained throughout the conflict by the government itself and the myriad of authorities carrying out its will.[22] Although the freedom of the subject was placed squarely in the hands of the government to respect or invade according to its own appraisal of the necessities of the moment, the encroachments upon this freedom were in fact rather trifling, even in the darkest days of the Nazi threat to the island. This was largely due to the virtual unanimity with which the British people faced the enemy and backed the Churchill government, but it cannot be denied that this government—particularly in the light of the crisis—

[20] Finer, *loc. cit.*, p.343. Churchill "could ignore Parliament. Instead he cultivates it"—Lindsay Rogers: "Legislative and Executive in Wartime," *Foreign Affairs*, XIX (1941), p.726.

[21] Mr. Mander, M.P., quoted in Greaves: *Pol. Q.*, XII, p.210. Or hear what Harold Laski had to say: "The House of Commons has not deserved better of the nation since it stood up to the challenge of Charles I just three centuries ago this year"—"Civil Liberties in Great Britain in War Time," *Bill of Rights Review* (Summer, 1942), p.250. The House of Lords, on the other hand, did nothing in particular in the war and did it very poorly, in contrast to the first World War.

[22] See generally Harold Laski, the article cited in note 21; "Civil Liberties in Great Britain and Canada During War," a note in *Harvard L.R.*, LV (1942), p.1006; Ronald Kidd: *British Liberty in Danger* (London, 1940), a rather critical account of the restrictions effected in the war; Paul B. Rava: "Emergency Powers in Great Britain," *Boston Univ. L.R.*, XXI (1941), pp.403, 411 ff.

could have abridged personal liberty far more than it did and still held the confidence of the nation.

The most radical invasion of a cherished English liberty was the tremendous potential restriction of freedom of person authorized by defense regulation 18B.[23] This regulation empowered the Home Secretary in effect to suspend the writ of habeas corpus and detain indefinitely any person in England if he had "reasonable cause" to believe that such person was (a) of hostile origin or associations, (b) had recently been concerned in acts prejudicial to the public safety, (c) was a member of an organization "subject to foreign influence or control" or in sympathy with "the system of government of any Power with which His Majesty is at war," or (d) had done things or said things "expressing sympathy with the enemy" in any area specified by the Home Secretary. An advisory committee was set up to recommend the disposition of detention cases, but the Secretary was not bound by its decisions. Actually about 80 per cent of its recommendations were accepted. Parliamentary control was maintained through the medium of monthly reports by the Home Secretary of those cases in which he had seen fit to disregard the advice of the committee, as well as of the total number detained.

The greatest number of persons detained at any one time under 18B was 1428, in August 1940, surely a trifling number considering the state of England's defenses at that time. By mid-1944 this number had been reduced to about 200. It was this dictatorial power which was employed for the protracted incarceration of such noted Britons as Sir Oswald Mosley and Capt. Archibald Ramsay, representative in the House of Commons of the Electors of Midlothian and Peebles. 18B was a severe break with the traditions of British liberty, and even though it was used with evident circumspection by Home Secretary Herbert Morrison, it was bitterly and repeatedly attacked on the floor of Commons, as well as in several dissenting court opinions.[24] The Churchill government let it be known at an early stage that it regarded this autocratic power as indispensable to the defense of England, and that its nullification would be considered a vote of no-confidence. Morrison, who clung to this power like a bulldog throughout the war, had been one of 18B's principal critics when in opposition in 1939. The bitter critic of

[23] This regulation and the others discussed in the pages to follow may be found in a publication of H. M. Printing Office: *Defence Regulations*, numerous editions of which were published throughout the war.
[24] See Allen: *Law and Orders*, pp.234 ff., for a review of some of the most arbitrary cases of detention under 18B as well as for a cogent attack on the regulation itself.

emergency powers always seems perfectly willing to use them himself when he in his turn gets the responsibility for defending the nation in crisis.

The Home Secretary's power of detention under 18B was most vigorously attacked and broadly upheld in the consequential case of *Liversidge v. Anderson*, decided in 1942.[25] The chief question was the interpretation of the phrase "if the Secretary of State has reasonable cause to believe," and the majority opinion of the Law Lords was that "reasonable cause" was something existing only in the mind of the Home Secretary, that it was for him alone to determine whether "reasonable cause" for detention existed, and that this decision was not subject to challenge for *ultra vires* or to judicial review. In other words, the reasonableness of any particular detention was a matter of responsible administrative discretion and not of judicial demonstration. This decision was of vital importance for the larger question of validity of actions taken under the defense regulations; it was a virtual abdication of the fortress of *ultra vires*. It was to the House of Commons, not to the courts that the people of Britain had to look for any relief from arbitrary action in wartime England. And as Professor C. K. Allen has written:

"It is important to remember that the effect of *Liversidge v. Anderson* is not confined to wartime detentions or to the wrongs, or supposed wrongs of a comparatively small group of persons whose loyalty is in doubt. It gives to executive discretion an almost unlimited charter for all time. . . . We shall not have heard the last of this case when the war is ended."[26]

Freedom of expression—of press and speech and assembly—suffered scant abridgment in wartime Britain, partly because the government made a conscious effort to fight a democratic war, partly because the people were almost unanimous in their support of the war, and partly because the persons most likely to foment printed or oral disloyalty were cowed or cooped up by 18B. Although its military and diplomatic reporting was heavily censored, the press was free to attack the government in the spirit of sincere, or for that matter carping criticism. The establishment of several new ministries, the departure of Chamberlain,

---

[25] (1942), A.C. 206. Lengthy extracts from the opinions in this case are to be found in Allen, *op. cit.*, app. 3, while other cases under 18B are reviewed pp.244 ff. See also app. 5 and Cecil T. Carr: "A Regulated Liberty," *Columbia L.R.*, XLII (1942), pp.339, 344 ff. Viscount Maugham delivered the majority opinion, Lord Atkin the vigorous dissent reminiscent of Justice Davis's decision in *Ex Parte Milligan*.

[26] *Op. cit.*, p.243.

and the Cabinet shake-up of February 1942 were a few of the important governmental reorientations in which the press played a leading role. The ultimate control of the press was vested in the Home Secretary by virtue of defense regulations 2C and 2D. Regulation 2C empowered him to proceed judicially against any person continuing (after a fair warning) to publish "matter . . . calculated to foment opposition to the prosecution to a successful issue of any war in which His Majesty is engaged," with a maximum sentence of seven years and £500 provided. Regulation 2D permitted him to proceed administratively and on his own responsibility to the absolute suppression of any publication engaged in the systematic printing of such matter. The arbitrary and complete censorship authorized by 2D was reluctantly approved by an aroused Parliament only after definite assurances had been made that it would be used in none but the gravest situations of national danger. It was under 2D that the Communist publications *The Week* and *The Daily Worker* were suppressed in the period before the Soviet Union went to war and converted it into one of the "holy" variety. Otherwise this dictatorial power was held in abeyance. The important fact is that it was authorized, and by an executive decree at that, even if it was used only twice. Such a regulation, along with 18B, would probably have been declared unconstitutional in the United States even at the height of the war effort. But then again, the United States was not a beleaguered fortress.

The freedoms of speech and assembly underwent even less invasion, although they too were at the mercy of the government, under such regulations as 39A, 39B, 39BA, and 39E. Regulation 39A provided for the prosecution of persons inciting Britons to disaffection or seducing them from their duties under the Crown; 39B did the same for false and malicious propaganda; 39BA authorized a penalty of one month's imprisonment and a fine of £50 for any person summarily convicted of publishing "any report or statement . . . likely to cause alarm or despondency"; and 39E gave the Home Secretary—poor Mr. Herbert Morrison—an absolute veto on any "processions" or meetings "likely to cause serious public disorder or to promote disaffection," another provision which the American people would have regarded as a shocking violation of their liberties, but which the British people (a few thousand miles nearer the sound of the guns) could hardly have spared their hard-pressed leaders. The spectacle of soap-box orators demanding a second front (since they didn't have to open it) before crowds in

Trafalgar Square provided conclusive proof that British democracy was still very much of a going concern.

Perhaps the worst blot on the British record in the second World War —and it is admittedly easier to call the affair a "blot" than to suggest how it might have been handled differently in the heat of the crisis—was the wholesale internment of enemy aliens over eighteen in the dark days of May 1940. The lessons of the fifth column were a bit too thoroughly learned by the government, and the result was the indiscriminate jailing of many well-known anti-Fascist refugees who were solidly behind the war effort. The press and Parliament were not slow to leap to their defense, and eventually the matter was straightened out.[27] The fact that this was the worst blot shows how excellent the record actually was.

The rights of labor—to seek better employment, to strike, or to stay home and work in the garden—were brought thoroughly into line with the government's policy of all-out production.[28] The point of departure for wartime control of labor in England was the drastic provision for industrial conscription in the Emergency Powers (Defence) Act of May 22, 1940. On this Act was grounded defense regulation 58A, which conferred upon the Minister of Labour and National Service the power to direct any person in Great Britain to perform any service of which the Minister thought him (or her) capable. A series of "Essential Work Orders" and other decrees were in turn issued under 58A, the net result being an absolute control of the employer-employee relationship in British industry. The employer could not hire or fire except under governmental supervision; the employee could not strike or be absent without cause, and was frozen to his job. On the other hand, he was guaranteed a job and a minimum wage.

The trade unions took the lead in the voluntary rejection of the right to strike, a pledge which became easier to honor after the admittance of Bevin, Morrison, Attlee and the rest to the government in 1940. Although there were some "wildcat" strikes of a local and short-lived nature, these were rare and were most bitterly condemned by the union leaders in and out of office. America's NWLB had its counterpart in the

[27] Otherwise the enemy alien problem was extremely well handled throughout the war. See M. Koessler: "Enemy Alien Internment," *Pol. Sci. Q.*, LVII (1942), p.98.

[28] The literature on British labor at war is enormous. See generally F. Wunderlich: *British Labor and the War* (New York, 1941); International Labor Office: *The Labor Situation in Great Britain* (Montreal, 1941); Eric H. Biddle: *Manpower. A Summary of the British Experience* (Chicago, 1942), and *The Mobilization of the Homefront* (Chicago, 1942); Mary E. Murphy: *The British War Economy* (New York, 1943), chap. 3.

five-man National Arbitration Tribunal, set up in 1940 as the final arbiter of any dispute not otherwise settled by normal methods of negotiation. The government outlawed all strikes and lock-outs unless the Minister of Labour had failed to refer the particular dispute to the Tribunal. That the government meant business was demonstrated in a 1942 strike of 1500 coal miners in Kent against an award of the Tribunal—1000 of the miners were fined and three of their leaders were imprisoned. Man-hours lost because of strikes hit an all-time low in the Ministry of Labour's statistics.

Many volumes have been written, and many more are doubtless on the way, covering one or all of the numerous aspects of governmental control of British industry in the second World War.[29] It must suffice here to trace the broad outlines of this problem. In the first place, there is little doubt that the government's control of industry, far as it went— and it certainly outstripped the American experience—would have gone further still had a government more in conformity with the temper of the British people been in power. Mr. Churchill's Tory spirit did not stand in the way of thoroughgoing governmental control of the nation's instruments of production, distribution, and supply, but it is of interest to speculate what a coalition government headed by Attlee and backed by a strong Labour majority in Commons might have done. Secondly, the British government had every bit as much trouble getting organized for the war of production as did the people in Washington. The creation of the office of Minister of Production in February 1942 as a sort of super-coordinator for industrial control was forced by the House of Commons. Like Mr. Roosevelt, Mr. Churchill's talents seemed better suited to the war abroad than the war at home.

In the third place, the governmental readjustments to meet the multiplying tasks of economic control followed a somewhat different pattern from that of the United States. All such control was headed up in the ministries themselves, not in a conglomeration of jerry-built commissions, boards, authorities, government-owned corporations, and presidential junior cabinets. In general the British war economy was organized along commodity lines, with a particular ministry responsible for licensing, price control, priorities, distribution, and other controls for a specific product or group of products. Although this made possible an

[29] The best single account is Mary E. Murphy: *The British War Economy*. See also Jules Backman: *Rationing and Price Control in Great Britain* (Washington, 1943); W. H. Wickwar: "Government and the Social Pattern in Wartime England," chap. 2 in *Government in Wartime Europe and Japan.*

effective integration of control over all aspects of a single product, it made for a lack of coordination between various ministries and their sub-agencies. The creation of the Lord President's Committee and the Ministry of Production went a long way toward correcting this situation.

Fourthly, the British system ended up as a conglomeration of cartels, for each major industry operated beneath its particular ministry through a supervisory committee largely made up of leaders of the industry itself. Finally, the whole structure of industrial control was erected on a defense regulation under the Emergency Powers (Defence) Act. Regulation 55 and its amendments are as clear a piece of executive lawmaking as could well be imagined. Not only did it set the general policy for industrial control in the broadest terms, but in its turn it delegated power to the various ministries to prescribe controls, hours, wages, profits, and prices for any plant engaged in any sort of war production.

It would hardly seem right to end this description of Britain's government of the second World War without some particular mention of the remarkable gentleman who symbolized and directed this epic war effort. Mr. Churchill has long since descended from his lofty pedestal to re-enter the arena of controversial politics (with his ungracious "Gestapo" speech of the 1945 campaign), and he deserves a heavy vote of thanks for coming down of his own accord. It is now a good deal easier to appraise his leadership in its proper perspective. Even so appraised, it is obvious that the conspicuous success of the British war government was in large part traceable to his unique courage and personality. As Lord Hankey has pointed out, Churchill was more than just an orator and a master politician; no man in English history ever brought so much sound experience in parliamentary and ministerial government to the post of the King's first minister. The heartfelt tribute paid by Clement Attlee on August 16, 1945 to the man—"there is a true leadership which means the expression by one man of the soul of a nation"—and to the man's words—"words at great moments of history are deeds"— was the most convincing testimony of all. Like the men of ancient Rome the British people turned to a man of the past to secure their future, and the man of the past did the dictatorial job as no one else could possibly have done it.

The way in which Britain's war government came to an end is common knowledge and need not be repeated here. Although Churchill had made a clear bid in March 1943 for continuance of all-party government after the war to carry through a four-year plan of social and economic reconstruction, the Labour Party had made it equally clear that they would have none of it. The War Cabinet itself came to an end in the weeks following V-E Day, and a "caretaker" Cabinet of sixteen Conservatives and non-party men was formed to prosecute the distant war against Japan. For reasons best known to himself, Churchill dissolved Parliament on June 15, 1945. The country indulged in a wonderful old-time party scrap, and the new temper of the British people was demonstrated July 5 in a sweeping Labour victory.

The Attlee government has functioned since 1945 on a peacetime basis. The Cabinet numbers some twenty men from the majority party, the House of Commons has reassumed a respectable portion of the legislative burden, and the most dictatorial of the wartime controls have been laid aside. Of particular importance in the return to normal ways is the manner in which the House of Commons has cast off its role as council of state and divided once again into definite party groupings. It was a splendid role for war, but as Ivor Jennings has keenly observed, the idea of such a Parliament in time of peace would be little better than "veiled fascism."[30] The democratic process just doesn't work that way.

The Emergency Powers (Defence) Acts came to an automatic end February 24, 1946, their final extension having been for only a six months period.[31] The most severe of the defense regulations were wiped out with the conclusion of the European war, and most of the others were gone by the end of the year. The Home Secretary was only too happy to announce to the House of Commons May 9, 1945 that an Order-in-Council had just revoked five special codes of regulations, 84 regulations in whole, and 25 in part. Among the departed were 2C, 2D, 18B, 39BA, 39E, and a host of others. Mr. Morrison thereby set an all-time record for the swift abandonment of instruments of constitutional dictatorship. A number of other regulations were revoked at the close of the war in the Pacific. The remaining decrees, dealing with economic problems, were absorbed into the postwar controls of the Attlee government. All remaining persons held under 18B were released immediately after V-E Day, and in December 1945 Sir Oswald's die-hards held a reunion dance—not in honor of 18B—at London's Royal Hotel.

[30] *Parliament Must Be Reformed*, p.17.
[31] The Emergency Laws (Transitional Provisions) Act, February 14, 1946 (9 & 10 Geo. VI, ch. 26), continued a few non-controversial controls through to December 31, 1947.

The most significant change worked by the war is the permanent establishment of government by administrative decree, the cutting edge of the sword of delegated legislation. In this instance as in many others, however, the experience of the war only capped a long and steady progress in this direction.[32] As for governmental control of industry, Britain's new Labour government has naturally been more disposed to a continuation and even partial reinstitution of wartime controls through the bitter economic crisis of the last two years than the authorities in Washington. In December 1945 the Attlee government secured the passage of the Supplies and Services (Transitional Powers) Act[33] which authorized a five-year extension of the war controls over labor, prices, transport, and materials. The Act was challenged heavily by the Conservative opposition, which strove to have it limited to two years, but went through Commons by a safe majority. In August 1947 the Attlee government moved even further into dictatorial territory with the obviously necessary Supplies and Services (Extended Purposes) Act,[34] a statute giving the Cabinet the power to issue decrees that might conceivably force every able-bodied Briton into productive work, whether he liked it or not. And meanwhile the socialization of Britain goes on apace. The arrival of a Socialist government in power has guaranteed that this time peace will mean more rather than less government control or ownership of British industry.

The future trend of crisis government in England seems obvious. The cleavage between the traditional and twentieth century patterns of emergency powers and government will doubtless become even more pronounced with the passage of the stormy years ahead. The day may well come when statutory martial law, an unvarnished English state of siege, will be instituted as a recognized part of British law and government. The stark facts of history, geography, economics, and science have snatched away from the British people their peculiarly blessed status as the sole European people free from the ravages of repeated crises. Whatever else has changed, the English political genius has not. In no country have the manifold problems of constitutional, democratic dic-

---

[32] See generally Allen: *Laws and Orders*, chap. 2, for a history of delegated legislation; pp.276 ff., for some excellent suggested reforms. In May 1944 the Home Secretary announced in Commons the government's intention of instituting a committee of the House (with Cecil T. Carr as legal adviser) to scrutinize all regulations requiring affirmative resolution of the House or merely its negative approval—D. W. Logan: "Delegated Legislation," *Pol. Q.*, xv (1944), p.185.

[33] 9 & 10 Geo. vi, ch. 10.   [34] 10 & 11 Geo. vi, ch. 55.

tatorship been so skillfully and resolutely brought to solution. The Emergency Powers Act of 1920, the unique and still viable concept of martial law, the enabling act, the Emergency Powers (Defence) Acts of 1939 and 1940, the infinite possibilities of cabinet dictatorship—all these weapons in the arsenal of British crisis government bear witness that the problem of emergency power has been well handled by the men who have ruled this country. The crisis importance of Commons as council of state, the fine regard of the government for the liberties of the people, the comparative ease with which government returned to normal after the recent war—all these demonstrations of British democracy bear equal witness that the problem of limitations on emergency power has been just as well handled.

The men who ruled England in 1940 possessed arbitrary power such as the Tudors themselves did not enjoy, and the men who rule it in 1948 are equally able to claim such power should the nation again come to the crisis of war. And yet this power has had and will continue to have but one reason for its existence: the maintenance of democracy and freedom within the realm of England.

Part Four

CRISIS GOVERNMENT IN THE
UNITED STATES

Tᴴᴱ United States of America occupies a unique position among the four large modern democracies. It is stretching the point considerably to say that any American government has ever been a constitutional dictatorship. The application of this book's title to American experiences with crisis government is little more than a convenient hyperbole. There have been four occasions in the history of the Republic—the Civil War, the World War, the Depression of 1933, and the second World War—when the government at Washington was forced to make use of highly irregular powers and procedures in the presence of a pronounced national emergency; yet in each of these instances the adherence to the pattern of peacetime government was tenacious. Perhaps the perils of the Civil War or the Great Depression might have been more speedily and efficiently routed if the government had been more dictatorial and less conventional. The truth is that these crises were mastered by governments which, when contrasted with emergency regimes in France, England, and Weimar Germany, appear to have acted in remarkably close conformance to the normal constitutional scheme.

It is the history of the United States, of course, which has made this possible. Since the founding of the Republic the people of this nation have been forced to deal with exactly one invasion and one revolution, while until 1933 the chief factor in overcoming the economic upheavals which have arisen periodically to plague American society was not resolute governmental action, but the resilient and unaided vitality of the nation's free economy. What is in large part true of America's major national crises is completely true of the many minor instances of social and economic unrest: ordinary methods of government, and often no governmental effort at all, have usually been sufficient to quiet the danger and restore normal times.

A second reason for this tenacious adherence to regular procedures of government is the constitutional nature of the government itself, which presupposes that it will continue to function in all its parts in any crisis of any sort. There are several other explanations of this two-fold verity of American history—the lack of serious crisis and the concomitant lack of crisis government—which should be mentioned in passing: the undeniable fact of geographic isolation, the hugeness and richness of the American continent,[1] the value of the frontier as a safety valve, and the remarkable buoyancy of the nineteenth century American economy. These historical facts have helped to swell the remorseless surge of the Republic's evolution; at the same time they have endowed the American people with a unique sense of security by inducing and indulging a healthy distrust of emergency departures from the normal ways of government, no matter how painful the stress of circumstance might be. Strong government and abnormal government alike are anathema to the traditional American philosophy of politics. Up until 1948 at least, the Americans have been able to get away with this ingrained distaste for emergency power. An institution like the state of siege or Article 48 has always been (and continues to be) a practical and constitutional impossibility in the United States.

Crisis government in this country has therefore been a matter of personalities rather than of institutions. Indeed, the one consistent instrument of emergency government has been the Presidency itself, a fact never more apparent than in the recent war. The study of constitutional dictatorship in the United States is not so much an analysis of institutions like martial law and the delegating statute as it is a history of Abraham Lincoln, Woodrow Wilson, and Franklin D. Roosevelt.

---

[1] In chapter 8 of his *Democracy in America*, de Tocqueville wrote that every presidential election in the United States was in itself a major crisis. The country managed to survive this periodic upheaval, he believed, only because of the wide expanse of territory which prevented scattered disturbances from eventuating into one great civil war!

CHAPTER XIV

The Constitution, the President, and Crisis Government

THE two basic features of the American governmental system of particular significance for the problem of constitutional dictatorship are these: that it is a government of limited powers functioning within the perimeter of a written Constitution, and that it is a government in which the executive power has been conferred upon an independent President not immediately beholden to the legislature in the prosecution of his constitutional and statutory duties. From these obvious features proceed in turn the three leading characteristics of American crisis government already put forward: the adherence to normality, the lack of conscious institutionalization, and the selection of the President, who operates through his personality as much as through recognized institutions and procedures, as the focal point of such government. The constitutional, presidential pattern of government has made crisis rule more difficult, and it has singled out the chief executive as the chief instrument of crisis authority.

The Constitution and Crisis Government

THE implications of the historical fact that the government of the United States has functioned for more than 150 years within the framework of a written, respected, and somewhat rigid Constitution are several and significant.[1] Constitutional dictatorship finds in the Constitution a barrier to strong and abnormal action far more hostile than the fundamental laws and charters of England, France, and Weimar Germany. Whatever men mean by "the Constitution"—whether it be the document itself, the scheme of government it establishes, the vigorous guarantee of "certain unalienable rights" it underwrites, the tradition of perfection it enjoys, or the psychology of constitutionalism it has created in the American people whether ruled or ruling—it has helped induce a widespread belief that there is something essentially wrong about emergency government. All other factors being equal—the intensity of

---

[1] For a discussion of this problem in relation to America's participation in the first World War, see Lindsay Rogers: "The Constitutional Difficulties of American Participation," *Contemporary Review*, CXII (1917), p.32.

the crisis, the desire of the government to face it boldly, the willingness of the people to make sacrifices to conquer it—constitutional dictatorship is still less of a possibility in the United States than in almost any other country on earth. The varieties of crisis government in Great Britain are infinite, as long as public opinion sustains a legally omnipotent Parliament. The varieties of crisis government in the United States are few and limited, for even if public opinion be willing, the Constitution will remain a repressive brake, and changes will be made only under the most terrific pressure of events. The old cry "It's unconstitutional!" is no joke.

The Bill of Rights, federalism, and the separation of powers are the three main constitutional barriers to the easy establishment of emergency dictatorship in the United States. These are the principles of the American system which must be in whole or in part suspended if such government is to be inaugurated in a national emergency. Although the last two have been considerably vitiated by the extraordinary events of this century and the exertions of the government in facing them, they remain even today undeniable obstructions to any emergency regime. The Constitution is no insurmountable barrier to the law of national self-preservation,[2] but it cannot be denied that it has in the past and will in the future put a curb on the probability of constitutional dictatorship not paralleled in the governmental system of any other country. More than this, emergency government has been a constitutional question to a degree quite unmatched in French, German, or English experience. It seems as important for the historian to ascertain whether Lincoln and Roosevelt acted constitutionally as it is to ascertain whether they acted greatly or wisely.

The traditional theory of the Constitution is clearly hostile to the establishment of crisis institutions and procedures. It is constitutional dogma that this document foresees any and every emergency, and that no departure from its solemn injunctions could possibly be necessary. It never seems to have been seriously considered in the Convention of 1787, the *Federalist*, or the debates in the state ratifying conventions that the men who were to govern in future years would ever have to go outside the words of the Constitution to find the means to meet any crisis. The provisions of the document and the government which they ordained were to be adequate for war as well as peace, for rebellion as well as internal calm,[3] and there was no Article 48! Hear for example

[2] See generally Edward S. Corwin: *Total War and the Constitution* (New York, 1947).
[3] This is essentially the argument of the *Federalist*—that the Constitution will be equal to any emergency. See in particular numbers 23, 26, 28, 41, 71.

what the Supreme Court of the United States has had to say on this point. Said Justice David Davis in *Ex Parte Milligan*, 1866:

"The Constitution of the United States is a law for rulers and people, equally in war and in peace, and covers with the shield of its protection all classes of men, at all times, and under all circumstances. No doctrine involving more pernicious consequences was ever invented by the wit of man than that any of its provisions can be suspended during any of the great exigencies of government. Such a doctrine leads directly to anarchy or despotism, but the theory on which it is based is false; for the government, within the Constitution, has all the powers granted to it which are necessary to preserve its existence. . . ."[4]

Chief Justice Charles Evans Hughes in *Home Building and Loan Association v. Blaisdell*, 1934, declared:

"Emergency does not create power. Emergency does not increase granted power or remove or diminish the restrictions imposed upon power granted or reserved. The Constitution was adopted in a period of grave emergency. Its grants of power to the Federal Government . . . were determined in the light of emergency and they are not altered by emergency."[5]

And Justice Frank Murphy, in his concurring opinion in the Hawaiian martial law case, February 25, 1946, quoted the first of these passages once again and said that "we must ever keep (it) in mind."[6] What has been said of the Milligan opinion—that it was an "evident piece of arrant hypocrisy"[7]—may also be said of the others, considering how far the Constitution has actually been stretched in emergencies by at least two of our strong Presidents. And yet these words do mirror faithfully the ideas of rulers and ruled alike throughout this nation's history. Nor is this view of the perfect Constitution the possession of the judges alone. Justice Davis's words have been quoted about as often and as approvingly as *Exodus*, xx, 14. Franklin D. Roosevelt, who brought the emergency power of the President to new heights in his efforts to carry the nation through two great crises, had this to say in his first inaugural address:

"Our Constitution is so simple and practical that it is possible to meet extraordinary needs by changes in emphasis and arrangement without loss of essential form. That is why our constitutional system has proved itself the most superbly enduring political mechanism the modern world has produced. It has met every stress of vast expansion of territory, of foreign wars, of bitter internal strife, of world relations."

[4] 4 Wallace 2, at 120-121. [5] 290 U.S. 398, at 425.
[6] *Duncan v. Kahanamoku* (327 U.S. 304, at 335).
[7] E. S. Corwin: *The President: Office and Powers* (2nd rev. ed., New York, 1941), p.165.

There was as much truth as rhetoric in the President's statement, for the Constitution has indeed been adequate to see this nation through its most perilous hours. There is a reasonable foundation for the tradition of constitutional perfection, and although the Constitution has been several times violated in times of severe emergency, its essence and provisions have generally worked to keep the government well within bounds.

In a sense, then, the entire text of the Constitution foresees crisis government, and none of its provisions must be overlooked in considering its adaptability to such government. There are, however, several clauses in the Constitution which may be singled out as of particular importance in times of national emergency. These are the crisis provisions of the American Constitution:

Preamble: We the people of the United States, in order to . . . insure domestic tranquillity, provide for the common defense. . . .

Art. I, 8: The Congress shall have power . . . to declare war . . . to raise and support armies . . . to provide and maintain a navy; to make rules for the government and regulation of the land and naval forces; to provide for calling forth the militia to execute the laws of the Union, suppress insurrections and repel invasions . . . to make all laws which shall be necessary and proper for carrying into execution the foregoing powers, and all other powers vested by this Constitution in the government of the United States, or in any department or officer thereof.

9: The privilege of the writ of habeas corpus shall not be suspended, unless when in cases of rebellion or invasion the public safety may require it.

Art. II, 1: The executive power shall be vested in a President of the United States of America. . . .

Before he enter on the execution of his office, he shall take the following oath or affirmation: "I do solemnly swear (or affirm) that I will faithfully execute the office of President of the United States, and will to the best of my ability, preserve, protect and defend the Constitution of the United States."

2: The President shall be commander in chief of the army and navy of the United States, and of the militia of the several States, when called into the actual service of the United States. . . .

3: He shall from time to time give to the Congress information of the state of the Union, and recommend to their consideration such measures as he shall judge necessary and expedient; he may, on extraordinary occasions, convene both Houses, or either of them . . . he shall take care that the laws be faithfully executed. . . .

Art. IV, 4: The United States shall guarantee to every State in this Union a republican form of government, and shall protect each of them against invasion; and on the application of the legislature, or of the executive (when the legislature cannot be convened) against domestic violence.

It is on these clauses that all instances and institutions of constitutional dictatorship in the United States must be based. The other parts of the Constitution are not to be overlooked—what they forbid, what they provide, what they fail to provide. For example, it is important to recall that the Bill of Rights presents an apparently (although not actually) unconditional guarantee against legislative encroachment on the freedoms therein asserted, and that legislation by any but the normal process is totally unforeseen. It is equally important to recall that the due process clauses of the Fifth and Fourteenth Amendments have been thrown up by the Supreme Court as imposing barriers to administrative and legislative action of a decisive and arbitrary character. The Constitution looks to the maintenance of the pattern of regular government in even the most stringent of crises.

Martial Law in the United States

WHATEVER else it may forbid or fail to foresee, the Constitution of the United States makes adequate provision for the use of armed force to keep the peace of the nation. Throughout the history of this country its government has never lacked the constitutional or legal authority to maintain public order and internal peace in every part of the land. The Civil War should be proof enough of this assertion. Although it has never been precisely determined just where the line is to be drawn between the respective constitutional powers of President and Congress in the employment of the nation's armed forces, it is nevertheless obvious that through legislative delegation and executive initiative the President occupies a predominant position today, and possesses an almost unrestrained competence to employ and deploy the armed might of this nation to maintain order and authority on every foot of American soil.

The statutes empowering the President "to call forth the militia of any or all of the States, and to employ such parts of the land or naval forces of the United States as he may deem necessary to enforce the faithful execution of the laws of the United States" go back to 1792,[8] and furnish graphic evidence that the American legislature, like all legislatures, has been forced by the cold logic of history to acknowledge the executive branch of the government as the only power qualified to act

---

[8] See *Revised Statutes*, secs. 5297-5300.

as an instrument of constitutional dictatorship. The most conspicuous example of presidential initiative in the use of the armed forces to keep the peace was, of course, Abraham Lincoln and the Civil War. President Cleveland's employment of federal troops in the Pullman Strike of 1894, despite the bitter and warranted protest of Governor Altgeld of Illinois, is perhaps the next most striking indication of the extent of this facet of presidential power.

From the Whiskey Rebellion of 1794 (in the course of which President Washington himself took the field) to the government's seizure of several strike-bound industries in 1946 this power has never been doubted, and it has always been for the President alone to decide when and how and to what extent it is to be employed.[9] The only effective restrictions upon his discharge of this fateful responsibility would seem to be his own political and moral sense and the remote possibility of impeachment. This federal power to keep the peace of the United States, lodged by historical and constitutional development in the elected leader of the American people, runs the gamut of dictatorial action from the mere threat of force to outright martial law.

It is well established that the institution of martial law, whether on the state or national level, is a legal possibility within the framework of the Constitution. Indeed, federal martial law, which like the state variety is patterned on the English institution, is contemplated by the Constitution.[10] The provision for the suspension of the writ of habeas corpus, a process of constitutional dictatorship whose uncertainties are well in the tradition of martial law, is evidence of this statement. The wording of the clause shows that this extraordinary power was understood to exist already and was merely being qualified. Although the history of martial law in the United States is almost exclusively one of its employment by state governments and thus falls outside the scope of this book, its importance as a federal device must not be overlooked.

Not only the institution of martial law itself, but also the confusion surrounding it in English practice and theory find their counterpart in American law and legal thought. Martial law as an instrument of emer-

[9] See the old case of *Martin v. Mott* (12 Wheat. 19). See generally Frederick T. Wilson: *Federal Aid in Domestic Disturbances*, Sen. Doc. no. 209, 57th Congress, 2nd sess. (Washington, 1903). This treatment has been brought up to date by Bennett M. Rich: *The Presidents and Civil Disorder* (Washington, 1941). For the military aspects of presidential and other civil use of troops in quieting disturbances, see *Military Aid to the Civil Power* (Fort Leavenworth, 1925).
[10] See R. S. Rankin: "The Constitutional Basis of Martial Law," *Constitutional Review*, XIII (1929), p.75; Frazer Arnold: "The Rationale of Martial Law." *Am. Bar Assn. Journal*, XV (1929), p.550.

216

gency government on the national level is a hazy mass of concepts, based largely on analogies from state practice. Nevertheless, the labors of Professors Fairman, Rankin, and Corwin have established beyond a doubt that the federal government does possess a power of martial law, that this power springs from the twin sources of the Constitution and the common law, and that the circumstances and qualifications of its initiation and use are, as in English theory, a matter of necessity and fact to be ultimately determined by the regular courts.[11] Professor Corwin asserts that the only test of martial law at the national level would be that of good faith,[12] and Professor Rankin makes clear that, although Congress can declare martial law under the necessary conditions of crisis,[13] the realities of government would seem to place this power almost exclusively in the hands of the President, particularly in view of his constitutional powers and duties as Commander in Chief and executor of the laws.[14] In the states the governors have always been able to declare martial law under circumstances considerably less than desperate.[15] Martial law is for the federal government a phenomenon only attending actual war, civil or foreign. Its existence as an adjunct of the powers of self-preservation inherent in this government cannot be doubted.

The Presidency and Crisis Government

THE implications of the fact that the government of the United States is one of the presidential variety are likewise several and significant. In the first place, since this country is no different from any other in that the use of emergency powers is fundamentally the province of the executive branch, it must follow that a serious crisis will result invariably in an increase in the prestige and competence of the President.[16] This is made doubly certain by the broad and flexible grants of power to the

[11] Charles Fairman: *The Law of Martial Rule* (2nd ed., Chicago, 1943); R. S. Rankin: *When Civil Law Fails* (Durham, 1939); Corwin: *The President*, pp.176-184; and "Martial Law, Yesterday and Today," *Pol. Sci. Q.*, XLVII (1932), p.95. See also W. W. Willoughby: *The Constitutional Law of the United States* (New York, 1929), III, chap. 87; F. B. Wiener: *A Practical Manual of Martial Law* (Harrisburg, 1940).

[12] Corwin, *op. cit.*, pp.182-184.

[13] See W. E. Birkhimer: *Military Government and Martial Law* (3rd rev. ed., Kansas City, 1914), chap. 23. He suggests that the congressional program of reconstruction after the Civil War was, in effect, legislative martial law.

[14] Rankin, *op. cit.*, pp.195 ff.

[15] Judicial sanction of the practice of *preventive* martial law was most strongly stated by Justice Holmes in *Moyer v. Peabody* (212 U.S. 78). But see *Sterling v. Constantin* (287 U.S. 387).

[16] See James Bryce: *The American Commonwealth* (2nd rev. ed., London, 1891), I, pp.50-51, 61.

President found in the Constitution. It was clearly recognized by the founding fathers that in moments of peril the effective action of the government of the United States would be channeled through the person of the chief executive. As Hamilton said in the *Federalist*, number 70:

"Energy in the executive is a leading character in the definition of good government. It is essential to the protection of the community against foreign attacks; it is not less essential to the steady administration of the laws; to the protection of property against those irregular and high-handed combinations which sometimes interrupt the ordinary course of justice; to the security of liberty against the enterprises and assaults of ambition, of faction, and of anarchy."

And his great antagonist wrote: "In times of peace the people look most to their representatives; but in war to the executive only. . . ."[17] Constitutionally, historically, and logically the office of the President is the focus of crisis government in the United States.

Presidential ascendancy in any condition of emergency is built squarely upon two solid foundations, initiative (the Constitution) and delegation (the laws). The Lockian theory of prerogative has found a notable instrument in the President of the United States, and executive initiative has come to be the basic technique of constitutional dictatorship in this country. If the Constitution is rigid, the executive power therein stated most certainly is not; and, although much of the President's power to act decisively in emergencies has proceeded from Congress, the strong Presidents have grounded most of their unusual actions in the broad terms of Article II. As Attorney General Murphy pointed out to the Senate in 1939, the President's constitutional powers in time of emergency defy precise definition, "since their extent and limitations are largely dependent upon conditions and circumstances."[18]

Important in this respect is Theodore Roosevelt's celebrated "Stewardship Theory," under which the first Roosevelt, following the lead of James Wilson, proclaimed himself competent to proceed to just about any action demanded by an evident national necessity—as long as it was not specifically forbidden him by the Constitution or by duly enacted laws of Congress.[19] This doctrine converts the Presidency into a

[17] Jefferson to Rodney, February 10, 1810, *The Writings of Thomas Jefferson*, v (Washington, 1853), p.500.

[18] XXXIX *Op. Att. Gen.* (1939), 343. "The domain of executive power in time of war constitutes a sort of 'dark continent' in our jurisprudence."—J. W. Garner: *"Le Pouvoir Exécutif en Temps de Guerre aux Etats-Unis,"* Rev. Dr. Pub., XXXV (1918), p.13.

[19] See his statement of this doctrine in *An Autobiography* (New York, 1913), pp.388-389. The looseness of the grant of executive power in the Constitution and its possibilities as a matrix for dictatorship were apparent long before T. Roosevelt, or even

mighty reservoir of crisis authority. President Taft opposed this revolutionary concept with a strict construction of the President's powers,[20] and the weight of theory is certainly on his side. A literal application of the Stewardship Theory would constitute a serious disruption of the American constitutional scheme. And yet, whatever the theory, in moments of extreme national emergency the facts have always been with Theodore Roosevelt and John Locke. The crisis actions of Abraham Lincoln and Franklin D. Roosevelt will be examined in due time, and this assertion will be conclusively demonstrated.

Secondly, Congress itself has recognized that the executive branch alone can properly exercise emergency powers. Delegations of unusual power for the duration of some particular crisis have been made repeatedly since the founding of the Republic. Moreover, throughout the nation's history but especially in this century, the President has been vested permanently with vast discretionary powers to be exercised in time of war or other national emergency, usually to be determined and proclaimed by himself. Few Americans realize just how far this practice of delegating power for future emergencies has gone. Even before 1939 Mr. Roosevelt, in an emergency *to be ascertained and declared by himself*, could have prohibited transactions in foreign exchange, seized power houses and dams, increased the army and navy beyond their authorized enlisted strength, devalued the dollar, forbidden all Federal Reserve transactions except under regulations which he approved, seized (in war or when war was imminent) any plant refusing to give preference to governmental contracts or to manufacture arms for a fair price, requisitioned any American vessel, and exercised complete control over all communications in the United States.[21]

These statutes are by no means a result of conscious congressional planning. Indeed, they are almost without exception "obvious leftovers

---

Lincoln. See Abel Upshur's significant comments in *A Brief Inquiry into the True Nature and Character of Our Federal Government*, pp.116-117, published in 1840. Professor Corwin: *The President*, p.24, notes that the Swiss, in framing their constitution in 1848, imitated the American charter in some respects, but "steered clear of the Presidency because they felt it to be conducive to dictatorship."

[20] *Our Chief Magistrate and His Powers* (New York, 1916), pp.139-147.

[21] A list of those statutes designed for presidential use in emergency is to be found in a valuable pamphlet issued by the Library of Congress Legislative Service and entitled *Acts of Congress Applicable in Time of Emergency*, bull. no. 5 (Washington, 1941). Supplements to this listing have since been issued. See also the letter from Attorney General Murphy to the President of the Senate: *Executive Powers Under National Emergency*, Sen. Doc. no. 133, 76th Congress, 2nd sess. See generally R. E. Hayes: "Emergencies and the Power of the United States Government to Meet Them," *Temple Univ. L.Q.*, XVI (1941), p.173.

from periods of actually existent emergency, and do not represent the considered judgment of Congress that they ought to be retained permanently."[22] Nevertheless, they remain on the statute books, and the President holds them as a ready reservoir of statutory supplementation to his constitutional powers. It is of interest to note that these and all other delegations of power to the President are effected by a simple majority of Congress, but can only be retracted, if the President insists upon making use of his veto power, by a two-thirds vote of each House. By statute as well as constitutional provision and inherent nature, the Presidency bears the major responsibility for the success of crisis government in this country. Small wonder that Lincoln, Wilson, and Roosevelt, the three great crisis Presidents, were "dictators" to the men who opposed them and even to many who supported them. (Even Buchanan was probably called a dictator by somebody.)

The natural difficulty (or even frustration) that presidential governments experience in securing the necessary harmony of executive and legislature in time of crisis finds one of its most striking examples in the government of the United States. The constitutional system conspires to set Congress and President apart from one another with no guarantee that the unity of purpose indispensable to many types of national emergency will be forthcoming.[28] More than this, the fact that the President is not, as is the Prime Minister of Great Britain, the elected agent of the legislature makes the passage of an emergency enabling act a much more difficult achievement. Although "the want of elasticity, the impossibility of a dictatorship, the total absence of a *revolutionary reserve*" in this government was clearly overstated by Walter Bagehot, the fact remains that the rigidities of a presidential government dedicated to the shade of "the celebrated Montesquieu" are not as conducive to successful emergency government as are the manifest flexibilities of the cabinet system. One of the most pressing problems in any crisis in this country has been and remains the erection and use of techniques whereby this constitutional separation of the executive and legislative branches may be effectively bridged. It was to this problem that Wilson and Franklin Roosevelt in particular devoted their attentions and personalities.

[22] Corwin, *op. cit.*, p.135.
[28] Walter Bagehot: *The English Constitution*, pp.98-100; Bryce, *op. cit.*, I, pp.288-289. For a recent statement of the problem see Thomas K. Finletter: *Can Representative Government Do the Job?* (New York, 1945), pp.9 ff. An antidote to these criticisms of the American system is furnished by Don K. Price: "The Parliamentary and Presidential Systems," *Public Admin. Rev.* (Autumn, 1943), p.317.

And as Bagehot further pointed out, the government and people of the United States lack a satisfactory way to get rid of an incompetent President in time of crisis. There is no guarantee that a man at all equal to the times will be in the White House. The cabinet system makes the substitution of a crisis executive for one more suited to the problems of peace a relatively simple matter. The presidential system makes such a substitution a virtual impossibility. Even though the United States has been fortunate enough to have a strong and able President in each of its major crises, still Bagehot was right when he wrote that "success in a lottery is no argument for lotteries." So far this country has had no cause to regret this continuing separation of the executive and legislative branches and the fixed terms for each. This is no guarantee for the future.

Throughout the first seventy years of the Republic under a constitutional and presidential government, the hopes of the founding fathers that the Constitution would work for a signal reduction in the occasions for crisis government, and would be able to comprehend and overcome such crises as would nevertheless arise, were thoroughly justified. Until the final outbreak of the Irrepressible Conflict, a genuine instance of emergency government can hardly be said to have existed on a national scale. Such insurrections, wars, or panics as there were, and there were enough, were successfully undergone and written into the pages of history without occasioning any important readjustment in the organization of the government or abridgment of the liberties of the people. President Washington's determined actions prevented the Whiskey Rebellion from becoming another Shays' Rebellion; Thomas Jefferson made his contribution with a significant union of executive and legislature in the face of difficult national problems, particularly in the one-day passage of the Embargo Act of December 22, 1807; the Non-Intercourse Act of 1809 presented an excellent example of the delegation of emergency power to the President; Andrew Jackson made it perfectly clear in the Nullification crisis that the government stood ready to preserve the Union of states and the constitutional supremacy of the federal government by outright war against its citizens;[24] and James K. Polk demonstrated pronounced abilities in the use of his constitutional power

[24] Said Jackson to a South Carolina congressman departing for home: "Tell them from me that they can talk and write resolutions and print threats to their hearts' content. But if one drop of blood be shed there in defiance of the laws of the United States, I will hang the first man of them I can get my hands on to the first tree I can find."—quoted in G. F. Milton: *The Use of Presidential Power* (Boston, 1944), p.91.

as Commander in Chief. But even these were isolated instances, and the emergencies were not exactly catastrophic in nature. And on the other side of the picture, John Adams attempted to transfer his title and powers as Commander in Chief to George Washington; Madison fumbled and faltered through a war which saw the nation's capitol burned; and Martin Van Buren maintained stoutly that the government was not supposed to lift a finger for any of its citizens ruined by a nation-wide depression.

Thus it was that the American government in 1861, brought face to face with the most exacting crisis this country has ever known, had no precedent in its history for emergency rule on a national scale, and no authority in the Constitution to exert extraordinary force in an extraordinary manner except in the inchoate and ill-defined powers of the President.[25] How Abraham Lincoln resorted to those powers and met the rebellion is the most significant chapter in the story of constitutional dictatorship in the United States, and indeed a unique instance in the history of this age-old phenomenon of constitutional government.

[25] On the general subject of the President's war powers, see Clarence A. Berdahl: *War Powers of the Executive in the United States* (Urbana, 1920) ; Corwin, *op. cit.*, chap. 5; J. W. Garner: *"Le Pouvoir Exécutif en Temps de Guerre aux Etats-Unis,"* *Rev. Dr. Pub.*, xxxv (1918), p.5; H. White: *Executive Influence in Determining Military Policy in the United States* (Urbana, 1925) ; Pendleton Herring: *The Impact of War* (New York, 1941), chap. 6; E. A. Gilmore: "War Power—Executive Power and the Constitution," *Iowa L.R.*, xxix (1944), p.463; M. K. White: "The War Powers of the President," *Wisc. L.R.* (March 1943), p.205.

CHAPTER XV

The Great American Crisis:
The Civil War

No threat to the continued existence of a nation and its government is so exacting, no species of political and social upheaval is so ominous, as the crisis of civil war. The attempt of a large and discontented segment of the population to seize power or win independence by force of arms is as potent a menace to constitutional government as can well be imagined. Thus it is that the War of 1861-1865, certainly one of the most bitter and bloody civil struggles in all recorded history, was the most dangerous emergency ever faced by a government of the United States. The four years of the Civil War remain even today the most critical in the life of the Republic. The principle and the institutions of constitutional dictatorship played a decisive role in the North's successful effort to maintain the Union by force of arms.

It was in this conflict that the peculiar pattern of crisis government in the United States was first set. It is remarkable how little change in the structure of the government and how little abridgment of civil liberty accompanied the prosecution of this bitter war. In the light of the crisis and in comparison with the experience of other democratic nations in similar situations, the government of the United States stayed surprisingly close to the peacetime constitutional scheme. The one major institutional readjustment effected in the course of the war was the astounding expansion of the powers of the Presidency, the enforced disclosure of the hitherto well-hidden emergency potentialities of this great office. The story of crisis government in the Civil War is the story of Abraham Lincoln.

The President's crisis actions fall chronologically into two distinct categories: those taken between the outbreak of armed rebellion on April 12, 1861 and the first subsequent meeting of Congress July 4, 1861, and those taken during the remainder of the war. The significant point is that the unusual powers which he had assumed in the absence of Congress were firmly established by the time the two Houses met, and, despite congressional efforts to pare them down, remained virtually intact throughout the four years of the war.

The Lincoln Dictatorship

THE eleven weeks between the fall of Sumter and July 4, 1861 constitute the most interesting single episode in the history of constitutional dictatorship. The simple fact that one man was the government of the United States in the most critical period in all its 165 years, and that he acted on no precedent and under no restraint, makes this the paragon of all democratic, constitutional dictatorships. For if Lincoln was a great dictator, he was a greater democrat. Whether this was the most effective way to have combatted the crisis no man can say. Whether what Lincoln did was strictly constitutional is for the history of the Civil War a rather minor issue. The important fact is that he assumed unprecedented authority on his own initiative, that he was supported in this radical conduct by the majority of public opinion, and that he thereby saved the Union and set a consequential historical and constitutional precedent for all future crises in this or any other democracy.

It is impossible to say just what powers the Lincoln of April 1861 thought that he constitutionally possessed to meet the actuality of armed rebellion. He had come to the office of President with scant preconception of the authority it embodied, "with little more than an acute understanding of his obligation to see to the due execution of the laws."[1] But he had sworn "an oath registered in Heaven" to defend the Constitution, and in his inaugural address he promised his fellow citizens to save the Union without which the Constitution would be nothing but a scrap of paper. The Union must be preserved, and, in direct contrast to the vacillating Buchanan who had asserted that as President he had no right to coerce a state to remain in the Union, Lincoln was ready to use military force to prevent secession. There was something greater than the Constitution, without which that charter had no meaning— the Union. "If the Union and the Government cannot be saved out of this terrible shock of war constitutionally, *a* Union and *a* Government must be saved unconstitutionally."[2] Thus might he have reasoned. He had little concern for the institutional form which his actions were to take; he meant only to act—as President, as Commander in Chief, as

[1] Norman J. Small: *Some Presidential Interpretations of the Presidency* (Baltimore, 1932), p.31. By far the best study of Lincoln as President is the admirable two-volume work of James G. Randall: *Lincoln the President* (New York, 1943).

[2] S. G. Fisher: *The Trial of the Constitution* (Philadelphia, 1862). This great book is an eloquent statement of the powers of emergency and self-preservation inherent in the Constitution and government. And in 1944 a Justice of the Supreme Court stated: "The armed services must protect a society, not merely its Constitution."—Justice Jackson in *Korematsu v. U.S.* (323 U.S. 214, at 244).

the man whose duty it was to secure the faithful execution of the laws, and as the sole possessor of the indefinite grant of executive power in Article II of the Constitution.

"It became necessary for me to choose whether, using only the existing means, agencies, and processes which Congress had provided, I should let the Government fall at once into ruin or whether, availing myself of the broader powers conferred by the Constitution in cases of insurrection, I would make an effort to save it, with all its blessings, for the present age and for posterity."[3]

It is impossible to dissociate Mr. Lincoln's personality, his mystic conception of the Union, and his comprehension of his duty as President from the extraordinary actions he took as constitutional dictator. Whatever he thought, it is certain that he acted as if his task were the dispersion of a gigantic mob. In the words of the Militia Act of 1795, the government was faced "by combinations too powerful to be suppressed by the ordinary course of judicial proceedings or by the powers vested in the marshals." It was therefore his plain duty to disperse these combinations. The rebellion was a colossal riot aimed at the existence of the nation, and he, as Commander in Chief and executor of the laws, could call up all the powers of self-preservation in the Constitution and call out all the loyal citizenry to give him aid in dispersing the persons disturbing the peace of the United States.

His first step was to issue an executive proclamation (April 15, 1861)[4] in which he declared that, inasmuch as the execution of the laws of the United States was being forcibly obstructed in the seven southernmost states, he was compelled to resort to his constitutional and statutory powers to call forth "the militia of the several States of the Union to the aggregate number of 75,000" in order to suppress the rebellion and guarantee the execution of the laws. In this same proclamation he put out a call to the Houses of Congress to convene in special session on July 4 "to consider and determine such measures as, in their wisdom, the public safety and interest may seem to demand."

This last point deserves consideration. It was a judicious resolution of the President not to have convoked a divided Congress in the period between his inauguration and the fall of Sumter. It was a rather arbitrary decision not to have done so immediately after April 12. It can only be interpreted as a considered determination to crush the rebellion

[3] James D. Richardson: *Messages and Papers of the Presidents* (Washington, 1897), VI, p.78.
[4] *Ibid.*, pp.13-14.

swiftly without the vexatious presence of an unpredictable Congress to confuse the narrow issue. It is highly probable that Lincoln expected the whole thing to be over by July 4. Whatever the judgment as to the rationale and wisdom of this audacious stroke, its significance for history cannot be doubted. He was allowed to proceed without external check to a series of unusual measures which he alone deemed necessary to lay the rebellion. Unlike Cincinnatus, this great constitutional dictator was self-appointed.

By a proclamation of April 19 Mr. Lincoln clamped a blockade on the ports of the seceded states, a measure hitherto regarded as contrary to both the Constitution and the law of nations except when the government was embroiled in a declared, foreign war.[5] On April 20 he ordered a total of nineteen vessels to be added immediately to the Navy "for purposes of public defense,"[6] and a few days later the blockade was extended to the ports of Virginia and North Carolina.[7]

It was on May 3 that the President for the first time passed well beyond the most latitudinarian construction of his constitutional powers and entered into one of the hitherto (and ever since) most jealously guarded fields of congressional power, those clauses of the Constitution which state that Congress shall have power "to raise and support armies" and "to provide and maintain a navy." Although he had been able to point to statutory authority allowing him to call out the militia of the several states, his proclamation of May 3 (appealing for "42,034 volunteers to serve for the period of three years" and enlarging the regular army by 23,000 and the navy by 18,000) was an out-and-out invasion of the legislative power of the Congress of the United States, an invasion hardly mitigated by the President's declared purpose of submitting these increases for the approval of Congress as soon as it should assemble.[8] This amazing disregard for the words of the Constitution, though considered by many as unavoidable, was considered by nobody as legal.

Nor was this the only unabashed presidential encroachment upon the power of Congress in these weeks. On April 20 he had directed Secretary of the Treasury Chase to advance two millions of dollars of unappropriated funds in the Treasury to three private citizens of New York who were absolutely unauthorized to receive it, "to be used by them in meeting such requisitions as should be directly consequent upon the military and naval measures necessary for the defense and support of

[5] Ibid., pp.14-15.
[7] Ibid., p.15.
[6] Ibid., p.78.
[8] Ibid., pp. 15-16.

226

the Government"—this despite the blunt constitutional provision that "No money shall be drawn from the Treasury but in consequence of appropriations made by law." This extraordinary and unconstitutional action, necessitated as Mr. Lincoln later explained by reason of the large number of disloyal persons in the various departments of the government—a fact which he regarded as permitting him to confide official duties to private citizens "favorably known for their ability, loyalty, and patriotism"—was not adequately recounted and elucidated by the President until a letter to Congress of May 26, 1862.[9] Another unprecedented act of a legislative character was the offer of a temporary loan, a pledging of the credit of the United States for a quarter of a billion dollars.

The actions of President Lincoln by which he undertook to maintain public order and suppress open treason in the loyal sections of the Union were even more astounding. The outstanding step of this nature was his proclamation of April 27 authorizing the Commanding General of the United States Army to suspend the writ of habeas corpus "at any point or in the vicinity of any military line which is now or which shall be used between the city of Philadelphia and the city of Washington." This was his answer to the violence being visited by the Baltimore mobs on the Washington-Philadelphia Railroad and the Northern regiments passing along it on their way to Washington.[10] A proclamation of July 2 extended this power to a similar area between Washington and New York.[11] This was done by the President in the face of almost unanimous opinion that the constitutional clause regulating the suspension of the writ of habeas corpus was directed to Congress alone, and that the President did not share in this power of suspension. Mr. Lincoln solved this particular problem by having Attorney General Bates work up an opinion championing his view that the President had the power and duty to take such action in case of necessity.[12] The still undecided question of the location of the power to suspend the writ of habeas corpus Lincoln decided in his own favor, and the only official judicial or legislative declaration ever to contradict his actions and the opinion of Bates, the brave decision of Chief Justice Taney in the circuit case of *Ex parte Merryman*,[13] was simply disregarded.

Finally, Mr. Lincoln directed that the Post Office be closed to "trea-

[9] *Ibid.*, pp.77-79.   [10] *Ibid.*, p.18.   [11] *Ibid.*, p.19.
[12] July 5, 1861; x *Op. Atty. Gen.*, 74.
[13] *Fed. Cases*, no. 9487 (1861). On the whole matter of the suspension of the writ of habeas corpus in the war, see S. G. Fisher: "The Suspension of Habeas Corpus during the War of the Rebellion," *Pol. Sci. Q.*, III (1888), p.454.

sonable correspondence" and "caused persons who were represented to him as being or about to engage in disloyal and treasonable practices to be arrested by special civil as well as military agencies and detained in military custody when necessary to prevent them or deter others from such practices."[14] In the light of the numbers and fervor of the "fifth column" behind the Union lines at this time and throughout the war, these measures, though clearly a deviation from established and constitutional American practice, hardly merit the opprobrium cast upon Mr. Lincoln by reason of their adoption.

These actions are the sum total of "the Lincoln dictatorship," an extraordinary eleven weeks of presidential activity unparalleled in the history of the United States. By the time Congress had come together, he had set on foot a complete program—executive, military, legislative, and judicial—for the suppression of the insurrection. When it is considered what forms of government have in recent years been labeled "dictatorships," the application of this word to Mr. Lincoln's few weeks of unrestrained power is a blatant exaggeration. Yet it cannot be denied that he had proceeded to acts of a radical, dictatorial, and constitutionally questionable character.[15]

On July 4 he greeted Congress with a special message,[16] a remarkable state paper in which he described frankly the steps he had taken, rationalized his more doubtful actions by reference to the "war power of the Government" under the Constitution (his phrase and evidently his idea), and invited whatever ratification Congress should think necessary to legalize them. This message is a significant assertion of the inherent crisis power of the President. Lincoln posed and answered with a forceful *yes* the fundamental question whether a constitutional government has an unqualified power of self-preservation, in this instance whether the government of the United States was constitutionally equal to the task of preserving the Union by force. More than this, he asserted that in the American government this power of self-preservation is centered in the office of the President.

Mr. Lincoln apparently entertained no doubts concerning the legality of his calling out the militia and the establishment of the blockade, nor did he find it necessary to explain why he had chosen to postpone the

[14] These actions are divulged and explained in an executive order of Secretary Stanton, February 14, 1862, concerning the release of political prisoners—Richardson, *op. cit.*, VI, pp.102-104.

[15] Carl Schmitt cites Lincoln as a *kommissarischer Diktator*, one who suspended the Constitution in order to save it.—*Die Diktatur*, p.136.

[16] Richardson, *op. cit.*, VI, pp.20-31.

emergency convocation of Congress to July 4. He asserted that the power to suspend the writ of habeas corpus could belong to him as well as to Congress, and tactfully left the subsequent disposal of this matter to the legislators. For his actions of a more legislative, and therefore constitutionally more doubtful character, he advanced a different justification:

"These measures, whether strictly legal or not, were ventured upon under what appeared to be a popular demand and a public necessity, trusting then, as now, that Congress would readily ratify them. It is believed that nothing has been done beyond the constitutional competency of Congress."

Thereby Mr. Lincoln subscribed to a theory that in the absence of Congress and in the presence of an emergency the President has the right and duty to adopt measures which would ordinarily be illegal, subject to the necessity of subsequent congressional approval. He did more than this; he seemed to assert that the war powers of the Constitution could upon occasion devolve completely upon the President, if their exercise was based upon public opinion and an inexorable necessity. They were then sufficient to embrace any action within the fields of executive or legislative or even judicial power essential to the preservation of the Union. The whole tenor of his message implied that this government, like all others, possessed an absolute power of self-defense, a power to be exerted by the President of the United States. And this power extended to the breaking of the fundamental laws of the nation, if such a step were unavoidable.

"Are all the laws *but one* to go unexecuted, and the Government itself go to pieces lest that one be violated? Even in such a case, would not the official oath be broken if the Government should be overthrown when it was believed that disregarding the single law would tend to preserve it?"

In other words, in an instance of urgent necessity, an official of a democratic, constitutional state will be acting more faithfully to his oath of office if he breaks one law in order that the rest may operate unimpeded.[17] This was a powerful and unique plea for the doctrine of paramount necessity. It established no definite rule for this or any other country, but it does serve as a superlative example of how a true democrat in power is likely to act when there is no other way for him to preserve the constitutional system which he has sworn to defend.

[17] Lord Bryce, in his *American Commonwealth*, I, p.289, n. 1, tells the widely quoted but probably apocryphal story that Lincoln said to Chase in the first days of the war: "These rebels are violating the Constitution to destroy the Union. I will violate the Constitution if necessary to save the Union; I suspect, Chase, that our Constitution is going to have a rough time of it before we get done with this row."

Congress, faced by a *fait accompli* that was in its nature irrevocable, registered approval of "all the acts, proclamations, and orders of the President respecting the army and navy of the United States and calling out or relating to the militia or volunteers from the United States" in an act of August 6, 1861.[18] Moreover, the Supreme Court, asked well over a year later in the *Prize Cases* to determine the legality of the presidential blockade, gave its direct sanction to this particular matter and its general blessing to Lincoln's extraordinary exercise of the war power. The subsequent congressional ratification of these actions was held to be unnecessary.

"Whether the President in fulfilling his duties as Commander-in-Chief, in suppressing an insurrection, has met with such armed resistance, and a civil war of such alarming proportions as will compel him to accord to them the character of belligerents, is a question to be decided *by him*, and this Court must be governed by the decisions and acts of the political department of the Government to which this power was entrusted. . . . He must determine what degree of force the crisis demands."[19]

What the Supreme Court held was simply this: that the President of the United States has the constitutional power, under such circumstances as he shall deem imperative, to brand as belligerents the inhabitants of any area in general insurrection. In other words, he has an almost unrestrained power to act toward insurrectionary citizens as if they were enemies of the United States, and thus place them outside the protection of the Constitution. This, it seems hardly necessary to state, is dictatorial power in the extreme. The Constitution can be suspended after all—by any President of the United States who ascertains and proclaims a widespread territorial revolt. "In the interval between April 12 and July 4, 1861 a new principle thus appeared in the constitutional system of the United States, namely, that of a temporary dictatorship."[20]

The Civil War Government After July 4, 1861

ONCE Congress had reassembled in answer to the President's call, the normal organization of the government began to function again, and continued to do so for the remainder of the war. Ordinarily in emer-

[18] XII *Stat.* 326.

[19] *Prize Cases* (2 Black 635, at 670). The dissenting justices clung to the view that a civil war, like any other, must be declared, and that Congress had not recognized the existence of this conflict until July 13, 1861.

[20] W. A. Dunning: *Essays on the Civil War and Reconstruction* (New York, 1898), p.20.

gency governments the inflation of executive power is accompanied by a deflation of legislative power, resulting from the transfer of legislative authority by means of a delegatory statute. This was not true of Lincoln and his Congress. It must be remembered that it was new, untapped power which the President had undertaken to wield, power he had seized on his own initiative. Congress gave him nothing but unenthusiastic acquiescence in his eleven weeks dictatorship, and unquestionably regarded itself as in no way degraded by this exertion of presidential power. In fact, it proposed to get its share.

Congress continued to grind out in the usual manner the entire legislative program by which the Union was governed at home and the armies kept in the field, and in this program Lincoln, by all modern standards, had remarkably little hand. The day of outright legislative leadership by the President as a crisis procedure was still in the future. Mr. Lincoln and his Congress went their respective ways throughout the war in a sort of reciprocal isolation incomprehensible to Bagehot and contrary to the essential nature of crisis government. Lincoln did not attempt to break down the barrier between the legislative and executive branches; he simply ignored it. Even in his annual messages to Congress his proposals of legislation were general and timid, and his action in presenting to Congress on July 14, 1862 a specific proposal for compensated abolition was regarded as even more audacious than some of his enterprises under the war power.[21] What cooperation did exist between the two branches was effected through Secretaries Stanton and Chase in conjunction with their followings in Congress. Mr. Lincoln was content with backing up their proposals, whether in public or in conference with congressional leaders. In short, the crisis of 1861-1865 failed completely to break down the separation of executive and legislative branches so painstakingly wrought in this country's constitutional pattern.

And while it fought continually and on the whole successfully to keep the President out of the acknowledged legislative sphere, Congress itself was not loathe to project its influence and power into the arena of war-making, which by his eleven weeks of solitary authority Mr. Lincoln had staked out as his own preserve. Congress was not without its advocates of war as primarily the business of the legislative branch and of the executive as an appendage to carry out the legislative will. Said Thad Stevens: "We possess all the powers now claimed un-

---

[21] The draft of his proposed bill—"the passage of which substantially as presented I respectfully and earnestly recommend"—is in Richardson, *op. cit.*, VI, p.84.

der the Constitution, even the tremendous power of dictatorship."[22] But after the failure of the radicals in Congress to work a readjustment in Lincoln's Cabinet in December 1862,[23] the success of the President's assertion to power could no longer be doubted. Unable to grasp for itself a respectable share of the emergency authority which he had found hidden in the Constitution and had exploited so boldly, Congress had to be content with maintaining its normal powers undiminished. This did not hinder the legislature from sniping away continually at Mr. Lincoln's position.

The congressional outpost from which it harassed the President was the Joint Committee on the Conduct of the War, an investigating commission consisting of three senators and four representatives.[24] It was created in December 1861, and continued to function throughout the war. Inquiring everywhere about everything that had to do with the conduct of the war, this Committee, led by Ben Wade and Zachariah Chandler, never ceased to assert the doctrine of congressional participation, if not supremacy, in the actual prosecution of military campaigns. For Lincoln the Committee was a constant irritant, questioning every general but Grant, disciplining and helping to unseat several of them, making lengthy and hostile reports (eight volumes of them) on all aspects of the war, virtually forcing the resignation of Cameron and dictating the appointment of Stanton as Secretary of War, exerting control over certain military operations, and fighting with the President over the dismissal of incompetents such as Hooker. Whether, in the long run, the Committee rendered valuable or harmful service to the cause of the Union is an undecided and much argued question. Its mere existence proves the unwillingness of Congress to acquiesce in Lincoln's conception of the relative crisis competence of the two branches.[25] Moreover, it set a precedent for the future. Congressional investigating committees are an accepted part of the crisis scene today.

[22] *Congressional Globe*, XXXVIII, 2nd sess., p.440. Said Senator Sumner: "He is only the instrument of Congress under the Constitution of the United States."—*Congr. Globe*, XXXVII, 2nd sess., p.2972.

[23] For the details, see Carl Sandburg: *Abraham Lincoln, the War Years* (New York, 1939), I, pp.636 ff. An excellent new appraisal of the relations of Lincoln with this group is T. Harry Williams: *Lincoln and the Radicals* (Madison, 1941). On Lincoln's relations with his Cabinet, see Burton J. Hendrick: *Lincoln's War Cabinet* (Boston, 1946).

[24] See generally W. W. Pierson: "The Committee on the Conduct of the Civil War," *Am. Hist. Rev.*, XXIII (1918), p.550; T. H. Williams: "The Committee on the Conduct of the War," *Journal of the American Military Institute*, III (1939), p.139.

[25] For an interesting account of the attacks on Lincoln, both in and out of Congress, see Charles Warren: "Lincoln's 'Despotism' as Critics saw it in 1861" in the *New York Times*, May 12, 1918, sec. 5.

It is a matter of history that the two Houses remained throughout the war the arena for some of the most bitter attacks upon the President and the whole war effort launched anywhere in the North. The Whig tradition of legislative supremacy and fear of the executive had carried over into the new Republican Party, and was voiced continually in Congress. That the Democratic minority, swollen to dangerous proportions by the elections of 1862, looked upon the President with undisguised disdain or fear, and generally voted accordingly, goes without saying. Lincoln was no dictator on Capitol Hill.

Meanwhile Mr. Lincoln went forward with his high resolve to see the war to the bitter end. He had brought the office of President to a new high of power and prestige, and he kept it there to the end. His interpretation of the war powers confided in him by the Constitution had become better defined and stabilized at an exalted level. It appears that he considered himself constitutionally empowered to do just about anything that the necessities of the military situation demanded. "As Commander in Chief of the Army and Navy in time of war I suppose I have a right to take any measure which may best subdue the enemy."[26] His uncertainties and his tendency to regard his war power as an interim one in the absence of Congress were now dispelled. The use of dictatorial force to save the Union became in his mind almost exclusively an executive affair.[27] He had read into the words of the Constitution the mystical term *Union*, and after 1861 he never doubted that his power to preserve the Union had no limits. Indeed, the only limitation on Lincoln's activity was "not the clear expression of the organic law, but the forbearance of a distracted people."[28]

Many of the President's acts were, of course, merely executory of the will of Congress. After the Acts of August 6, 1861 and July 17, 1862 all proceedings in the confiscation of rebel property could be regarded as presidential executions of congressional desires. This is likewise true of all presidential suspensions of the writ of habeas corpus after the Act of March 3, 1863.[29] In many of his other actions, however, Mr. Lincoln continued to exercise unprecedented authority, based on

[26] Quoted in Nicolay and Hay: *Abraham Lincoln, a History* (New York, 1890), VI, pp.155-156.
[27] See the note in Corwin: *The President*, pp.382-383, speculating on the influence which William Whiting's celebrated *War Powers under the Constitution* (43rd ed., Boston, 1871) may have had on Lincoln's conception of his war powers. This book, the work of a solicitor in the War Department, is probably the most extreme American statement of governmental and presidential absolutism in time of war.
[28] Dunning, *op. cit.*, p.15.
[29] These acts are, respectively: XII *Stat.* 319, 589, 755.

his latitudinarian interpretation of his war powers under the Constitution. Not only did he do things that were regarded by most people as within the exclusive field of Congress's power, but he went further and asserted his competence to do things in an emergency that Congress could never do at all, maintaining that his designation as Commander in Chief allowed him to adopt measures that in normal times could only be effected by an amendment to the Constitution. This was a revolutionary and unique reading of the war clauses of that document, an unparalleled precedent for some equally extraordinary crisis act by a future President of the United States. His most eventful use of this sort of war power was the Emancipation Proclamation of September 22, 1862,[30] "as absolute an exercise of power as the ukase of the Czar which freed the serfs of Russia."[31] In this proclamation he seems to have asserted that, whereas Congress (which incidentally had just adjourned) could only deal with slavery by the method of compensated abolition, he as President could proclaim any or all the slaves free without compensation to their owners, if such a step were regarded as indispensable to the prosecution of the war. It was his expectation that this freeing of the slaves in rebel territory would add immeasurably to the strength of the Union cause; as such he considered it within his powers as Commander in Chief. He might have based this epic measure on the Confiscation Acts; instead he preferred to go to the Constitution, the fundamental charter, for his authority.

He further resorted to his constitutional war powers to initiate a program of limited conscription under the Militia Act of 1862;[32] to promulgate a complete code embodying the rules of war applicable to the armies in the field (in direct derogation of Article I, section 8, clause 14, of the Constitution, which empowers Congress "to make rules for the government and regulation of the land and naval forces"),[33] to set up military and even permanent governments in conquered territories,[34] and

[30] Richardson, *op. cit.*, VI, pp.96-98. The final proclamation of January 1, 1863 is on pp.157-159. For the details, see Sandburg, *op. cit.*, I, pp.555 ff.; II, pp.8 ff.

[31] H. J. Ford: *The Rise and Growth of American Politics* (New York, 1900), p.280.

[32] Richardson, *op. cit.*, VI, p.120.

[33] The celebrated "Lieber's Code" is to be found in General Orders, no. 100, *Official Records, War of the Rebellion*, ser. III, vol. 3.

[34] The power of the President to provide for the military government of conquered territories is undoubted, but whether this power extends to aiding the people in areas where an insurrection has been suppressed to resurrect republican and loyal governments is another question. Congress refused to seat the senators and representatives sent to Washington in 1864 by the presidentially-reconstructed government of Arkansas. On the general problem of military government in the Civil War, see A. H. Carpenter: "Military Government of Southern Territory, 1861-1865" in *Reports, American Historical Assn.* (1900), I, p.465; Birkhimer, *passim*; Whiting, *op. cit.*, pp.259 ff.

to issue plans for reconstruction. It need hardly be mentioned that he took his constitutional designation as Commander in Chief literally and exercised considerable control and direction of the military prosecution of the war.[35]

Lincoln and Civil Liberties

THE President not only asserted that the crisis brought him unique executive, legislative, and even constituent power; he further assumed authority of a judicial nature. Throughout the war the governmental control of individual liberty, such as it was, was almost completely in his hands, not because Congress had decided that this would be a good policy, but because he as President undertook such responsibility on his own initiative. The entire program to suppress treason was based on the presidential suspension of the writ of habeas corpus. Although Lincoln had invited congressional ratification of his suspensions during the eleven weeks dictatorship, he had also made clear that he considered this dictatorial power to belong to him as well as to Congress under the terms of the Constitution. He was able to maintain this stand in defiance of Chief Justice Taney and all precedent; nor was Congress itself ever able effectively to gainsay this claim.[36] His most sweeping cancellation of the writ, on September 24, 1862, was effected without even a reference to Congress.[37] This proclamation is all the more remarkable in its assertion of presidential power to institute martial law proceedings for persons indicted for aiding the rebellion.[38] It stated in part:

"... be it ordered, first, that during the existing insurrection, and as a necessary measure for suppressing the same, all rebels and insurgents, their aiders and abettors, within the United States, and all persons discouraging volunteer enlistments, resisting militia drafts, or guilty of any disloyal practice affording aid and comfort to rebels against the authority of the United States, shall be subject to martial law and liable to trial and punishment by courts-martial and military commissions; second, that the writ of habeas corpus is suspended in respect to all persons arrested, or who are now or hereafter during the rebellion shall be imprisoned in any fort, camp, arsenal, military prison, or other place of confinement by any military authority, or by the sentence of any court-martial or military commission."

[35] See Richardson, *op. cit.*, VI, pp.100-101, for two orders of the President in regard to the actual movement into combat of the armed forces.

[36] See G. C. Sellery: *Lincoln's Suspension of Habeas Corpus as Viewed by Congress* (Madison, 1907).

[37] Richardson, *op. cit.*, VI, pp.98-99.

[38] On martial law in the Civil War, see Fairman: *The Law of Martial Rule*, pp.109, 178; James G. Randall: *Constitutional Problems Under Lincoln* (New York, 1926), chap. 8.

Mr. Lincoln had declared a state of siege in Union territory. Here indeed was a "perfect platform for a military despotism,"[39] but more than a platform it never became. In the entire course of the war there were not more than 25,000 arrests of this nature. There were doubtless unwarranted abuses of this power by subordinate officials, but it is certain that no government in mortal struggle ever dealt less severely with traitors, or went so far as to proclaim a general and almost unconditional release of political prisoners in the very middle of the conflict, as was done by Lincoln's order of February 14, 1862.[40] In all this suspension of civil liberty he had the acquiescence of Congress and the overwhelming support of the loyal population. This does not mask the fact that he was exercising dictatorial power. It was not until the Act of March 3, 1863 that Congress itself authorized the President to suspend the writ of habeas corpus, and incidentally ratified his past actions in this regard. As far as Lincoln was concerned, this statute was simply an expression of congressional opinion, having no effect on his past or future activities.

The possibilities of widespread martial law foreseen in his proclamation of September 24, 1862 were never realized, and only in locales where disorder and treason were rampant—as in Indiana, southern Ohio, and Missouri—did martial law and trial by military commission exist in any real sense. Even in these regions trials by military commissions were rare, and the notorious Vallandigham and Milligan cases were unique in the extent to which they were carried. Arrest without warrant, detention without trial, release without punishment—this was the program by which civil liberty was restricted in the Civil War.[41] Lincoln not only withdrew the right to civil trial from those few citizens apprehended for sedition; in most cases he withdrew the right to military or any trial at all. Men were imprisoned and released without ever facing any charges or court. As he himself explained, his whole purpose was precautionary and preventive, not punitive or vindictive. That it was an exercise of arbitrary power there can be no doubt, and yet little injustice resulted. The moderation which Lincoln exhibited in the use of this power and his clemency towards Northern advocates of rebellion are a matter of historical record.

Freedom of speech and press flourished almost unchecked, and no

[39] Dunning, *op. cit.*, p.40.
[40] Richardson, *op. cit.*, VI, pp.102-104.
[41] See Randall, *op. cit.*, chap. 7, and works there cited for the problem of arbitrary arrest. See generally George F. Milton's interesting *Abraham Lincoln and the Fifth Column* (New York, 1942).

leader of a country at war ever received such shocking and vituperative treatment from prominent citizens and journals alike as did Abraham Lincoln. The President forbore this with a remarkable exhibition of tolerance and clemency. Pro-Union forces often criticized him for this patience and leniency more severely than did his enemies for his summary actions under the war power. There were no judicial prosecutions of verbal assaults on the government, outright verbal treason being dealt with in flagrant cases by detention without trial.[42] The one conspicuous (and well-warranted) interference with the freedom of speech in all these years was the arrest and conviction to imprisonment in 1863 of Clement Vallandigham.[43] When the President learned of the case, he commuted the sentence to banishment to the South. Vallandigham was allowed to return to Union soil some months later, and from this time forward continued unmolested in his violent public tirades against Lincoln and the Union cause.

Despite the transitory and clearly deserved suspension of publication of several prominent newspapers,[44] the control by the government of the telegraph lines (a rude and unsuccessful method of censoring military news), the detention of certain seditious editors, and the denial of mailing privileges to their journals, the liberty and indeed the license of the Northern press suffered no restriction whatsoever. The policy of the President and his administration towards the free expression of opinion, a policy of forbearance of all but the most treasonous assaults upon the government, is summed up in this letter written by Lincoln to General Schofield:

"You will only arrest individuals and suppress assemblies or newspapers when they may be working palpable injury to the military in your charge, and in no other case will you interfere with the expression of opinion in any form or allow it to be interfered with violently by others. In this you have a discretion to exercise with great caution, calmness, and forbearance."[45]

[42] Congress passed a Treason Act in 1862 (XII *Stat.* 589) softening the existing penalty for treason to imprisonment or fine as a possible substitute for death, but it went virtually unused.

[43] See the case of *Ex Parte Vallandigham* (1 Wallace 243), in which the Supreme Court beat a prudent retreat to the fortress of technicality and declined to hear an appeal from the sentence of the military commission, on the ground that the latter was not a court of record of which it could take cognizance.

[44] For the most famous of these suspensions, that for three days of the New York *World*, which had printed on May 18, 1864 a bogus proclamation of the President, see T. F. Carroll: "Freedom of Speech and of the Press during the Civil War," *Virginia Law Rev.*, IX (1923), pp.516, 526 ff.

[45] Nicolay and Hay: *Works*, IX, p.100. The whole question of freedom of speech and press in this period is treated exhaustively by Randall, *op. cit.*, chap. 19.

In other respects the relations between the people and their government were equally normal. Although the individual citizen faced stiffer and more comprehensive taxes, and although a young man who lacked $300 might be conscripted to fight in the army, otherwise he went about his business saying and doing what he pleased, and need hardly have known that a fateful war was in progress. Moreover, he was given full opportunity on November 8, 1864 to vote his "dictatorial" President right out of office. The congressional elections of 1862 and 1864 and the presidential election of 1864 were probably the first general elections ever held in a nation at war since manhood suffrage was adopted.

As far as business and industry went, it was only in the matters of transportation and communication that the government went outside its usual sphere of activity. The President took over the railroads and telegraph lines on the basis of congressional authorization.[46] Otherwise business was only unusual in the profits that unscrupulous men were able to make out of the cause.[47]

This was the government of the United States in its darkest hour. Need it once more be insisted that the agony of the crisis worked little change in this government charged with the defense of the nation's existence, and that it was in the person of Abraham Lincoln that the constitutional dictatorship was almost completely reposed? Through his bold initiative, through his unprecedented methods of action, through his unique interpretation of his war power under the Constitution, and through the only outright plea of necessity in American history, Mr. Lincoln raised the office and powers of the President to a position of constitutional and moral ascendancy that left no doubt where the future burden of crisis government in this country would rest. The Supreme Court spoke out against him, in the Milligan Case almost two years after his death, but the words there uttered in protest of his extraordinary power have been adequately disposed of by Professor Corwin:

"To suppose that such fustian would be of greater influence in determining presidential procedure in a future great emergency than precedents backed by the monumental reputation of Lincoln would be merely childish."[48]

What Lincoln did, not what the Supreme Court said, is the precedent

[46] Act of January 30, 1862; XII *Stat.* 334. Lincoln's proclamations assuming possession of telegraph and railroad systems are in Richardson, *op. cit.*, VI, pp.108, 113.

[47] On business and industry in the North, see generally E. D. Fite: *Social and Industrial Conditions in the North during the Civil War* (New York, 1910).

[48] Corwin, *op. cit.*, p.166. See generally Samuel Klaus: *The Milligan Case* (New York, 1929).

of the Constitution in the matter of presidential emergency power. Lincoln's actions form history's most illustrious precedent for constitutional dictatorship. There is, however, this disturbing fact to remember: he set a precedent for bad men as well as good. It is just because Lincoln's reputation is so tremendous that a tyrant bent on illegal power might successfully appeal to this eminent shade for historical sanction of his own arbitrary actions. If Lincoln could calmly assert: "I conceive that I may, in any emergency, do things on a military ground which cannot constitutionally be done by Congress,"[49] then some future President less democratic and less patriotic might assert the same thing. The only check upon such a man would be the normal constitutional and popular limitations of the American system. They were not too rigid to prevent Lincoln's noble actions; time alone will tell whether they will be rigid enough to prevent a tyrant's despotic actions.[50]

[49] Nicolay and Hay: *Works*, IX, pp.120-121.

[50] It is obvious that this discussion, limited in space and purpose, has omitted mention of two other crisis governments that arose in and from this bitter war. The Confederate States of America were certainly an emergency government, one that exhibited many characteristics similar to those of the Union government. The government of the South after the war under Congress's policy of reconstruction is another type of crisis rule, of an entirely different nature from any of the emergency regimes considered in this book. It was a government of conquest, not defense.

CHAPTER XVI

The Government of the United States in the First World War

ALTHOUGH crisis government on an important scale was not instituted again in this country until the outbreak of the war with Germany, there were several periods of national emergency between 1865 and 1917 which evoked governmental procedures out of harmony with the normal operation of the constitutional scheme. The most conspicuous use of emergency powers during these years was President Cleveland's dispatch of federal troops to Chicago during the Pullman Strike of 1894.[1] The vigorous actions of the President in defense of the mails and commerce and the subsequent pronunciamento of the Supreme Court in the Debs case reaffirmed in fact and theory the extraordinary extent of his discretionary power to keep the peace of the United States. In his arbitrary action in overriding Governor Altgeld's protest, Cleveland demonstrated further that the federal principle presents no barrier to the exercise of this power. Said Justice Brewer in the Debs case[2]: "The entire strength of the nation may be used to enforce in any part of the land the full and free exercise of all national powers and the security of all rights entrusted by the Constitution to its care." The marshalling and employment of the "strength of the nation" are matters for the President's discretion; and if there is any immediate way to control this discretion, it is not yet apparent.

Strikes and Wall Street panics, however, were not crises that resulted in thorough-going emergency government, and normality was the keynote in Washington from 1865 to 1917. Indeed, it is somewhat of a misrepresentation of history to cite the World War government of the United States as a clear-cut example of constitutional dictatorship. This country had not been invaded as France had been, nor even threatened with invasion as was England, and the crisis of a war fought 3,000 miles away is of a far different nature from the crisis of a war

---

[1] See Cleveland's account of this event in his *Presidential Problems* (New York, 1904). See also Almont Lindsey: *The Pullman Strike* (Chicago, 1942); B. M. Rich: *The Presidents and Civil Disorder*, chap. 6. The actions of President Hayes in the railroad strikes of 1877 are equally instructive and precedental. See Rich, *op. cit.*, chap. 5. Samuel Yellen: *American Labor Struggles* (New York, 1936), tells graphically of these and other great American strikes.

[2] 158 U.S. 564. On the "peace of the United States," see *In Re Neagle* (135 U.S. 1).

fought to defend one's own soil from the threat or presence of enemy aggression. This is not to say that America did not have extraordinary problems to be solved only by extraordinary means. The United States did face an emergency in 1917-1919, an emergency of which people and government alike were conscious, but it was not the trial endured by France or England. It was not, as was the Civil War, a matter of life and death for the nation.

The nature of the crisis permitted the United States again to pass through a period of national danger with very little alteration in the organization of the government, certainly less than might have been expected by observers of contemporary British and French practice, or than might have been thought advisable for the successful prosecution of the war. The decline of the British Parliament was not paralleled in the American Congress, nor did the state of siege and DORA have American counterparts. The most important alteration in the federal government was the expansion of its administrative branch to fight the war of production; the chief readjustment in the relations of people and government was the control exercised by this administration over American business and industry.

The Presidency remained the chief instrument of crisis government in the United States. The expansion of the administration was first of all an expansion of the President's own power, and Woodrow Wilson was as much the pivot of the World War government as Lincoln had been of the Civil War administration. Neither the precedent of that first great crisis nor the basic canon of emergency government—that the executive branch is primarily responsible for mastering a situation of national danger—was departed from in the World War. Although Wilson came by his power in a different way and was forced by the complexities of the times to share it with others to an extent that Lincoln never desired nor was required to do, nevertheless it is only in terms of his actions as President that the constitutional dictatorship of this second great American crisis can be understood.

Wilson and the War

WORLD WAR publicists and politicians were as free in the use of the words "dictator" and "dictatorship" in discussing Wilson's personality and powers as their predecessors of 1861 had been in discussing Lincoln's. In Woodrow Wilson was concentrated infinitely more power than had ever been given to an American President. In absolute terms it far exceeded Lincoln's, for it extended to a control of the nation's economic life that would have caused a revolution in 1863. One American authority pictured Wilson to the subscribers of a noted English periodical as King, Prime Minister in control of legislation, actual Commander in Chief of the armed forces, active party leader, economic dictator, Secretary of State for Foreign Affairs, and general supervisor of administration all rolled into one.[3]

The most significant feature of the Wilsonian dictatorship is the way in which the President acquired his vast powers. The preponderance of his crisis authority was delegated to him by statutes of Congress. In brief, the most important single emergency device in the World War government was the delegatory statute. Confronted by the necessity of raising and equipping a huge army to fight overseas rather than by a sudden and violent threat to the Republic, Wilson chose to demand express legislative authority for almost every unusual step he felt impelled to take. Lincoln had shown what the office of President was equal to in crises calling for solitary executive action. Now Wilson was to show its efficacy as a crisis instrument working along with the legislative branch of the government. The basis of Lincoln's power was the Constitution, and he operated in spite of Congress. The basis of Wilson's power was a group of statutes, and he cooperated with Congress.[4]

This is not to say that President Wilson failed to make use of his acknowledged competence as Commander in Chief of the armed forces. On the contrary, he undertook several important steps on the basis of his constitutional authority: he armed American merchantmen in February 1917, created the famed Committee on Public Information for propaganda and censorship purposes, dealt in an arbitrary manner with German nationals and firms, established a cable censorship, and set up several other emergency agencies, particularly the War Industries Board. Most of his actions, however, had statutory authority behind them. The President preferred to ask for his power, even though he might have it anyway. The episode of the arming of the merchantmen is the leading case in point. Although he undoubtedly had the constitutional power to do this, he nevertheless thought it politic to ask Congress for statutory authority for such a serious step. When a senatorial fili-

[3] Lindsay Rogers: "Presidential Dictatorship in the United States," *Quarterly Review*, CCXXXI (1919), pp.127, esp. 139-140.
[4] For a general comparison of the two war administrations and their respective leaders, see J. G. Randall: "Lincoln's Task and Wilson's," *So. Atl. Q.*, XXIX (1930), p.349.

buster prevented the delegation, he proceeded to arm these ships on his own initiative.

Among the important statutory delegations to the President were acts empowering him to take over and operate the railroads and water systems, to regulate or commandeer all ship-building facilities in the United States, to regulate and prohibit exports, to raise an army by con-scription, to allocate priorities in transportation, to regulate the conduct of resident enemy aliens, to take over and operate the telegraph and telephone systems, to redistribute functions among the executive agen-cies of the federal government, to control the foreign language press, and to censor all communications to and from foreign countries.[5]

The largest single delegation of power was effected by the Lever Act of August 10, 1917.[6] Under the terms of this statute the President, through whatever agencies he cared to establish, could regulate the importation, manufacture, storage, mining, and distribution of any necessaries; could requisition foods, fuels, and other supplies necessary for any public use connected with national defense; could purchase, store, and sell certain foods; could fix a reasonable and guaranteed price for wheat, based on a statutory minimum; could take over and operate factories, mines, packing houses, pipe lines and similar industrial institutions important to national defense; could fix the price of coal and coke and regulate their production, sale, shipment, distribution, and storage; and could regulate or even forbid the use of food materials in the manufacture of intoxicants.

There is another feature of presidential emergency power that must not be overlooked in this contrast between Lincoln and Wilson—the technique of legislative leadership. Executive direction and control of the lawmaking process is an extremely important factor in any consti-tutional dictatorship which extends over a period of time, particularly one in which the executive branch must be delegated broad emergency powers. The separation of executive and legislature ordained in the Constitution presents a distinct obstruction to efficient crisis govern-ment, and it is primarily the President's job to bridge the gap, by lead-ing Congress to the enactment of his emergency program. In countries

---

[5] Most of these delegating statutes are in XL *Stat.* They are summarized in C. G. Fenwick: *Political Systems in Transition*, chaps. 7-8; Berdahl; *War Powers of the Executive in the United States*, chaps. 10 and 12. The American experience with delegated legislation in the war is treated by Herbert Tingsten: *Les Pleins Pouvoirs*, pp.151-174, and is shown to fall short of the practice of the other democracies in the war.

[6] XL *Stat.* 276.

where cabinet government flourishes, executive leadership of the legislative process is a regular peacetime feature, and is merely strengthened in time of crisis. In presidential governments the executive and legislature may be of opposing political beliefs and must remain so at least until the next election. As a result, the harmony between the two branches that is taken for granted in England may be extremely difficult to achieve in the United States. It seems hardly necessary to point to the implications of presidential leadership of Congress for the problem of the delegation of power in crisis conditions. An unbidden Congress will not readily abdicate its normal lawmaking functions. A President who seeks extraordinary powers through a delegatory statute must ask for them specifically.

This is exactly what Woodrow Wilson did. Throughout his two terms he considered himself a sort of prime minister in relation to Congress, and always regarded the forthright suggestion of desired legislation as one of his principal functions.[7] As a teacher of politics he had conceived a President who would ignore the rigid theory of the separation of powers and provide Congress with vigorous leadership, even in normal times.[8] As a practitioner he was a President much after the model he had drawn. In his first term he became an acknowledged leader of legislative activity. In his second, as the emergency sharpened, this facet of presidential authority became even more important. He never let himself forget what he had written of the President in his *Constitutional Government*: "The Constitution bids him speak and times of stress must more and more thrust upon him the attitude of originator of policies."[9]

For each of these two important ingredients of his constitutional dictatorship—delegated power and legislative leadership—President Wilson had some precedent, although in the extent to which he used these techniques he was breaking new ground. The sources of his leadership of the legislative process are to be found in his own well-known writings and in the several, though not always openly avowed attempts of strong Presidents like Washington (acting through Hamilton),

[7] See his letter to Rep. Mitchell, printed in the appendix to H. J. Ford: *Woodrow Wilson, the Man and His Work* (New York, 1916).

[8] See his *Constitutional Government in the United States* (New York, 1908), chap. 3. See also Small: *Some Presidential Interpretations of the Presidency*, pp.46-54, and chap. 5; Lindsay Rogers: "President Wilson's Theory of His Office," *Forum*, LI (1914), p.174.

[9] *Op. cit.*, p.73.

Jefferson, Jackson, Lincoln, Cleveland, and especially Theodore Roosevelt, to lead the way to congressional action.[10]

Delegated power as an emergency institution in this country had precedents in the several militia acts empowering the President to call out and deploy the armed forces of state and nation to execute the laws and keep the peace, in the various embargo and non-intercourse acts of the Jefferson and Madison administrations, in the delegations to Lincoln,[11] and in a number of scattered statutes empowering the President to do certain things in times of emergency. An interesting if little-known precedent for emergency delegation was the action of the Continental Congress in granting temporary powers of requisition, recruitment, expenditure, and summary arrest to General Washington.[12]

Whatever his precedents, whatever his theories, it is a matter of history that Woodrow Wilson took a far different path to crisis power from the dangerous and unbroken trail blazed by Abraham Lincoln. The importance of Wilson's personality and political dogmas in his wartime "dictatorship" can hardly be overestimated.

Congress and the War

THE Congress of the United States flourished even more importantly in the World War than it had in the dark days of 1861-1865. Once again the augmentation of presidential power, whether by delegation or executive initiative, did not necessarily entail a concomitant reduction of congressional authority. The expansion of executive power in this crisis was into the economic field, one that Congress itself had not chosen or been able to invade to any pronounced degree. In a sense the power of the legislative branch was increased in the very act of delegat-

[10] See generally Small, *op. cit.*, chap. 5; Corwin: *The President*, chap. 7; H. C. Black: *The Relation of the Executive Power to Legislation* (Princeton, 1919), esp. chap. 3. Absolute executive leadership of the lawmaking process in time of war was advocated strongly by H. J. Ford: "The War and the Constitution," *Atlantic Monthly*, CXX (1917), p.485; "The Growth of Dictatorship," *Atlantic Monthly*, CXXI (1918), p.632.

[11] For the delegations to Lincoln, none of them of a strictly legislative character, see James Hart: *The Ordinance-making Powers of the President* (Baltimore, 1925), pp.92-96.

[12] See W. C. Ford and Gaillard Hunt, eds.: *Journals of the Continental Congress, 1774-1789* (Washington, 1904-1914); resolutions of December 27, 1776 (VI, p.1045); September 17, 1777 (VIII, p.752); October 8, 1777 (IX, p.784); November 14, 1777 (IX, p.905). See also the speech of Randolph in the Virginia ratifying convention, Elliot's *Debates*, III, p.79; also II, pp.357-361, concerning certain proposals forwarded in New York and Virginia during the Revolution to create an omnipotent dictator to prosecute the rebellion.

ing wide authority to the President to direct the war activities of the nation's economy.

At no time did Congress consider renouncing any sizable portion of its normal legislative functions. In the light of previous American practice some of the important delegating statutes of this period, especially the Lever Act and the Overman Act of May 1918,[18] were radical departures from peacetime legislative procedure. In no sense, however, can these acts be regarded, even collectively, as true enabling acts. The President certainly did not enjoy the legislative capacity of the English ministries under the Defence of the Realm Acts.

Although the Wilsonian leadership was adequate to secure the program necessary to wage a vigorous war, the contemporary parliamentary situation in England, where cabinet government was demonstrating all its latent crisis possibilities, was not paralleled in the United States. The President knew better, even had he been prepared, than to introduce a bundle of vital statutes into Congress on the day of the declaration of war and expect their immediate passage. Congress was not that sort of legislature, nor did anyone expect or encourage it to be.

The debates of both Houses were as vigorous and fundamental as ever, and the President was often criticized quite bitterly. His leadership in the lawmaking process was always difficult to maintain, and was hardly recognized by Congress as the indispensable instrument of crisis government which he considered it to be. No important war statute was excused from the rigors of normal congressional procedure, and some bills were altered materially against the desires of the President. For example, in its final form the Overman Act was a considerably less far-reaching delegation of power than the original bill the President had requested. Even the complexities of the committee system were retained almost intact. Except for a somewhat changed attitude towards its duties and a sensible voluntary abbreviation of the lawmaking process, Congress played its important role in the war government in much the same way it operated in peacetime. There was no reason why it should have abdicated, there was ample reason why it should have continued to function, to prove that democracy can fight a foreign war through regular processes and institutions.

The attempts of the Civil War Congress to project its influence into the executive field of war-making had their counterparts in the World War. Several ventures were made by certain groups in Congress to emu-

[18] XL Stat. 556.

late the Committee on the Conduct of the Civil War, but in the face of Wilson's strong opposition all such proposals were abandoned.[14] The attempt of the radicals to force a reconstruction of the Lincoln Cabinet in 1862 also had its sequel, in Senator Chamberlain's proposal of January 21, 1918, that a war cabinet to be composed of "three distinguished citizens of demonstrated ability" (one of whom was certain to be ex-President Roosevelt) be set up by President and Senate as a super-agency to be entrusted with the over-all direction of the war effort.[15] In this instance too the President was successful in preventing any weakening of his position as the focus of crisis government in the United States.[16]

The Administration and the War

IT was in the administrative branch that the most important wartime departures from the normal procedures and organization of the federal government were concentrated. The necessity that seems to arise in all modern wars for strict governmental control or operation of the nation's instruments of production, supply, and transportation was for the first time brought home to the American people.[17] The citizen of France was most conscious of the war by reason of the state of siege, the citizen of England by DORA and his palsied Parliament, the citizen of the United States by the migration of private citizens to Washington and the erection there of a complexity of boards, commissions, and agencies to control his economic life.

It was conclusively demonstrated that large-scale modern war was just as much a socializing influence in the United States as in any other so-called "free enterprise democracy." Through direct governmental

[14] See his letter to Rep. Lever in R. S. Baker: *Woodrow Wilson, Life and Letters* (New York, 1927-1939), VII, pp.185-186.

[15] The text of this proposal is in *Congr. Rec.*, LVI, pp.1077-1078.

[16] An interesting treatment of this whole affair, written from the point of view of "Roosevelt or Wilson," is in W. E. Dodd: *Woodrow Wilson and His Work* (New York, 1920), chap. 12. See also J. M. Leake: "The Conflict over Coordination," *American Political Science Review*, XII (1918), p.365.

[17] See generally W. F. Willoughby: *Government Organization in Wartime and After* (New York, 1919): F. L. Paxson: "The American War Government, 1917-1918," *Am. Hist. Rev.*, XXVI (1920), p.54; G. B. Clarkson: *Industrial America in the World War* (Boston, 1923). The most concise account is by Carl B. Swisher: "The Control of War Preparations in the United States," *Am. Pol. Sci. Rev.*, XXXIV (1940), p.1085. The studies on specific phases of war administration are numberless. Walker D. Hines: *War History of American Railroads* (New Haven, 1928), is an excellent survey of this extremely important encroachment on free enterprise in the war. The chief supporting actor tells the story of the war administration—Bernard M. Baruch: *American Industry in the War* (new ed., New York, 1941).

administration of privately-owned businesses and industries (especially the railroads and the telephone and telegraph systems), through governmental entrance into the field of private business (for example, the shipbuilding industry), and through control and direction of industries still owned and operated by their private managers, the administration at Washington regulated the entire scheme of American enterprise in a manner incompatible with all previous American conceptions of the proper relations of government and business. The most important of these three methods was the third—administrative control and direction of privately owned and operated industry by means of a myriad of new agencies, particularly the War Industries Board headed by Bernard M. Baruch, the Fuel Administration headed by Harry A. Garfield, and the Food Administration headed by Herbert Hoover. The regulation of industry and commerce was effected by means of voluntary cooperation of corporations to conform to the standards and requests of the administration, as well as by systems of licensing, priority regulations, and price-fixing. The methods of securing obedience to the orders of the different agencies were the so-called "indirect sanctions"—appeals to patriotism, publicity, threats of higher taxes, and occasionally outright coercion. The ultimate sanction of the administration's activities was the executive power of the federal government centered in the President, particularly his authority to commandeer any recalcitrant business organization. This was rarely necessary, for cooperation between industry and the government was generally whole-hearted and successful.

The important constitutional aspect of this expansion of the administrative activity of the government was its basis: the power and authority, constitutional or delegated, of the President of the United States. While the national economy was brought under the control of the administration, the administration remained under the control of the President. In his name and by his authority did all these agencies function. None was ever set up against his wishes, none which he desired ever failed to be created. The decisions to erect new boards or commissions, as well as their organization, powers, personnel, and relations to the other transient or permanent agencies of the administration, were matters for the President's judgment. Most of the delegating statutes, concerning such problems as food, fuel, espionage, trading with the enemy, and communications, granted power to the President alone, without suggesting any agency to exercise this power. It was understood that he in his turn would institute some sort of administrator or board.

248

For example, the establishment of the Fuel and Food Administrations under the Lever Act was purely a matter of presidential discretion.

Other agencies were completely informal and without statutory foundation. Neither the Committee on Public Information, the War Labor Board, nor the all-important War Industries Board was foreseen in any way by congressional action. Most of the important agencies were the offspring of earlier unofficial and advisory boards appointed by the President, presumably on the basis of this general executive power. Finally, under the Overman Act the President was given complete authority over whatever administrative machinery had been or could be legally established for the prosecution of the war. This statute was used by the President as a sort of threat, to insure coordination of this complex administration. Actual resorts to it for authority were scarce.

The precedent established by Abraham Lincoln, that the chief executive is to be the central and dominant figure in war governments in the United States, was even more firmly fixed by Woodrow Wilson. He demonstrated beyond a doubt that not only the business of actual war, but also the job of preparation, production, and mobilization for war is fundamentally a problem for the President to solve. He is the man who will be praised for success and blamed for failure, whether in the battles waged in the actual theater of war or in the equally important battles waged by America's instruments of production. In this undoubted leadership the Congress must and did acquiesce, with its statutory delegations and its refusal to meddle actively in matters of administration. The clash between President and Congress, which was set off by Chamberlain's proposal and concluded in the passage of the Overman Act, was definitely resolved in favor of the former. Even if he had created chaos, it was for him alone to make it cosmos. The parallel between the gropings toward an effective war administration in 1917-1918 and the similar efforts of the early years of this most recent war confutes the aphorism that history never repeats itself. Given a certain situation of crisis, American democracy pretty generally reacts in identical patterns of thought and action.

That modern war is socialistic, that it entails for the American government a tremendous expansion of administrative activity, that this activity is fundamentally for the President to control and direct, that Congress realizes this and delegates the President those extraordinary powers which he does not feel qualified to seize upon his own initiative

—these are the lessons of the first World War that were not forgotten in 1941 and 1942, and will not be forgotten again.

The People and the War

NEITHER actually nor potentially were the liberties of the American people abridged to any serious degree in the course of the first World War. Removed from the theater of war and governed by a legislature which, if not completely obstructed, was nonetheless hampered by a written and respected Bill of Rights, the American people were forced to undergo precious little suppression of their peacetime liberties. It is a fact of history that mob intolerance cut far more deeply into the freedoms of speech, press, and assembly than did official federal, state, and local action.[18] But then again, it always does.

The most sizable restriction of traditional American liberty was worked by the controls set up by the administration over the nation's economic life. An example of this control which impinged directly upon the people themselves was the war prohibition effected by Wilson's decrees of December 8, 1917 and September 16, 1918 under the Lever Act.[19] This abridgment of an important American liberty (or license) was carried over into time of peace, first by the wartime Prohibition Act of October 28, 1919, and later by the Eighteenth Amendment.[20] A conscription program that did not permit anyone to buy his way out of compulsory service in his country's forces was another significant departure from the privileged status enjoyed by the American citizen. So too was an extraordinarily heavy and comprehensive scheme of taxation. Rights such as those of public assembly and inviolable domicile remained untouched by federal action.

The right to strike and the right to work where and when one pleased were not restricted by governmental action in the World War. It is a matter of record that there were more strikes in 1917 than ever before in American history. Although there were fewer strikes in 1918, the number of workers involved was about the same in each of these years.[21]

[18] See the publication of the National Civil Liberties Bureau: *Wartime Prosecutions and Mob Violence* (New York, 1919), for an excellent, though somewhat one-sided story of both official and popular suppression of civil liberty in the World War.

[19] U.S. *Stats.*, 65th Congr., 2nd sess., Procls. 84, 204.

[20] XLI *Stat.* 305.

[21] U.S. Dept. of Labor (Bureau of Labor Statistics): *Monthly Labor Review* (June 1919), pp.303-325. On labor in the war, see generally Gordon S. Watkins: *Labor Problems and Labor Administration in the United States in the War* (Urbana, 1919).

No repressive legislation was enacted by the federal government, nor was any such method as compulsory arbitration instituted. The reduction of the number of strikes in essential defense industries was wholly a product of public opinion and the mutual desire of labor, management, and government to cooperate in a successful war effort.

Not until April 9, 1918, after numerous gropings at the problem,[22] was a central labor agency created—the National War Labor Board, headed by ex-President Taft and Frank P. Walsh and including representatives of management, labor, and the public. The Board was not based on congressional authority; its decisions therefore found their sanction in public opinion.[23] A month later a War Labor Policies Board under Felix Frankfurter was created to formulate general rules for the government employment of labor. Under certain statutes the President could seize companies failing to cooperate with the government and could withdraw draft exemptions from employees adopting a similar attitude. Three times in the course of the war he took over the operation of industries refusing to abide by the decisions of the War Labor Board. Through one means or another, strikes were not allowed to interfere seriously with American production for war, but the rights of labor themselves were never governmentally suppressed.

The only outright limitations on American liberty during the war were those placed upon the twin freedoms of speech and press. The methods adopted by the federal government to meet the threat of outspoken disloyalty were significantly different from those of the Civil War.[24] President Lincoln had, without reference to Congress or resort to the regular courts, dealt personally with sedition of persons and periodicals, mainly through the procedure of arrest without warrant and detention without trial. Only the most arrant disloyalty was thus suppressed. The World War government was faced with a war far removed and a disloyalty and espionage problem far less perilous than that of the Civil War period. A suspension of the writ of habeas corpus by President or Congress or the use of other Lincolnian methods was obviously unnecessary, unconstitutional, and highly inadvisable. The President made it clear that he was opposed to military trial of sedition

[22] See L. C. Marshall: "The War Labor Program and Its Administration," *Journal of Pol. Eco.*, XXVI (1918), p.425.

[23] For the work of this board and pertinent statistics, see the publication of the Bureau of Labor Statistics: *The National War Labor Board* (Washington, 1922); Alexander M. Bing: *Wartime Strikes and Their Adjustment* (New York, 1921).

[24] On this point, see W. A. Dunning: "Disloyalty in Two Wars," *Am. Hist. Rev.*, XXIV (1919), p.625.

and espionage cases as unconstitutional and bad policy. The problem was approached in a vastly different manner.

Congress itself, at the behest of the President, took the formal initiative. The various treason laws of the United States in force at the outbreak of the war were supplemented and strengthened by the Espionage Act of June 15, 1917 and the stringent "Sedition Law" amendment thereto of May 16, 1918, as well as by provisions in such statutes as the Selective Service Act and the Trading with the Enemy Act.[25] Taken as a whole, these statutes made it a penal offense not only to aid the enemy or hinder the United States by false reports, incitement to disloyalty, or obstruction to recruitment; but also to "willfully utter, print, write, or publish any disloyal, profane, scurrilous, or abusive language" about the American form of government, the armed forces, the flag, the President, and the Constitution, or language designed to bring these into "contempt, scorn, contumely, or disrespect." The Committee on Public Information itself had to admit that "few more sweeping measures have ever found their way to the national statute book."[26] It was through governmental prosecution in the federal courts that these statutes were enforced and disloyalty and sedition punished. This sort of action was paralleled by similar laws and proceedings in many of the states.[27]

It was for the President to decide how severely these laws should be applied. Mr. Wilson passed on this competence to the Attorney General and his Department of Justice. In place of the confusion of authorities executing the will of Mr. Lincoln, there was a well-organized, omnipresent Department of Justice operating throughout the land. More than two thousand indictments were presented to the courts for oral or printed violations of the above acts, and in about half of these, convictions were obtained. In many instances the convictions and penalties went far beyond the necessities of the case.[28] The fact remains that each injustice was committed by a court of the United States, on the recommendation of a jury of citizens. The general oversight and clemency exercised by Lincoln were sadly lacking in this war, and the

[25] These statutes are, respectively: XL *Stat.* 217, 553, 76, 411.

[26] Paxson, Corwin, and Harding (eds.): *War Cyclopedia* (1st ed., Washington, 1918), p.88.

[27] For a discussion of state espionage acts in the World War, see Zechariah Chafee, Jr.: *Freedom of Speech* (New York, 1920), pp.110 ff.

[28] For a trenchant criticism of the Espionage Acts and their application, as well as for a thorough consideration of freedom of speech in the war, see Chafee: *Freedom of Speech*, esp. chaps. 1 and 2; *Free Speech in the United States* (Cambridge, 1941), chaps. 3 and 4. See also Berdahl, *op. cit.*, chap. 11.

comparison of Vallandigham openly seditious and Debs sentenced to ten years in jail is more than odious. A presidential directive could have limited the Department of Justice to prosecutions of utterances of only the most harmful nature; a presidential statement could have put a stop to much of the witch-hunting which went on throughout the war. Neither the directive nor the statement was ever forthcoming.

No censorship of the press was established during the World War, and all demands by the executive or members of Congress for anything smacking of prior censorship were defeated. Such control of the printed word as did exist was effected in several ways: through prosecutions under the Espionage and Sedition Acts, the closing (under Title XII of the Espionage Act) of the mails to printed matter violating the tenets established in those acts,[29] federal censorship of cables and other means of communication to and from foreign countries, a rather complete discretionary censorship of the foreign language press in the United States (under section 19 of the Trading with the Enemy Act), and voluntary self-censorship by all newspapers and periodicals in the United States. This latter procedure was effected largely through the cooperation of the press with the famed Committee on Public Information. This powerful organization headed by George Creel was set up by an executive order of August 14, 1917 and was never recognized by Congress except by a statute of 1918 making an appropriation for its expenses. Its chief task was that of propaganda and publicity, but it also acted in conjunction with the other federal authorities concerned with the suppression of vital information and seditious utterances in such a way that it became a sort of extra-legal, over-all directing body for the American press. The policies and standards which it advised were not flouted by the newspapers.[30]

On the whole, it cannot be said that the suspension of civil liberty was a very important emergency technique in the World War. Although blatant disloyalty and treason were judicially punished, much more severely and unnecessarily than in the Civil War, the average citizen and newspaper continued to speak and act pretty much as usual. The limitations on American liberty in World War I were ridiculously few.

The return of peace was followed by an abandonment of practically all the new procedures and agencies which had been created to meet the

[29] The importance of the Post Office Department in the matter of war censorship is emphasized by Lindsay Rogers: "Freedom of the Press in the United States," *Contemporary Rev.*, CXIV (1918), p.177.

[30] The standard treatment of the CPI as a censorial board is James R. Mock: *Censorship 1917* (Princeton, 1941).

demands of war, as well as by a reaction to executive power similar to that which followed the death of Lincoln. Most of those statutes and agencies which did not cease operation under the terms of their limited statutory duration were repealed or abolished by the Act of March 3, 1921.[31] In the summer of 1920 Congress passed a bill—343 to 3 in the House, unanimously in the Senate—repealing sixty wartime measures delegating powers to the President. Wilson killed it by a pocket veto, and thereby provided the Republican Party with a stock of campaign ammunition against "executive dictatorship." And yet the Republican candidate himself had stated during the war that "what the United States needs and what it must have if it is to win the war is a supreme dictator, with sole control of and sole responsibility for every phase of war activity. . . . The sooner it comes the better for all of us. . . . For supreme dictator at the present moment, there is but one possible man, the President of the United States."[32]

Finally, it need only be mentioned in passing that the Constitution itself presented no direct barrier to all these abnormal legislative and administrative measures. Only one important case involving the validity of war legislation came before the Supreme Court during hostilities; in *Arver v. United States* the Selective Service Act was unanimously and vigorously upheld.[33] In a number of other decisions after the war a latitudinarian conception of the Constitution-at-War was manifested,[34] and in no case did the Court intimate that the tremendous wartime delegations of power had been unconstitutional. *Inter arma silet curia suprema.*

[31] XLI *Stat.* 1359.
[32] *New York Times*, February 10, 1918.
[33] 245 U.S. 366.
[34] *Hamilton v. Kentucky Distilleries* (251 U.S. 146); *Schenck v. U.S.* (249 U.S. 47); *Abrams v. U.S.* (250 U.S. 616); *Block v. Hirsch* (256 U.S. 135). In *Chastleton Corp. v. Sinclair* (264 U.S. 543), decided in 1923, the Court overturned any further continuance of rent controls in Washington, the emergency in its opinion having long since passed. See also *U.S. v. Cohen Grocery Co.* (255 U.S. 81).

CHAPTER XVII

The New Deal and the Great Depression

WHETHER the depression which reached its peak in 1933 was a crisis in the life of the American Republic as perilous as the Civil War or World War is a matter of dispute. That there was a serious crisis, and that it was acknowledged as such by both government and people, is a matter of history. A world-wide depression had dealt the American economy a staggering blow. Unemployment, industrial stagnation, and social unrest were all unmistakable symptoms of the most serious economic emergency in American history. The nation's economy had suffered grievous blows in the past and had recovered almost unaided by governmental intervention, but the year 1933 was a different story for two reasons. First, the day of the "positive state" had definitely arrived, and the federal administration was no longer expected to sit back and watch the people of the United States battle through their trials without governmental assistance. Secondly, the unusually grave condition of the nation's economy made it doubtful whether its vaunted powers of self-recuperation could bring it back to normal within any reasonable length of time.

The crisis of 1933 was one of spirit as well as substance. The people of the United States were thoroughly bewildered, even frightened, and in their bewilderment they turned to the federal government for aid. They found a government most willing to give it. "For many months the people had looked to Government for help, but Government had looked away. I promised action,"[1] said the leader of the incoming Democratic administration, and history records that he meant what he said. The Roosevelt administration which took office March 4, 1933 was the first in American history that set about deliberately to rout a depression through direct governmental action—to rescue the federal government, the states, business and industry, agriculture, and the people generally from the economic prostration which menaced the whole of American society.

---

[1] *Papers and Addresses of Franklin D. Roosevelt* (New York, 1938), II, 16. The outgoing Hoover government had caused or permitted to be enacted several important emergency measures, *inter alia* the Reconstruction Finance Act (XLVII *Stat.* 5) and the Emergency Relief and Reconstruction Act (XLVII *Stat.* 709).

Neither the necessity for the New Deal of 1933 nor the degree of its success in mastering the economic crisis is a subject of discussion here. This chapter's one concern with this controversial period in American history is to answer this simple question: what were the elements which made the government of the United States in 1933 a positive crisis government? The answer is: the personality of Franklin D. Roosevelt and five recognized crisis techniques—executive initiative, executive leadership of legislation, an abbreviated legislative process, the delegation of powers by statute, and an expansion of the administrative branch. In brief, the crisis government of 1933 was marked by an unprecedented breakdown of the constitutional barriers separating Congress and the President. In this respect it was following the pattern of all economic emergency governments.

The personality of Franklin Roosevelt was as inseparable from the crisis of 1933 as the personality of Abraham Lincoln from the crisis of 1861, and his was an emergency government not least because he chose it to be one. In Roosevelt the voters had chosen the most crisis-minded public figure in American history, a man who thrived on crises, emergencies, dangers, perils, and panics.[2] His long tenure of office was a continuous emergency, and not just for the Republicans. Nor did he fail to admit or take advantage of the fact. "I *love* a good fight." Like Murat he rode ever toward the sound of the guns. He was preeminently "a man proposing, not prudence, but the deliberate assumption of risks in the hope of great gains."[3] The resort to extraordinary power in extraordinary circumstances was instinct for this extraordinary man, and his character is not to be overlooked in any estimate of the crisis government of 1933. He was as much the government of the United States in this grave national emergency as Lincoln and Wilson had been in those of the past.

These warlike passages from his memorable inaugural address sound the keynote of this administration:

". . . I assume unhesitatingly the leadership of this great army of our people dedicated to a disciplined attack upon our common problems. . . .

I am prepared under my constitutional duty to recommend the measures that a stricken Nation in the midst of a stricken world may require. These measures, or such other measures as the Congress may build out of its ex-

[2] Volume II of the President's papers is entitled *The Year of Crisis*. Rep. Bruce Barton issued a list in March 1939 (*New York Times*, March 17) showing that, according to the President, the country was in its thirty-ninth emergency in six years!
[3] G. W. Johnson: *Roosevelt: Dictator or Democrat?* (New York, 1941), p.214.

perience and wisdom, I shall seek, within my constitutional authority, to bring to speedy adoption.

But in the event that the Congress shall fail to take one of these two courses, and in the event that the national emergency is still critical, I shall not evade the clear course of duty that will then confront me. I shall ask the Congress for the one remaining instrument to meet the crisis—broad Executive power to wage a war against the emergency, as great as the power that would be given me if we were in fact invaded by a foreign foe."[4]

It was on the day of this address that the economic crisis reached the peak of its intensity, evidencing itself in a sharply felt attendant emergency: the run on the banks and the concomitant threat to the whole private banking structure. To meet this threat the new President had resort to the essential element of the Lincoln dictatorship—executive initiative. In one respect, this whole emergency regime was based on the President's initiative, for it was his decision that the United States should have an unvarnished crisis government. The emergency convocation of Congress on March 9 and the executive leadership of legislation in this Congress were also examples of the crisis initiative of a strong executive. The outstanding example of this technique, however, was his proclamation of March 6, 1933 referring specifically to the existence of a "national emergency," decreeing a bank holiday, forbidding the export of gold and silver, and prohibiting transactions in foreign exchange.[5] This declaration of a financial state of siege was based on the questionable authority of section 5b of the Trading with the Enemy Act of October 6, 1917, empowering the President to "investigate, regulate, or prohibit, under such rules and regulations as he may prescribe, by means of licenses or otherwise, any transactions in foreign exchange and the export, hoarding, melting, or earmarkings of gold or silver coin or bullion or currency. . . ." The President was later to admit that this step was taken only with considerable premeditation and concern. The best legal authority he could discover for the extraordinary action of proclaiming a national bank holiday and a gold embargo was this provision of a statute passed in and for war, and generally regarded as defunct. His selection for Attorney General, Senator Walsh of Montana (who died on March 2), behaved like a good Attorney General and assured his chief that the law was still in effect, and that it was more plausible authority for the bold step he was about to take than the constitutional fact that he was President of the United States. It was therefore on the basis of this provision alone that

[4] *Papers and Addresses,* II, pp.11-16.
[5] *Ibid.,* pp.24-26.

Mr. Roosevelt acted March 6.[6] It is interesting to speculate what authority Mr. Lincoln would have called up for this action.

Having issued an important proclamation on the doubtful authority of an act regarded as defunct and dealing only with a state of war, the President took a leaf out of Mr. Lincoln's book by asking in effect that Congress ratify his questionable action. The Emergency Banking Act of March 9,[7] passed by the Houses of Congress in the exact form in which it was presented and on the same day, validated the proclamation of March 6 and all other acts of the President and Treasury in the five days since the inauguration, and reenacted in amended form the pertinent provision of the Trading with the Enemy Act. The President was given undoubted authority, "during time of war or during any other period of national emergency declared by the President" to do those things which he had already done. A proclamation of the same day extending the bank holiday "until further proclamation by the President" was based upon the amendment.[8] The President's move had been a bold one, and undoubtedly beyond the purview of the Act of 1917, but it had also been necessary. A drastic crisis demanded a drastic remedy, and the crisis arm of the government supplied it. Presidential initiative, even in defiance of the law and agreed constitutional theory, remains this country's fundamental emergency instrument.

The President and Congress

"I AM not speaking to you in general terms. I am pointing out a definite road."[9] These words from President Roosevelt's economy message to Congress of March 10, 1933 characterize accurately the relations between executive and legislature in the famed Hundred Days special session of 1933. The problem facing the President was the fulfillment of his crisis pledge to the American people "to wage war against the emergency." The power he needed could come only from Congress, and the success of this crisis government hinged upon his ability to lead the two Houses to a speedy enactment of his legislative wishes. He knew,

[6] See the note appended to the text of this proclamation, *ibid.*, pp.26-29. There is no doubt that the law was only designed for a state of war. In fact, it had been construed in its entirety as such—*Stoehr v. Wallace* (255 U.S. 239, 241-242). For a discussion of the legal points of this action, see Ellingwood: "The Legality of the National Bank Moratorium," *Ill. L.R.*, XXVII (1933), p.923.

[7] XLVIII *Stat.* 1. Not more than a handful of Congressmen had even seen the bill, and it is said that it was represented in the House by a folded newspaper! The bill was introduced at 3 P.M. and was signed by the President after dinner.

[8] *Papers and Addresses*, II, p.48.

[9] *Ibid.*, p.49.

as Wilson had known, that the vast display of power which he felt impelled to wield would not be bestowed upon him by an unbidden Congress. He had to ask for it specifically and directly, and see the fulfillment of his request through to the end. This he was nothing loathe to do. To a degree never before matched in American history, the President became a prime minister.[10] He proposed to Congress a complete and detailed program of emergency legislation, and, although this program entailed unprecedented grants of legislative and administrative power, he was able to obtain its enactment substantially without change and in record time. The President had a rousing majority in each chamber begging for leadership; he had an abnormal amount of patronage to dole out to the well-starved Democrats;[11] he had the mandate of an aroused people to get something done;[12] he was able to work more intimately with congressional leaders in both Houses than any President in history; he exploited masterfully the new technique of the radio in his appeals to the people as executive leader of this emergency law-making program—and the result was an unparalleled feat of legislative leadership. Mr. Roosevelt would seem to have taken his text from page 68 of Woodrow Wilson's *Constitutional Government*: "The nation as a whole has chosen him, and is conscious that it has no other political spokesman. His is the only national voice in affairs." The roll call on every government bill was a test vote, and he never failed to get his vote of confidence.

In answer to an exigent national demand and this strong presidential ascendancy, Congress responded with one of the most unusual sessions in history.[13] The Congress of the Hundred Days was practically a war-

[10] Pendleton Herring: *Presidential Leadership* (New York, 1940), p.53.

[11] This point is emphasized by W. E. Binkley: *The Powers of the President* (New York, 1937), pp.271 ff. He reminds the reader how important the dispensation of patronage was for the maintenance by Lincoln of his solitary and unprecedented power. See H. J. Carman and R. H. Luthin: *Lincoln and the Patronage* (New York, 1943).

[12] Frank Kent in an article in *Virginia Q. R.*, IX (1933), p.372, entitled "White House Technique," attributes Roosevelt's success during the Hundred Days to the impact of a "thoroughly scared country" on a "thoroughly scared Congress." As Harold Laski has observed about abnormal times in the United States: "In a crisis, to put it shortly, public opinion compels the abrogation of the separation of powers. There is only one will in effective operation, and that is the will of the President."—*The American Presidency* (New York, 1940), pp.154-155. See his precise statement of the problems facing the "crisis President" in his review of Mr. Roosevelt's *Papers and Addresses*, *Chicago L.R.*, IX (1942), p.383.

[13] A measured account and appraisal of this session is given by Pendleton Herring: "The First Session of the Seventy-third Congress," *Am. Pol. Sci. Rev.*, XXVIII (1934), p.65. The best account of these early months is still Raymond Moley's *After Seven Years* (New York, 1939), chaps. 5 and 6. See also Garet Garrett: "The Hundred Days" in *Sat. Eve. Post* (August 12, 1933). The literature of the New Deal is, of course,

time legislature. The forms of lawmaking were observed, but all along the line there was a sensible abbreviation of the many steps in the legislative process. In both House and Senate debates were shortened and kept to the point. The average debating time in the House for each of the eleven most important bills was three and two-thirds hours. Special steering committees were established to channel the flood of business, and they were able to jam the government bills through with about the same speed and ease that a government bill goes through in Commons. Only in regard to several radical items in the Agricultural Adjustment Act and the highly political matter of the reduction of veterans' compensation did the Roosevelt program meet with any serious opposition, with a resultant compromise. In the House of Representatives most of the administration's bills were considered under stringent rules prohibiting amendments from the floor, or any amendments save those approved by one of the regular or extraordinary steering committees. Congress did not degenerate into a machine for rubber-stamping presidential edicts. There were loud and angry protests voiced continually from the floors of both Houses against the executive domination which was resulting in wholesale and precipitate delegation. These, however, were the protests of a minority; on the whole the two Houses (which, incidentally, included an unusual percentage of freshman congressmen) proceeded with remarkable docility to enact the President's desires. Never in the history of this government has the gap between the two political branches been so completely and effectively bridged. Without a real crisis, this would not have been possible.

The tangible results of the Hundred Days were a group of emergency statutes delegating the President unprecedented power to wage war on the economic front. Taken as a whole, the dozen or so important statutes enacted in the special session constitute the largest single instance of delegated power in American history. It is important to remember that, whatever has happened since 1933, this first batch of New Deal delegating statutes consisted of strictly emergency measures; both the President and Congress were in agreement that it was temporary power that was thus sweepingly delegated. It is significant to note too that the emergency delegations of 1933 were granted to the President or to a direct subordinate, while the permanent reform measures en-

tremendous. One of the best brief accounts is Arthur Schlesinger: *The New Deal in Action* (New York, 1939). See also Chas. Beard and George Smith: *The Future Comes: A Study of the New Deal* (New York, 1933); Basil Rauch: *The History of the New Deal* (New York, 1944).

acted under the New Deal program usually established independent commissions to wield the delegated power of Congress.

The emergency portions of the legislative output of the Hundred Days were: the Emergency Banking Act of March 9, the Economy Act of March 20, the Unemployment Relief Act of March 31, the Agricultural Adjustment Act of May 12, the Thomas "Inflation Amendment" of May 12, the Emergency Farm Mortgage Act of May 12, the Federal Emergency Relief Act of May 12, the Home Owners Loan Act of June 13, the Farm Credit Act of June 16, the Emergency Railroad Transportation Act of June 16, and the all-inclusive National Industrial Recovery Act of June 16.[14]

These statutes were typical examples of the emergency technique of delegated legislative power. All of them embodied provisions limiting their duration; for example, the National Recovery Act was to be in effect for two years unless earlier terminated by the President, while the Agricultural Adjustment Act was to lose validity "whenever the President finds and proclaims that the national economic emergency in relation to agriculture has been ended." The Emergency Banking Act, on the other hand, although passed for immediate use and to ratify previous executive action, was in the nature of a permanent statute giving any President the power to act as Mr. Roosevelt had acted, in case of war or other national emergency. Each of them spoke in specific terms of the great national emergency and the particular aspect thereof to which it was directed. Said the declaration of policy in the National Recovery Act:

A national emergency productive of widespread unemployment and disorganization of industry, which burdens interstate and foreign commerce, affects the public welfare, and undermines the standard of living of the American people, is hereby declared to exist.

To summarize the manifold activities of the President and his associates which were authorized by the terms of these statutes would require a separate treatise. The tremendous administrative effort under the National Recovery Act is example enough of the scope of this delegated emergency power, as well as of the vast expansion of the administration which accompanied its exercise.[15] The terms of this statute

[14] XLVIII *Stat.* 1, 8, 22, 31, 41, 51, 55, 128, 257, 211, 195. The messages of the President recommending these various bills are in vol. II of *Papers and Addresses.* An article by J. F. Essary: "Long Live the King" in the *American Mercury* (September 1933), lists 77 important delegations in the Hundred Days. The measures adopted in this session as lasting reforms were the Securities Act of May 27, the TVA Act of May 12, and the Banking Act of June 16—XLVIII *Stat.* 74, 58, 162.

[15] See generally L. S. Lyon *et al.*: *The National Recovery Administration* (Washington, 1935).

were so broad as to confer upon the President plenary power to prescribe the trade practices and labor policies of almost the whole of
American business and industry. The lawmaking activity of General
Hugh Johnson and his associates, all of it carried on in the name of the
President and by his authority, included the formulation of over 700
codes of fair competition filling 18 volumes of some 13,000 pages and
governing minutely the entire economic life of the nation. The administrative orders interpreting and executing these codes were numbered in the tens of thousands. In one respect, this unprecedented
emergency delegation was not as complete as the French enabling acts
of the 1930's. The President was not actually making laws, that is,
statutes of the United States; he was merely filling out in an administrative manner the emergency statutes already enacted by Congress.
To be sure, many of his important orders under the delegatory statutes
were as basic and far-reaching as regular laws. In contrast, the decrees
of the French Cabinet issued under the enabling acts were regarded by
Parliament and people as actual laws, and were promulgated as such.
In another respect, however, the NRA delegation was unique; the administrative codes, which were based ultimately on the approval of the
President, were in fact drafted by private persons or trade groups
working under the supervision of the administration. The NRA was a
remarkable instance of government by administrative decree.

To execute this vast project for the rehabilitation of the American
economy, hundreds of authorities and agencies were instituted on the
basis of a single clause in the Act empowering the President to establish
the machinery for its execution "without regard to the Civil Service
laws." This astounding exhibition of presidential legislative and administrative power, based on the most ill-defined and general expressions
of Congress's desires, was paralleled in regard to the other fields of
American society over which the power of the government had been
extended by the legislative program of the Hundred Days. The government itself was not exempted from the exercise of delegated power, for
the Economy Act gave the President wide powers not only to cut
salaries and pensions and other expenses, but to reorganize or consolidate the executive agencies of the government or abolish them altogether, subject to congressional disapproval within sixty days. Finally,
the authority granted to the President (under Title II, the National
Recovery Act) to spend over three billions of dollars through an
emergency public works administration, though hardly unusual in the

light of subsequent practice, was for the time a radical delegation of spending power.

This is the way in which the government launched its attack upon the grave economic emergency of 1933. The chief institutional elements through which the separation of powers was nullified as an obstruction to unified and vigorous governmental action were the same two devices which Wilson had exploited for his wartime dictatorship—legislative leadership and delegated power. A thoroughly chastised people had demanded and received strong governmental leadership to guide them out of the dangerous economic wilderness into which they had strayed. It was clearly an emergency government, but it was not really dictatorship. There was no suppression of rights, no complete abdication by a demoralized legislature, no thoroughgoing enabling act. The Roosevelt emergency program did involve extraordinary delegation of lawmaking authority, but it fell short of the magnitude and character of the French enabling acts of the 1930's. For the normal-minded people of the United States, however, it was unalloyed crisis government.

It is significant to note that it was a strictly party President and government to whom this power had been delegated, contrary to the practice of England, France, and Weimar Germany in their experience with enabling acts. As a matter of fact, coalition Cabinets have never thrived in this country since Washington's failure to keep both Jefferson and Hamilton in his government. Wilson fought the attempts to saddle him with a coalition war cabinet, and neither the Democrats in Lincoln's Cabinet nor the Republicans in Roosevelt's made them in any true sense coalition groups. The fact is that a coalition regime is of little if any meaning in a presidential crisis government.

Two important features of the emergency government of 1933, neither of them of any particular significance for America's other two crisis regimes, remain for brief consideration: the problem of limitations and the problem of permanent governmental alteration. One of the leading characteristics of the Civil War and World War governments was the fact that the limitations on the use of emergency powers remained the normal limitations of the American constitutional and political system. Moreover, these limitations were weakened, for the Supreme Court refused during and after both crises to pass unfavorably upon any of the extraordinary legislative or executive acts—with the single and comparatively harmless exception of the Milligan Case in 1866. This was not true of America's third emergency government. The limitations on executive and legislative power in the year 1933 itself remained the usual political and constitutional responsibility of the two branches; but shortly thereafter the Supreme Court, asked to interpret parts of this legislation which were infinitely more controversial than the popular war acts of the other two crisis governments, was not loathe to inform the government that some of the New Deal crisis statutes had passed beyond the bounds of two great American constitutional principles: federalism and the separation of powers. Specifically, the AAA was voided on the first of these counts, the NRA on both of them.[16] Even though all this happened two years or more after the passage of these statutes, they were still in operation at the time; thus the decisions did work a sizable if belated check on the government's crisis activity. Just how effective a limitation on crisis action this makes of the Court is hard to say. In the light of the recent war, the Court today would seem to be a fairly harmless observer of the *emergency* activities of the President and Congress. It is highly unlikely that the separation of powers and the Tenth Amendment will be called upon again to hamstring the efforts of the government to deal resolutely with a serious national emergency.

The two war governments, although they set important precedents for future crisis action, had remarkably little permanent impact on the normal operations of the government. This was not true of the New Deal government of 1933, for the emergency practices of the Year of Crisis wrought several lasting alterations in the constitutional structure: important permanent delegations of crisis power, such as the Emergency Banking Act; a greatly expanded administration; a marked breakdown of the federal principle; and a general increase of presidential power based on executive leadership of the lawmaking process and the delegation of power. The succeeding years of the New Deal carried on each of these changes as permanent techniques and institutions of government. Almost all the crisis laws of 1933 were later extended, and some are still in operation today. The economic emergencies of the twentieth century have had definite lasting effects on democratic, constitutional government.

[16] In *U.S. v. Butler* (297 U.S. 1; January 6, 1936) the AAA was declared unconstitutional; in *Panama Refining Co. v. Ryan* (293 U.S. 388; January 7, 1935) the NRA had been assaulted, and in *Schechter Poultry Co. v. U.S.* (295 U.S. 495; May 27, 1935) it was destroyed completely.

CHAPTER XVIII

The Government of the United States in the Second World War

THE people of the United States are just now casting off the last of the wartime controls imposed upon their lives and pursuits by the fourth of their great crisis governments. Although the administration of 1948 prosecutes its difficult tasks through the medium of recognized peacetime procedures, the strong government of 1941-1945 is still more than just a memory. For the second time in this century the American Republic took the final plunge into the maelstrom of total war; the inevitable result was a government which made continuous use of emergency powers and techniques in its effort to mobilize the nation for total victory. As in the case of Great Britain, an outstanding characteristic of this crisis government was its adherence to the pattern traced in the first World War. The mould of 1917-1918 was rarely broken; the grooves were simply cut a little deeper.

The pattern of 1941-1945 was roughly this: a President who went beyond Wilson and even Lincoln in the bold and successful exertion of his constitutional and statutory powers; a Congress which gave the President all the power he needed to wage a victorious total war, but stubbornly refused to be shunted to the back of the stage by the leading man; a multitude of presidentially created boards and bureaus which regulated the nation's entire economic life and which, for all the false starts and mistakes and prophecies of doom, could point to the most incredible triumphs of production, research, and supply in the history of man; a governmental record of non-interference with the political liberties of the American people that would have been well-nigh perfect but for one dictatorial performance, the evacuation of 70,000 American citizens of Japanese descent from the Pacific Coast area; and finally, a Supreme Court that once again *durante bello* gave judicial sanction to whatever powers and actions the President and Congress found necessary to the prosecution of the war, and then *post bellum* had a lot of strong but unavailing things to say about the limits of the Constitution-at-War.

Roosevelt and the Crisis

FUTURE historians will record that in the course of the second World War the Presidency of the United States became the most powerful and distinguished constitutional office the world has ever known. It seems hardly necessary to declare that Franklin D. Roosevelt was as much the spearhead of the attack and the symbol of the cause as Abraham Lincoln and Woodrow Wilson had been in their great moments of national trial and triumph. From his proclamation of a "limited" national emergency September 8, 1939 through his proclamation of an unlimited emergency May 27, 1941 and on to December 7, 1941, Mr. Roosevelt personally led a disunited nation down the inevitable road to total war.[1] From the day of "infamy" through the great offensives in Europe and the Pacific and on to the threshold of victory, he just as personally led a united nation down the inevitable road to total victory. The people who lived during Mr. Roosevelt's third term could well echo the considered sentiment of Charles Evans Hughes that "there is no more impressive spectacle than that of the President of the Republic in time of war."[2]

The President's sources of emergency authority were, of course, his own broad reading of his constitutional war powers and the immense delegations of discretionary power which he already enjoyed or which Congress gave him for the duration of the crisis. The most significant emergency actions which he undertook on the basis of his constitutional powers were: the two proclamations of emergency, the second of which was aimed squarely at the Axis; the exertions in aid of the beleaguered Allies in 1940 and 1941, particularly the famed "destroyer deal" with Great Britain; the erection of the huge war administration; the Executive Order of February 19, 1942 which served as the basic authority for the uprooting of 70,000 Japanese-American citizens and 40,000 Japanese aliens from their Western homes and pursuits; the unqualified approval of the declaration and maintenance of martial law in Hawaii; the creation of the military commission to try the Nazi saboteurs apprehended by the FBI in June 1942;[3] and the continuance of the Wilso-

---

[1] The emergency proclamations are respectively nos. 2352 and 2487. For an English view of Mr. Roosevelt's leadership *into* total war, see the magnificent tribute "Bereavement in Victory," *Round Table* (June 1945), p.195.

[2] *War Powers under the Constitution*, Sen. Doc. no. 105, 65th Congress, 1st sess. (Washington, 1917), p.8.

[3] Upheld by the Supreme Court in *Ex Parte Quirin* (317 U.S. 1). See R. E. Cushman: "The Case of the Nazi Saboteurs," *Am. Pol. Sci. Rev.*, XXXVI (1942), p.1082; Cyrus Bernstein: "The Saboteur Trial," *Geo. Wash. L.R.*, XI (1943), p.131.

nian technique of "indirect sanctions" as the means of enforcing the war administration's orders and decisions, the most notable instance being the seizure of Montgomery Ward and Company in 1944. Another evident piece of presidential initiative, not quite within the limited scope of this book, was his decision to play the world strategist and his frequent appearances in the role. As usual Mr. Roosevelt had words to match his deeds—particularly the remarkable statement of his war power which he made in his Labor Day speech to Congress in 1942. Most of these manifestations of presidential power are more properly discussed below under other sections of this chapter; the first two and the Labor Day speech merit consideration here.

The proclamations of emergency of 1939 and 1941 were in keeping with the best conceptions of the President's constitutional authority and even more in keeping with the love of crisis which Mr. Roosevelt was never bashful in exhibiting. The idea of a "limited" national emergency as declared in September 1939 was the President's own; it is completely unrecognized by statute or constitutional practice. Under this proclamation he was able to make use of various emergency statutes, particularly those allowing him to expand the peacetime army and navy, without getting the public too excited and inviting the accusation that he was trying to get the nation into war. It is important to remember that in each of these proclamations the President was untying his own hands and giving himself permission to make use of the large arsenal of presidential emergency powers which had been accumulated during the crises of the past. Many people feel strongly that Congress alone should possess this power, just as Congress alone possesses the constitutional power to declare war; and it is interesting to speculate just when those proclamations would have been made by the Congress of 1939-1941. The American dictators, constitutional though they may be, are still largely self-appointed.

The story of the effective manner in which Mr. Roosevelt extended a helping hand to the embattled Allies in the two years before Pearl Harbor is also somewhat outside the scope of this chapter.[4] It should be sufficient to recall that the President not only gave repeated verbal support to the democratic cause, but also pushed the American people

[4] See Forrest Davis and E. K. Lindley: *How War Came: An American White Paper* (New York, 1942). A measured account of the President's actions in this period is given by Louis W. Koenig: *The Presidency and the Crisis* (New York, 1944). On the presidential use of armed force in instances "short of war" and the way in which he can commit the nation to war, see James G. Rogers: *World Policing and the Constitution* (Boston, 1945).

right to the brink of war (where they belonged anyway) with such extraordinary exertions of executive initiative as the call for the Lend-Lease Act, the occupation of Iceland, the Atlantic Charter, the initiation of the American convoys (particularly the extension of the neutrality patrol almost to England in April 1941), the "shoot at sight" order of September 1941, and the destroyer deal of September 1940. Despite the confirming opinion of the Attorney General and the vigorous defense put up by the Roosevelt supporters in the storm of legal controversy which the destroyer deal stirred up,[5] a majority of the nation's constitutional authorities agree that Mr. Roosevelt acted in derogation from the law of nations and disregarded at least two laws of the land,[6] not to mention the constitutional provision (Article IV, section 3, clause 2) that "Congress shall have power to dispose of . . . property belonging to the United States." But his vigorous show of initiative in swapping the fifty overage destroyers for some badly-needed Atlantic bases was generally applauded and was never effectively challenged. This was the "Stewardship Theory" in action, with both of the barriers set up by the first Roosevelt completely trampled down.

The broadest statement of his presidential powers that Mr. Roosevelt ever made—a statement able to stand comparison with the most extreme of President Lincoln's assertions—may be found in his address to Congress of September 7, 1942. In demanding that Congress repeal a provision of the Price Control Act of January 30, 1942, which prohibited ceilings on food products until farm prices had risen to the 110 per cent level over parity, the President stated:

"I ask the Congress to take this action by the first of October. Inaction on your part by that date will leave me with an inescapable responsibility to the people of this country to see to it that the war effort is no longer imperiled by threat of economic chaos.

In the event that the Congress should fail to act, and act adequately, I shall accept the responsibility, and I will act.

At the same time that farm prices are stabilized, wages can and will be stabilized also. This I will do.

The President has the power, under the Constitution and under Congressional acts, to take measures necessary to avert a disaster which would interfere with the winning of the war. . . .

[5] The text of Mr. Jackson's opinion appears in the *New York Times*, September 4, 1940, p.16. See particularly the three articles by Herbert W. Briggs, Quincy Wright, and Edwin Borchard in *Am. Jour. Int. Law.* XXXIV (1940), pp.596, 680, and 690 respectively. The deal was unquestionably a violation of American neutrality. See *U.S. Code*, tit. 5, sec. 3.

[6] See *U.S. Code*, tit. 34, secs. 492, 493a, 456c.

The American people can be sure that I will use my powers with a full sense of my responsibility to the Constitution and to my country. The American people can also be sure that I shall not hesitate to use every power vested in me to accomplish the defeat of our enemies in any part of the world where our own safety demands such defeat.

When the war is won, the powers under which I act automatically revert to the people—to whom they belong."

In other words, the man charged by the Constitution to "take care that the laws be faithfully executed" announced to the makers of one of those laws, a law which he himself had approved, that he was about to act in direct disregard of its terms if they didn't repeal it immediately! It is unfortunate for the history of constitutional dictatorship that Congress finally gave in to the President's peremptory threat; it would have been interesting indeed to see what action he would have taken and what authority he would have cited. The Attorney General's opinion would also have made instructive reading. Even though this unique assertion of presidential emergency power remained in the form of words and was never transformed into deeds, it is still of considerable significance for the doctrine here expressed that the President's initiative is this nation's ultimate weapon of national salvation. The President's power to act as a dictator in time of crisis may henceforth be regarded as a gift from the sovereign people of the United States![7]

The most important new delegations of power to the President in the second World War were the Lend-Lease Act of March 11, 1941 and the First and Second War Powers Acts of December 18, 1941 and March 27, 1942.[8] The Emergency Price Control Act of January 30, 1942 was another thoroughgoing delegation of lawmaking power,[9] but in this instance the power was conferred upon the price administrator called for in the terms of the Act. Although each of these statutes devolved extreme discretionary authority upon the President or his administration, none is comparable to Britain's Emergency Powers (Defence) Acts in the scope of legislative power actually granted.

The Lend-Lease Act was the broadest delegation of spending power

[7] In his article "War-Time Powers of the American Presidency as Conceived by Thomas Jefferson," *Lawyers Guild Review* (September 1942), p.13, Mitchell Franklin argues that the President's extraordinary message was "rooted in the concrete, historical, and flexible thought of the democratic Jefferson." See also his "War Power of the President," *Tulane L.R.*, xvii (1942), p.217. The message and its implications are held up as a horrible example by Henry Hazlitt in his case for *A New Constitution Now*, pp.vii-ix.

[8] lv *Stat.* 31; lv *Stat.* 838; lvi *Stat.* 176, respectively.

[9] lvi *Stat.* 23.

in American history. Passed by a Congress upon which the President was forced to exert his every weapon of legislative leadership, this statute and its repeated extensions[10] gave the chief executive authority to turn over billions of dollars worth of goods, or credits for their purchase, to any country whose defense he should deem vital to the defense of the United States. From first to last, the Office of Lend-Lease Administration, set up under presidential order[11] and headed through most of the war by Edward Stettinius, disposed of some fifty billions to some fifty countries, and no small part of Mr. Roosevelt's renown as "architect of victory" may be ascribed to this bold and unprecedented program.

The two War Powers Acts were rag-bags into which were tossed all manner of provisions dealing with such emergency problems as administrative reorganization for war, censorship of overseas communications, alien property, defense contracts, the power to penalize priorities violations, trading with the enemy, the governmental acquisition of property, and free postage for the armed forces. The statutory basis for the war administration's "government by decree" of the nation's essential business and industry was this clause in the Second War Powers Act:

Whenever the President is satisfied that the fulfillment of requirements for the defense of the United States will result in a shortage in the supply of any material or of any facilities for defense or for private account or for export, the President may allocate such material or facilities in such manner, upon such conditions and to such extent as he shall deem necessary or appropriate in the public interest or to promote the national defense.

The Lend-Lease Act and the Second War Powers Act set definite calendar limits to the period of their validity and had to be several times extended. The First War Powers Act stated its term of operation as the duration of the war plus six months. It is of interest to note that in these statutes Congress empowered itself to revoke any of the granted powers at any time by a mere concurrent resolution. Whether the power of recall thus shrewdly asserted by Congress could be validly exercised is a matter of considerable dispute. There was no test of the matter in connection with these statutes.[12]

[10] The last was April 16, 1945. See generally E. R. Stettinius: *Lend-Lease; Weapon for Victory* (New York, 1944).

[11] Executive Order 8926, October 28, 1941.

[12] See H. White: "The Concurrent Resolution in Congress," *Am. Pol. Sci. Rev.*, xxxv (1941), p.886, and "Executive Responsibility to Congress via Concurrent Resolution," *Am. Pol. Sci. Rev.*, xxxvi (1942), p.895.

The full compass of the President's war powers is yet to be depicted. But can there be any doubt of the extent of those powers? The most unreconstructed Republican would have given assent at any time in the war to this statement of presidential wartime ascendancy, delivered during the first World War:

"When . . . millions of our citizens are constituted in an army, the will of its supreme commander will be in fact our law until the mission of that army is accomplished. Often we shall doubtless suspect his motives, question his judgment, resent his methods; but on penalty of losing civilization itself by the triumph of our enemies, his commands we must obey."[13]

Congress and the War

THE British Parliament in the first war was a stripped-down "machine for registering magisterial edicts"; the British Parliament in the second war was a respected council of state. Congress in both wars was Congress. This time just as last time the crisis was of such a nature that the American legislature, once it had voted the President the astronomical funds and broad powers needed to wage a victorious war, could act generally in a manner quite indistinguishable from its peacetime methods and habits. What was said of Lincoln may be said of Roosevelt. Whatever he was in the White House or in Yalta, he was no dictator on Capitol Hill. Most of the essential parts of his annual programs were enacted in due time, but some demands were casually ignored (his 1943 plea for an extension of the Bituminous Coal Act of 1937), and others were just plain voted down (his 1945 call for legislation "for the total mobilization of all our human resources"). The independence of the legislative branch was most vigorously asserted in the mad rush of the House and Senate to override the President's vetoes of the Smith-Connally Anti-Strike Bill (War Labor Disputes Act of June 1943)[14] and the Revenue Bill of 1943,[15] which was repassed by the enraged legislators February 25, 1944. In the Public Debt Act of 1943, moreover, Congress included a rider specifically repealing the President's controversial order of October 6, 1942 limiting salaries to $25,000 after tax deductions.[16] This undisguised rebuff Roosevelt allowed to become a law without his signature.

[13] W. A. Dunning: "The War Power of the President," *The New Republic* (May 19, 1917).

[14] LVII *Stat.* 163.   [15] LVIII *Stat.* 21.

[16] LVII *Stat.* 63. The presidential order was Executive Order 9250, rather lamely grounded on section 4 of the Emergency Price Control Amendment Act of October 2, 1942. LVI *Stat.* 766.

The spirit of Ben Wade and Senator Chamberlain was carried on rather half-heartedly by Senator Vandenberg, but to no apparent avail. His early proposal for a Joint Committee on the Conduct of the War was never seriously considered, although in the light of Congress's periodical disregard of some of the President's most ardent wishes, the erection of such a committee would have occasioned no great surprise. In lieu of one overall investigating body, the standing committees busied themselves constantly with hearings on various aspects of the war effort, and there were also a number of special committees active throughout the war, the most noted and effective being the Truman (Senate Special War Investigation) Committee and the Tolan (House) Committee on National Defense Migration.[17] The hearings and reports of all these committees form a small library.

It is easy to criticize Congress for its role in the recent war, particularly for such incidents as the House's 1942 one-week debate on fan-dancers in the OCD and the 1944 Senate filibuster on the anti-Poll Tax Bill. It would certainly have been more in keeping with the facts and traditions of democracy if Mr. Roosevelt's exertions in mobilizing the nation for war had been given positive congressional sanction— for example, if the WPB and the NWLB had been set up on a clear statutory basis, with their organization, competence, and methods of enforcement laid down in the law of the land. Moreover, not one of the President's extraordinary domestic or military actions—with the single minor exception of his $25,000 salary limit—was ever repudiated by Congress, although individuals on Capitol Hill occasionally called him to task for his cavalier treatment of statutes and precedents.

Perhaps Congress could have acted a little more nobly and a little less politically, but this is unimportant for the problem at hand. What is important is that Congress acted as usual,[18] and under the circumstances it doesn't seem to have made much difference. Whether it acts badly or not, the national legislature should never give up any power or alter any procedure in an emergency unless such a step appears to be absolutely necessary. It was in pursuance of this basic principle of constitutional dictatorship that the American legislature played its part in the government of World War II.

[17] See L. V. Howard and H. A. Bone: *Current American Government* (New York, 1943), pp.89 ff.

[18] See the comprehensive series of articles by Floyd M. Riddick on the sessions of the War Congress in *Am. Pol. Sci. Rev.*, XXXVI (1942), p.290; XXXVII, p.290; XXXVIII, p.301; XXXIX, p.317; XL, p.256. See also Howard and Bone, *op. cit.*, chap. 5. An excellent survey of the legislation enacted is L. Turrentine and S. D. Thurman: "Wartime Federal Legislation," *California L.R.*, XXXIV (1946), p.277.

The War Administration

THE efforts of President Roosevelt and his administration to mobilize the home-front for total war went a good deal further in disrupting the lives and pursuits of the American people than had the similar efforts of the Wilson government in the first World War. The exorbitant demands placed upon American industry and agriculture by the great global conflict made the problems of the short first war seem almost trifling by comparison. It is not the purpose of this chapter to present any connected picture of the galaxy of emergency and regular agencies which controlled the war activities of the nation—to trace in any detail the first timid undertakings of 1940, the laborious gropings of 1941-1942, or even the bewildering yet somehow coordinated structure of 1943-1946. That job has been too well done too many times already to call for any repetition in these pages.[19] What this discussion can do is to indicate broadly the salient constitutional and political facts underlying the war administration, and perhaps deduce certain lessons that may be of value in predicting or planning future American experiences in emergency economic dictatorship. (*Absit omen.*)

In the first place, it seems hardly necessary to repeat that the President of the United States was, and will remain in any future crisis, the sole director of the nation's emergency administration. The war of production was as much the responsibility of the Commander in Chief as the war of bombs and shells, and if there was any overall coordination in the bewildering administrative structure, it was this: that every agency could follow its line of responsibility up to and its line of authority down from the man in the White House.

In keeping with this paramount fact of presidential authority and responsibility, almost every war agency which the American people came to know so well was created out of the whole cloth of Mr. Roosevelt's war powers under the Constitution, with hardly a reference to statutory provision. The single important exception was the Office of Price Administration, which found its legal basis in the Emergency Price Control Act of 1942, and which remained independent of the

[19] See particularly the Government's own story—*The United States at War* (Washington, 1947). See also Luther Gulick: "War Organization of the Federal Government," *Am. Pol. Sci. Rev.*, XXXVIII (1944), p.1156; D. O. Walter: *American Government at War* (Chicago, 1942), chaps. 1 and 2; Howard and Bone, *op. cit.*, chaps. 3 and 10; James Hart: "National Administration," *Am. Pol. Sci. Rev.*, XXXVII (1943), p.25; "Organizing for Total War," *The Annals of the American Academy of Political and Social Science* (March 1942); E. Stein *et al.*: *Our War Economy* (New York, 1943). A heavy criticism of the confusion and false starts is made by John Burnham: *Total War* (Boston, 1943).

President's immediate authority throughout the war—mostly because it acted exactly the way Mr. Roosevelt wanted it to act. The other major agencies—the War Production Board, the Office of War Mobilization, the War Shipping Administration, the Office of Defense Transportation, the War Manpower Commission, the Office of War Information, the War Labor Board, and all the rest—wielded their individual portions of the totality of presidential power within the framework of the Office for Emergency Management. The OEM is of particular significance as the coordinating agency set up to aid the President in the oversight of this multitude of boards and bureaus which functioned in his name and by his authority. It was established in the Executive Office of the President by an administrative order of May 25, 1940, which in turn was based on the congressionally approved Executive Order of September 8, 1939 providing that there should be "in the event of a national emergency, or threat of a national emergency, such office for emergency management as the President shall determine."[20] The OEM functioned throughout the war as a general advisory, investigating, and coordinating office within the President's immediate entourage.

Thirdly, it is disturbing to note just how far Congress stayed out of the picture of production, consumption, and supply. The initiative Mr. Roosevelt displayed in the destroyer deal was matched on the domestic side by the initiative he displayed, dilatory though it may have been, in setting up the WPB; and in neither instance was there the slightest shred of evidence that it is Congress, not the President, which is constitutionally charged with the determination of the public policy of this nation. The long-range demands of constitutionalism and the short-range demands of dictatorship would both have been more efficiently answered by thoroughgoing statutes providing undoubted legal sanctions and penalties for the decisions and directives of the welter of authorities operating under the OEM; but the President did not ask for, nor did Congress feel compelled to give, such authority—except in certain unconnected and vague clauses in the Selective Service Act, the War Powers Acts, and the Price Control Act. If anyone is to blame for the haphazard and often constitutionally questionable systems of direct and indirect and legal and extra-legal means whereby the WPB and the WLB secured obedience to their edicts,[21]

[20] Section 1 (6) of Executive Order 8248.
[21] On the President's power to use "indirect sanctions" on the basis of the Second War Powers Act and his constitutional authority, see J. L. O'Brian and M. Fleischmann: "The War Production Board: Administrative Policies and Procedures," *Geo. Wash. L.R.*, XIII (1944), p.1.

Congress must accept a healthy share. The OPA, the Truman Committee, and the quarterly reports of the Lend-Lease Administration notwithstanding, Congress occupied a back seat in this wartime economic dictatorship.

A fourth lesson arising from the administrative experiences of the second war was the continued failure of the American government to plan adequately or plan at all for periods of emergency readjustment and operation. The stubborn refusal of the American mind to understand that governmental long-range planning and democratic free enterprise are not incompatible bore bitter though hardly fatal fruit in this war. What plans for war there were in this country—for example, the War Department's Industrial Mobilization Plan of 1939[22]—failed to foresee boldly the unique demands that a global war would place upon the American economy. It is in this respect that the "between wars" work of the British Committee of Imperial Defence forms a good object lesson for the United States.

On the other hand, it has been convincingly argued that the pragmatic, searching methods of Mr. Roosevelt and his aides were after all the best under the political and social circumstances peculiar to the United States. Could any large blueprint have foreseen the final demands of this total war, or taken into account the fact that the President was after all a political figure and had to deal with many of his chief domestic problems in a political way? The method actually adopted throughout the war—setting up each new control agency as the particular need became plainly apparent and each new coordinating agency as the confusion became too great—was typically American; and although the end-product was neither neat nor systematic, still there was no agency not engaged in meeting some definite and essential need. It was Mr. Roosevelt's groping methods which thrust Congress out of this important field of policy-determination. A need would arise and an office to fill it would be created months before an unbidden Congress would have acted.

The President's administration met the practical test of global war and met it reasonably well. The incredible triumphs of American production are not to be as exclusively ascribed to the genius and skill of America's industrialists and technicians as a few of those gentlemen would have the nation believe. The work was done in the offices and factories and fields, but the direction came from Washington. Perhaps the confusion was more apparent than real.

[22] The text of this plan is in H. J. Tobin and P. M. Birdwell: *Mobilizing Civilian America* (New York, 1940), p.237.

The War and the People's Liberties

THE political liberties of the American people—the freedoms of person, speech, press, and assembly—suffered less invasion in this war than in either the Civil War or the World War, with one major exception. A number of reasons have been suggested for this heartening feature of the last few years—most important among them being the virtual unanimity of the nation (after Pearl Harbor) on the necessity of the war, the federal assumption and state surrender of the major responsibility for dealing with the problem of subversive print and speech, and the conscious effort of the Roosevelt administration not to repeat the uncalled-for excesses of the last war.[23] This was easily the most popular war the American people ever fought; the problems of civil liberty were therefore comparatively easy to solve.

There were two important statutes dealing with free speech and press in the recent war, both of them still in effect at the time of this writing: the Espionage Act of 1917 and the Alien Registration Act of June 1940.[24] The latter made it unlawful to advise or urge insubordination, disloyalty, or refusal of duty in the armed forces of the United States, or to distribute any printed or written matter advising such disaffection; to advise, advocate, or teach the desirability of overthrowing or destroying any government in the United States by word or print; or to organize or affiliate with any group or society advocating the overthrow of lawful government.

On several occasions the government proceeded against and secured convictions of out-and-out enemy agents; on several other occasions the government proceeded against certain colorful representatives of the fascist lunatic fringe, usually on the narrow grounds of having attempted to cause insubordination in the armed forces or to obstruct recruiting, and on most of these occasions was thoroughly repulsed. In *Hartzel v. U.S.* the Supreme Court overturned by a 5-4 margin the lower court conviction of a man who had printed and mailed articles to

[23] See R. E. Cushman: "Civil Liberties," *Am. Pol. Sci. Rev.*, xxxvii (1943), p.56, and "Civil Liberty after the War," *Am. Pol. Sci. Rev.*, xxxviii (1944), p.1; Wiley Rutledge, T. R. Powell, J. Edgar Hoover *et al.*: "A Symposium on Constitutional Rights in Wartime," *Iowa L.R.*, xxix (1944), p.379; Roscoe Pound: "Civil Rights during and after the War," *Tenn. L.R.*, xvii (1943), p.706; Howard and Bone, *op. cit.*, chap. 7; O. K. Fraenkel: "War, Civil Liberties, and the Supreme Court. 1941 to 1946," *Yale L.J.*, lv (1946), p.715. See generally the wartime issues of *The Bill of Rights Review* and the many publications of the American Civil Liberties Union.

[24] XL *Stat.* 217, reenacted with increased penalties for peacetime violations in March 1940 (LIV *Stat.* 79); LIV *Stat.* 670, respectively. The noxious Sedition Act of the last war was repealed in 1921.

service men and persons of draft age portraying the war as a betrayal of America, slandering the English and the Jews, and denouncing the President's honesty and patriotism.[25] This decision was based on the technical ground that there was insufficient evidence that he had done this "willfully" within the meaning of the Espionage Act. The indictments for sedition brought against such worthies as William Dudley Pelley, Elizabeth Dilling, and George W. Christians in 1942 were finally dropped in 1946 after a course of events bordering on the fiasco. An attempt by the Department of Justice to indict the *Chicago Tribune* for the unauthorized publication of secret information relative to the Battle of Midway was blocked when the grand jury failed to indict. One governmental action which evoked a good deal of well-aimed criticism was that taken by the Postmaster-General (under the Espionage Act and at the request of the Department of Justice) in barring from the mails a large group of seditious and near-seditious publications, *inter alia* the Radio Priest's *Social Justice*, the *Galilean*, and the *Philadelphia Herold*. Admittedly these suppressions were long overdue; nevertheless the Postmaster-General's summary action should have been subject to a closer survey by the courts. The discretion that he exercises in refusing the second-class mailing privilege received a beneficial curb in the noted case of *Hannegan v. Esquire.*[26]

Censorship in the second World War was the province of Byron Price and his Office of Censorship, set up by an Executive Order of December 19, 1941 to carry out those provisions of the First War Powers Act which granted the government an absolute discretion in the censorship of all communications with foreign countries.[27] The domestic press and radio were controlled on a strictly voluntary and extra-legal basis under the sensible terms of a Censorship Code issued by Mr. Price in early 1942. On the whole, the problem was well handled throughout the war, although there were instances—such as the President's tour of the nation's industries in September 1942—when the press felt that it was being unnecessarily stifled. Six members of the President's Cabinet were included in an advisory Censorship Policy Board. The other job of the first World War's Committee on Public Information—the publicizing and propagandizing of the war at home and abroad—was carried on by Elmer Davis's Office of War Informa-

[25] 322 U.S. 680.   [26] 327 U.S. 146.

[27] No. 8985. See generally Elmer Davis and Byron Price: *War Information and Censorship* (Washington, 1943); Byron Price: "Governmental Censorship in War-Time," *Am. Pol. Sci. Rev.*, XXXVI (1942), p.837; H. C. Shriver and Cedric Larson: "Office of Censorship," *Bill of Rights Rev.* (Spring, 1942), p.189.

tion, set up in June 1942 to consolidate the hitherto unconnected activities of such groups as the Office of Facts and Figures and the Foreign Information Service.[28]

The great and victorious war of production was fought without a single significant restriction upon the rights of labor. The right to strike, the right to picket, and the right to leave one job and go after another were left untouched by the government, although the exertions of Paul McNutt's War Manpower Commission to solve the continuing problems of labor shortages sometimes appeared to be grounded in governmental compulsion, especially after the December 1942 transfer of the Selective Service System into Mr. McNutt's area of responsibility.[29] Despite the early and sincere pledges of William Green and Philip Murray, minor strikes continued throughout the war, but the percentage of man-hours lost was infinitesimal.

The chief emergency agency erected to deal with the problem of wartime industrial disputes was the twelve-man National War Labor Board, headed at one time or another by William H. Davis, Wayne Morse, Lloyd Garrison, and George W. Taylor.[30] The NWLB, on which labor, management, and the public were equally represented, was set up within the OEM by the President's order of January 12, 1942.[31] In the course of the war this emergency agency settled literally hundreds of thousands of cases through arbitration or mediation. As it finally evolved, the NWLB sat in Washington and acted as a policy-determining "supreme court of labor" to which one of its twelve regional miniature boards could refer any decision it was unable to enforce. Moreover, the Board was granted wage-approving powers under the amended Price

[28] Executive Order 9182. The entire Spring 1943 issue of the *Public Opinion Quarterly* is devoted to the OWI. See also H. L. Childs: "Public Information and Opinion," *Am. Pol. Sci. Rev.*, XXXVII (1943), p.56.

[29] By Executive Order 9279. On manpower in the war see W. H. Nicolls and J. A. Vieg: *Wartime Government in Operation* (Philadelphia, 1943); J. J. Corson: *Manpower for Victory* (New York, 1943).

[30] The literature on the general problem of labor and the war and the particular problem of the NWLB is almost frightening in its volume. Recommended in particular are L. B. Boudin: "The Authority of the National War Labor Board over Labor Disputes," *Mich. L.R.*, XLIII (1944), p.329; Howard and Bone, *op. cit.*, chap. 11; Wayne Morse: "The NWLB puts Labor Law Theory into Action," in *A Symposium on Labor Law in War Time, Iowa L.R.*, XXIX, p.175, and "The NWLB, Its Powers and Duties," *Oregon L.R.*, XXII (1942), p.1; C. V. Shields: "The Authority of the War Labor Board," *Wisconsin L.R.* (May 1943), p.378; C. E. Warne, ed.: *War Labor Policies* (New York, 1945).

[31] Executive Order 9017. The NWLB replaced the ineffectual National Defense Mediation Board, created March 19, 1941.

Control Act of 1942,[32] as well as certain responsibilities in the enforcement of the unfortunate War Labor Disputes Act of 1943.

From first to last, it was the constitutional authority of the President of the United States which secured adherence to the decisions of the Board. Publicity and governmental seizure were the most important "indirect sanctions" used against recalcitrant labor or management. Labor was further dealt with by the withholding of union dues, union security, or retroactive pay raises, management by the denial of essential materials, fuel, and transportation. In only about twenty-five instances was it found necessary to seize and operate strike-bound plants. The most publicized cases were the presidential seizures of Mr. McNear's Toledo, Peoria, and Western Railroad and Mr. Avery's Montgomery Ward and Company.[33] The order setting up the NWLB spoke of its power to settle cases "finally," *i.e.* without appeal to the federal judiciary. The concerted attempt by Montgomery Ward to fight the seizure in the courts was doomed to failure. The two lower courts disagreed on the validity of the government's action, and with the cessation of hostilities the Supreme Court held the case moot. The instructive fact in all this is that McNear, Avery, and certain intransigent unions defied the NWLB as long as they did, not that they were finally brought to task. Things were different in Great Britain.

The economic liberties of the American people did not fare as well in the course of the war, although it would be ridiculous to assert that price-fixing, rationing, and government control of industry were anything but the democratic way to fight the war at home. Considering the sacred-cow character of the law of supply and demand in this country, however, price control can certainly be regarded as emergency dictatorship of an extreme nature. Of all the time-honored Anglo-Saxon liberties, the freedom of contract took the worst beating in the war.

The fierce political battle that centered about the OPA in the two years after the war should not obscure the yeoman service rendered by Prentiss Brown and Chester Bowles in their unceasing wartime efforts to "hold the line" against inflation and to see that poor and rich alike got their fair share of the nation's scarce commodities. The OPA derived its independent existence and its power over prices from the Emergency Price Control Act of January 30, 1942, its power over rationing from a presidential order of April 7, 1942 based on Title III of the Second

---

[32] LVI *Stat.* 765, on which Executive Order 9250 of October 3, 1942 was based.
[33] See the immensely entertaining *Investigation of Seizure of Montgomery Ward and Company*, Select Committee to Investigate the Seizure of Montgomery Ward and Company, House of Representatives, 78th Congress, 2nd sess. (Washington, 1944).

War Powers Act.[34] The Price Control Act and the broad authority of the OPA to enforce its regulations and decisions both administratively and judicially were upheld by the Supreme Court in the leading case of *Yakus v. U.S.*[35] The exclusive jurisdiction of the Emergency Court of Appeals to determine the validity of price control orders was also strongly approved in this case.[36] A second important litigation involving the OPA was the case of *Steuart and Co. v. Bowles*,[37] in which the Court decided that the OPA could punish violators of its lawful orders by withholding rationed materials and goods, the strongest judicial approval of the whole arsenal of "indirect sanctions." Legislative control over the OPA was maintained through a statutory provision that comprehensive reports be laid before Congress every ninety days. The Act itself set a definite time limit to its own validity (June 30, 1943), and as the nation well remembers, it had to be extended several times. Finally, the manner in which the purposes of the Price Control Act were carried out was the war's best illustration of what is meant by the phrase "government by administrative decree." For the normal-minded people of America, this was delegation of power and dictatorship of free economy in the extreme.[38]

The Case of the Japanese-Americans

THE two most forceful and controversial assertions of dictatorial power in the second World War were the evacuation of the Japanese-Americans from the West Coast and the maintenance of martial law in the Territory of Hawaii from December 1941 to October 1944. The salient facts of the Japanese-American case are these.[39] On February 19,

[34] Executive Order 9125.

[35] 321 U.S. 414. The rent control provisions of the Price Control Act were upheld in *Bowles v. Willingham* (321 U.S. 503). See generally R. A. Sprecher: "Price Control in the Courts," *Columbia L.R.*, XLIV (1944), p.34.

[36] See also *Lockerty v. Phillips* (319 U.S. 182).   [37] 322 U.S. 398.

[38] The scholarly articles on the OPA are as numerous as the country's law, economics, and political science journals. See in particular: Julius Hirsch: *Price Control in the War Economy* (New York, 1943); D. D. Holdoegel: "The War Powers and the Emergency Price Control Act of 1942," *Iowa L.R.*, XXIX (1944), p.454; J. W. Willis: "The Literature of OPA. Administrative Techniques in Wartime," *Mich. L.R.*, XLII (1942), p.235; George P. Adams: Wartime Price Control (Washington, 1942); Paul M. O'Leary: "Wartime Rationing and Governmental Organization," *Am. Pol. Sci. Rev.*, XXXIX (1945), p.1089.

[39] See generally Eugene V. Rostow: "The Japanese American Cases—A Disaster," *Yale L.J.*, LIV (1945), p.489, and the thorough bibliography in his notes; Carey McWilliams: *What About Our Japanese-Americans?* (New York, 1944) and *Prejudice. The Japanese-Americans* (Boston, 1944). See also the voluminous hearings and reports of the Tolan Committee, which made a thorough and admirable investigation of the whole affair.

1942 President Roosevelt signed Executive Order 9066 which endowed the Secretary of War "and the military commanders whom he may from time to time designate" with broad discretionary authority to establish military areas in the United States "from which any or all persons" might be excluded in order to prevent espionage and sabotage. The following day Secretary of War Stimson delegated this authority to Lt. General J. L. DeWitt, commanding the so-called Western Defense Command, and General DeWitt in his turn established by proclamation "Military Areas Nos. 1 and 2," consisting of the three westernmost states and part of Arizona. By a series of 108 separate orders he then proceeded to remove every single person of Japanese ancestry from these two areas, and by August 7, 1942 both the coastal and eastern portions of the designated states had been cleared of the 110,000 persons who answered this racial criterion. Fully 70,000 of this number were full-fledged citizens of the United States, by every legal, constitutional, and moral standard enjoying all the rights and privileges of any other citizen of the United States.

The official explanation for this enforced mass evacuation—which as the nation knows worked grievous personal and financial hardships on the unfortunate people thus uprooted—was that it was "a matter of military necessity." The "military necessity" which the army had specifically in mind was the possibility of a Japanese assault upon the Pacific Coast. In such an event, it was asserted, the presence of thousands of disloyal or unpredictable people of Japanese descent might easily prove an element of confusion which the enemy could exploit to excessive advantage. To the suggestion that the loyal and disloyal should have been separated by individual examination, as Britain had done with the enemy aliens in its midst, the answer was made that there was not enough time. (The main Exclusion Order was issued *five* months after Pearl Harbor.) The criterion for exclusion was thus not the rational one of disloyalty but the undemocratic one of race.

The President himself was within the limits of the "good faith" criterion affirmed by the Supreme Court in the leading case on preventive martial law, *Moyer v. Peabody*,[40] relying particularly on General DeWitt's appraisal of the situation. The General's appraisal, however, seems to have been influenced by the illiberal anti-Japanese propaganda of the Hearst newspapers and such organizations as the Native Sons of the Golden West, the still fresh object lesson of Admiral Kimmel and General Short, and his soldier's appraisal of the relative importance

[40] 212 U.S. 78.

of the freedom of unpopular minorities in the American scheme. The February 13, 1942 recommendation to the President by the West Coast delegation in Congress that he evacuate "all persons of Japanese lineage" carried much weight too. It is no reflection on the democratic character of Mr. Roosevelt's leadership to say that in this instance he took the easy and popular way out of a nasty situation and "let the people down." Congress played its part in the tragedy, and the role was one of full support for the President. An Act of March 21, 1942 in effect ratified and confirmed Executive Order 9066 by making a federal misdemeanor (punishable by a $5000 fine and a year in jail) of any action in violation of the restrictions laid down by the President, the Secretary of War, or designated military subordinates.[41]

The Supreme Court in its turn was given full opportunity to declare the evacuation unconstitutional and proffer the injured Japanese-Americans some belated relief. This the Court steadfastly refused to do, despite the fact that its decisions were rendered in June 1943 and December 1944, when judicial invalidation of the evacuation scheme would have had no more effect on the war effort than *Ex Parte Milligan* had on the course of the Civil War. In *Hirabayashi v. U.S.* the Court upheld General DeWitt's curfew order under which a University of Washington senior had been convicted, and neatly evaded judicial examination of the validity of the general evacuation order.[42] In *Korematsu v. U.S.* the Court went a good deal further in support of the executive and military authorities and accepted as final the General's judgment that the necessities of the moment demanded the complete evacuation of all persons of Japanese ancestry, and that there was no time in early 1942 to examine the suspected members of the Japanese-American community on an individual basis.[43] The punishment of this loyal citizen of the United States was sanctioned by the highest court of the land; his crime: sitting in his own home. Bitter dissents from this decision were entered by Justices Murphy and Roberts, a milder one by Justice Jackson. In *Ex Parte Endo* the Court decided unanimously that a Japanese-American citizen of proven loyalty was entitled to an unconditional release from the inland camp to which she had been sent. The great constitutional issue was again sidestepped.[44]

[41] LVI *Stat.* 173.   [42] 320 U.S. 81.   [43] 323 U.S. 214.
[44] 323 U.S. 283. The War Relocation Authority was set up within the OEM by Executive Order 9102 of March 18, 1942 to handle the twin problems of evacuation and relocation. For an interesting account of how the problem was handled at the camps see A. H. Leighton: *The Governing of Men* (Princeton, 1945). About 70,000 of these people were still in the camps three years after the evacuation.

The implications of this dictatorial evacuation and the refusal of the Supreme Court to declare it unconstitutional are, as far as they can be ascertained, extremely disturbing.[45] Its pros and cons will doubtless be argued as thoroughly as was Lincoln's suspension of the writ of habeas corpus. The important lessons for the problem of constitutional dictatorship in the United States are these: that the President's unlimited range of dictatorial crisis power was again exerted without legislative, judicial, or popular contradiction; that the Supreme Court demonstrated its continued unwillingness to get in the way of the war power of the United States; and that the most basic rights of a large group of American citizens were grossly flouted under conditions considerably less than desperate, and can be again. The next time it may be a slightly larger minority group. Whatever it was for its citizens of English, German, Jewish, or Chinese descent, the government of the American Republic was a naked dictatorship for its 70,000 Japanese-American citizens of the Pacific Coast.[46]

There are many Americans who would not agree with the writer's appraisal of this affair and would argue that the hindsight of 1948 should not be used to judge a difficult military decision of 1942. There are others who would agree with the appraisal and would brand it the most arbitrary and unnecessary invasion of American rights in the nation's history. But wherever the truth of this matter may rest, this cold fact stands forth undisputed: the government of the United States, in a case of military necessity, can be just as much a dictatorship as any government on earth.

As to the implications of the Japanese-American relocation, the final word is not with Justice Black's sorry "Hardships are a part of war, and war is an aggregation of hardships," nor even with Justice Murphy's brave "Such exclusion goes over 'the very brink of constitutional power' and falls into the ugly abyss of racism." It is with Justice Jackson's coldly realistic

[45] The most trenchant criticism of this whole affair is Eugene V. Rostow: "Our Worst Wartime Mistake," *Harper's* (September 1945), p.193. He suggests financial indemnification and a Supreme Court reversal of the Korematsu decision. He states further that there was not a single conviction of a person of Japanese descent for sabotage in Hawaii or the Pacific States throughout the entire war.

[46] And for the thousands of loyal Japanese enemy aliens too. On the whole the alien problem was handled very well indeed by the Department of Justice. All aliens were registered under the Alien Registration Act of 1940. Regional boards examined about 10,000 suspected enemy aliens, and about 4,000 were interned. This problem and many of the others considered in this chapter are excellently treated in a series of lectures entitled *War and the Law* (Chicago, 1944), Ernest Puttkammer, ed. See also Walters, *op. cit.*, chap. 5; Howard and Bone, *op. cit.*, chap. 8.

"If the people ever let command of the war power fall into irresponsible and unscrupulous hands, the courts wield no power equal to its restraint. The chief restraint upon those who command the physical forces of the country, in the future as in the past, must be their responsibility to the political judgments of their contemporaries and to the moral judgments of history."

The story of martial law in Hawaii is considerably less disturbing and has a slightly happier ending. On December 7, 1941 Governor J. B. Poindexter, acting upon a clear grant of authority in the Organic Act of the Territory of Hawaii,[47] suspended the writ of habeas corpus, declared martial law throughout the islands, and turned over to the Commanding General, Hawaiian Department, the exercise of all his normal powers "during the present emergency and until the danger of invasion is removed." A telegram was dispatched to the President asking for confirmation of his action, and this confirmation was immediately forthcoming. Under the confused circumstances of the moment this swift establishment of martial law was a judicious and warranted measure. Despite a rising wave of criticism in the months following the Battle of Midway against the continuation of martial law, it was not terminated fully until October 1944. The strong protests of Governor Stainback had resulted in the return of eighteen functions of civil government to the civil authorities in March 1943, but the military continued to maintain a qualified martial law.

Not until February 25, 1946 did the the Supreme Court get a chance to review the constitutionality of the extension of martial law after the initial Japanese threat had passed. The *Ex Parte Milligan* of this war was *Duncan v. Kahanamoku.*[48] The simple question for decision was the validity of two prison sentences imposed by military tribunals upon civilians for civilian crimes—one on a 1942 charge of embezzlement, the other on a 1944 charge of assault upon two Marine sentries in the Pearl Harbor Navy Yard. The Court held by a 6-2 decision that the

[47] Sec. 67, xxxi *Stat.* 141.
[48] Also *White v. Steer* (327 U.S. 304). The prolongation of martial law in the Islands received its scathing due in the country's law reviews during the four years that preceded the Court's final decision. See particularly Charles Fairman: "The Law of Martial Rule and the National Emergency," *Harv. L.R.*, IV (1942), p.1253; R. S. Rankin: "Hawaii under Martial Law," *Jour. of Pol.*, V (1943), p.270, and "Martial Law and the Writ of Habeas Corpus in Hawaii," *Jour. of Pol.* VI (1944), p.213: Garner Anthony: "Martial Law, Military Government, and the Writ of Habeas Corpus in Hawaii," *Calif. L.R.*, xxxi (1943), p.477. J. P. Frank's provocative article: "Ex Parte Milligan v. The Five Companies: Martial Law in Hawaii," *Columbia L.R.*, xliv (1944), p.369, asserts that martial law was unduly perpetuated in order to keep Hawaii's labor under military control.

military courts had no jurisdiction in either instance, and that the prisoners should be released from custody. The particular constitutional doctrine announced in the Milligan case—that military courts have no jurisdiction over civilians in areas where no imminent danger threatens and the regular courts are able to discharge their duties—was thus vigorously reasserted. Justice Black's majority opinion judiciously refrained from reciting once again the unqualified statement of the crisis validity of the Constitution delivered by Justice Davis in the Milligan case. Justice Murphy, one of the dissenters in the Korematsu case, was able to sing the old refrain without laying himself open to the charge of rank hypocrisy. Two men got some belated but welcome relief, and the Court upheld the Constitution. But the people of Hawaii lived under martial law until October 1944. The Duncan case will be even less of a controlling precedent than the Milligan decision.

There is little that needs to be added to this account of America's most recent constitutional dictatorship concerning the events of the past two or three years, so fresh in the public's mind are the leading events of the Truman administration. The similarities between 1945-1948 and 1918-1921 are countless. The battles over the retention or abandonment of controls between President and Congress, the hasty demise of some of the most important wartime agencies, the lingering death-pains of others, the general popular and legislative reaction to presidential power (accompanied by loud cries of "dictatorship!" and "police state!"), the surge of industrial strife and domestic politics—all these things the nation has been through before. Although most of the wartime statutes have expired, a few controls are still in effect, most particularly rent control. At the present writing, neither President Truman nor Congress has made a move to end the overall state of emergency in which the nation has been since before Pearl Harbor. Considering the present state of the nation and the world, it is no wonder that at least a few of the trappings of constitutional dictatorship will be part of the governmental scheme for several years to come.

In conclusion, it is important to recognize that a considerable degree of permanent change has been worked in the structure and powers of the government of the United States by these four experiences in constitutional dictatorship. Except in the particular matter of the statutory delegation of powers for presidentially-declared emergencies, the scope of this lasting impact defies precise determination. Yet it is certain that many of the pronounced deviations in the present system from the pattern of 1789 owe much of their extent, if not their genesis, to the crisis administrations of Lincoln, Wilson, and Roosevelt. The rise of the President to a dominant position in the structure of the federal government; the firm establishment of those closely related weapons of the strong President of the twentieth century, legislative leadership and delegated power; the concomitant impairment of the carefully ordained separation of powers and functions between the executive and legislative branches; the general weakening of the federal principle; the extension of governmental supervision or control over large areas of American free enterprise; and with all this the continued expansion of the Constitution as a living document—all these contemporary features of the American government would probably have come in time had there never been a crisis government in the United States, but each of them was hastened and intensified to a significant extent by the Republic's periods of emergency.

Each of the modern democracies studied in this book has contributed an outstanding institution of constitutional dictatorship. Germany's Article 48, France's state of siege, and Great Britain's cabinet dictatorship are all bold answers to the knotty question of constitutional emergency powers. In comparison with the emergency experiences of any one of these three European countries, the crisis history of the American Republic is still hardly impressive enough to make the phrase "constitutional dictatorship in the United States" anything more than a figure of speech.

Nevertheless, the United States in its turn does offer a striking example of a potent crisis institution: the independent President. Whether or not it was planned this way makes little difference; the fact is that the Presidency today, when properly handled, is as powerful an instrument of constitutional dictatorship as the office of Prime Minister of Great Britain. Its power is the boundless grant of executive authority found in the Constitution, supplemented by broad delegations of discretionary competence from the national legislature; its limitations are the political sense of the incumbent and the patience of the American people; its effectiveness rests in the personality and energy of the President himself and the circumstances with which he has to deal. To a Van Buren, a Buchanan, or a Taft the Presidency is an instrument of government whose powers and status are virtually the same in peace, war, rebellion, or depression. To a Lincoln, a Wilson, or a Roosevelt it becomes in time of national crisis a mighty weapon of freedom, absolute in its authority and conditioned only by its purpose: the preservation of the American constitutional system and American liberty.

Because it is so ideal a matrix for constitutional dictatorship, the Presidency does present a serious potential danger to the American people. It is for them to be eternally vigilant, to demand that this vast display of power be wielded in their behalf, as hitherto it always has been, and not against them. It is not too much to say that the destiny of this nation in the Atomic Age will rest in the capacity of the Presidency as an institution of constitutional dictatorship.[49]

[49] Of timely interest is this gloomy observation of the gloomy Oswald Spengler, made shortly following the close of the first World War: "As for America, hitherto lying apart and self-contained, rather a region than a State, the parallelism of President and Congress which she derived from a theory of Montesquieu has, with her entry into world politics, become untenable. It must in times of real danger make way for formless powers, such as those with which Mexico and South America have long been familiar."—*The Decline of the West* (American ed., New York, 1939), II, p.416.

CHAPTER XIX

Constitutional Dictatorship: The Forms, The Dangers, The Criteria, The Future

THE universal significance of constitutional dictatorship should need no further demonstration. The crisis experiences of the Roman Republic and the four large modern democracies are mirrored in the history of every constitutional state. The more complex the constitutional structure and the more assured the rights of the people, the more necessary and severe the practice of constitutional dictatorship has been. The history of Rome bears witness to this assertion. The mere adoption of dictatorial powers and procedures carries with it no guarantee that any particular emergency will be successfully put to rout. Dictatorship is no sure panacea for a democratic nation's woes, especially in an economic crisis. Other things being equal, however, a great emergency in the life of a constitutional democracy will be more easily mastered by the government if dictatorial forms are to some degree substituted for democratic, and if the executive branch is empowered to take strong action without an excess of deliberation and compromise.

In terms of power, crisis government in a constitutional democracy—whatever the character of the emergency and whatever the dictatorial institutions temporarily adopted—entails one or two, or more probably all, of three things: *concentration*, *expansion*, and *liberation*. Generally these three features are fused together and evidence themselves as an increase in the authority and prestige of the state and a decrease in the liberty and importance of the individual.

The concentration of governmental power in a democracy faced by an emergency is a corrective to the crisis inefficiencies inherent in the doctrine of the separation of powers. In most free states it has generally been regarded as imperative that the total power of the government be parceled out among three mutually independent branches—executive, legislature, and judiciary. It is believed to be destructive of constitutionalism if any one branch should exercise any two or more types of power, and certainly a total disregard of the separation of powers is, as Madison wrote in the *Federalist*, no. 47, "the very definition of tyranny." In normal times the separation of powers forms a distinct obstruction to arbitrary governmental action. By this same token, in abnormal times it may form an insurmountable barrier to decisive emergency action in behalf of the state and its independent existence. There are moments in the life of any government when all powers must work together in unanimity of purpose and action, even if this means the temporary union of executive, legislative, and judicial power in the hands of one man. The more complete the separation of powers in a constitutional system, the more difficult and yet the more necessary will be their fusion in time of crisis. This is evident in a comparison of the crisis potentialities of the cabinet and presidential systems of government. In the former the all-important harmony of legislature and executive is taken for granted; in the latter it is neither guaranteed nor to be too confidently expected. As a result, cabinet dictatorship is more easily established and more trustworthy than presidential dictatorship.

The atomism of political power found in every constitutional state has been expressed geographically as well as organizationally. Federalism, regionalism, municipal freedom, local self-government—all of these are institutional devices whereby the total power of the state has been further divided and subdivided in the name of liberty. Almost as important as the democratic idea that the executive should not make laws is the democratic idea that the central government should have as little as possible to do with the regimes installed by the people for their governance on a local, city, state, departmental, or other regional level. In the United States the phrase "state rights" has been for many people synonymous with "liberty." But federalism and local self-government, be they important as in the United States or Switzerland, or rather less significant as in France, present distinct barriers to effective crisis action, and in a great emergency they will be broken down. Constitutional dictatorship must mean a concentration of power, no matter how it is divided.

The expansion of power is an equally significant feature of constitutional government in crisis. In areas where it already exists—taxation, the control of public businesses, the punishment of public crimes, the maintenance of internal order—the power of the state manifests itself in stronger and more arbitrary control, administration, and adjudication. Into areas normally forbidden to it—the ordinary exercise of civil and economic liberties, the management or ownership of industry, the regulation of manpower—the power of the state is extended. The crisis expansion of governmental power is most clearly evidenced in the contraction of civil and economic freedom which it works. Whether the emergency be that of war or rebellion or depression, the government finds it necessary to abridge the rights of citizens to speak freely, assemble peaceably, maintain an inviolate domicile, strike, escape military service, or even vote their representatives out of office. In war or depression, moreover, the constitutional democracy of the twentieth century is further constrained to regulate the business, industry, and transportation of the nation to a degree that would be decried as "bolshevism" in time of national or economic peace. Into whatever forbidden fields of freedom the necessities of crisis may force the leaders of a constitutional government to go, go they must or permit the destruction of the state and its freedom.

"When it comes to a decision by the head of the State upon a matter involving its life, the ordinary rights of individuals must yield to what he deems the necessities of the moment."[1]

"However precious the personal liberty of the subject may be, there is something for which it may well be to some extent sacrificed by legal enactment, namely national success in the war or escape from national plunder or enslavement."[2]

The power of the state in crisis must not only be concentrated and expanded, it must also be freed from the normal system of constitutional and legal limitations. One of the basic features of emergency powers is the release of the government from "the paralysis of constitutional restraints."[3] The military police are not required to have a warrant to search a citizen's house, the prime minister is not forced to submit to the usual barrage of questions and votes of confidence, the courts may often proceed to the trial of public offenses by summary procedure and without the possibility of appeal—everywhere the wielders of public power are relieved of normal restrictions and responsibility. The classic example of the liberation of governmental power from the chains of constitutionalism is the Roman dictatorship.

The Forms of Constitutional Dictatorship

THERE are three general forms of modern crisis government that may be deduced from the many emergency regimes considered in this book: the executive dictatorship, the legislative dictatorship, and the war government. The institutions and techniques of government adopted

[1] Mr. Justice Holmes in *Moyer v. Peabody* (212 U.S. 78, 85).
[2] Lord Atkinson in *King v. Halliday* (1917), A.C., 271-272.
[3] F. M. Watkins: *The Failure of Constitutional Emergency Powers under the German Republic* (Cambridge, 1939), p.36.

under each of these three categories are remarkably similar in all constitutional democracies.

The executive dictatorship, which finds its classic model in the Roman dictatorship and its modern expression in the institutions of martial law and the state of siege, is the most venerable form of constitutional emergency government. This is the type of constitutional dictatorship reserved for crises of a sudden and violent character, particularly the danger of armed rebellion. Its military origin and nature are manifest in the terms martial law and state of siege; the ultimate significance of each is that it sanctions a lawful declaration of war by the government upon any portion of the citizenry substantial enough to foment an armed rebellion. To this end the executive is empowered by law or custom to proceed to arbitrary action in defense of the state: to suspend some or all rights of some or all citizens; to use troops to maintain or restore order; to institute military courts for the summary trial and punishment, even by execution, of crimes against the public safety and order.

In Weimar Germany, the United States, France, Great Britain, and all other constitutional countries, the executive possesses this dictatorial power to repel forcible attacks against the state with whatever amount of force is necessary to subdue the insurrectionary forces. The points of difference between martial law and the state of siege are of some importance, particularly in regard to their rationale and their traditional methods of limitation,[4] but their similarities of purpose and effect are far more significant. The character of martial law and the state of siege as purely executive institutions is evidenced by the fact that neither of them authorizes emergency executive legislation. Legislative activity is unnecessary in a true condition of martial rule, and the legislature stays in session (if session is possible) merely to act as supervisor of this extraordinary power.

---

[4] It is interesting to note some of the theories advanced for this cleavage between martial law and the state of siege. A typical comment is that of Reinach in *De L'Etat de Siège*, p.9, in which he asserts that any difference in the emergency institutions of one nation from those of another "is in accord with the character of the different peoples." Muth: *Das Ausnahmerecht*, pp.20 ff., advances the belief that martial law arises from the principles of Democracy and Equality, while the state of siege is based upon the principles of Liberalism and Individual Liberty. It is because the citizen fears the government more in France than in England that he has authorized the establishment of constitutional dictatorship in the law. Carl Friedrich: *Constitutional Government and Politics*, p.215, seems to have exactly the opposite idea. The liberty of the individual is emphasized under the English, not the continental practice. Watkins: *Constitutional Dictatorship*, pp.346 ff., contributes an excellent short review of the differences between the state of siege and martial law. Are not the contrasting facts of French and English political and legal history sufficient explanation of these differences?

The second variety of modern emergency government, the legislative dictatorship, is chiefly available for crises of an economic nature, whether transient or sustained. The fundamental process of this form of emergency government is that of executive legislation, the simplest (often too simple) solution to the problem of parliamentary incapacity or unwillingness to face difficult questions demanding legislative treatment.

There are three recognized bases for executive lawmaking in an emergency.[5] First, there are constitutional provisions such as Article 48 or those found in the old German state constitutions. This particular procedure has been avoided by most constitutional states as one whose dangers far exceed its value. In those constitutions in which emergency legislation has been authorized, the absence of the parliament is the normal prerequisite for executive action, and its immediate convocation to register positive approval of executive ordinances is almost always provided. An interesting variation upon this means of providing for emergency legislation in the absence of the parliament was Article 54 of the pre-1939 Czech Constitution, which authorized the issuance of crisis ordinances by a joint legislative committee of twenty-four members following the recommendation of the Cabinet and the approval of the President. Both judicial and legislative review were stipulated.

Secondly, there are examples in all constitutional democracies of permanent statutes delegating ordinance power to the executive, to be exercised in emergencies ordinarily ascertained and declared by himself. An instance of this is the power of the President of the United States to raise or lower the value of the dollar within certain limits or of the Crown-in-Council to forbid certain imports and exports. A third basis, the one most frequently adopted in modern states, is that of temporary delegation for a specific emergency. The practice of the temporary or permanent delegating statute for emergency purposes, only one facet of the larger problem of the delegation of power, has been thus officially justified:

"In a modern state there are many occasions when there is a sudden need for legislative action. For many such needs delegated legislation is the only convenient or even possible remedy. . . . It may not be only prudent but vital for Parliament to arm the executive Government in advance with almost plenary power to meet occasions of emergency, which affect the whole nation. . . . as in the extreme case of the Defence of the Realm Acts in the Great War, where the emergency had arisen; or in the Emergency

[5] See the excellent note by James Hart: "The Emergency Ordinance: A Note on Executive Power," *Col. L.R.*, XXIII (1923), p.528.

Powers Act, 1920, where the emergency had not arisen but power was conferred to meet emergencies that might arise in the future. . . . There is in truth no alternative means by which strong measures to meet great emergencies can be made possible; and for that reason the means is constitutional."[6]

Examples of the practice of emergency delegation are the German enabling acts of 1923-1924, the English delegating statutes of 1931, the National Industrial Recovery Act of 1933, and the French enabling acts of the 1930's. This institution is under a cloud today in democratic countries, as well it might be. The indiscriminate employment of the enabling act in the last years of the French Republic as a cure for the peculiar crisis of parliamentary irresponsibility, paralleled by a similar use and abuse of Article 48 in Germany, illustrated all too clearly the dangers which attend the use of this controversial crisis institution.

Finally, in all constitutional states there remains the continuing possibility that in a case of extreme necessity the executive will resort to action of a legislative character in derogation from or addition to existing statutes. There is no legal or constitutional basis for this sort of emergency lawmaking, and the great precedents—such as those set by Lincoln in 1861 and Pitt in 1766—have been so scattered as to have failed to make this practice an institution of any regularity. Executive legislation without constitutional or legal authority is a dictatorial practice reserved for only the most stringent of crises. In the absence of the legislature and in the presence of an overwhelming necessity, the executive in any constitutional democracy will "legislate"—of that there can be no doubt. This may not be constitutional law, nor even an unwritten and extreme constitutional convention, but it is historical fact. The President of the United States has no constitutional authority whatsoever, nor has the Crown any prerogative, to issue emergency ordinances with the force of law, but if the life of the state calls for illegal and unconstitutional action, then such action will be taken by any President or Prime Minister true to his constitutional duty.

The third type of crisis regime, the war government, may be regarded as the ultimate, if somewhat chaotic expression of the theory of constitutional dictatorship. Given an undeniable necessity, no institution of dictatorial government can properly be withheld from the authority of the men charged with the defense of a constitutional state engaged in total war. The state of siege or martial law, declared by executive or legislature as the circumstances require; the general or specific, com-

[6] *Report of the Committee on Ministers' Powers* (1932), Cmnd. 4060.

plete or partial delegation of lawmaking power to the executive; the suspension of whatever individual rights and privileges whose full enjoyment would impair the efficient prosecution of the war, and to whatever extent necessary; the invasion by an expanded administration of the ordinarily bitterly defended areas of free enterprise;[7] the suspension of elections by the elected themselves, the imposition of confiscatory taxes, and the conscription of manpower; the institution of special or even military courts for the trial of citizens accused of public offenses; the general relaxation of popular and legal controls on all public officials; the admission of the military to the high councils of the land in a manner not paralleled in peacetime; the relegation of the legislature to a secondary or even humiliating status; and finally, the inflation of executive power through delegation and initiative to permit arbitrary action of executive, legislative, or judicial character—these are the dictatorial forms and procedures that were to be found, some or all of them, in the democratic governments of the first and second World Wars.

The Dangers of Constitutional Dictatorship

CONSTITUTIONAL dictatorship is a dangerous thing. A declaration of martial law or the passage of an enabling act is a step which must always be feared and sometimes bitterly resisted, for it is at once an admission of the incapacity of democratic institutions to defend the order within which they function and a too conscious employment of powers and methods long ago outlawed as destructive of constitutional government. Executive legislation, state control of popular liberties, military courts, and arbitrary executive action were governmental features attacked by the men who fought for freedom not because they were inefficient or unsuccessful, but because they were dangerous and oppressive. The reinstitution of any of these features is a perilous matter, a step to be taken only when the dangers to a free state will be greater if the dictatorial institution is not adopted.

The most obvious danger of constitutional dictatorship, or of any of its institutions, is the unpleasant possibility that such dictatorship will abandon its qualifying adjective and become permanent and unconstitutional. Too often in a struggling constitutional state have the institutions of emergency power served as efficient weapons for a coup d'état. Not without reason did the followers of Marshal MacMahon

---

[7] See generally A. C. Pigou: *The Political Economy of War* (rev. ed., London, 1940); H. W. Spiegel: *The Economics of Total War* (New York, 1942); Horst Mendershausen: *The Economics of War* (New York, 1941).

advise him to declare the state of siege in his attempt to restore the monarchy in France, and Napoleon III used the state of siege to destroy a constitution even more effectively than the World War government used it to defend one. The dolorous and instructive history of Weimar Germany and its ill-famed Article 48 is the most conspicuous instance of a constitutional dictatorship being converted into a steppingstone to permanent absolutism.

The institutions of constitutional dictatorship are not only uniquely available as instruments for a coup d'état; they are also ideal for the purposes of reactionary forces not so much interested in subverting the constitutional order as they are in thwarting all legal and electoral attempts to dislodge them from their entrenched positions of power. This was the significant criticism leveled at the Roman dictatorship—that it was more than once employed by the patrician party to obstruct the normal constitutional progress of the Republic. Moreover, there have been numerous occasions in British and American history when martial law has been instituted and civil rights suspended, supposedly because of some internal crisis, but actually for no other reason than the maintenance of some privileged group in power. General Peron owes a heavy debt to the Argentine version of the state of siege. Revolution and reaction are infinitely more possible with the aid of crisis institutions such as martial law, executive legislation, or the suspension of civil rights. Therein lie the great and continuing dangers of constitutional dictatorship.

A third risk inherent in the constitutional employment of dictatorial institutions is the simple fact that changes less than revolutionary, but nonetheless changes, will be worked in the permanent structure of government and society. No constitutional government ever passed through a period in which emergency powers were used without undergoing some degree of permanent alteration, always in the direction of an aggrandizement of the power of the state. It is entirely possible that changes of this nature might be welcome as propitious to the cause of freedom and good government. It took the crisis of 1933 to convince Congress that the federal government ought to have certain expanded powers in the field of agriculture, and this may have been an advisable permanent change. The dictates of constitutional democracy demand, however, that all lasting alterations be deliberated upon and initiated in less troubled times, not under the compulsion of a raging crisis. Alterations in the structure of a constitutional government may be wrought and made permanent that do not represent the mature and collected

295

judgment of the representatives of the people, alterations that in their nature are far more difficult to disestablish than they were to institute. Federalism and free enterprise will serve as examples of institutions easy to break down in crisis and infinitely more difficult to restore thereafter, and a legislature relegated to the background in a great national emergency will not easily prove its claims to a restored status of power and prestige.

Professor Rappard has pointed out that the concentration of power in the executive, the governmental invasion of the field of free enterprise, and the increasing encroachment of the state upon the liberties of its citizens are changes characteristic of all modern democracies, even in normal times.[8] The aspect of his reminder most significant for the problem of constitutional dictatorship is that each of these trends is a feature of democracy in crisis, and it is obvious that much of their impetus has been gained from the repeated emergencies of the last thirty years. There are those who believe that these twentieth century departures of democratic government will aid the cause of human freedom. Nevertheless, all three are clearly repugnant to the western democratic tradition; any particular step in their direction should be instituted as a permanent policy only by the elected representatives of the people and only after full deliberation and popular acquiescence, not in the confusion of some national crisis.

A further danger to democracy is inherent in the implicit and even positive acknowledgment that the regular institutions of constitutional government do not have the virility to protect the state from the dangers of war, rebellion, or economic collapse. The wartime abandonment of such features of constitutional government as the maintenance of jury trial for all crimes or the separation of the functions of legislation and administration cannot help but weaken their peacetime prestige and efficacy. It is in regard to the maintenance of normal parliamentary government that this danger is most ominous and consequential. The man who is prone to overemphasize the petty activities of modern legislatures may too easily be convinced in a crisis, where the parliament is relegated to a secondary position, that this arrangement should be continued as a permanent feature of his constitutional government.

Finally, it is obvious that individual abuses of public power are more likely to occur under conditions of crisis and in the prosecution of extraordinary duties than in normal times and in pursuit of normal duties. Even the best of public officials charged with a task under a

[8] William E. Rappard: *The Crisis of Democracy* (Chicago, 1938), chap. 3.

state of martial rule may not be able to avoid needless injury to the rights and lives and property of loyal citizens, while the worst will make use of their unwonted authority in such a manner as to defeat the very purposes for which this institution of constitutional dictatorship is called into action. This abuse of executive emergency powers is often paralleled in the matter of delegated legislative power; oppressive ordinances are issued by the executive that would have no chance of passage in a legislature responsible to a discerning public. "If hard cases make bad law, emergencies may make worse."[9] Once a constitutional dictatorship is initiated, it is inevitable that the men charged with its success will seek more extraordinary powers or demand more procedural readjustments than are necessary or even expedient. Unwarranted suspensions of rights and unnecessary alterations of governmental procedure, as well as individual abuses of emergency power, are dangers that must be consistently opposed by public opinion.

The Criteria of Constitutional Dictatorship

THE facts of history demonstrate conclusively that constitutional dictatorship has served repeatedly as an indispensable factor in the maintenance of constitutional democracy. For all the formidable dangers they present, for all the knotty problems they pose, the accepted institutions of constitutional dictatorship are weapons which the democracies will henceforth renounce at their own peril. In the Atomic Age upon which the world is now entering, the use of constitutional emergency powers may well become the rule and not the exception. This may not be a happy prospect, but it is a very possible one. This brings the free people of this earth face to face with some perplexing problems. How are they to insure that emergency powers will preserve and not destroy their liberties and free government? How are they to make their system of government better prepared for the shock of future crises? In short, how are they to maximize the efficiency and minimize the dangers of constitutional dictatorship? These are questions which can be answered only in the most general terms. There is no set formula for the success of the basic principle or any one of the major or minor institutions of constitutional dictatorship, any more than there is one for the regular procedures of constitutional government. The present discussion will nevertheless attempt to do two things: first, offer the American people (or any other free people, for that matter) certain criteria with which

[9] Cecil T. Carr: *Concerning English Administrative Law* (New York, 1941), p.165.

to test the worth and propriety of any future resort to emergency powers in their behalf; and second, put forward a few suggestions for the more precise and candid institutionalization of American constitutional dictatorship.

In the first chapter of this book the ends of constitutional dictatorship were broadly defined as the preservation of the independence of the state, the maintenance of the existing constitutional order, and the defense of the political and social liberties of the people; and the precise duty of constitutional dictatorship was summed up in the simple precept: end the crisis and restore normal times. With these ends in mind, the essential criteria of constitutional dictatorship may be presented and analyzed. No institution of constitutional dictatorship will ever conform perfectly to all of these prescriptions, but the complete disregard of any one of them is also a disregard of the theory of constitutional emergency powers and the fundamental principles of democracy. A free people should certainly be educated and encouraged to demand that the use of emergency powers in their defense conform to these standards. In general, they may be separated into three categories: those criteria by which the initial resort to constitutional dictatorship is to be judged, those by which its continuance is to be judged, and those to be employed at the termination of the crisis for which it was instituted. In the first category may be considered the following:

1. *No general regime or particular institution of constitutional dictatorship should be initiated unless it is necessary or even indispensable to the preservation of the state and its constitutional order.* This is the first and great commandment of constitutional dictatorship. As far as may be feasible, the salvation of a constitutional democracy in crisis should be worked out through its regular methods of government. Only when the benefits to be assured by a resort to constitutional dictatorship clearly outweigh the dangers to be expected should emergency powers be called into action. In Rousseau's words: "However, none but the greatest dangers can counterbalance that of changing the public order, and the sacred power of the laws should never be arrested save when the existence of the country is at stake."[10]

Martial rule and executive legislation in particular should be reserved for only the most ominous crises. Whether the margin for error is to be conceded to the demands of normality or to the demands of the emergency is a problem to be solved only by the most acute and farsighted statesmanship. The crisis history of the modern democracies demon-

[10] *Social Contract*, IV, 6.

strates that executives will usually ask for more power than they really need, and that courts are powerless to obstruct or even mitigate their demands. The immediate defense of this criterion will therefore rest with the national legislature, while the burden of proof must be placed squarely upon those who demand the initiation of the particular constitutional dictatorship. It is in respect to this criterion that the German use of Article 48 and the French use of the enabling act are most heavily to be condemned.

2. A criterion which suggests itself from Roman practice is this: *the decision to institute a constitutional dictatorship should never be in the hands of the man or men who will constitute the dictator.*[11] In other words, no constitutional dictator should be self-appointed. That this criterion has not been uniformly observed in modern experiences with emergency powers is obvious. The greatest of constitutional dictators was self-appointed, but Mr. Lincoln had no alternative. Few Americans seem to realize that almost all of the President's lengthy catalogue of emergency powers go into operation upon the declaration of an emergency ascertained and proclaimed by himself alone. This unquestionably leads to an increased frequency in the use of these powers. And as Professor Friedrich has suggested,[12] there might well have been no crisis in 1933 if President Roosevelt had been required to appoint another to wield the abnormal display of power which he seemed to find so necessary at the moment. The contrast between the German and Roman constitutional dictatorships in respect to this criterion is particularly instructive.

Although in most democracies the legislature is nominally charged with the final authority to decide on the initiation of a constitutional dictatorship, in fact it seems always to be the wielders of crisis powers themselves who decide that an emergency exists. This is especially true when, as is so often the case in many countries, the executive branch is supported in the legislature by a solid and disciplined party majority. In such instances it is hardly practicable to look to the legislature for an independent decision that emergency powers be called into action, or for an independent check upon their employment. In theory at least, the French state of siege conforms most closely to the requirements of this second criterion. The ascertainment and declaration of the emergency

[11] See Friedrich: *Constitutional Government and Politics*, pp.210 ff. Another criterion based on the Roman dictatorship would seem to be that the dictatorial power should never be transferred by the dictator to another.
[12] *Ibid.*, p.217.

are lodged with the legislature, the use of emergency powers with the executive.

3. *No government should initiate a constitutional dictatorship without making specific provision for its termination.* As the American people know only too well, it is far more difficult to end a period of national emergency than it is to declare one. The instructive example of the Roman dictatorship, with its rigid six-month limit and its equally rigid convention that the dictator was to lay down his power immediately upon the completion of the task for which he had been called up, is not quite valid for the twentieth century, but it does serve as a significant moral warning that a time limit of some sort should always be fixed on the use of constitutional emergency powers. The duration of the state of siege is to be determined in the declaratory statute; the validity of the Emergency Powers Act is fixed at one month; war powers in the United States are generally granted "for the duration of the present war" or an actual calendar date is set for the termination of their validity; the enabling acts in all constitutional democracies set rigid time limits only to be extended by positive action of the national legislature—through provisions such as these the modern constitutional dictatorships are brought into reasonable conformity with this third criterion. In the last resort, the efficacy of these provisions can only be guaranteed if a residual power is left somewhere to halt the dictatorship and break up the temporary concentration of power. (And where else can it be left except in the national legislature?)

4. A criterion of cardinal importance both before and during a period of constitutional dictatorship is: *all uses of emergency powers and all readjustments in the organization of the government should be effected in pursuit of constitutional or legal requirements.* In short, constitutional dictatorship should be *legitimate.* It is an axiom of constitutional government that no official action should ever be taken without a certain minimum of constitutional or legal sanction. This is a principle no less valid in time of crisis than under normal conditions. The constitutional dictatorship should be instituted, as was the Roman dictatorship, according to precise constitutional forms; it should be continued in no less a spirit of devotion to constitutional provisions and principles. Give a government whatever power it may need to defend the state from its enemies, but ground that power in the constitution or the laws and make the dictatorship lawful—this is a fundamental requirement of constitutional dictatorship.

The criterion of legitimacy would seem to demand an answer to the question long haggled over by French and English jurists: how thoroughly should a constitutional democracy in time of peace provide for dictatorial action in time of crisis? The extreme French view was that unusual powers are often necessary to the defense of the constitutional order and will in fact be adopted by the magistrates charged with that defense; therefore, lest the law be broken and disrespect for it created, provision must be made for every eventuality. A constitution which fails to provide for whatever emergency action may become necessary to defend the state is simply defective. A carefully elaborated state of siege, a recognized procedure for the suspension of rights, constitutional provision for and qualification of emergency executive legislation —this would be the irreducible minimum of crisis institutions in every constitutional state. The text is from Machiavelli:

"Now in a well-ordered republic it should never be necessary to resort to extra-constitutional measures; for although they may for the time be beneficial, yet the precedent is pernicious, for if the practice is once established of disregarding the laws for good objects, they will in a little while be disregarded under that pretext for evil purposes. Thus no republic will ever be perfect if she has not by law provided for everything, having a remedy for every emergency, and fixed rules for applying it."[13]

On the other hand, too much provision for constitutional dictatorship comprises a positive danger to a constitutional state, not only because unscrupulous men who happen to come into authority may be able to pursue their nefarious ends in a legitimate manner, but also because the use of emergency powers will become more common. This would lead to a violation of the first and basic criterion, that a clear necessity should precede the initiation of any institution of constitutional dictatorship. Eventually the rulers of the state would turn to emergency powers for a solution to every difficult problem, thereby increasing many times over the possibility of the several dangers of constitutional dictatorship. The history of Article 48 is evidence enough of the evil consequences of too broad a provision for the use of emergency powers. A dictatorship was simply too easy a matter in Weimar Germany.

The history of Article 48 is also evidence of the evil consequences of too *loose* a provision for constitutional emergency powers. If a state decides that an emergency institution is to be provided for in law, then the purpose, powers, effects, and limitations of that institution ought to be clearly qualified. The Emergency Powers Act of 1920 is an excellent example of such qualification, while the "unprecedented loose-

[13] *Discourses,* I, p.34.

ness" of Article 48 was an important contributing factor in its misuse. Of course, it is not possible to foresee in detail the conditions which will obtain in a period of emergency. To quote again from the *Social Contract*, "It is a highly necessary part of foresight to be conscious that everything cannot be foreseen." It would be sheer folly to attempt to codify the crisis possibilities of the English cabinet system or the American Presidency. The leaders of a country blessed by a virile constitutional morality can be granted considerable leeway to act dictatorially in time of crisis. Nevertheless, all emergency action should have some basis in the law. A system of martial rule is the one institution of constitutional dictatorship that ought to be, and indeed has been provided in every constitutional state. Whether other constitutional provisions and statutes are to increase the capacity of the government to strike hard in an emergency is a question for each country to decide according to its necessities and its essential democratic strength. In point of fact, rarely if ever has a constitutional democracy provided for an instrument of emergency powers except under the compulsion of some present crisis.

5. The first and most important of three criteria to be observed during the prosecution of a constitutional dictatorship is: *no dictatorial institution should be adopted, no right invaded, no regular procedure altered any more than is absolutely necessary for the conquest of the particular crisis.* Certain it is that no normal institution ought to be declared unsuited to crisis conditions unless the unsuitability be painfully evident. The more dictatorial a government becomes, the more exposed it will be to all the dangers of constitutional dictatorship.

The institution which ought to be most resolutely defended before the demands of those in favor of unalloyed emergency dictatorship is the national legislature. There may be conditions of transient crisis when it is impossible for the legislature to sit. In any protracted national emergency, however, the dictates of constitutional government would seem to make imperative the continuous session of the nation's representatives. It is the legislature which is the chief instrument of criticism and control of executive activity in modern constitutional dictatorships;[14] it is the legislature alone which can translate these criteria into effective limitations.

[14] "I hold it to be our bounden duty, impressed upon us by our position here, to keep an anxious, watchful eye over all the executive agents who are carrying on the war at the direction of the people, whom we represent and whom we are bound to protect in relation to this matter." Senator William P. Fessenden to the Senate of the United States, December 9, 1861; quoted in Lindsay Rogers: "Legislature and Executive in Wartime," *Foreign Affairs*, XIX (1941), p.717.

"An emergency, however, is no time to dispense with or even unduly to subordinate a legislature. It may have to change its activities, but it can play a high, albeit a difficult, role in making a militant representative government more vigorous and effective."[15]

The contrast of the British Parliament of 1942 with the Parliament of 1917, as well as of their comparative efficacy in aid of the war effort, furnishes sufficient evidence that a legislature can be an indispensable part of a great crisis machine. It was the continued absence of the Reichstag which permitted the pernicious abuse of Article 48; its continued presence might have forestalled the destruction of the Republic. It is a difficult role that the legislature has to play in modern crisis government, but it is a role which the stage managers of democracy will dispense with at their peril. The fact that the mark of constitutional democracy at peace is a robust legislative assembly should be prima facie evidence that it ought to be maintained as far as practical in time of war, not be carelessly discarded as unfit for crisis service. "War cannot be waged by debating societies,"[16] but the mere fact of war is no reason for the automatic suspension of their activities.

6. *The measures adopted in the prosecution of a constitutional dictatorship should never be permanent in character or effect.* Emergency powers are strictly conditioned by their purpose, and this purpose is the restoration of normal conditions. The actions directed to this end should therefore be provisional. For example, measures of a legislative nature which work a lasting change in the structure of the state or constitute permanent derogations from existing law should not be adopted under an emergency enabling act, at least not without the positively registered approval of the legislature. Permanent laws, whether adopted in regular or irregular times, are for parliaments to enact. By this same token, the decisions and sentences of extraordinary courts should be reviewed by the regular courts after the termination of the crisis.

But what if a radical act of a permanent character, one working lasting changes in the political and social fabric, is indispensable to the successful prosecution of the particular constitutional dictatorship? The only answer can be: it must be resolutely taken and openly acknowledged. President Lincoln found it necessary to proceed to the revolutionary step of emancipation in aid of his conservative purpose of pre-

[15] *Ibid.*, p.715.
[16] Lindsay Rogers: "Presidential Dictatorship in the United States," *Quarterly Review*, CCXXXI (1919), p.136.

serving the Union; as a constitutional dictator he had a moral right to take this radical action. Nevertheless, it is imperative that any action with such lasting effects should eventually receive the positive approval of the people or of their representatives in the legislature.

7. *The dictatorship should be carried on by persons representative of every part of the citizenry interested in the defense of the existing constitutional order.* This is the criterion which motivates the persistent demand that crisis government should be coalition government. In Germany, France, and Great Britain it was consistently a prerequisite of the passage of an enabling act that the cabinet be of a coalition or nonpartisan character. As a leading journal stated of the enabling act in France:

"We have always held to the principle that the power to legislate by decree should in no case and under no pretext be given to a party government. *Pleins pouvoirs* must not be used to pit ideologies or passions against one another, or to favor this or that political conception at the profit of its opposite. They must be used in the name of all, in the interest of all, which comes down to saying that if one may give them occasionally to governments of union and concord, it is necessary to refuse them to governments of combat."[17]

The circumstances of crisis and the fact that constitutional dictatorship is often a one-man affair make this criterion often nothing more than a moral reminder to an emergency regime that it is defending the whole community and maintaining an established order. The old Tory doctrine of virtual representation must be resurrected and twisted to democratic ends. Every loyal citizen of 1942 was entitled to regard himself as represented in the extraordinary efforts of Mr. Roosevelt and his lieutenants to save American democracy. The converse of this proposition was that President Roosevelt and his lieutenants were constrained to regard their unwonted authority as something to be wielded with impartiality in behalf of all loyal Americans, not just those who voted the straight Democratic ticket. Such authority must never be exercised to the advantage of one part of the population. There is obviously no sure way to guarantee the observance of this criterion, especially in a country with a presidential system of government. Except in the matter of enabling acts and cabinet dictatorship it remains a pious hope and nothing more. But if expressed loudly and

[17] *Le Temps*, December 1936; quoted by Lindsay Rogers: "Personal Power and Popular Government," *Southern Review*, III (1937), p.240.

often enough on the floor of the nation's legislature, it is a hope that might have considerable practical effect.

There are four criteria which are particularly valid at the close of any period of constitutional dictatorship:

8. *Ultimate responsibility should be maintained for every action taken under a constitutional dictatorship.* This criterion is directed against one of the chief dangers of constitutional dictatorship: the transient abuses wrought and the needless dictatorial steps adopted by persons charged with extraordinary powers in time of crisis. It is manifestly impossible and even detrimental to demand that an official entrusted with some unusual duty under martial rule be made to answer in the heat of the crisis for actions taken in pursuit of that duty. It is imperative that he be held responsible for them after its termination. The knowledge of a future reckoning may make him overcautious in his emergency actions, and it is often unfair to judge the measures adopted in the turmoil of a grave national danger by the standards of official conduct which prevail in the period of popular reaction to strong government which usually follows the end of an emergency. Nevertheless, it would seem to be a categorical principle of constitutional democracy that every public act must be a responsible one and have a public explanation. The plea of necessity for any dictatorial action will almost always be honored by the courts, the legislature, and the people. Officials who abuse authority in a constitutional dictatorship—in other words, men who were charged with defending democracy but instead profaned it—should be ferreted out and severely punished.

To pursue this criterion from a different angle, general elections in such countries as the United States and Great Britain should be held as scheduled unless the crisis is of such intensity as to render this an actual impossibility. The British people may easily be excused for having permitted the life of their wartime Parliament to be prolonged until mid-1945. On the other hand, the American people may take some pride in the elections of 1862, 1864, 1942, and 1944. It is interesting indeed to remember that two of America's three great constitutional dictators faced the necessity for reelection in the midst of their crises and were both returned to office by substantial majorities.

9. *The decision to terminate a constitutional dictatorship, like the decision to institute one, should never be in the hands of the man or men who constitute the dictator.* This is a direct corollary of the second and third criteria. Congress, not the President, Parliament, not the Crown, ought to declare the beginning and end of all emergencies in

which the executive is to be given abnormal powers, so far as is practicable and possible. It is in this respect that the permanent statutes delegating emergency powers to the American President are to be most heavily criticized.

10. *No constitutional dictatorship should extend beyond the termination of the crisis for which it was instituted.* It is the crisis alone which makes the dictatorship constitutional; the end of the crisis makes its continued existence unconstitutional. If the purpose of constitutional dictatorship is to defend constitutional democracy in time of peril, then it follows that an extension of the dictatorship beyond the cessation of the peril is directed to another purpose and becomes a dangerous display of unwonted power. The story of Cincinnatus should be required reading for all officials active in modern crisis government. This is one lesson of the Roman dictatorship which remains eternally valid.

11. Finally, *the termination of the crisis must be followed by as complete a return as possible to the political and governmental conditions existing prior to the initiation of the constitutional dictatorship.* It is, of course, impossible to reestablish perfectly the scheme of things in practice at the time the crisis first erupted. Every emergency leaves its mark on the pattern of constitutional government and democratic society. Every period of democratic autocracy leaves democracy just a little more autocratic than before. But better to become one-tenth of a permanent dictatorship in a successful attempt to maintain the rest of the constitutional order than to become a whole dictatorship or an enslaved nation by refusing to take a chance on the dangers of lasting change which attend the constitutional use of dictatorial institutions and powers.

It is in the observance of these criteria that the democratic and constitutional character of a democratic and constitutional dictatorship is to be tested. The listing of them may be doctrinaire in the extreme, but their validity and significance cannot be doubted.

The Future of Constitutional Dictatorship in the United States

THAT constitutional dictatorship does have a future in the United States is hardly a matter for discussion. Dismal and distressing as the prospect may be, it seems probable that in the years to come the American people will be faced with more rather than fewer national emergencies. Even if Manhattan Project had not been crowned with quite the awful success that it was, the continuing tensions of a world of sovereign nations and the irrepressible economic convulsions of the twentieth century would have made it plain that the second World War was not to be the last but only the latest of the American Republic's great national crises. The possibility of an atomic war only establishes emergency government a little more prominently in the frightening array of this nation's problems. Not that martial law is going to save us from an atomic attack; still, it may be the only glue available when it comes time to pick up the pieces.

That this nation's present-day institutions and procedures of emergency government present considerable room for improvement seems equally beyond dispute. Admittedly the American people are groping for the answers to questions a good deal more pressing and perplexing than the fashioning of more efficient and responsible instruments of emergency government. Nevertheless, the political scientists and the practicing politicians might well devote a little thought to the question: what are the practicable alterations that can be worked in the Constitution and laws of the United States to make this a government better fitted to meet national emergencies with determined and responsible action in defense of the American people and their democratic freedom? What can actually be effected for "the more precise and candid institutionalization of American constitutional dictatorship?"

It is obvious that any overhauling of this government's weapons of constitutional dictatorship is only one small part of a larger and more essential whole—the renovation of the entire constitutional structure and the creation of a national government capable of dealing resolutely and effectively with the bewildering problems of this twentieth century world. The frequent and penetrating proposals for the streamlining of Congress, the reorganization of the federal administration, the reform of the electoral college, the formalization of the President's leadership of the lawmaking process, the nullification of the filibuster as an obstruction to decisive senatorial action, and the recasting of the presidential succession are all symptoms of a widely-held belief that the government of the United States—however well it may have served in the past century and a half, and however sound it may still be in its fundamental structure and functions—is nevertheless in conspicuous need of an exhaustive rehabilitation.

Although it is not the province of this book to survey or evaluate the general question of governmental reform, it should certainly be pointed out that any reform which renders any part of the American government a more efficient and accountable unit renders it at the same time a more effective and trustworthy repository of constitutional emergency powers. The principal ends of the general reform of the American government are an increase in responsibility and an increase in efficiency; the principal ends of the particular reform of the government's instruments of constitutional dictatorship are identical. In short, constitutional dictatorship in the United States must be made more constitutional and more dictatorial. Both the limitations and the powers are in need of strengthening, and paradoxical as this may at first sight appear, the attainment of one of these ends by no means precludes the attainment of the other.

There are two general proposals which this book has to offer. The first is not so much a reform as it is a defense of the status quo. The inherent emergency power of the President of the United States— the power used by Lincoln to blockade the South, by Wilson to arm the merchantmen, and by Roosevelt to effect the destroyer deal—should be left intact and untrammeled. Granted that the indefinite vastness of this power presents a potential threat calling for unceasing vigilance on the part of Congress and the electorate; granted that some uses of this power, for instance federal martial law and the system of "indirect sanctions" created by Wilson and Roosevelt, might at least be defined and given statutory basis; granted even the cogency of Henry C. Lockwood's anguished "Woe to that country whose destinies are involved in the fortunes of any one man, however great and pure he may be!"[18]— still, the memorable deeds of Lincoln, Wilson, and Roosevelt are persuasive reminders that if there must be an ultimate authority in the government of the United States to take unprecedented, dictatorial, or even unconstitutional action in moments of extreme national danger, it must rest with the President.[19] The steady increase in executive power is unquestionably a cause for worry, but so too is the steady increase in the magnitude and complexity of the problems the President has been

[18] H. C. Lockwood: *The Abolition of the Presidency* (New York, 1884), p.195.
[19] Of some interest are these words of Secretary of War Newton D. Baker: "Laws passed in anticipation of war hampered more than helped the prosecution of the World War. What needed to be preserved was the implied power of the President, under the Constitution, to prosecute the war to the fullest extent in keeping with conditions obtaining at the time. Implied powers were seldom broadened, but rather restricted, by laws interpreting them." *New York Times*, March 12, 1931. As a matter of fact, laws of Congress may *supplement* a strong President's constitutional ability to act as steward of the people in a national emergency; it is highly unlikely that they could ever *limit* it. Mr. Roosevelt demonstrated this in the destroyer deal.

called upon by the American people to solve in their behalf. They still have more to fear from the ravages of depression, rebellion, and especially atomic war than they do from whatever decisive actions may issue from the White House in an attempt to put any such future crises to rout. What was declared at the conclusion of the last chapter may well be repeated here: it is not too much to say that the destiny of this nation in the Atomic Age will rest in the capacity of the Presidency as an institution of constitutional dictatorship.

The second general proposal is of equal importance and even more present significance. If Congress is to play a salutary part in future emergency governments in this country, then its functions of legislation, investigation, and control must be streamlined and strengthened. It is particularly in respect to the reorganization of Congress that the various proposals for general reform—only partially realized in the La Follette-Monroney Act of 1946—will be as beneficial to emergency government as they will be to regular government. If it is the President's duty to make emergency government more effective and dictatorial, it is Congress's to make it more responsible and constitutional. If some future strong-minded President is not to run wild in his choice of extraordinary ways and means of exercising his vast powers as constitutional dictator, then Congress is going to have to turn out legislation which will define without constricting and codify without emasculating some of the President's constitutional and statutory powers for emergency action. As was stated in the last chapter, if anyone is to blame for the haphazard and often constitutionally questionable systems of direct and indirect and legal and extra-legal means whereby the WPB and the WLB secured obedience to their edicts in the recent war, Congress must take its full share.

The congressional investigating committee is another case in point. Judiciously handled, this vital weapon of congressional control could go a long way toward rendering any crisis administration more effective and responsible in the use of constitutional emergency powers; but if wartime congressional investigating committees continue to be as political as the Joint Committee on the Conduct of the War of 1861-1865, as aimless as the House committee which investigated the seizure of Montgomery Ward, or miss the point as completely as the Wood-Rankin Committee on un-American activities, then the blame for inefficient and irresponsible administrative action will continue to rest as much on Congress as on the administration itself. It is in the debates, the committees, and the roll-calls of the House and Senate that the doctrinaire criteria of constitutional dictatorship advanced in this chapter can take on practical significance. The independent status of Congress gives it a chance to play an invaluable role in any constitutional dictatorship in the United States; it is entirely up to Congress itself whether this shall be done.

In addition, there are six specific proposals of reform which might be considered as contributions to more effective and responsible constitutional dictatorship in the United States. First, the entire catalogue of the President's statutory emergency powers could well be scrutinized and overhauled. These laws are for the most part left-overs from former major or minor national emergencies; as such they are in no sense the products of a reflective congressional judgment that the nation's welfare calls for such a panoply of presidential emergency powers. Some of them are entirely unnecessary, some are badly drafted, some are virtual dead-letters anyway. On the other hand, there might well be a few additions to the President's arsenal. It would be a great service to the cause of constitutional government if an expert congressional committee should undertake to examine carefully and recast precisely the present-day delegated emergency powers of the President. A statute delegating the President a general provisional power to issue ordinances with the force of regular laws would be going too far. His present statutory and constitutional powers would seem to be sufficient to cover almost any situation demanding emergency legislative action, and it is doubtful whether even the present Court would uphold an act breaking so violently with American legal and constitutional history.

Second, a more precise means of declaring and ending national emergencies should be established in law. The declaration of a national emergency has three important effects: it makes available the whole array of statutory emergency powers; it gives moral sanction to those of the President's emergency actions which he bases on his constitutional powers; and it helps put the American people in a frame of mind more readily disposed to look with equanimity or even approval on unusual administrative and legislative measures. It is obvious that a declaration of the existence or termination of a national emergency involves a major statement of national policy. Therefore, Congress should be more closely associated with such declarations, particularly those which initiate a period of emergency government. A solution which would answer both the second criterion of constitutional dictatorship and the peculiar character of America's presidential government would be: the President should have a provisional power of declaring national emergencies;

Congress, however, should have the final decision; and the rules of Congress should be so amended that a presidential demand for confirmation of his declaration of a national emergency would be put to an immediate vote. The termination of an emergency should be entirely in the hands of Congress.

Third, the Office for Emergency Management should be established as a permanent adjunct of the Executive Office of the President. The OEM exists today in a state of suspended animation and seems doomed to extinction from simple neglect. This is an unfortunate turn of events, for a revived OEM could provide expert assistance and advice for the President in his efforts to meet the nation's major and minor crises, could organize and coordinate the activities upon which he devolves his constitutional and statutory duties as executor of the laws and protector of the peace of the United States, and could make plans to deal with future emergencies. As an American counterpart of Britain's Committee of Imperial Defence the OEM could be an invaluable addition to the governmental scheme, a frank and wholesome recognition of the increasing importance of the problems of constitutional dictatorship. The President would be doing the Republic in general and the cause of constitutional government in particular a great favor if he would reactivate and finance this neglected war agency on a permanent basis. The way has already been shown by Mr. Roosevelt in his administrative order of January 7, 1941 which devolved upon the OEM the responsibility for advising and assisting the President in the discharge of his duties in any war, threat of war, flood, drought, or "other condition threatening the public peace or safety." The President could well use a permanent trouble-shooter, and a revived OEM with one of his executive assistants at its head would fill the bill admirably.

Fourth, the possibilities of an American version of the British Emergency Powers Act should be thoughtfully considered by Congress. The emergency actions taken by the government in the disastrous coal strikes of 1946, which went a long way toward mitigating the severity of the shock suffered by the community at large, were mostly grounded in the war powers temporarily delegated to the President. It would be more difficult to secure these results in time of peace, and an American Emergency Powers Act would give the administration permanent legal power to adopt measures designed to soften the effects of great strikes in the nation's basic industries. Its terminology and purposes, however, should be equally as well-guarded and limited as those of the Emergency Powers Act. President Truman virtually admitted the necessity of such

311

a statute when he confessed that the termination of the recent emergency would have come a lot sooner if he hadn't needed the war powers to deal with the strikes of 1946.

Fifth, in conjunction with the above statute it seems unfortunately imperative that the President of the United States be given an undoubted peacetime power to seize strike-bound industries of such importance as the coal mines, telephones, and railroads. Here again the statute should be precise and limiting, but it should be made perfectly clear that there are strikes that are positive national calamities, and that the President should have the power in peace as well as war to deal with them resolutely in behalf of the nation's best interests. Periodic strikes in the great national industries may be part of the price we must pay for our constitutional democracy; still, the public should not be made to suffer unnecessarily. The unfortunate emergency bill proposed by President Truman through which he forced a conclusion to the railroad strike of 1946 is not the sort of statute that is here recommended.

The sixth specific suggestion is one about which the writer himself is quite undecided, namely the codification of martial law at the national level. That the President has the power of martial law is obvious; that martial law is an uncertain institution is equally obvious. If the federal power of martial law can be left as forceful and effective as ever, while at the same time some of its effects can be more precisely defined—particularly in respect to such matters as the jurisdiction and penalties of courts-martial and a system of redresses for persons who claim to have been injured or restricted beyond the necessities of the case—then such a law would be an asset to constitutional dictatorship and thus to constitutional government.[20] The definition of a power by no means signifies that it will be any less effective; it does signify that it will be more responsible.

All of these are proposals of a controversial nature. Many people feel that the President's inherent emergency power should be left not only unembarrassed but undefined, and that the vigilance of Congress and the electorate, not laws which try to limit what is essentially illimitable, must be relied upon to keep his feet in the paths of constitutional righteousness. Others would criticize these proposals on the theory that most of them, particularly such items as the codification of martial law, represent too violent a break with the traditions of the American constitutional system. Still others would wish to proceed on the alto-

[20] Max Radin regards an American state of siege as feasible in his "Martial Law and the State of Siege," *California L.R.*, xxx (1942), p.634.

gether understandable principle that the less we talk about and admit the principle of constitutional dictatorship, the better it will be for the freedom of the American people. Then again, the cynics, or perhaps we should call them the "realists," will assert that the necessity for these reforms, like the necessity for all reforms, is more apparent than real; that the road of constitutional progress is littered with abandoned reforms as excellent and as impractical as these; and that if the President and Congress devoted their time and energies to only a fraction of the well-meaning proposals of governmental revision put forward as "absolutely indispensable to the maintenance of constitutional democracy in the United States," they would never have time for anything else. The force of such arguments cannot be denied, but neither can the historical fact that many of constitutional democracy's greatest gains were registered only because the "impractical reformers" had beaten their drums long and loud enough to wake the people from their usual condition of political repose.

One final word. In describing the emergency governments of the western democracies, this book may have given the impression that such techniques of government as executive dictatorship, the delegation of legislative power, and lawmaking by administrative decree were purely transitory and temporary in nature. Such an impression would be distinctly misleading. There can no longer be any question that the constitutional democracies, faced with repeated emergencies and influenced by the examples of permanent authoritarian government all about them, are caught up in a pronounced, if lamentable trend toward more arbitrary, more powerful, and more "efficient" government. The instruments of government depicted here as temporary "crisis" arrangements have in some countries, and may eventually in all countries, become lasting peacetime institutions.

Nevertheless, it remains the belief of this writer that the accepted pattern of constitutional democracy in the United States, England, and France can still be considered the norm. A technique of government like the delegation of power (despite the ever-increasing validity of its claims to being a normal governmental procedure) will remain for a time at least essentially an emergency technique—in short, an instrument of constitutional dictatorship. Each twentieth century crisis leaves the governments of the United States, England, and France, and the valiant small democracies as well, a little less democratic than before, at least by traditional standards. The heartening fact remains that these nations are still constitutional democracies, and that most of the arbitrary procedures and compulsions adopted in the recent global war have since been done away with rather completely. The western democracies are still democracies, and the twentieth century has been since Hiroshima practically the twenty-fifth century; the need for more effective and responsible institutions of constitutional dictatorship is therefore more insistent than ever before.

Constitutional dictatorship is today, and will continue to be in the stormy years before us, one of the most urgent problems to be solved by the men of the constitutional democracies. It is more than just a problem; it is a compelling and anxious reality. For who in this year 1948 would be so blind as to assert that the people of the United States, or of any other constitutional democracy, can afford again to be weak and divided and jealous of the power of their elected representatives? The Bomb has settled once and for all the question whether the United States can go back to being what Harold Laski has labeled (a little too contemptuously) a "negative state." You can't go home again; the positive state is here to stay, and from now on the accent will be on power, not limitations.

Power, however, does not necessarily mean despotism, and merely because we are to have a government strong enough to deal with the Atomic Age does not mean that we are henceforth to be slaves. Not at all, for if the crisis history of the modern democracies teaches us anything, it teaches us that power can be responsible, that strong government can be democratic government, that dictatorship can be constitutional. From this day forward we must cease wasting our energies in discussing whether the government of the United States is to be powerful or not. It is going to be powerful or we are going to be obliterated. Our problem is to make that power effective and responsible, to make any future dictatorship a constitutional one. No sacrifice is too great for our democracy, least of all the temporary sacrifice of democracy itself.

A 2
B 3
C 4
D 5
E 6
F 7
G 8
H 9
I 0
J 1